SCOTS LAW FOR STUDE
AN INTRODUCTION

SCOTS LAW FOR STUDENTS: AN INTRODUCTION

General Editor

Dale McFadzean

Programme Leader for Law, University of Paisley

DUNDEE UNIVERSITY PRESS
2007

First published in Great Britain in 2007 by
Dundee University Press
University of Dundee
Dundee DD1 4HN

www.dundee.ac.uk/dup

ISBN 978–1–84586–015–8

No natural forests were destroyed to make this product;
only farmed timber was used and replanted.

British Library Cataloguing-in-Publication Data
A catalogue record for this book is available on request from the British Library

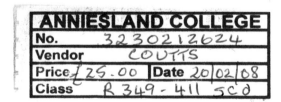
Typeset by Waverley Typesetters, Fakenham
Printed and bound by Bell & Bain Ltd, Glasgow

CONTENTS

PREFACE

Scots Law for Students: An Introduction is the first book of its kind to be tailor made for the growing number of students who undertake the study of law outwith the traditional LL.B. path. Many students now study law at various levels, from the B.A. Law degree to the H.N.C. in Legal Services. Students of accountancy, business and human resource management, to name some, undertake the study of business-related law modules and so, as Programme Leader for Law at the University of Paisley, I felt it was time to produce a text which clearly matched the curricula of non-LL.B. courses.

To this end, working with Dundee University Press, we assembled a team of experienced academics from both further and higher education and from a variety of institutions. It has been our aim to provide a text which is user-friendly, readable and, I hope, enjoyable. The chapters carefully match the range of subjects which will be studied by those undertaking the Cert./Dip. H.E. Law, H.N.C. Law or the B.A. Law degree. The book is also suitable for those students dipping into legal study from other disciplines, and is well suited for courses such as the Cert./Dip. H.E. Accounting and the B.A. Accounting degree.

The text is presented in a clear and accessible manner. Each chapter contains paragraph numbering for ease of use and also a set of essential facts and cases as a revision aid. I hope that students find this text to be an invaluable tool for facilitating their learning and enjoyment of the law.

DALE McFADZEAN
August 2007

TABLE OF CASES

TABLE OF STATUTES

TABLE OF STATUTORY INSTRUMENTS

TABLE OF EUROPEAN AND INTERNATIONAL LEGISLATION

1 SOURCES OF SCOTS LAW

WHAT IS LAW?

The definitions of law are wide and varied. It has been described by White and Willock **1.1** as "... the words of someone in authority who has the power to intervene in other people's affairs ... and if they do not comply something unpleasant is liable to befall them",[1] while the *Oxford English Dictionary* describes law as a "... body of rules, whether proceeding from formal enactment or custom, which a particular state or community recognises as binding on its members or subjects".[2] Law may have many descriptions but it has only one main practical purpose – to restrict and regulate certain kinds of behaviour. The fact that there are laws which most people obey means that you can generally go about your business secure in the knowledge that someone is not going to assault you, or steal your belongings, or generally put your life in danger by failing to take proper care. If someone does carry out this kind of behaviour then the law creates legal consequences. If you commit a crime then you could be fined or sent to prison. If you have injured someone through negligence then you may be forced to pay compensation or damages.

CATEGORISING THE LAW

PUBLIC AND PRIVATE LAW

Scots law deals with many specific subject areas, such as criminal law, the law **1.2** of contract, and the law of delict, among others. Each of these areas is known as a "branch" of law. For simplicity, each of these branches is further categorised into two distinct groupings: public law and private law. There is no real technical reason for these groupings. It is simply a useful way of categorising the various branches of law under separate headings.

With "public law", the involvement of the state is paramount. Public law relates **1.3** to the operation of government and the regulation of the relationship between government and citizens. It also regulates other public bodies such as the courts, the Scottish Parliament, local government, and even the police. Key branches of public law include constitutional law, administrative law and criminal law.

On the other hand, with "private law" the involvement of the State is minimal. **1.4** Instead, private law is more concerned with the regulation of relationships between individual citizens and/or companies and organisations. For example, when a

---

[1] White and Willock, *The Scottish Legal System* (2nd edn, 1999).
[2] *Oxford English Dictionary*, vol VI.

legal relationship between individuals breaks down, such as a contract, this concerns private law. Key branches of private law include contract law, delict and family law.

CIVIL AND CRIMINAL LAW

1.5   As well as categorising the various branches of law into both public and private, the law can also be described in terms of civil or criminal. The main difference between civil and criminal law is that a different court structure is used to regulate each.[3] Under criminal law, a special set of criminal courts exists which aims to punish criminal behaviour and impose sanctions on individual liberty. Cases brought before the criminal courts are known as prosecutions and are brought by officials representing the state. In Scotland these are the Procurator Fiscal, the Lord Advocate, or one of their deputies (known as Depute Procurators Fiscal and Advocates Depute). The person against whom the prosecution is brought is called the *accused*. The standard of proof in a criminal prosecution is "beyond all reasonable doubt". This means that if a jury has a reasonably held doubt, based upon the evidence, as to the accused's guilt, then they must acquit. The standard of proof is set at a high level in order to safeguard the liberty of the accused who may ultimately face imprisonment.

1.6   Under civil law, a special set of civil courts exists which deals with disputes arising between two or more parties, where the conduct of one party has caused unjustified loss to another. Such disputes are known as civil cases and when brought before the civil courts they are referred to as "litigation". The person bringing the case to court is known as the pursuer and the person against whom the action is taken is called the *defender*. Examples of civil cases include a DIY company damaging your home while fitting a new bathroom suite, or a driver running into your vehicle and causing you to suffer from whiplash. In each of these examples, the aggrieved party may attempt to sue the other party before the civil courts if they have failed to fulfil their obligations or pay compensation for any damage caused by their actions. Under the civil law, courts have no power to interfere with individual liberty. Instead of punishment through imprisonment or fine, the civil courts focus upon reparation whereby aggrieved parties are financially recompensed for any loss suffered. As such, the standard of proof is lower than that of the criminal courts and is based upon the "balance of probabilities".

Overlap between civil and criminal law

1.7   Often there can be an overlap between the civil and criminal law. This can happen when a type of behaviour occurs which is both criminal and civil in nature. For example, if an individual assaults another person in the street, that individual has committed a crime which can then result in a prosecution taking place before the criminal courts. However, that assault can also be dealt with under the civil law,[4] in that the victim could attempt to sue his assailant for compensation, using the civil courts.

---

[3] See further Chapter 2.
[4] Specifically under the branch of delict.

SOURCES OF LAW

INTRODUCTION

All legal systems must have sources of law. It is these sources which give authority **1.8** to the rules and principles within any given system. However, the approach to creating and defining these sources will differ according to the type of legal system. Civil law systems, on the whole, are codified. They have been heavily influenced throughout the ages by Roman law and are based upon codified rules and principles logically set out in often encyclopaedic documents. These "codes" are the main source of law.

Common law systems, on the other hand, have developed quite independently of **1.9** the influence of Roman law. Instead of reliance upon codes as a source of law, they rely upon judicial precedent. As a source of law, precedent consists of the decisions of judges made in cases which are heard before them. From these decisions, legal principles can be drawn from the judges' written decisions which together form a major source of law. Common law systems have been greatly influenced by English law which was little affected by the spread of Roman law.

There is a third type of legal system which is known as the *hybrid* system. This is **1.10** the system to which Scots law adheres and it has developed in such a way that it does not conform exclusively to either civil or common law. Instead, it is a mixed system in which one can discern elements of civil or Roman law but also the influence of common law and precedent. This is certainly true of Scotland where, for example, the branch of criminal law is almost wholly derived from common law whereas other branches, such as company law, rely almost entirely on Acts of Parliament which codify them.

FORMAL SOURCES OF SCOTS LAW

Within the Scottish legal system, there are a number of formal sources of law. Each of **1.11** these sources has varying importance and can effectively be "ranked" in terms of their authority. In order of importance the sources are:

(1) legislation;
(2) judicial precedent;
(3) institutional writings;
(4) custom; and
(5) equity.

Legislation

Legislation is the most important source of law within the Scottish legal system. **1.12** It emanates ultimately from the authority of a legislature and includes Acts of Parliament as well as legislation passed by delegates such as the Scottish Parliament or local authorities. It also includes European Union legislation. Despite its having its own Parliament, arguably the most important legislation in Scotland is still that of the UK Parliament. Despite the Scottish Parliament having law-making powers by virtue of the Scotland Act 1998, the doctrine of the supremacy of Parliament remains in place and the law-making powers of the UK Parliament remain unaffected for Scotland.[5] The doctrine of the supremacy of Parliament also applies to European legislation.

UK parliamentary legislation

1.13   Parliamentary legislation is initiated mainly by the Government and tends to introduce changes to society which reflect the policies of a particular Government. Proposals for an Act of Parliament take the form of a Bill and, during the opening ceremony of Parliament, the Queen will generally outline the forthcoming Bills for the year ahead. Bills themselves fall into three distinct categories. Public Bills are the most important and take up the majority of parliamentary time since they deal with matters of important principle and generally affect society as a whole.

1.14   There are two types of Public Bill: Government Bills and Private Members' Bills. Government Bills are introduced by the ruling government of the day and generally reflect current policy or manifesto commitments.[6] The majority of Acts passed by Parliament originate from Government Bills; Private Members' Bills, on the other hand, generally originate from an individual MP. These Bills will more often than not deal with an area which does not receive Government backing or is controversial and they often reflect personally held beliefs of MPs.[7] In some cases, controversial measures for which a Government does not want to take responsibility may be introduced by back-benchers, with the Government secretly or openly backing the measure and ensuring its passage. Such Bills are sometimes known as "Government handout Bills"; the Abortion Act 1967 was passed in such a manner. This type of Bill ensures that back-benchers have more input into the legislative process of Parliament, but the success of such Bills is very limited.[8] Most Private Members' Bills fail to become an Act.

1.15   The second category of Bills is known as Private Bills. These contain proposals which generally affect the interests of specified persons or localities. They are introduced through petition by the persons or organisations who desire the Bill. Private Bills are commonly introduced by local authorities or public corporations and seek to give statutory powers to those bodies which they would otherwise not have. For example, the Transport for London Bill is currently before Parliament and seeks to give the London Assembly and the Greater London Authority increased powers relating to the regulation of transport. Private Bills follow a slightly different procedure in their enactment from other Bills and there is often very little discussion of such Bills within Parliament.[9]

1.16   The third and final category of Bills is called Hybrid Bills. These are normally Government Bills which specifically affect particular individuals or groups. They are therefore treated in many ways like Private Bills. An example of such a Bill can be found

---

[5] Scotland Act 1998, s 28(7). For further discussion of the supremacy of Parliament, see para 8.29.

[6] For example, the Constitutional Reform Act 2005 was introduced as a Government Bill reflecting the Labour Government's enthusiasm for judicial reform.

[7] Recent examples of Private Members' Bills include the Female Genital Mutilation Act 2003 and the Gangmasters (Licensing) Act 2004.

[8] For example, in the 2003–04 session of Parliament, 38 Public Bills received Royal Assent; of these, only five were Bills introduced by back-bench Members.

[9] For a detailed discussion of Private Bill procedure, see further A W Bradley, and K D Ewing, *Constitutional and Administrative Law* (13th edn, 2003), pp 193–194.

in the Channel Tunnel Bill of 1986, now the Channel Tunnel Act 1987. The Bill was generally public in nature, given that it set out to create the Channel Tunnel, however, certain sections of the Act gave the Government powers of compulsory purchase to buy areas of land in Kent required to build the tunnel. Since these sections specifically affected only Kent landowners, the Bill was hybrid in nature.

Parliamentary stages of Bills. Bills may be introduced in either the House of Commons   **1.17** or the House of Lords. However, there are a number of Bills which must always originate in the Commons, such as Money Bills and Bills of constitutional importance. A Bill which originates in the House of Lords will progress through the same stages as those in the House of Commons. The stages of a Bill as it passes through Parliament are as follows:

- **First Reading**

The first stage consists of a number of formalities where the Bill is announced and its short title is read out. A date is set for the Second Reading of the Bill and from here the Bill will be printed and distributed.

- **Second Reading**

At this stage, the House will debate the general principles contained in the Bill. At the end of the debate, the motion is put to a vote. It is very rare for a Government Bill to lose a vote, although it is not unheard of. For example, the Shops Bill 1986 was lost at the Second Reading.

- **Committee Stage**

During the Committee Stage, most Bills are passed over to a Standing Committee which is created for the specific purpose of dealing with the Bill.[10] Standing Committees generally consist of between 18 and 50 MPs and reflect the state of the parties represented in the House of Commons. At this stage, the Bill is subjected to a thorough line-by-line examination and any of its clauses may be amended where necessary.

A small number of Bills at this stage are passed over to a Committee of the Whole House as opposed to a Standing Committee. During such a Committee, each clause of the Bill is debated on the floor of the House of Commons by all MPs. Such a Committee is used for Bills of constitutional significance, such as the Scotland Bill during 1999. It is also used to pass Bills which require a rapid enactment, such as the annual Finance Bill.

- **Report Stage**

If a Bill has come from a Committee of the Whole House, then this stage is purely a formality. However, for the majority of Bills, this stage will involve a review of any amendments made during the Committee Stage. All members of the House have an opportunity to debate at this stage, making it rather more democratic than the Committee Stage where the scope for debate is rather limited. There is no vote at this point.

---

[10] A new Standing Committee is appointed for each Bill and will disband after it has completed its work.

- **Third Reading**

  Here, the House examines the final version of the Bill. The Bill is debated in principle and a vote taken. This stage is usually very brief since no major amendments may be made.

A key problem with the legislative process of the Commons is the amount of time it takes. The more amendments a Bill receives, the longer it will take to pass through Parliament. Consequently, many Bills are subject to what is called a "guillotine" motion. Such a motion will quickly bring the debate on a Bill to an end, allowing it to proceed more quickly. Since 1999, the Commons has also used a new procedure known as the "programme" motion. Using this motion, a programme or timetable is put before the House, agreeing the amount of time allocated to stages of a Bill and dates for progression.

- **Lords Stages**

  Once the Commons stages have been completed, the Bill is sent to the House of Lords, where the whole procedure is repeated. The Lords stages are similar in many ways to those of the Commons, except for a few key differences. The Committee Stage in the Lords always consists of a Committee of the Whole House and there is no use of "guillotine" or "programme" motions which allow for unrestricted debate on the principles of a Bill. It is also possible to table amendments during the Third Reading in the Lords.

  Changes made to a Bill in the House of Lords result in an extra stage in the Commons known as "Lords Amendments Considered". This is necessary in order to approve any amendments made by the Lords.[11] Occasionally, the two Houses will not agree on a Bill. In such circumstances, the Lords can exercise its delaying power and refuse to accept the proposals of the House of Commons.[12] However, this delaying power is limited by the Parliament Act 1911, as amended by the Parliament Act 1949, which states that the Lords can delay a Bill only for up to 1 year. Using the Parliament Acts, the House of Commons can then submit a Bill for Royal Assent without the consent of the House of Lords. Thus, the power of the House of Lords to block legislation permanently is curtailed.[13] Unless the House of Commons invokes the Parliament Acts, then both Houses of Parliament must always agree in order for the final Bill to progress.

- **Royal Assent**

  This is the final stage of a Bill, where the Crown must formally assent to the Bill in order for it to become an Act of Parliament and pass into law. In modern times this has become something of a formality since the UK is a constitutional monarchy and the sovereign is bound to assent to any Bill, except in extraordinary circumstances. The last time assent was given by the Crown in person was in 1854 and assent has not been refused since 1707 when Queen Anne refused to consent to the Scottish Militia Bill.

---

[11] The Commons will generally accept around 90% of Lords amendments since most are non-controversial.

[12] A recent example of this can be found in the Sexual Offences (Amendment) Bill, now the Sexual Offences (Amendment) Act 2000 (c 44).

[13] For a useful analysis of the Parliament Acts, see the decision in *Jackson* v *Attorney-General* [2005] 3 WLR 733.

Reading a statute 1

Murder (Abolition of Death Penalty) Act 1965 2

1.17

1965 CHAPTER 71 3

An Act to abolish capital punishment in the case of persons convicted in Great Britain of murder or convicted of murder or a corresponding offence by court-martial and, in connection therewith, to make further provision for the punishment of persons so convicted.

[8th November 1965] 5

4

Be it enacted by the Queen's most Excellent Majesty, by and with the advice and consent of the Lords Spiritual and Temporal, and Commons, in this present Parliament assembled, and by the authority of the same, as follows:

6

1.—(1) No person shall suffer death for murder, and a person convicted of murder shall, subject to subsection (5) below, be sentenced to imprisonment for life. Abolition of death penalty for murder.

Abolition of 7
death penalty
for murder.

(2) On sentencing any person convicted of murder to imprisonment for life the Court may at the same time declare the period which it recommends to the Secretary of State as the minimum period which in its view should elapse before the Secretary of State orders the release of that person on licence under section 27 of the Prison Act 1952 or section 21 of the Prisons (Scotland) Act 1952.

1952 c. 52.
1952 c. 61.

(3) For the purpose of any proceedings on or subsequent to a person's trial on a charge of capital murder, that charge and any plea or finding of guilty of capital murder shall be treated as being or having been a charge, or a plea or finding of guilty, of murder only; and if at the commencement of this Act a person is under sentence of death for murder, the sentence shall have effect as a sentence of imprisonment for life.

(4) In the foregoing subsections any reference to murder shall include an offence of or corresponding to murder under s 70 of the Army Act 1955 or of the Air Force Act 1955 or under section 42 of the Naval Discipline Act 1957, and any reference to capital murder shall be construed accordingly; and in each of the said sections 70 there shall be inserted in subsection (3) after paragraph (*a*) as a new paragraph (*aa*)—

1955 c. 18.
1955 c. 19.
1957 c. 53.

"(*aa*) if the corresponding civil offence is murder, be liable to imprisonment for life".

(5) In section 53 of the Children and Young Persons Act 1933, and in section 57 of the Children and Young Persons (Scotland) Act 1937, <u>there shall be substituted</u> for subsection (1)—

1933 c. 12.
1937 c. 37.

"(1) A person convicted of an offence who appears to the court to have been under the age of eighteen years at the time the offence was committed shall not, if he is convicted of murder, be sentenced to imprisonment for life, nor shall sentence of death be pronounced on or recorded against any such person; but in lieu thereof the court shall (notwithstanding anything in this or in any other Act) sentence him to be detained during Her Majesty's pleasure, and if so sentenced he shall be liable to be detained in such place and under such conditions as the Secretary of State may direct."

2. No person convicted of murder shall be released by the Secretary of State on licence under section 27 of the Prison Act 1952 or section 21 of the Prisons (Scotland) Act 1952 unless the Secretary of State has prior to such release consulted the Lord Chief Justice of England or the Lord Justice General as the case may be together with the trial judge if available.

Release on licence of those sentenced for murder.
1952 c. 52.
1952 c. 61.

11   **3.**—(1) <u>This Act may be cited</u> as the Murder (Abolition of Death Penalty) Act 1965.

(2) The enactments mentioned in the Schedule to this Act are hereby repealed to the extent specified in the third column of that Schedule.

(3) This Act, except as regards courts-martial, shall not extend to Northern Ireland.

(4) This Act shall come into force on the day following that on which it is passed.

4. This Act shall continue in force until the thirty-first day of July nineteen hundred and seventy, and shall then expire unless Parliament by affirmative resolutions of both Houses otherwise determines: and upon the expiration of this Act the law existing immediately prior to the passing of this Act shall, so far as it is repealed or amended by this Act, again operate as though this Act had not been passed, and the said repeals and amendments had not been enacted:

Short title, repeal, extent and commencement.

Duration.

Provided that this Act shall continue to have effect in relation to any murder not shown to have been committed after the expiration of this Act, and for this purpose a murder shall be taken to be committed at the time of the act which causes the death.

SCHEDULE   **12**

ENACTMENTS REPEALED

Section 2.

Chapter	Short Title	Extent of Repeal
33 Hen. 8. c. 12.	The Offences with the Court Act 1541.	Section 2, so far as relates to the punishment of persons found guilty of murder.
25 Geo. 2. c. 37.	The Murder Act 1751.	In section 9 the words from "or rescue", where secondly occurring, to "during execution".
4 Geo. 4. c. 48.	The Judgment of Death Act 1823.	In section 1 the words "except murder".
24 & 25 Vict. c. 100.	The Offences against the Person Act 1861.	Section 1 (but without prejudice to the operation of sections 64 to 68).

Chapter	Short Title	Extent of Repeal
		In section 71 the words "otherwise than with death".
31 & 32 Vict. c. 24.	The Capital Punishment Amendment Act 1868.	The whole Act, except as applied by any other enactment.
50 & 51 Vict. c. 35.	The Criminal Procedure (Scotland) Act 1887.	In section 55 the words from "in cases in" to "conviction, or". In section 56 the words from "except on conviction" to "1829".
3 & 4 Eliz. 2. c. 19.	The Army Act 1955.	In section 70(3)(*a*) the words "or murder" (and the words added by the Homicide Act 1957). In section 125(2) the words "and any rules made under section seven of that Act."
3 & 4 Eliz. 2. c. 18.	The Air Force Act 1955.	In section 70(3)(*a*) the words "or murder" (and the words added by the Homicide Act 1957). In section 125(2) the words "and any rules made under section seven of that Act."
5 & 6 Eliz. 2. c. 11.	The Homicide Act 1957.	Sections 5 to 12. In section 13, in subsection (1) the words from "and" to "Part III", and subsection (2). Section 15. Schedule 1.
5 & 6 Eliz. 2. c. 53.	The Naval Discipline Act 1957.	In section 42(1), in paragraph (*a*) the words from "or" to "1957" and in paragraph (b) the word "other". In section 80(2) the words "and any rules made under section seven of that Act".

KEY

1. The *Royal seal* is simply to show that, by the Royal Assent having been given, the Act is one associated with Her Majesty. Bills, as proposals for Acts which are not yet passed, have no Royal seal. On a lighter note, it is also there for decoration!   **1.19**

2. The *short title* gives a broad indication of the scope of the Act. The word "Scotland" in brackets means that the Act applies to Scotland only. This is often shortened to a capital letter "S", full stop. Ideally the short title should be prosaic, but often it is political or emotive. For example, the Tenants' Rights etc (Scotland) Act 1980 was essentially a Housing Act; why was it not named so?

3. The *chapter number.* This means that the Act was the 71st passed in 1965. The system is straightforward and was adopted by the Acts of Parliament Numbering and Citation Act 1962. Prior to that, the reference was to the session of Parliament in which the Act was passed, the session being numbered according to the length of reign of the existing monarch, for example the Factories Act 1961 (9 & 10 Eliz II c 34).

4. The *long title* states in more detail the objectives of the Act, but still in fairly general terms (the phrase "... and for connected purposes" is often used). The long title will also state whether the Act is a consolidating or codifying Act, if

either. A consolidating Act is one that repeals or re-enacts the provisions of a number of statutes dealing with the same subject into a single Act, for example the Sale of Goods Act 1979. A codifying Act brings all the earlier law (both statutes and precedent) together into one Act, often with changes to the pre-existing law, for example the Legitimation Act 1968.

5. The *date of Royal Assent* is the date upon which the provisions of the Act come into effect unless otherwise stated elsewhere in the Act. This is known as the date of commencement.

6. The *enacting formula* is a standardised formula which verifies the statute as a true Act of Parliament. It shows that the House of Commons, the House of Lords and the Queen must all be consulted and must approve it. Since the Parliament Acts of 1911 and 1949, the House of Commons has been able to override the will of the House of Lords. If the Lords makes amendments to a Bill, or rejects it completely, then, provided that the House of Commons can pass its own version of the Bill twice in one parliamentary session, this will become law; the European Parliamentary Elections Act 1999 was passed in such a way. These Acts have a slightly different enacting formula and include "... as prescribed by section 4(1) of the Parliament Act 1911 as amended ...".

7. A *marginal note* performs many functions, such as indicating the general scope or purpose of a section (as in this Act where the note reads "Abolition of death penalty for murder", showing the effect of s 1 of the Act), or citing the reference to another Act. For example, in this Act, s 1(2) refers to the Prisons (Scotland) Act 1952, and the marginal note cites "1952 c 61".

8. A *section* is the main form of division in an Act, here s 1. It is indicated in citations by a small letter "s" followed by a full stop.

9. A *subsection* is the next level of division below a section. It is shown by numerals in brackets, for example "s 1(2)".

At this point the reader should also be aware of the existence of the *paragraph* and the *sub-paragraph*, not shown on the Murder (Abolition of Death Penalty) Act 1965. A paragraph is the third level of division below a section and is shown by lower-case letters in brackets, for example s 3(1)(a) of the Scotland Act 1998, illustrated below:

"3. – (1) The Presiding Officer shall propose a day for the holding of a poll if –
(a) the Parliament resolves that it should be dissolved and, if the resolution is passed on a division, the number of members voting in favour of it is not less than two-thirds of the total number of seats for members of the Parliament, or (b) any period during which the Parliament is required under section 46 to nominate one of its members for appointment as First Minister ends without such a nomination being made."

A sub-paragraph is the fourth and lowest division below a section. It is shown by lower-case Roman numerals, for example s 2(1)(c)(i) of the Prevention of Terrorism (Temporary Provisions) Act 1989, illustrated below:

"2. – (1) Subject to subsection (3) below, a person is guilty of an offence if he –
(a) belongs or professes to belong to a proscribed organisation,

(b) solicits or invites support for a proscribed organisation other than support with money or other property; or

(c) arranges or assists in the arrangement or management of, or addresses, any meeting of three or more persons (whether or not it is a meeting to which the public are admitted) knowing that the meeting is—

    (i) to support a proscribed organisation;

    (ii) to further the activities of such an organisation; or

    (iii) to be addressed by a person belonging or professing to belong to such an organisation."

10. An *amending provision* is part of an Act which amends the law in a pre-existing Act by deleting, inserting or substituting certain words, phrases or paragraphs.

11. The *short title*, extent and commencement section contains a number of sub-sections which have a variety of purposes. Here, s 3(1) contains the short title of the Act. This states how the Act may be referred to in other Acts, case reports and textbooks. It accordingly follows that two Acts in the same year 10 introduction to law and legal obligations will not be called the same thing, as this would cause unnecessary confusion. If the same title is used, the use of the words "(No 2)" in brackets can be employed, for example the Education and Education (No 2) Acts 1986.

The territorial extent of the Act can be found in s 3(3). This determines whether the Act, and if so which parts of it, applies to specific areas of the UK. The most usual areas are Northern Ireland, England and Wales, and Scotland. If no extent is mentioned, the Act is assumed to extend in entirety to the whole of the UK.

The commencement subsection can be seen in s 3(4). Here, the most common form of commencement is used, ie that the Act will come into force on the day of Royal Assent, or one or more specified days thereafter (here, it is on the following day). An Act may also come into force on a specific date, such as 22 June 2006. The date will be specifically mentioned within the section in such cases. It is also possible for an Act to come into force when a commencement order is made by a subordinate person or body (usually a Secretary of State) if the Act expressly allows for this. Finally, an Act or a provision of it may come into force upon the coming into effect of another Act.

12. A *Schedule* can be used in a variety of ways. Here, it is used to show what parts of old legislation are to be repealed (got rid of!) by the passing of the new Act. Repeals can be of the whole Act, any part, section, subsection, paragraph, sub-paragraph, phrase or even single word, or any combination of them. Schedules may also be used to give more detail to an Act, for example detail as to membership of bodies in Sch 7 to the Local Government etc (Scotland) Act 1994. They can also provide guidance as to the interpretation of a provision within the Act, for example Sch 2 to the Unfair Contract Terms Act 1977. If legislators wish to show the form of something (for example, the ballot paper in the referendum held under the Scotland Act 1978) they may use an Appendix instead of a Schedule.

Subordinate legislation. It is common for Parliament, through an Act, to confer on **1.20** Ministers or other executive bodies the power to make rules and regulations which have the force of law and are thus properly called legislation. The phrase "subordinate legislation" covers every exercise of such power and is sometimes also known as "delegated legislation". The power to enact this kind of legislation comes from an authorising or "parent" Act which will be an Act of Parliament. There are many types of subordinate legislation but the most common are statutory instruments and Orders in Council. More than 3,000 of these are passed every year and they have a number of advantages and uses:

- Parliament has time to concern itself only with the broad principles of Acts. Detailed regulations and rules should be dealt with by the administration. The Road Traffic Acts are a good example. The Road Traffic Act 1972 empowered the Secretary of State to make regulations for the use of vehicles on public roads; such detail cannot possibly be set out in an Act of Parliament. Thus subordinate legislation can save parliamentary time.

- Subordinate legislation allows the knowledge and experience available outside Parliament to be utilised through appropriate consultation. For example, in issuing regulations under the Dangerous Dogs Act 1991, the Secretary of State must consult with the British Veterinary Association.

- In times of emergency, it is impossible to pass an Act of Parliament quickly enough to deal with the situation. Subordinate legislation can be passed rapidly and allows responsiveness to emergencies. For example, the Secretary of State for the Environment could restrict the movement of livestock if there was an outbreak of Foot and Mouth Disease.

- Subordinate legislation is also used to give effect to Acts of Parliament. Often an Act of Parliament will state that all, or some, of the Act is to come into force on a date to be set by the Secretary of State. This is done using a statutory instrument known as a "commencement order".

1.21   *Statutory instruments*. Statutory instruments are also known as "Regulations" or "Rules" and the power to make them will be delegated to a Minister by an Act of Parliament. Most statutory instruments are "laid" before Parliament. However, they are not scrutinised to any great extent. If the authorising Act states that an instrument is to be passed using the negative procedure, then it will come into force in 40 days unless either House of Parliament resolves that it should be annulled. This is a fairly weak form of control.

1.22   The second method of laying an instrument before Parliament involves the *affirmative* procedure. Under this method, the instrument requires parliamentary approval before it can come into force. This is achieved through a 90-minute debate in Parliament. If a resolution to pass the instrument is not achieved then it will be taken back and amended in order for re-submission. This is obviously a slightly stronger form of control than the negative procedure.

1.23   Many statutory instruments have no laying requirement at all. This is not uncommon and regularly applies to commencement orders.

1.24   *Orders in Council*. Orders in Council refer to the Privy Council which advises the Queen on matters of constitutional importance. There are two types of Order in Council: those made under the authority of the Royal Prerogative, and those which are delegated to Ministers through an Act of Parliament. The first is an Order which is made without requiring the consent of Parliament. Such Orders are usually reserved for matters of constitutional importance, such as the dissolution of Parliament. They are made by the Privy Council with the authority of the Queen; although the Queen's assent today is purely formal and in reality is exercised by Ministers on her behalf. The second type of Order is authorised by an Act of Parliament and cannot be made without parliamentary approval. Such an Order was used to transfer powers from the UK Ministers to the Scottish Parliament under the devolution settlement.

Orders in Council do not really differ in status from that of statutory instruments **1.25** but are considered through custom and convention to be more dignified and are therefore used for matters of constitutional importance.

Control of subordinate legislation. Challenge in the courts is not possible for Acts of **1.26** Parliament, but it is for subordinate legislation. This is because the legislative powers of the UK Parliament are unlimited, whereas those of Ministers and subordinate bodies are not. There are two main grounds of challenge in the courts:

(1) that the content or substance of the legislation is *ultra vires* the parent Act. (In other words, it goes beyond the powers authorised by the Act); and

(2) that correct procedures have not been followed in the making of the legislation.

Scottish parliamentary legislation

Legislative competence. On 1 July 1999, the Queen officially opened the Scottish **1.27** Parliament. The Scotland Act 1998 (SA 1998) created the Scottish Parliament by devolving various powers from the UK Parliament and handing them over to the Scottish Parliament.[14] Of those devolved powers, arguably the most important is the power to make law. The Scotland Act states that the "... Parliament may make laws, to be known as the Acts of the Scottish Parliament"[15] but the power to make such laws is not unlimited.

The Scottish Parliament is a creature of statute and can only pass laws in areas **1.28** where it has legislative competency. This is because the UK Parliament has not passed all of its law-making powers to the Scottish Parliament. SA 1998 does not state which powers have categorically been given to the Scottish Parliament since the Scotland Act subscribes to the retaining model of devolution. Under this model, everything is devolved to the Scottish Parliament except a number of specific areas which are "retained". These retained areas are listed within the Scotland Act and dictate the legislative competence of the Scottish Parliament.

The legislative competence of the Scottish Parliament is clearly spelled out in SA **1.29** 1998, s 29:

• the Scottish Parliament may not legislate for another territory;

• the Scottish Parliament may not legislate on a matter reserved to the UK Parliament by virtue of Sch 5;

---

[14] For more discussion on Scottish devolution, see para 3.77.
[15] SA 1998, s 28(1).

- the Scottish Parliament may not legislate in breach of the restrictions contained in Sch 4;[16]
- Acts of the Scottish Parliament must be compatible with the Human Rights Act 1998 and the European Communities Act 1972; and
- the Scottish Parliament may not remove the office of Lord Advocate.

1.30 In terms of Sch 5 to the Scotland Act, there are a number of areas which are known as "reserved" areas and here the Scottish Parliament has no power. The reserved areas are split into both "general" and "specific" reservations.[17] General reservations deal with subjects such as defence, social security and foreign affairs. These are areas where the law generally needs to be uniform across the UK or must be retained in order to fulfil international obligations. Specific reservations are very detailed and provide particular named areas where the Scottish Parliament has no power. The list is long and includes such areas as abortion; space exploration; interference with time zones; and xeno-transplantation.

1.31 **Bills and parliamentary stages**. Like Acts of the UK Parliament, Acts of the Scottish Parliament must begin as Bills. A Bill may be introduced by a member of the Scottish Executive, a Committee of the Scottish Parliament, or an individual MSP. Prior to the introduction of a Bill, a member of the Scottish Executive must make a statement that the provisions of the Bill are within the legislative competence of the Parliament.[18] The Presiding Officer must also consider the provisions and make a similar statement to the Parliament as to whether or not the Bill is competent.[19]

1.32 There are four main categories of Bill which can be brought before the Scottish Parliament. These are Executive Bills, Committee Bills, Members' Bills and Private Bills. As a general rule, there is extensive consultation and pre-legislative scrutiny on a Bill before it is introduced to the Parliament. All Bills on introduction must be accompanied by a Financial Memorandum setting out estimates of the administrative and compliance costs of the Bill. Furthermore, all Government Bills must be accompanied by explanatory notes summarising the provisions of the Bill, and a Policy Memorandum which sets out the policy objectives of the Bill. The parliamentary process that a Bill follows will vary depending on the type of Bill but the most common procedure is that used for Executive Bills which consist of three stages:

- **Stage 1**: the Bill is referred to the relevant subject committee, known as the "lead committee", for consideration of its general principles. The lead committee can take evidence at this stage and other committees with an interest in the Bill may also be involved in putting forward their views, for example the Finance Committee. The lead committee prepares a report which is submitted to the Parliament where a debate and vote are held on the principles of the Bill;
- **Stage 2**: after a period of at least 2 weeks, the Bill is sent to one or more committees to receive more detailed line-by-line consideration. The lead committee will

---

[16] Schedule 4 states that particular statutes of constitutional note cannot be amended or repealed by the Scottish Parliament, eg the Acts of Union 1707, the European Communities Act 1972 and SA 1998.

[17] See SA 1998, Sch 5, Pts I, II.

[18] SA 1998, s 31(1).

[19] SA 1998, s 31(2).

generally draw together the observations of any other committee involved at this stage. It is also possible for a Bill to be sent to a Committee of the Whole Parliament. At this stage, amendments may be proposed and made to the Bill;

- **Stage 3**: following a further 2-week period, the amended Bill returns to the Parliament for further consideration and amendment. The Parliament must decide whether the Bill in its final form should be passed and at least a quarter of all MSPs must vote.

Following the final vote in the Parliament there must be a 4-week period before the Bill is submitted for Royal Assent. This time gap allows certain Law Officers, namely the Advocate General, the Lord Advocate and the Attorney-General, to have a role in the scrutiny of Bills. During this period, if any of the Law Officers doubts whether any provision is within the legislative competence of the Scottish Parliament, then they may refer the issue to the Judicial Committee of the Privy Council (JCPC).[20] This power may be similarly exercised by a Minister of the UK Parliament.[21] If the JCPC finds that the Bill is outwith the legislative competence of the Parliament, then the Bill must be returned to the Parliament in order for amendments to be made. If the amended Bill is then subject to no further challenge, the Presiding Officer submits it to the Queen for Royal Assent. **1.33**

Committee Bills. Committee Bills are seen as an innovation of the Scottish Parliament and a modern addition to the law-making process. The White Paper *Scotland's Parliament*[22] suggested that legislation should be initiated by committees of the Scottish Parliament, in keeping with the spirit of giving more MSPs a greater role in the legislative process of the Parliament. Committee Bills allow a committee of the Parliament to conduct inquiries into an area of law where it is perceived that change is required. The committee may then submit a report on this to the Parliament. With the agreement of the Parliament, the Scottish Executive then has 5 days to decide whether or not to support the report and propose legislation. If the Executive does not itself agree to bring forward legislation in line with the committee's proposals, then the Parliament may decide to adopt the Bill and bring forth draft legislation. The draft Bill would then be introduced to the Parliament and be subject to a general debate on its principles. If approved in principle, then the Bill would generally follow the same procedure outlined for an Executive Bill. The first Committee Bill was introduced by the Justice 1 Committee in 2001 and was enacted as the Protection from Abuse (Scotland) Act 2001. **1.34**

Members' Bills. These are similar to Private Members' Bills within the UK Parliament. Individual MSPs are entitled to bring forward proposals for legislation before either the Parliament or a relevant committee. If an MSP submits proposals to a committee, then the committee may hold an inquiry in order to assess whether the legislation is required. If the committee decides to proceed with the proposals then the Committee Bill procedure will be used. Alternatively, if an MSP submits proposals to the Parliament, then they must have the support of at least 11 other MSPs. After lodging **1.35**

---

[20] SA 1998, s 33.
[21] SA 1998, s 35.
[22] *Scotland's Parliament* (Cm 3658, July 1997).

the Bill with the Parliamentary Clerk, if the Bill receives 11 signatures within 1 month, then it will proceed following the Executive Bill procedure. One of the most high-profile Members' Bills was the Protection of Wild Mammals (Scotland) Bill introduced by Lord Watson which subsequently received Royal Assent in 2002.

1.36 **Private Bills**. Private Bills may be introduced by a person, body or association in order to gain powers in a specific area. They may be introduced to the Parliament on any sitting day. Private Bills generally follow the Executive Bill procedure, however, during Stage 1, the committee may require additional information and may ask the proposer to advertise the Bill in order to allow for any objections. The Committee must then prepare a report which deals with the need for such legislation and incorporates any public objections. The first Private Bill introduced in the Parliament was the Robin Rigg Offshore Wind Farm (Navigation and Fishing) (Scotland) Bill which received Royal Assent in 2003.

1.37 **Subordinate legislation of the Scottish Parliament**. The Scotland Act 1998 conveys powers to make subordinate legislation upon Scottish Ministers, Ministers of the Crown and Her Majesty in Council.[23] This is necessary for the same reasons that the UK Parliament requires power to enact statutory instruments and Orders in Council. Statutory instruments of the Scottish Parliament are known as Scottish statutory instruments or SSIs. Although Scottish Ministers normally make subordinate legislation only in areas where the Parliament has legislative competence, provisions exist which also allow them to legislate in areas where the Parliament has no competence. SA 1998 allows a UK Minister to transfer functions, by Order in Council, to Scottish Ministers and these functions may then be exercised insofar as they relate to Scotland.[24] There are some restrictions placed upon the power to make subordinate legislation. Such legislation cannot create serious criminal offences,[25] and it is also subject to the same principles of challenge as UK subordinate legislation, for example the *ultra vires* doctrine.

Byelaws

1.38 As well as subordinate legislation emanating from both the UK and Scottish Parliaments, there exists another form of subordinate legislation which is known as a byelaw. Byelaws are rules made by an authority subordinate to Parliament for the regulation, administration or management of a certain district and/or property. In Scotland, byelaws are made by local authorities and certain other public bodies such as railway authorities. However, the vast majority of byelaws are enacted by local authorities by virtue of the Local Government (Scotland) Act 1973.[26] The 1973 Act states that local authorities may make byelaws for the good rule and government of their area. A common example is the "anti-drinking" byelaw adopted by most Scottish local authorities which bans the consumption of alcohol within certain public areas. Such

---

[23] SA 1998, Pt IV. For a detailed overview of subordinate legislation in the Scottish Parliament, see J McFadden and M Lazarowicz, *The Scottish Parliament: An Introduction* (3rd edn, 2003), Chapter 5.
[24] SA 1998, s 63.
[25] SA 1998, s 113(10).
[26] Sections 201–204.

byelaws must satisfy a number of conditions. They must be within the authority of the authorising statute and must not be contrary to the general law of the land. In addition, they must be certain in their enactment and not unreasonable. Byelaws are capable of being challenged in court as *ultra vires*[27] if they fail to adhere to these conditions and have not been made by following the prescribed procedure.

Byelaws have the same effect as any other law, provided that they are validly **1.39** enacted. Before being deemed valid, a byelaw must be confirmed by a relevant Scottish Minister. Prior to confirmation, the local authority must inform members of the public of its intention to legislate. This is done by printing a notice in the local newspaper and informing the public where copies of the draft byelaw can be obtained. This procedure allows citizens to lodge any relevant objections. Such objections must be taken into account by the Scottish Ministers who then have the power to confirm, modify or refuse the byelaw. Once a byelaw has been confirmed, it must be publicised in the area concerned. Local authorities are also obliged to keep a register of byelaws for their area in order to allow public inspection.

European legislation

European law has become increasingly important in the UK. As a result of its **1.40** membership of the European Union, the UK has agreed to be bound by European law. The European Communities Act 1972 ensures the applicability of European law in the UK and states that all directly effective EU legislation creates an enforceable right within the UK and must be enforced by all courts and tribunals. It also states that all UK law must be applied subject to European law. Therefore, European law overarches our system of national law and, if there is any conflict, it is European law which prevails.

These provisions are fairly revolutionary in that they fundamentally undermine **1.41** the concept of parliamentary sovereignty and the supremacy of the UK Parliament. The implications of the European Communities Act 1972 were discussed in great detail in the case of *R* v *Secretary of State for Transport, ex parte Factortame (No 2)*.[28] On appeal, it was affirmed by the House of Lords that an Act of Parliament contradicting EU legislation could not be enforced in the courts of the UK. Furthermore, since EU law had to be enforced, courts were entitled to issue orders to such effect. In effect, the 1972 Act allows European legislation to take precedence over that of the UK. There have been many positive effects of this principle, and some areas of UK law have been fundamentally changed for the better due to the influence of European law.[29]

Sources of European law. There are two main sources of European law. These are **1.42** primary legislation and secondary legislation. Primary legislation consists of the Treaties which originally established the European Economic Community (EEC) and

---

[27] See further J McFadden, *Local Government Law in Scotland: An Introduction* (2004), Chapter 4.
[28] [1990] 3 CMLR 375.
[29] For example, under UK law, separate legal protections used to exist for full-time and part-time workers. These were held to be discriminatory under EU law and so abolished. Also, female employees of the armed forces who became pregnant used to be instantly dismissed. This too was held to be discriminatory and abolished.

subsequently amended and altered its constitution. Since the EEC was created in 1957 it has greatly developed and expanded in its form and membership, becoming the European Community (EC) and now the European Union (EU). Upon joining the EU, Member States agree to be bound by the provisions of the Treaties. It is through the authority of the Treaties that secondary legislation is created. Some of the key European Treaties are as follows:

- the *Treaties of Rome 1957* led to the creation of the European Economic Community and the European Atomic Energy Authority;
- the *Treaty of Accession 1972* marked the entry of the UK to the EEC and further enlargement through the membership of Ireland and Denmark;
- the *Maastricht Treaty 1992* created the European Union;
- the *Amsterdam Treaty 1997* set new objectives for the European Union;
- the *Treaty of Nice* 2001 saw the creation of the EU Charter of Fundamental Rights.

1.43   Secondary legislation consists of Regulations, Directives and Decisions. European Regulations are of general application and become law within all Member States automatically. Member States do not have to pass any national legislation to apply the Regulations and they supersede any national law. Such Regulations are described as having "direct effect" within the Member States.

1.44   European Directives, on the other hand, state objectives to be achieved by Member States and it is up to each individual state to enact or amend national legislation in order to comply. A Directive does not, therefore, have direct applicability. There is normally a time limit within which a Directive must be implemented. If a Directive is sufficiently clear and specific, and if the time limit for implementation has elapsed, then the Directive will have direct effect. This means that a citizen can rely on the Directive to challenge the failure of the UK Government to comply.

1.45   Decisions are issued by the European Commission. The Commission is the administrative body of the EU and is responsible for all aspects of decision-making within the EU. The Commission ensures that Member States uphold their obligations to implement EU laws. Failure to implement obligations can result in enforcement proceedings being taken against a Member State. This involves the Commission investigating an alleged breach and issuing a reasoned opinion or decision on the matter. Decisions are binding upon the state to whom they are addressed and may also be issued to a public body, a private company or an individual.

Judicial precedent

1.46   Judicial precedent is the most important source of law after legislation. It is sometimes also known as case law, or common law. Precedent is not created by Parliament; instead, it emanates from the decisions of judges in cases heard before them. As such, precedent can often be difficult to find and interpret since it must be extracted from the written judgment of cases. With legislation, many drafters are involved in creating the most precise wording and form possible to avoid any ambiguities. However, judges will often produce their decisions in various styles, and some more clearly than others. Nonetheless, when a precedent is extracted from a case it forms part of the body of law in that area and can be regarded as authoritative. The relationship between precedent and legislation is an important one and worthy of note. Since legislation is the most important source of law, its position is supreme. Through the doctrine of the supremacy of Parliament, legislation cannot be altered by any kind of judicial precedent. Conversely, it is possible for legislation to alter precedent. For example, Parliament may decide to legislate for an area which has been traditionally governed by common law and the law of precedent. In England and Wales, for example, the Theft Act 1968 codified the common law of theft. This meant that the Theft Act superseded the pre-existing common law in that area.

The rules of precedent

Judicial precedent operates under the principle of *stare decisis* which literally means **1.47** "to stand by decisions". This principle means that a court must follow and apply the law as set out in the decisions of higher courts in previous cases. In this way a consistent body of precedent can be created and applied with some certainty. But not all precedents are binding, and there are a number of rules which are applied by the judiciary in ascertaining the status of a precedent.

If a precedent is to be followed by a judge in a current case, then first it must be **1.48** "in point". This means that the question of law answered in the previous case must be the same as the question before the current judge. It is not the facts of the case which must be similar but the actual point of law being dealt with in relation to those facts. In deciding whether a precedent is "in point", a judge needs to identify the *ratio decidendi* of the original decision. The *ratio* is the point of law which led to the decision. Sometimes judges will make it clear what the reason for the decision was in a case, by clearly stating so. More often, however, they will not and thus finding the *ratio* of a precedent can be a difficult task. There may also be statements made in a case which are *obiter dicta*, meaning "things said by the way". These do not form part of the reasoning for the decision or part of the *ratio*. They are often hypothetical questions or issues which illustrate how different facts in the case could lead to a different decision. *Obiter* remarks are never binding; they are merely persuasive on a judge. Their degree of persuasiveness will depend upon the authority of the judge who made the remarks.

If a precedent is not "in point" then it becomes merely "persuasive". A precedent **1.49** which is persuasive is not binding upon a judge and it may be distinguished. If a judge decides to distinguish a precedent then he is not bound to follow it. This leads to the development of the law in dealing with new situations. On the other hand, if a precedent is "in point", then it may be binding and the judge will be obliged to follow and apply the *ratio* of that decision. Yet this is ultimately dependent upon the position of the court within the hierarchy.

Precedent and the court hierarchy

It is not simply enough that a precedent be "in point" in order for it to be binding. **1.50** The relationship between the court where a precedent originated from and that of the court making the current decision is also crucial. As a general rule, in Scots law, a court will only be bound to follow the precedent of a court of higher status.[30] Decisions from

---

[30] For the position of courts within the Scottish court hierarchy, see Chapter 2.

courts with lower status are, as a rule, only persuasive. Precedents from courts outwith Scotland can also be considered but, apart from decisions of the House of Lords, none of these precedents is binding. On matters of European law, all UK courts are bound by precedents of the European Court of Justice. Here follows a brief overview of the principles of *stare decisis* in operation:

Criminal courts

1.51
- The *district court*, being the lowest criminal court, is bound by the decisions of the High Court of Justiciary (both as an appeal and as a trial court).
- The *sheriff court* is bound by the decisions of the High Court of Justiciary (both as an appeal and as a trial court).
- The *High Court of Justiciary (trial court)* is bound by the decisions of the High Court of Justiciary sitting as an appeal court. A decision of one Lord of Justiciary in the trial court does not bind another Lord of Justiciary in the trial court.
- The *High Court of Justiciary (appeal court)*, being the highest and most authoritative of the criminal courts, is not bound by its own precedents. However, any precedent which was questioned would have to be reviewed by a larger number of judges. A Full Bench of judges could easily overrule a precedent set by three appeal court judges.

Civil courts

1.52
- The *sheriff court*, being the lowest civil court, is bound by the decisions of the Inner House of the Court of Session and by the decisions of the House of Lords in Scottish appeals. A decision by one sheriff does not bind another sheriff, although sheriffs are bound by the sheriffs principal of that sheriffdom. A decision by a sheriff principal does not bind another sheriff principal.
- The *Court of Session (Outer House)* is bound by the decisions of the House of Lords in Scottish appeals and by decisions of seven or more judges.[31] Lords Ordinary are also bound by decisions of the Inner House of the Court of Session. The decision of a Lord Ordinary in the Outer House does not bind another Lord Ordinary in the Outer House.
- The *Court of Session (Inner House)* is bound by the decisions of the House of Lords in Scottish appeals. Either Division, or an Extra Division of the Inner House, is bound by its own previous decisions. Any precedent called into question can be overruled by a Full Bench of judges.
- The *House of Lords* sits as a final court of appeal in Scottish civil matters. Decisions of the House of Lords are binding on all Scottish civil courts. The House normally considers itself to be bound by its own precedents but may depart from them when circumstances dictate.[32]

Institutional writings

1.53   Institutional writings, also known as authoritative writings, are the works of writers who first brought together the principles of Scots law into legal texts. These institutional

---

[31] *Munro's Trustees* v *Munro* 1971 SC 280.
[32] See Lord Chancellor's Practice Note at [1966] 3 All ER 77.

writers lived mostly during the 17th and 18th centuries but their work has proved to be highly influential in the development of Scots law. Although their influence has dwindled somewhat in modern times, a statement made by an institutional writer will settle the law if there is no statute or judicial precedent covering the area in question. Some of the most important institutional writers are as follows:

- *James Dalrymple, Viscount Stair* (1619–95) is probably the most well known of all the institutional writers. Former Lord President of the Court of Session, his Institutions of the Law of Scotland was first published in 1681. Stair's work was based upon the principles of custom, feudal and Roman law, and Biblical law.
- *Professor John Erskine* (1695–1768) was responsible for producing *An Institute of the Law of Scotland*. Second only to Stair in terms of influence, this work was highly authoritative and set out the principles of Scots common law prior to the impact of judicial precedent and legislation.
- *Baron David Hume* (1757–1843) is famous for his treatise on Scots criminal law. His *Commentaries on the Law of Scotland respecting the Description and Punishment of Crimes* was first published in 1797 and still has relevance today in many aspects of criminal law in Scotland.

Custom

While custom was historically a very important source of law, it plays a far lesser role **1.54** today and is unlikely to be recognised in terms of creating new principles of law. Most older customs became embodied in the works of institutional writers and from there were incorporated into law by the courts as part of the common law. In modern, well-developed legal systems, custom has also been superseded by increasing amounts of parliamentary legislation. Nonetheless, it is still technically possible for custom to be accepted as a new source of law. In order for this to happen, four conditions must be fulfilled. First, the custom must be an exception to the general law but still be generally consistent with it. Second, there must have been a long acquiescence with the custom for it to be generally accepted as law. Third, it must be definite and certain and, finally, it must be fair and reasonable.

Equity

The use of the term "equity" in Scots law means justice, fairness and reasonableness. It **1.55** refers to the equitable power of the Court of Session and the High Court of Justiciary to provide a remedy in the interests of justice where otherwise there is none. This power is known as the *nobile officium* and is not often used by the courts. The *nobile officium* power of the Court of Session allows the law to operate in circumstances where otherwise a technicality would prevent it. In the case of *Ferguson, Petitioner*,[33] an electoral registration officer wrongly deleted the names of prospective voters from the draft electoral register. There was no common law or statutory remedy available which would allow the names to be placed back on the register. Therefore, in the interests of justness and fairness, the court invoked the *nobile officium* and ordered the names to be reinstated in order that the petitioners could vote in an imminent election.

---

[33] 1965 SC 16.

1.56   The *nobile officium* power also allows the High Court of Justiciary to declare certain acts to be criminal in nature where previously they were not. This is known as the declaratory power of the High Court of Justiciary. In the case of *Khaliq* v *HM Advocate*,[34] a shopkeeper was convicted of selling "glue-sniffing kits" to children. The named offence was unknown to Scots criminal law but the High Court decided that it was behaviour of a type which was harmful and should be criminalised. This power is seldom used today.

ESSENTIAL FACTS

1.57

- Law can be categorised as either public law or private law. Public law deals with the operation of government and the regulation of the relationship between government and citizens. Private law is concerned with the regulation of relationships between individual citizens and/or companies and organisations.

- The law may also be described as civil law or criminal law. The main difference is that each has a different court structure for its regulation. Criminal law deals with the punishment of criminal behaviour while civil law deals with disputes arising between private individuals, where the conduct of one party has caused unjustified loss to another.

- Legislation is the most important source of law. It consists of Acts of the UK Parliament, Acts of the Scottish Parliament, European Community legislation and various forms of delegated legislation.

- The UK Parliament is the supreme law-making body in the UK. UK legislation begins as a Bill and must then pass through the scrutiny of the House of Commons and the House of Lords. A Bill must then be submitted for Royal Assent before it can become an Act of Parliament. Such Acts are commonly known as statutes.

- The Scottish Parliament has devolved power to enact legislation for Scotland by virtue of the Scotland Act 1998. Its law-making power is limited in that certain areas are "reserved" to the UK Parliament. The Scottish Parliament may not pass any laws in these areas.

- Subordinate legislation arises when Parliament confers the power to make laws on Ministers or other delegated bodies. The product of exercising such power is sometimes also known as "delegated legislation". There are many types of subordinate legislation but the most common are statutory instruments, Orders in Council and byelaws. All subordinate legislation is subject to the *ultra vires* doctrine and the control of the courts.

- European legislation has become increasingly important in the UK as a result of its membership of the European Union. The European

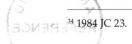

---

[34] 1984 JC 23.

Communities Act 1972 ensures the applicability of European law in the UK and states that all directly effective EU legislation creates an enforceable right within the UK and must be enforced by all courts and tribunals. There are two main sources of European legislation: primary and secondary. Primary legislation consists of the founding Treaties of the EU, whereas secondary legislation consists of Regulations, Directives and Decisions issued under the authority of those Treaties.

- Judicial precedent or "common law" is the second most important source of law in the UK. Utilising the rules of precedent and the doctrine of *stare decisis* (standing by decisions), court decisions become a source of law by building up a body of binding decisions. Superior courts generally bind inferior courts within the court hierarchy but decisions become binding only if a case is "in point" and a previously decided *ratio decidendi* is the same as the *ratio* in the present case. The *ratio* is the legal principle upon which a case is decided. Hypothetical comments made in a decision are said to be made "by the way" or *obiter dicta*. They are not binding upon future cases and are merely persuasive.

- Institutional writings, also known as authoritative writings, are the works of writers who first brought together the principles of Scots law into legal texts. The institutional writers lived mostly during the 17th and 18th centuries but their work has proved to be highly influential in the development of Scots law. Their influence has dwindled in modern times with the growth of legislation and judicial precedent.

- Custom was historically a very important source of law but there is little scope for it today in the creation of new legal principles. For this to happen, four conditions must be fulfilled. First, the custom must be an exception to the general law but still be generally consistent with it. Second, there must have been a long acquiescence with the custom for it to be generally accepted as law. Third, it must be definite and certain and, finally, it must be fair and reasonable.

- Equity in Scots law relates to justice, fairness and reasonableness. It refers to the equitable power of the Court of Session and the High Court of Justiciary to provide a remedy in the interests of justice where otherwise there is none. This power is known as the *nobile officium* and is not often used by the courts.

2 SCOTTISH LEGAL SYSTEM

The purpose of this chapter is to give the reader a detailed overview of the Scottish **2.1** court structure and of the people who work within the legal profession in Scotland. As discussed in Chapter 1, Scots law can be described in terms of both civil law and criminal law and each has a different court structure for its regulation. A useful starting point is to examine the civil and criminal court structures in some detail.

SCOTTISH CIVIL COURT SERVICE

The civil courts in Scotland are the sheriff court, the Court of Session and the House of **2.2** Lords. Civil cases are known as litigation and are adversarial in nature. They involve a judge considering evidence submitted by all parties to the case and then issuing a judgment based upon the "balance of probabilities".[1]

THE SHERIFF COURT

The majority of civil litigation in Scotland is dealt with by the sheriff court. This is the **2.3** lowest of the civil courts and deals with a wide range of civil cases. Scotland is divided into six sheriffdoms based upon the groupings of the old local government areas. The current sheriffdoms are:

- Lothian and Borders;
- South Strathclyde, Dumfries and Galloway;
- Glasgow and Strathkelvin;
- North Strathclyde;
- Tayside, Central and Fife; and
- Grampian, Highland and Islands.

Each sheriffdom has a sheriff principal who has the general duty of securing the **2.4** speedy and efficient disposal of business within the courts of the sheriffdom. The sheriff principal is a full-time judge and is assisted by a number of sheriffs. Sheriffs and sheriffs principal are required to be solicitors or advocates of at least 10 years' standing and are appointed by the Queen on the recommendation of the First Minister after consultation with the Lord President.

Each sheriffdom is divided into several sheriff court districts. There are currently **2.5** 49 such districts and each is staffed by as many sheriffs as are required to deal with

---

[1] See para 1.5 for an explanation of the differing standards of proof in civil and criminal law.

the volume of litigation for each court. The largest sheriff court in Scotland is Glasgow. This is one of the busiest courts in Europe and has in excess of 23 sheriffs.

Jurisdiction

2.6   In civil actions, the sheriff court is both a court of first instance and a court of appeal. Its jurisdiction is wide and encompasses actions ranging from debt recovery to breach of contract, and divorce. The sheriff court has exclusive jurisdiction over certain matters. This is known as *privative* jurisdiction, and an example includes actions which involve a sum of money less than £5,000. In terms of deciding geographically where an action should be raised, the general rule is that a case should be heard by the court which has jurisdiction over the defender. This rule is embodied in the Latin maxim *actor sequitur forum rei* – meaning "the pursuer follows the court of the defender". The defender must either be resident within the relevant sheriffdom or have a place of business there. Cases coming before the sheriff court are categorised according to their monetary value. There are three different types, namely *small claims; summary causes;* and *ordinary causes.*

Small claims

2.7   The small claims procedure was introduced by the Law Reform (Miscellaneous Provisions) (Scotland) Act 1985. The procedure deals with actions for payment worth no more than £750[2] and was created to assist citizens in resolving minor disputes. It is relatively informal in nature and seeks to make the court process more user friendly by relaxing the normal rules of evidence and procedure. The normal rules about court expenses are also relaxed and generally the procedure seeks to encourage individual citizens to raise or defend small claims with little assistance. Cases are heard before a sheriff sitting alone and the pursuer does not require legal representation.

2.8   The unique feature of a small claim is the preliminary hearing at which it is determined whether the action requires to go to a full hearing or whether it can be dealt with there and then. Both the pursuer and the defender must advise the sheriff of the points which are in dispute between them and the sheriff must take a note and deliberate on these. The hearing is relatively informal and strict rules of evidence do not apply, allowing self-representation.[3]

2.9   An appeal against the decision of a sheriff in a small claim is made to the sheriff principal only and must be based upon a point of law.

Summary cause

2.10   The summary cause was introduced to provide citizens with an efficient and cheap means of procedure. It is used for cases with a monetary value of over £750 up to a limit of £1,500 and its jurisdiction is exclusive and final in such cases. Actions are heard by a single sheriff who is assisted by a sheriff clerk in terms of administrative

---

[2] Proposals to raise this limit to £1,500 are currently being considered by the Scottish Parliament. See para 2.23 below for further discussion.

[3] Nonetheless, legal representation still remains commonplace within small claims and can seriously affect the likelihood of success. It should be noted that legal aid is not available for small claims.

functions. A summary cause does not normally involve written pleadings, unlike an ordinary cause.

An appeal against the decision of a sheriff in a summary cause is made to the **2.11** sheriff principal on a point of law. A further appeal can be made with leave to the Inner House of the Court of Session and then to the House of Lords.

Ordinary cause

This procedure is used for actions over £1,500, with no upper limit upon the value of **2.12** the claim. It is the most expensive and time-consuming procedure within the sheriff court and can be heard by a sheriff, sheriff principal or an assessor. Ordinary actions are conducted by way of formal written pleadings, which are full and detailed. An ordinary cause may be remitted to the Court of Session if the case is of sufficient complexity or importance and any of the parties to the case have requested so.

An appeal from a sheriff in an ordinary cause can be made to the sheriff principal, **2.13** and then to the Inner House of the Court of Session. A further appeal to the House of Lords can be made on a point of law only. Alternatively, an appeal can be made directly to the Inner House of the Court of Session, essentially usurping the sheriff principal. This is likely to happen when the issue being dealt with is one of importance and therefore requires a decision from a more authoritative court or where both parties to the case are determined to appeal against the sheriff principal, regardless. However, an appeal to the Inner House is expensive, as an advocate or solicitor-advocate is required for representation. Thus, in order to avoid escalating costs, most parties are content with an appeal to the sheriff principal.

THE COURT OF SESSION

The Court of Session was established in 1532 and sits only in Parliament House, **2.14** Edinburgh. It is a supreme court which has jurisdiction over the whole of Scotland and has both original and appellate jurisdiction. It generally deals with civil actions which involve very large sums of money[4] or important points of law which require a more authoritative judgment than that of a sheriff. Judges of the Court of Session are officially known as either Senators of the College of Justice or Lords of Council and Session and there are currently 32 such judges. The most senior Court of Session judges are the Lord President and the Lord Justice-Clerk, in order of seniority. They are appointed by the Queen on the nomination of the Prime Minister from a recommendation of the First Minister. The remaining judges are appointed by the Queen on the recommendation of the First Minister following consultation with the Lord President. The judges can be sheriffs or sheriffs principal of at least 5 years' standing, or advocates or solicitor-advocates with at least 5 years' right of audience in the Court of Session. All Court of Session judges are also judges within the High Court of Justiciary where the Lord President becomes known as the Lord Justice-General.

The Court of Session is divided into two distinct parts, namely the Outer House and **2.15** the Inner House. The names of these two parts do not have any technical explanation – merely a historical and geographical one. In centuries past, the most senior judges would sit in an inner chamber of Parliament House while more inexperienced

---

[4] For example, £100,000 or more.

judges would sit in other "outer" chambers of the building. When a party to an action was unhappy with a decision emanating from a judge in an outer chamber then it was common for an appeal to be made to the more experienced inner chamber judges. Thus the Inner and Outer House distinctions were created.

Outer House

2.16 The Outer House is a court of first instance, meaning that cases can be heard there for the first time. Cases are normally heard before a single judge but it is possible in some cases to seek a jury trial within the Outer House. This is rare, however, and is limited to cases such as an action for defamation or damages for personal injury. If a jury is used in such cases it consists of 12 members of the public selected at random from the electoral role.

2.17   The jurisdiction of the Outer House extends to all kinds of civil action except those which are excluded by statute or privative to another court. It is the only court in Scotland which can hear actions for judicial review of administrative action. This is known as the controlling power of the Court of Session and is used widely to review acts of persons and bodies who have been given delegated power from Parliament, for example local authorities and other government bodies. Decisions from the Outer House can be appealed to the Inner House of the Court of Session.

Inner House

2.18 The Inner House is primarily a court of appeal for civil actions raised in either the sheriff court or the Outer House. It also has some first instance jurisdiction but in extremely limited circumstances, for example an appeal against certain tribunals. The Inner House has two divisions, namely the First Division and the Second Division. Each has equal authority and jurisdiction. The First Division consists of the Lord President and three senior Lords of Session, while the Second Division comprises the Lord Justice-Clerk and three other Lords of Session. In practice, only three of the four judges actually sit in each division and it would only be in extraordinary circumstances that a Full Bench of four would sit.

2.19   In order to deal with heavy workloads, the Lord President may appoint any three judges to convene an Extra Division of the Court of Session. Also, in important or complicated cases, the First and Second Divisions may combine to form a more authoritative court of seven judges. Final judgments of the Inner House may be appealed to the House of Lords.

THE HOUSE OF LORDS

2.20 The House of Lords is an appellate court and is the final court of appeal in Scottish civil cases. It will normally only hear appeals on important or complex questions of law, and sometimes fact. There are 12 Lords of Appeal in Ordinary who hear appeals and they are commonly known as "Law Lords". In recent years, it has become customary to have at least two Law Lords who are of Scottish origin.[5] The quorum for hearing

---

[5] In that they have Scottish qualifications and have been prolific in practice within Scotland throughout their career.

appeals is three judges, but they are regularly heard by five and sometimes, in the most important cases, by seven Law Lords. It is a convention that at least one Law Lord should be of Scottish origin when hearing a Scottish civil appeal case, although this is not always possible and is subject to circumstance.

In an appeal from the Inner House of the Court of Session, the appellant must **2.21** petition the House of Lords, "praying" that the decision of the Inner House be altered. A decision of the House of Lords is not an operative judgment since it must be returned to the Court of Session where a decree from the Inner House will apply that judgment. Decisions of the House of Lords are ultimately binding upon all lower civil courts but the House itself is not bound by its own decisions and may depart from them when appropriate.

CIVIL JUSTICE REFORM

Recently, a number of changes have been introduced which will have a significant **2.22** impact upon the existing Scottish civil court structure. Of these probably the most significant are changes to the jurisdictional limits within the sheriff court and, more importantly, the creation of an entirely new court which will be known as the Supreme Court.

DEVELOPMENTS IN THE SHERIFF COURT

In July 1998 the Scottish Courts Administration issued a consultation paper[6] which **2.23** sought views on increasing the jurisdictional limits in the sheriff court. A number of reforms were put forward which were aimed at making the small claims procedure more accessible and which it was hoped would reduce the volume of ordinary causes. Thus, the Justice and Home Affairs Committee of the Scottish Parliament announced that small claim limits, fixed at £750 since 1988, are to be increased to £1,500 and summary cause limits are to be raised to £5,000. Consequently, ordinary causes will be reserved for more expensive actions exceeding £5,000. In addition, personal injury claims are to be specifically excluded from the small claim procedure. At the time of writing, these changes are awaiting approval by the Scottish Parliament.

A SUPREME COURT FOR THE UNITED KINGDOM

In recent years there have been mounting calls for the creation of a new, independent **2.24** Supreme Court, separating the highest appeal court from the House of Lords and removing the Law Lords from the legislature. On 12 June 2003 the Government announced its intention to do so and, in late 2004, the Constitutional Reform Act 2005 received Royal Assent.

The Government believes that the new Supreme Court will reflect and enhance the **2.25** independence of the judiciary from both the legislature and the executive. The decision to create the Supreme Court does not imply any dissatisfaction with the previous performance of the House of Lords as the UK's highest court of appeal; indeed, its

---

[6] Scottish Courts Administration, *Proposals to Increase Jurisdiction Limits in the Sheriff Court* (1998).

judges have conducted themselves with the utmost integrity and independence throughout the years. However, the Government believes that the time has come to establish a new court regulated by statute as a body separate from Parliament. This will allow the UK to adhere more rigidly to the doctrine of the separation of powers and will allay fears of potential conflict with the Human Rights Act 1998 and the right to a fair trial.

2.26   The Supreme Court will be a United Kingdom body, legally separate from the courts of England and Wales, which will take over the judicial functions of the Law Lords in the House of Lords and from the Judicial Committee of the Privy Council. The Supreme Court will be the final court of appeal in all matters under English law, Welsh law (to the extent that the Welsh Assembly makes laws for Wales that differ from those in England) and Northern Irish law. It will also be a court of record for appeals from the Court of Session in Scotland (there is no right of appeal beyond the High Court of Justiciary for criminal cases except in so far as devolution issues arise). The new Supreme Court is not based upon the United States model and will have no power to overturn legislation.

2.27   The court will be located in a building separate from the Houses of Parliament and, after a lengthy survey of suitable sites, including Somerset House, the location for the new court will be Middlesex Guildhall, in Parliament Square, Westminster, which is currently a Crown Court. The court is expected to hold its first hearing in 2009.

SCOTTISH CRIMINAL COURT STRUCTURE

2.28 The criminal courts in Scotland are the district court, the sheriff court and the High Court of Justiciary. Criminal cases are known as prosecutions and are adversarial in nature. There are two types of criminal procedure in Scotland, namely *summary* procedure and *solemn* procedure. Summary procedure is used for more minor cases such as breach of the peace or speeding, whereas solemn procedure is used for more serious offences such as assault or murder. The major difference between the procedures is that summary cases are heard by a judge sitting alone whereas solemn cases involve a trial before a jury of 15 members of the public as well as a judge. The standard of proof required in a criminal trial is "beyond all reasonable doubt", making it much higher than that of the civil courts.[7]

2.29   All criminal prosecutions in Scotland are taken through the system of public prosecution which is embodied in the Crown Office and Procurator Fiscal Service (COPFS). The most senior public prosecutor is the Lord Advocate who is assisted by the Solicitor General and around 15 Advocates Depute. At sheriff court and district court levels, prosecutions are normally undertaken by the procurator fiscal or a depute. Reports of offences are made chiefly by the police to the COPFS where it must be considered whether there is enough evidence and whether it is in the public interest to bring forth a prosecution. The procedure for bringing prosecutions is contained in the Criminal Procedure (Scotland) Act 1995.[8]

---

[7] See further paras 1.5 and 1.6.
[8] For a discussion of the criminal justice system, see further D McFadzean and K Scott, "Scottish Criminal Justice and the Police" in D Donnelly and K Scott (eds), *Policing Scotland* (2005).

DISTRICT COURT

The district court was created by the District Courts (Scotland) Act 1975. There are **2.30** currently 30 district courts in Scotland which roughly correspond with local authority areas. The district court is the lowest of the criminal courts and deals only with minor criminal matters, thus utilising only summary procedure. The district court is a lay court and is presided over by lay members known as justices of the peace (JPs). JPs are partially appointed by local councils, who may appoint up to one quarter of their members as justices. The remainder are upstanding members of the community who have been recommended by local committees for appointment by the Scottish Ministers. Any JP who sits on the bench of a district court is assisted by a legally qualified clerk of court[9] who will act as a legal assessor and give advice to the justice. In Glasgow, work is shared by JPs and legally qualified stipendiary magistrates. Such magistrates are unique to Glasgow and are not found in any other district courts. They are appointed by local authorities from among legally qualified practitioners in the area.

The sentencing powers of the district court reflect the minor nature of the offences **2.31** it deals with. A justice of the peace has the power to impose a prison sentence of up to 60 days and/or a fine of up to £2,500.[10] A stipendiary magistrate has the power to impose a prison sentence of 3 months (or up to 6 months in cases which involve a previous conviction of theft or dishonesty, or personal violence) and/or a fine of up to £5,000.

An appeal from a decision of the district court can be made to the High Court of **2.32** Justiciary only.

SHERIFF COURT

The jurisdiction of the sheriff court covers most criminal offences committed within **2.33** the sheriffdom except for those which are privative to other courts.[11] Thus, many cases which come before a district court could also be brought before the sheriff court. The decision on whether a case should ultimately be dealt with in the sheriff court is made by the procurator fiscal. As with civil actions before the sheriff court, cases are heard by either a sheriff principal or a sheriff, with or without a jury depending on what procedure is being used.

Summary procedure

This is used for the most minor offences and cases are heard by a sheriff sitting alone. **2.34** The decision on whether a minor offence should be brought before the sheriff court rather than the district court is made by the procurator fiscal and is based upon issues such as seriousness, sentencing and expediency. The sentencing powers of a sheriff under summary procedure are the same as those for a stipendiary magistrate, namely 3 months' imprisonment (or up to 6 months' for those with a previous conviction of theft or dishonesty, or personal violence) and/or a maximum fine of £5,000. The court

[9] The Clerk of Court must be qualified as a solicitor or an advocate.
[10] Note that some statutory offences will have a prescribed level of punishment to which the court must adhere.
[11] Eg parking offences must be dealt with by the district court, and murder or rape must be tried by the High Court of Justiciary.

also has the power to order disqualification from driving and in practice deals with most road traffic-related cases where disqualification or endorsement is involved.

Solemn procedure

2.35   Solemn procedure is used to deal with more serious offences such as robbery or assault. The sheriff will sit with a jury of 15 persons who will decide on the guilt of the accused. Three verdicts are available to a jury in Scotland, namely guilty; not guilty; and not proven. This last verdict has the same effect as an acquittal in that the accused is freed without sentence. It is regarded by many as a wholly unsatisfactory verdict since it indicates that the jury thought the accused was not entirely innocent but because there was insufficient evidence they could not convict "beyond all reasonable doubt". If the accused is found guilty, the sheriff has the power to impose a prison sentence of up to 3 years and/or an unlimited fine. It should be noted that the sheriff court also has the power to remit a case to the High Court of Justiciary for sentence, should it believe that its own powers are unduly restrictive.

Appeals

2.36   Appeals from the sheriff court may be taken, with leave, to the High Court of Justiciary for both summary and solemn cases. Unlike the civil jurisdiction of the sheriff court, it should be noted that there is no right of appeal from a sheriff to the sheriff principal in criminal matters.

HIGH COURT OF JUSTICIARY

2.37   Established in 1672, the High Court of Justiciary is the highest criminal court in Scotland and is both a court of first instance and an appellate court. It is presided over by the Lord Justice-General, the Lord Justice-Clerk and the Lords of Session as Lords Commissioners of Justiciary. It has jurisdiction over all crimes committed in Scotland except those which are privative to other courts or are excluded by statute. The High Court has exclusive jurisdiction with respect to a small number of offences which are known as the "Crown crimes", namely murder, rape, treason and incest.

Court of first instance

2.38   As a trial court, the High Court of Justiciary sits in Edinburgh but also has the power to go out on circuit as required. As a circuit court, the High Court can sit in locations throughout Scotland, using the local sheriff court as its base. While there are a number of towns which have regular sittings, such as Kilmarnock and Paisley, the circuits are not restricted to these towns and a sitting may be held wherever it is deemed convenient. Glasgow has a permanent sitting of the High Court because of the exceptionally high number of cases emanating from that area.[12]

2.39   The judges of the High Court of Justiciary are the same as those in the Court of Session, although they are known as "Lords Commissioners of Justiciary" in their

---

[12] Approximately half of all High Court cases originate from the Glasgow area.

criminal capacity. They sit alone, with a jury of 15 members of the public who decide upon the guilt of the accused. In particularly difficult or important cases, it is possible for three judges to sit; however, this is very rare and has occurred in only a handful of cases in the last century. The sentencing powers of the High Court are unlimited in terms of both imprisonment and fine. However, there are certain offences which have a sentence prescribed by statute. For example, by virtue of the Murder (Abolition of Death Penalty) Act 1965, any person convicted of murder must receive a sentence of life imprisonment.

Appeals from the High Court of Justiciary as a court of first instance can be made **2.40** to the High Court of Justiciary sitting as the Court of Criminal Appeal.

Court of Criminal Appeal

The High Court of Justiciary is also the highest court of criminal appeal in Scotland **2.41** and all criminal appeals must be heard before it. It should be noted that there is no right of appeal in Scottish criminal cases to the House of Lords.[13] Appeals from courts of summary criminal jurisdiction consist of appeals from the sheriff or district court against conviction, sentence or both. For appeals against conviction, the court consists of three or more judges and the determination of any question is according to the majority of members of the court sitting. Each judge is entitled to pronounce their own opinion. A lesser quorum of two judges is competent to hear appeals against various sentences. Appeals under solemn proceedings have similar grounds and procedure for those narrated above for summary. They are brought by way of a written note of appeal stating all of the grounds of appeal, ie conviction, sentence or both.

The court has wide powers of disposal for an appeal against conviction or **2.42** sentence. It can allow an appeal and quash a conviction, or it may amend a verdict, or modify a sentence. It also has the power to authorise the Crown to conduct new proceedings. It is worth noting that the Crown also has the right of appeal, albeit on a point of law against acquittal or sentence.

COURTS WITH SPECIAL JURISDICTION

THE EUROPEAN COURT OF JUSTICE

The European Court of Justice (ECJ) has jurisdiction over issues relating to matters **2.43** covered by the European Treaties. When such an issue arises in a case before a UK domestic court, the direction of the ECJ must be sought, or if a decision already exists on the issue then the precedent of the ECJ must be applied. Essentially, it is the job of the ECJ to ensure that European law is applied by Member States. Cases can be brought by individuals or can be referred to the ECJ from national courts for rulings on matters affecting the validity or interpretation of European law.

---

[13] *Macintosh v Lord Advocate* (1876) 3 R (HL) 34.

THE JUDICIAL COMMITTEE OF THE PRIVY COUNCIL

2.44 Historically, the Judicial Committee of the Privy Council was of little specific relevance to Scotland. The role of the Privy Council was to advise the monarch, to review decisions of certain professional bodies such as the General Medical Council, and to act as a final court of appeal from the colonies of the British Empire and from Commonwealth countries.[14] However, since the setting up of the Scottish Parliament in 1999, the Privy Council has had an increased profile in the administration of justice. The Scotland Act 1998 states that the Judicial Committee shall have the power to determine the legislative competence of a Bill of the Scottish Parliament prior to Royal Assent.[15] It also has the power to act as court of last resort in determining "devolution issues". Schedule 6 to the Scotland Act defines "devolution issues" as:

- a question as to the functions of the Scottish Executive, the First Minister or the Lord Advocate;
- whether the exercise of a function is within devolved competence;
- whether the exercise of a function is compatible with European law or the European Convention on Human Rights; and
- any other question regarding whether the exercise of a function is within devolved competence or any other question relating to reserved matters.

2.45 The Privy Council also hears appeals against devolution issues which arise in the lower courts, ie in Scotland the Inner House of the Court of Session or the High Court of Justiciary.[16] Decisions as to devolution issues are binding upon the lower courts.

STATUTORY TRIBUNALS

2.46 Although not technically courts, statutory tribunals are worthy of note and play an important supplementary role to the work of the courts within the UK. From the Second World War onwards, there has been an explosion in the size and complexity of the Welfare State in Britain. As a result, the state has become involved in more areas of everyday life than ever before. Consequently, this has led to a massive increase in the number of complaints and disputes which arise from the application of rules and regulations by various organs of the state. These disputes could be settled using the existing courts, however, the court system already struggles to cope with ever increasing litigation in other areas. As a result, Parliament decided to create special bodies, known as tribunals, for resolving certain categories of dispute between citizens and the state. It also created a number of tribunals with jurisdiction over disputes between citizens, for example in the area of employment law. Most tribunals are set up by statute and the powers and scope of the tribunal are contained either within the statute or in regulations issued under the authority of the statute.

2.47 Today, there are around 2,000 tribunals in the UK. They cover a wide range of disputes and include immigration appeals, employment tribunals, disability living

---

[14] Few countries retain this link but there are still some who use the Privy Council as their final court of appeal, eg Mauritius and the Bahamas.
[15] Scotland Act 1998, s 33.
[16] Scotland Act 1998, s 98 and Sch 6.

allowance tribunals, and benefit appeals, among many more.[17] The position of tribunals within the justice system was clarified in 1958 by the Franks Committee[18] and the recommendations of the Committee were embodied in the Tribunals and Inquiries Act 1958, now consolidated in the Tribunals and Inquiries Act 1992. The Franks Report was instrumental in the development of the modern tribunal system and stated that all tribunals should be open, fair and impartial, meaning that they should be free from government interference, have clear and consistent procedures and should be held publicly, giving clear and reasoned decisions. Tribunal proceedings differ greatly from those of a court in that they are very informal. Hearings tend to be held in office buildings, with proceedings being inquisitorial rather than adversarial, and a party to an action may represent themselves.[19]

Appeals from tribunals differ according to the governing legislation for each one. **2.48** There are no hard and fast rules as to the routes of appeal, however, many statutes convey a right of appeal to the sheriff court and then to the Inner House of the Court of Session. Where a right of appeal is given to a sheriff and the statute gives no indication about review of the sheriff's decision then it is presumed that the sheriff's decision is final.

LAW PERSONNEL

The Scottish legal system consists of a number of different offices and appointments, **2.49** including judges, solicitors, advocates and the police. The purpose of the following sections is to give a general overview of the key members of the legal profession.

SOLICITORS

Solicitors were previously known as "writers" or "law agents" and today are sometimes **2.50** known simply as "lawyers". They are members of an ancient profession within Scotland, and have a varied professional role within the legal system. Their work involves representing clients in the lower civil and criminal courts,[20] giving all kinds of legal advice, drafting wills and agreements and providing conveyancing services, among other things. Solicitors can work on their own as a sole practitioner, with other solicitors as a partnership, or for large multi-partner companies, or local authorities. All solicitors must have a practising certificate which is renewable each year.

The requirements for becoming a solicitor and the regulations as to how they may **2.51** carry out their practice are to be found in the Solicitors (Scotland) Act 1980 (as amended). In order to become a solicitor in Scotland, an individual must have successfully completed

---

[17] For a list of the key statutory tribunals, see H R W Wade and C F Forsyth, *Administrative Law* (9th edn, 2004), Chapter 24.

[18] Report of the *Committee on Administrative Tribunals and Inquiries* (Cmnd 218, 1957).

[19] It should be noted that legal aid is unavailable for tribunals with the exception of the Employment Appeals Tribunal and the Lands Tribunal for Scotland. However, a person can seek financial help for the costs of preparing a case under the advice and assistance scheme ABWOR (Advice by Way of Representation).

[20] Solicitors may not make an appearance within any of the Supreme Courts, namely the Court of Session, the High Court of Justiciary, the House of Lords and the Judicial Committee of the Privy Council. This is because they have a limited "right of audience" and are restricted to practice within the lower courts only.

an LL.B. degree from a recognised institution[21] as well as the Diploma in Legal Practice. From here, a potential solicitor must secure a legal traineeship with a firm of solicitors or other body such as a local authority. The traineeship lasts for two years where the individual will generally receive training and experience in specialist areas of law as well as sitting further examinations such as the Professional Competence Course. On completion of the traineeship, an individual may then be admitted to the Law Society of Scotland as a solicitor and will receive their first practising certificate.

2.52   As a profession, solicitors are regulated and governed by the Law Society of Scotland. All practising solicitors must be a member of the Society. It has a number of key functions which include setting the education, training and admission requirements for the profession, ensuring that professional standards and discipline are maintained and administering the Guarantee Fund[22] which is available to compensate clients if they have suffered financial loss through a dishonest solicitor. By far the most controversial function of the Law Society of Scotland is that of maintaining standards and discipline. Historically, the profession has been self-regulating, with complaints handled by the Society, free from government interference or regulation. This system has been criticised over the years as being biased and lacking openness and transparency. Consequently, the Scottish Parliament has recently reformed this area, in co-operation with the Law Society. The Legal Profession and Legal Aid (Scotland) Act 2007 introduces a number of widespread reforms, including the establishment of a new Scottish Legal Complaints Commission. The Commission will be an independent body with a number of key functions including the investigation of service complaints against solicitors. Conduct complaints, however, will remain with the Law Society.[23]

SOLICITOR-ADVOCATES

2.53   Until 1993, solicitors had no right of audience before the supreme courts. Despite being intimately involved in the preparation of a case, they would not be allowed to appear within any of the superior courts and would have to pass this work on to an advocate. This would also result in increased legal fees for the solicitor's client. In an attempt to erode the monopoly held by advocates in this area, the Government decided to extend rights of audience to certain solicitors. In order to gain extended rights of audience in either the civil or criminal courts, a solicitor must have a minimum of 5 years' experience in court practice. They must then undertake a course of specialised training and examinations provided by the Law Society of Scotland in order to prove that they are worthy of the right of audience. On completion of the training, a panel of five solicitors will then examine the application and make a recommendation to the Law Society.

2.54   A solicitor-advocate gains the same rights of audience as an advocate but is not allowed to work as a junior to a Queen's Counsel. The creation of solicitor-advocates

---

[21] The LL.B. degree is offered by a number of Scottish universities subject to accreditation by the Law Society of Scotland. The Law Society also allows graduates of other disciplines to complete its own examinations in law in order to qualify.

[22] All solicitors must contribute to the Guarantee Fund as well as being covered by a master policy of professional indemnity covering acts of negligence.

[23] For an overview of the main provisions of the Legal Profession and Legal Aid (Scotland) Act 2007, see "Countdown Phase" LSS (2007) 52(1) at 10–11.

was not welcomed by the Faculty of Advocates and it has issued a ban on working with solicitor-advocates in an attempt to preserve its monopoly.

ADVOCATES

An advocate is a specialist court practitioner who is a member of the Faculty of **2.55** Advocates. They have rights of audience in all Scottish courts and, unlike solicitors, they must work independently. Advocates are not allowed to enter into partnerships, however they do subscribe to an agency known as Faculty Services Ltd which is a company set up by the Faculty of Advocates to assist advocates with administrative work such as collecting fees and receiving instructions from clients. There are currently around 420 practising advocates in Scotland who may be instructed by solicitors and certain other organisations to appear on their behalf in the supreme courts. They are specialist pleaders but may also provide written or verbal advice on the legal merits of a case. This is known as "counsel's opinion" and is used regularly as a means of settling a case outside of court.

To become an advocate, a candidate must have at least a second class LL.B. honours **2.56** degree, or a second class honours degree in another subject plus an ordinary LL.B. degree, or an ordinary LL.B. degree with distinction as well as a Diploma in Legal Practice. Candidates are known as "intrants" and must go through a matriculation process for admission to the Faculty of Advocates. Intrants must then successfully complete the Faculty's training requirements which includes a process known as "devilling" where an intrant will undertake their training and examinations under the supervision of a senior advocate known as a "devil-master". It is a difficult process to become an advocate since the intrant must pay for all of their expenses, entry fees and equipment and essentially be unsalaried during the training process which takes around one and a half years. Newly qualified advocates become known as "junior counsel" and after many years' practice they may apply to become a Queen's Counsel; this is known as "taking silk".

Advocates, like solicitors, are essentially self-regulating. The Faculty of Advocates **2.57** sets its own education and admissions requirements and is free from government interference. The Faculty is also responsible for the maintenance of standards and discipline within the profession and has traditionally dealt with its own complaints. However, this system has recently been reformed by the Legal Profession and Legal Aid (Scotland) Act 2007 and advocates will be subject to the same new regulatory regime as solicitors.

LAW OFFICERS FOR SCOTLAND

The Law Officers for Scotland are the Lord Advocate, the Solicitor-General for Scotland, **2.58** and the Advocate-General for Scotland. The Law Officers assist with the handling of government affairs and advise and represent the Crown in civil cases. The Lord Advocate is head of the system of criminal prosecutions and investigation of deaths in Scotland. He decides whether a prosecution should take place and has control over the Procurator Fiscal Service. He can also issue direction to the police in the investigation of crimes. The Lord Advocate and the Solicitor-General may personally prosecute an offence themselves, however it is rare for them do so and in practice advocates-depute are appointed to prosecute on their behalf.

2.59   The Lord Advocate and the Solicitor-General for Scotland are appointed by the Queen on the recommendation of the First Minister and approval of the Scottish Parliament. Both Law Officers are members of the Scottish Executive. The Advocate-General for Scotland is a special office created by virtue of the Scotland Act 1998. The Scottish Advocate-General is responsible for advising the UK Government on matters of Scots law and the propriety of the Scottish Parliament within its devolved spheres of power.

2.60

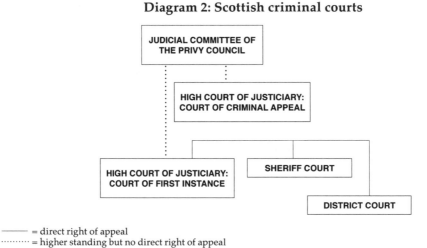

Diagram 1: Scottish civil courts

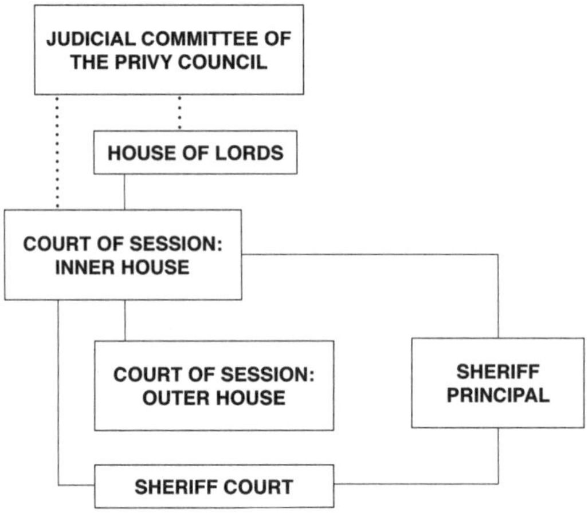

──────── = direct right of appeal
·········· = higher standing but no direct right of appeal

2.61

Diagram 2: Scottish criminal courts

──────── = direct right of appeal
·········· = higher standing but no direct right of appeal

ESSENTIAL FACTS

- The Scottish court hierarchy has two separate court structures for dealing with the civil and criminal law.

2.62

THE CIVIL COURT STRUCTURE

- Sheriff courts are organised into six sheriffdoms and 49 sheriff court districts. They have a wide civil jurisdiction and are presided over by sheriffs and sheriffs principal. There are three main procedures within the sheriff court, namely the small claim, the summary cause and the ordinary cause.

- The Court of Session sits in Edinburgh and consists of the Inner House and the Outer House. The Outer House is a court of first instance and its jurisdiction extends to all kinds of civil action except those which are excluded by statute or privative to another court. Cases are normally heard before a single judge but it is possible in some cases to seek a jury trial, although this is rare. The Inner House is primarily a court of appeal and is split into two divisions which hear appeals from the Outer House and the sheriff courts.

- The House of Lords is the highest court in the UK and is the final court of appeal in Scottish civil cases. It will normally only hear appeals on important or complex questions of law, and sometimes fact. There are 12 Lords of Appeal in Ordinary who hear appeals and they are commonly known as "Law Lords".

THE CRIMINAL COURT STRUCTURE

- District courts are the lowest courts within the hierarchy and have jurisdiction over minor crimes. They are presided over by lay justices of the peace, except in Glasgow where there are also qualified stipendiary magistrates. A justice of the peace has the power to impose a prison sentence of up to 60 days and/or a fine of up to £2,500. A stipendiary magistrate has the power to impose a prison sentence of 3 months (or up to 6 months in cases which involve a previous conviction of theft or dishonesty, or personal violence) and/or a fine of up to £5,000.

- Sheriff courts deal with more serious criminal offences and utilise either summary or solemn procedure depending upon the severity of an offence. Under summary procedure, a sheriff hears a case alone and has the same sentencing powers as a stipendiary magistrate. Under solemn procedure, a sheriff decides on the law while a jury of 15 members of the public decide on the facts and the guilt or innocence of an accused. A solemn sheriff has the power to impose a prison sentence of up to 3 years and/or an unlimited fine.

- The High Court of Justiciary is the highest criminal court in Scotland. It is a circuit court and deals with the most serious crimes such as murder, rape and treason. Cases are heard before a Lord Commissioner of Justiciary sitting with a jury of 15. The sentencing powers of the High Court are unlimited in terms of both imprisonment and fine.

- The High Court is also an appellate court when it sits as the Court of Criminal Appeal. A panel of three or more judges may hear appeals from the High Court itself, the sheriff courts and the district courts.

EUROPEAN COURT OF JUSTICE

- The European Court of Justice has jurisdiction over issues relating to matters covered by the European Treaties.

- Cases can be brought by individuals or can be referred to the ECJ from national courts for rulings on matters affecting the validity or interpretation of European law.

JUDICIAL COMMITTEE OF THE PRIVY COUNCIL

- By virtue of the Scotland Act 1998, the Judicial Committee of the Privy Council has the power to determine the legislative competence of a Bill of the Scottish Parliament. It also has the power to act as court of last resort in determining "devolution issues".

- The Privy Council also hears appeals against devolution issues which arise in the lower courts, ie in Scotland the Inner House of the Court of Session or the High Court of Justiciary.

LAW PERSONNEL

- There are many professionals who work within the Scottish legal system, including members of the judiciary, advocates, solicitor-advocates and solicitors.

- Solicitors practise widely in diverse areas of law and generally represent clients in the lower civil and criminal courts. They are regulated by the Law Society of Scotland and all solicitors must be enrolled as members.

- Advocates are specialist court practitioners who are members of the Faculty of Advocates. They are regulated by the Faculty and have rights of audience in the superior Scottish courts. Advocates may also issue "counsel's opinion" on particular points of law.

3 DELICT

The law of delict is concerned with civil wrongs, that is to say, the law governing **3.1** compensation or reparation for damage which one individual inflicts on another. The person injured invokes the law of delict in order to obtain compensation for injury which is caused to him. An obligation is imposed upon the person who injures another to compensate that other person. The obligation which is imposed arises *ex lege* (by law) as opposed to *ex contractu* (that is, by way of contract).

The law imposes a unilateral obligation on the person who committed the **3.2** wrongful act to compensate the person who is injured. That injury may take many forms. It may take the form of physical injury to one's person. This would be the case in relation to injury which is inflicted in a road accident, or an injury which is sustained in the workplace because of the negligence of a fellow road user or a fellow worker, respectively. However, the injury or damage for which I seek reparation may take other forms. I might sustain financial loss because I have relied on negligent advice. For example, if my financial adviser were to suggest that I invest money in the purchase of shares in a newly floated company and the company then goes into liquidation, the consequence of which is that I lose money, my loss would be purely financial. However, the injury for which the law of delict can also be invoked may take more subtle forms. For example, the injury could comprise loss of my reputation or hurt feelings as a result of what has been said or written about me. The law of defamation (which is part of the law of delict) allows one to recover in certain circumstances for such injury. Again, the injury could take the form of my being unable to enjoy the comfort of my house because my next-door neighbour persists in playing his drums all hours of the day. In such circumstances the law of nuisance can provide a remedy.

However, not every human act which causes injury or harm allows one to recover in **3.3** terms of the law of delict. For example, a small corner shop may be put out of business after a large supermarket is built in the vicinity. In this case the courts would not allow one to recover, since there is no wrongful act in the eye of the law.

There are a number of theories on the function and role of the law of delict. The **3.4** theories overlap to some extent. Occasionally, judges expressly refer to the theories in their judgments. In the majority of cases they do not.

Some argue that the law of delict operates to control the behaviour of people **3.5** before they perform a particular act which has the potential to cause harm. Therefore, I refrain from drinking before I set out on a journey in my car because I know that if I injure someone I could be sued. I refrain from assaulting you for the same reason. However, it could be argued that in such cases it is not the fear that I may be required to compensate my victim that makes me act in a non-delictual way but rather the fear of sanction under criminal law. I might be sent to jail for drunk driving or for assaulting you! One could also argue that another reason for my refraining from acting in a delictual way is not fear of any form of legal sanction, whether civil or criminal, but rather fear of public opprobrium.

3.6   Another function of the law of delict is based on distributive justice. This is founded on the premise that by spreading the loss from an individual victim to those who benefit from an activity, the loss is more easily borne in terms of society as a whole. For example, a public utility which is forced to compensate someone injured in a gas explosion is able to absorb the cost by raising the price of its service among those who benefit from it, in other words, the public. Another example of the principle of distributive justice is seen in the concept of vicarious liability where an employer (who can more easily bear the legal obligation to compensate the victim) is held strictly liable (in other words, liable without fault) for the delicts of his employees. The same principle applies to a situation in which a product injures a consumer. The producer can spread his loss (represented in terms of his obligation to compensate the victim) by raising the price of his products. Some are of the view that the requirements of distributive justice can also be satisfied simply by allowing the loss to lie where it falls. In *McFarlane* v *Tayside Health Board*[1] the pursuers were negligently advised that a vasectomy had rendered the husband infertile. The couple relied on that advice and ceased to take contraceptive precautions. A child was born to them and the couple sued the health board for the financial loss which they would incur in bringing up the child. The House of Lords rejected their claim. Lord Steyn was of the view[2] that such losses were those which society (some members of whom wanted, but could not have, children, others of whom have to bring up disabled children) as a whole had to bear. It would not be morally acceptable for the law to transfer the loss in respect of which the pursuer claimed compensation to the health board.

3.7   However, the main function of the law is to compensate the victim for the damage or injury which he has sustained, whether the damage sounds in terms of economic loss or physical injury. Again, the injury for which the pursuer seeks compensation may take less obvious forms. This would, for example, be the case were I to seek compensation from the courts in respect of the sleepless nights which I have endured as a result of the all-night parties which my next-door neighbour has been having for the past several months.

3.8   The law of delict, unlike, for example, the law of evidence or the law of succession, consists of a number of separate delicts. Some delicts, such as assault and intentional interference with contractual relations, comprise intentional acts on the part of the defender. Others, such as negligence, do not. In some delicts, such as the law of nuisance and defamation, there often exists an element of intention and also negligence in relation to the conduct which forms the factual basis of the action. For example, in relation to the law of nuisance, I may intend to carry out building operations on my land the consequence of which is that neighbouring proprietors are inconvenienced by the noise. The reason why this is so is that I have failed properly to ascertain the potential impact of my actions and thus acted negligently.

3.9   There are thus various delicts which are recognised by law. One concentrates on the more important delicts from a practical viewpoint.

---

[1] [2000] 2 AC 59.
[2] At 82.

The most important delictual wrong for which pursuers seek compensation from **3.10** the courts is in relation to negligent conduct on the part of the defender, to which we now turn.

NEGLIGENCE

Negligence actions form the vast bulk of civil actions which are brought before the **3.11** courts, and negligent conduct can take various forms. It can consist of my sustaining an injury on the road by virtue of negligent driving. It could also consist of my sustaining an injury at work by virtue of the negligence of my employer. The negligence which forms the basis of an action could also consist of negligent advice tendered by my financial adviser.

What we have to look at here is how the courts have attempted to ascertain whether **3.12** liability exists by harm caused by negligent acts. We will see that the courts, for policy reasons, are more willing to allow a negligence claim to succeed for certain types of injury than for others.

In order to recover for damage which is caused by negligent conduct, one requires **3.13** to establish that:

1 the defender owes the pursuer a *duty of care* in law;
2 the *standard of care* which the law demands of the defender has been breached; and
3 the negligent act in question *caused* the requisite injury to the pursuer.

We shall now look at each of these requirements in turn.

(1) THE DUTY OF CARE

In order to ascertain if I am liable in law for the damage which I have caused, the **3.14** courts have first to determine whether I owe the injured person a duty of care.

During the course of the 19th century, with the advent of road and rail transport **3.15** and industrialisation in general, negligence actions were increasingly being brought before the courts. By the end of the century the courts had already established that a doctor owed a duty of care to a patient in respect of the treatment which was given to the patient; a road user owed a duty of care to another road user for the former's conduct on the road; and an occupier of land owed, in certain circumstances, a duty of care to those who visited his land. However, the courts had never really worked out a general formula whereby one could establish whether the defender owed a duty of care to the pursuer in a novel situation, that is to say, a situation or circumstances which had not previously come before the courts.

Judges had indeed made several attempts to work out such a formula but the real **3.16** breakthrough came with the landmark decision of the House of Lords in *Donoghue* v *Stevenson*.[3] In that case Mrs Donoghue went into a café in Paisley. Her friend bought her an ice cream and ginger beer which had been manufactured by Stevenson. The café proprietor poured some of the ginger beer into her glass and Mrs Donoghue consumed some of the contents. Her friend then poured the remainder of the ginger

---

[3] [1932] AC 562.

beer into her glass. As she did so, the remains of a decomposed snail floated out of the bottle. Mrs Donoghue claimed that she suffered nervous shock and gastro-enteritis as a consequence. Mrs Donoghue, of course, did not have a contract with Stevenson, as her friend had bought the ginger beer from the café proprietor. Therefore, in order to succeed, she had to sue Stevenson in the law of delict. The question which the court had to answer was whether the manufacturer of the beer, Stevenson, owed a duty of care to Mrs Donoghue as the consumer. The House of Lords held that a duty of care was owed by the former to the latter. Lord Atkin stated:[4]

> "The rule that you are to love your neighbour becomes in law, you must not injure your neighbour … You must take reasonable care to avoid acts or omissions which you can reasonably foresee would be likely to injure your neighbour. Who then is my neighbour? … persons who are so closely … affected by my act that I ought reasonably to have them in contemplation as being so affected when I am directing my mind to the acts or omissions which are called into question."

In other words, according to Lord Atkin, if one could reasonably foresee that one's conduct could harm the pursuer, a duty of care would arise.

3.17   A good example of the Atkinian foreseeability test being applied is seen in *Beaumont* v *Surrey CC*.[5] In this case a teacher discarded a long piece of elastic in an open bin. The elastic was used in horseplay between pupils and the claimant lost an eye. The education authority was held liable since it was foreseeable that such an accident would take place. The Atkinian test was used again in a quite different situation in *Ministry of Housing* v *Sharp*.[6] In this case the clerk of a local land registry issued an erroneous certificate to the purchaser of land in respect of which the claimants had a charge.[7] The consequence of this was that when the land was purchased the claimant automatically lost its interest over the land concerned. The land registry was held liable for the negligence of its clerk on the basis that it was foreseeable that the claimant would suffer such a loss. Several years later the House of Lords used the foreseeability principle to establish liability in *Home Office* v *Dorset Yacht Co*.[8] In that case a party of borstal trainees were working on Brownsea Island in Poole Harbour, under the supervision and control of three borstal officers. During the night, seven of the trainees escaped and went aboard a yacht which was anchored nearby. They could not navigate properly, which resulted in a collision and damage to a yacht which was owned by the Dorset Yacht Company who successfully sued the Home Office in negligence. The gist of the House of Lords' holding that a duty of care existed was that such an occurrence was foreseeable if the boys were not properly supervised. Lord Reid stated:[9]

> "the time has come when we can and should say that [Lord Atkin's neighbour principle] ought to apply unless there is some justification or valid explanation for its exclusion".

It can be seen that Lord Reid is suggesting here that the law should impose a duty of care if one can foresee that one's conduct will injure someone else. However, he also states that such a duty should not be imposed if policy reasons dictate the contrary.

---

[4] At 580.
[5] (1968) 66 LGR 580.
[6] [1970] 2 QB 223.
[7] Ie they had real rights over the land in question.
[8] [1970] AC 1004.
[9] At 1027.

The scene was therefore set for the next stage in the development of the law relating to the duty of care: the two-staged approach.

Two-staged approach

The development of the concept of duty of care came with the decision in *Anns* v *Merton LBC*.[10] In that case a builder negligently constructed the foundations of a building and the walls began to crack. The owner of the building sued the local authority who were responsible for ensuring that the building works complied with the relevant building control legislation. The House of Lords ruled in favour of the claimant, with Lord Wilberforce enunciating a two-staged approach to the duty of care. In his view, if the court were confronted with a novel situation (that is to say, one which had not already come before the courts) it should approach the concept of duty of care in the following way: **3.18**

(a) first, if a sufficient relationship of proximity exists between the parties then *prima facie* a duty of care arises; and

(b) second, if such a duty does arise, it is then necessary to consider whether there are any considerations which ought to negative, reduce or limit the scope of such duty.

In deciding if there was a sufficiently close relationship, one would still rely on the foreseeability test of Lord Atkin in *Donoghue* v *Stevenson*. If one formed the view that a duty of care arose, one would ascertain if there were any policy grounds for excluding liability. We can see here that such an approach to the duty of care allows a court to extend the boundaries of the law of negligence fairly readily. **3.19**

However, this expansive approach to the duty of care was relatively short-lived. Indeed, there were signs that the courts were beginning to take stock of their somewhat generous approach to the law of negligence in *Governors of the Peabody Fund* v *Sir Lindsay Parkinson*[11] where the House of Lords held that the finding of a duty of care must depend on all the circumstances of the case. Several years later, in *Yuen Kun-Yeu* v *Attorney-General of Hong Kong*,[12] individuals who had deposited money in a bank sued the Government, for, in effect, failing to regulate the bank properly, resulting in their losing money. The Privy Council was of the view that the law should develop novel categories of negligence incrementally and by analogy rather than by a massive extension of a *prima facie* duty of care restrained only by indefinable considerations which ought to negative or to reduce or limit the scope of the duty or class of person to whom it is owed. In other words, the Privy Council advocated an approach in which more sanctity would be accorded to previously decided cases. If a novel factual set of circumstances were presented before the court it would ascertain if the courts had decided a case which was analogous to the present facts. In any case the law should allow the boundaries of the duty of care to be expanded gradually or incrementally. **3.20**

The final nail in the coffin, as it were, for the two-staged approach to the duty of care came with the decision in *Caparo* v *Dickman*[13] which concerned an action by **3.21**

---

[10] [1977] 2 WLR 1024.
[11] [1985] AC 210.
[12] [1987] 2 All ER 705.
[13] [1990] 2 WLR 358.

shareholders against auditors. Caparo claimed that the latter had negligently prepared an audit the consequence of which was that the shareholders had purchased shares, in reliance on the relevant report, and had suffered financially. The House of Lords held that no duty of care was owed by the auditors to the shareholders. A relationship of proximity or neighbourhood was required to exist. The court had also to consider it fair, just and reasonable that the law should impose a duty of a given scope. Foreseeability and proximity were different things. Foreseeability was a necessary but not a sufficient requirement to establish a duty of care in negligence.

3.22   The current approach to the duty of care enunciated in *Yuen Kun-Yeu* and *Caparo* is well illustrated in *Hill* v *Chief Constable of West Yorkshire*[14] in which the mother of one of the Yorkshire Ripper's victims sued the Chief Constable for failure to apprehend the Ripper. It was held that no duty of care was owed even though it was it was reasonably foreseeable that if Sutcliffe, the Ripper, was not apprehended, he would inflict serious injury on members of the public. Lord Keith was of the view that it was against public policy to hold the police civilly liable for failure to apprehend a criminal. He stated:

> "A great deal of police time, trouble and expense might be expected to have to be put into the preparation of the defence to the action and attendance of witnesses at the trial. The result would be a significant diversion of police manpower and attention from their most important function, that of suppression of crime."[15]

Again, in *X* v *Bedfordshire CC*[16] the House of Lords had to decide whether or not to impose common law liability in negligence for failing to take appropriate measures to protect the claimant from, among other things, abuse. It was held that the imposition of a common law duty of care would discourage the due performance of the local authority's statutory duties. Similarly, in *Mariola Marine Corporation* v *Lloyds Registration of Shipping (The Morning Watch)*[17] the plaintiff was a US company which had purchased the *Morning Watch*, a steel-hulled motor yacht. The yacht had just been surveyed by a Lloyd's surveyor and had been given a clean bill of health. In fact, the ship had serious defects. The court accepted that it was reasonably foreseeable that Mariola Marine might rely on the survey result. Foreseeability was not enough to establish a duty of care in law. There must also be a sufficient degree of proximity between the defender and the pursuer and it must be just and reasonable to impose on the defender a duty of care to the pursuer. The court also added that there was no universal test to determine whether the necessary proximity existed.

3.23   An interesting case where the modern approach to ascertaining if a duty of care is owed is *P* v *Harrow LBC*.[18] The claimant was sent by the defendant local authority to an independent school for boys with emotional behavioural difficulties. He was sexually abused by the headmaster of the school. There had been no complaints about the school but was the local authority liable? It was held that this was a "no duty" situation. There was no foreseeability that the harm in question would occur and there was no proximity between the local authority and the claimant in terms of

---

[14] [1989] AC 53.
[15] At 63.
[16] [1995] 2 AC 633.
[17] [1990] 1 Lloyd's Rep 547.
[18] *The Times*, 22 April 1992.

the latter's physical safety. It was also against public policy to hold the local authority liable, on the basis that it would make such authorities adopt a defensive approach to their duties of the type which centred round this action. Finally, when one looked at the purpose or intention of the relevant Education Acts under which the local authority had acted, there was no purpose or intention in such legislation that the local authority should be liable. This last factor illustrates the point that in order to ascertain if liability lies in law, account must be taken of the relevant statutes to ascertain whether it was Parliament's intention that the pursuer be compensated at common law. In the last analysis, however, one could argue that this would often seem futile given the fact that Parliament never gave any thought to potential civil suits when drafting the legislation in question.

There are several other cases which one can use to illustrate the modern **3.24** incremental approach to the duty of care. In *Barrett* v *Ministry of Defence*[19] a naval airman engaged in a bout of heavy drinking at a naval establishment. He became inebriated and then unconscious. He was later found dead, having asphyxiated on his own vomit. It was held by the court that the Ministry of Defence was not liable as it did not owe the deceased a duty of care in law. The fact that it was foreseeable that the claimant would sustain injury if he drank too much was insufficient to ground liability. It was fair, just and reasonable for the law to leave a responsible adult to assume responsibility for his own actions in consuming alcoholic drink. Beldam LJ stated:[20]

> "To dilute self-responsibility and to blame one adult for another's lack of self-control is neither just nor reasonable and in the development of the law of negligence an increment too far."

An important question which fell to be answered in the wake of the incremental **3.25** approach to the duty of care was whether, in determining whether a duty of care applies in law, one should adopt the same approach to claims pertaining to physical injury as one does to economic loss. In *Marc Rich & Co AG* v *Bishop Rock Marine Co Ltd*[21] it was held that the courts should not draw any distinction between the type of damage which the pursuer sustains in terms of the duty of care. A good example of this approach to the duty of care as well as that of the current incremental approach in general can be seen in *Watson* v *British Boxing Board of Control*.[22] This case concerned head injuries which were received by Michael Watson, a professional boxer, in his title fight with Chris Eubank. The fight was regulated by the British Boxing Board of Control (BBBC). Watson claimed that the BBBC had failed to take adequate measures to ensure that he received immediate and effective medical attention should he receive injury during the fight. It was held that there was sufficient proximity between the parties to ground a duty of care in law. Since the BBBC had complete control over the contest it was fair, just and reasonable to conclude that a duty of care existed. In his judgment Lord Phillip MR set store[23] by the following:

---

[19] [1995] 1 WLR 1217.
[20] At 1224.
[21] [1996] AC 211.
[22] [2001] 2 WLR 1256.
[23] At 1281.

1 Watson was one of a defined number of boxing members of the BBBC.

2 A primary stated object of the BBBC was to look after its boxing members' physical safety.

3 The BBBC encouraged and supported its boxing members in the pursuit of an activity which involved inevitable physical injury.

4 The BBBC controlled the medical assistance which would be provided.

5 The BBBC had access to specialist expertise in relation to medical care.

6 If Watson had no remedy against the Board, he had no remedy at all.

7 Boxing members of the BBBC, including Watson, could reasonably rely on the former to look after their safety.

The factual duty of care

3.26 What we have been looking at so far in terms of the duty of care is best described as the notional or nominal duty of care. That is to say, that the courts have analysed a particular series of facts and determined whether a duty of care is owed by the defender to the pursuer. However, what also requires to be established is whether *on the very facts of the case* the conduct of the pursuer actually imperilled or posed a risk to the pursuer. This is well illustrated in the leading case of *Bourhill* v *Young*.[24] There, a pregnant fishwife had just alighted from a tram when she heard the sound of a road accident. The accident had been caused by the negligence of a motor cyclist, John Young, who was overtaking the tram in which Mrs Bourhill had been travelling. He collided with a car which was turning right and into his direction of travel. Mrs Bourhill did not see the accident taking place but, nevertheless, suffered nervous shock. The House of Lords held that, whereas motorists and cyclists who use the roads owe a duty of care to fellow road users and pedestrians, on the facts of the case, the defender did not owe the pursuer a duty of care. The former could not reasonably foresee that someone where Mrs Bourhill was situated when the accident took place would have sustained nervous shock.

Conclusions on the duty of care – the general part

3.27 What we have been looking at above can best be described as the general part of the duty of care. There are, however, certain areas where the courts have had to refine the rules which we have looked at, for a number of reasons, often to reduce the number of potential claims which could be made. These will now be considered.

Pure economic loss

3.28 The general rule is that there is no liability for causing pure economic loss, in other words loss which is not prefaced on physical injury or damage. This approach is well illustrated in *Spartan Steel and Alloys Ltd* v *Martin and Co (Contractors) Ltd*.[25] The claimants operated a steel factory. The factory obtained electricity by direct cable from a power station. Martin was a building contractor. It used power-driven tools in

---

[24] 1942 SC (HL) 78.
[25] [1972] 3 All ER 557.

carrying out excavating works. A shovel fractured a cable and the electricity supply to the factory was shut off, causing a "melt" to be damaged. It was also established that during the time when the electricity was unavailable the claimant could have put more melts through the furnace. The claimant brought an action against Martin in order to recover all damages which had been incurred. It was held that the claimants were only entitled to recover for the loss to the particular melt and not for the economic loss or loss of revenue or productivity which was represented by a loss of other melts which might have been put through the furnace had the power supply not failed. According to Lord Denning MR:[26]

> "if claims for pure economic loss were permitted for this particular hazard there would be no end of claims. Some might be genuine but many might be inflated or even false. A machine might not have been in use anyway, but it would be easy to put it down to the cut in supply. It would be well-nigh impossible to check the claims".

A good illustration of the reluctance of the courts to allow claims which sound in terms of pure economic loss is the previously mentioned case of *McFarlane* v *Tayside Health Board*[27] where the pursuers failed in their action since this loss – the cost of bringing up an unwanted child – ranked simply as pure economic loss. **3.29**

Negligent statements

If I drive my car negligently on the road or if I conduct myself negligently at work, I certainly can injure those who are within the relevant risk area. However, the actual number of people who can be affected is normally likely to be small. That being said, as far as liability for negligent statements is concerned, the potential number of people who could be affected by relying on the statement is limitless. For example, if I were to place an advertisement on the Internet to the effect that one should invest in a new company which proves to be financially unsound, the message could in theory reach hundreds of thousands, if not millions, of people. In the leading case on liability for negligent statements, *Hedley Byrne* v *Heller*,[28] Lord Pearce stated: "Words are more volatile than deeds. They travel fast and far afield. They are used without being expended."[29] The question of liability for unlimited sums of money to an unlimited class of individuals is something that the courts are unwilling to encourage. In effect, the law therefore has to introduce some sort of check in order to cut down the possible number of claimants. This is a policy decision on the part of the courts. In *Hedley Byrne* v *Heller*[30] Easypower, a firm, asked Hedley Byrne do some work for it. In order to ascertain whether Easypower could afford to pay the claimant, it asked its bank, National Provincial, to enquire of Easypower's bank, namely Heller, whether Easypower could afford the services of Hedley Byrne. Heller informed Hedley Byrne that Easypower was financially sound but at the same time expressly disclaimed liability for the accuracy of the information which it imparted. Easypower was not, in fact, financially sound and Hedley Byrne lost money. It therefore sued Heller and the House of Lords held that in the absence of **3.30**

---

[26] At 38.
[27] 2000 SCLR 105.
[28] [1964] AC 465.
[29] At 534.
[30] [1964] AC 465.

a disclaimer the defendant would have been liable. According to Lord Morris, a duty of care will arise if someone possessed of a special skill undertakes, quite irrespective of a contract, to apply that skill.[31] However, Lord Devlin stated that in order for a duty of care to arise in terms of the making of a negligent statement, the relationship between the maker of the negligent statement and the recipient must be equivalent to that existing under a contract. In other words, the relationship must be close. The House of Lords also held that there must be assumption of responsibility on the part of the maker of the statement and also reliance on the part of the recipient. In the previously mentioned case of *Caparo v Dickman*[32] Lord Oliver was of the view that in order to be liable for the making of a negligent statement, the necessary relationship between the defender and the pursuer requires to have four features:

3.31 (1) the advice is required for a purpose either specific or generally described which is made known to the adviser at the time the advice is given;
(2) the defender knows the advice will be communicated to the advisee either individually or as a member of an ascertained class in order that it should be used by the advisee for that purpose,
(3) the defender knows that the advice is likely to be acted upon without independent enquiry; and
(4) the pursuer acts on the advice.

3.32 It is not sufficient that the defender knows that his advice will be relied on.[33] The law must hold that there is a special relationship between the maker of the statement and the person who relies on the statement. Generally speaking, there will be no liability for statements which are made on a purely social occasion since the maker of the statement implicitly accepts no responsibility for the statement.[34] It is also critical that the defender knows that the pursuer will be likely to rely on the statement without obtaining independent advice.[35] Moreover, it is not essential that the person to whom the statement is made relies solely on the statement and thereby incurs a loss.[36] Finally, it is not necessary that the statement be made directly to the person who sustains the loss in question. The statement can be made to a third party who relies on the statement and acts on it to the detriment of the pursuer.[37]

Psychiatric injury

3.33 According to Professor Fleming in *The Law of Torts*, to treat nervous shock in the same way as equivalent to external injuries from physical impact would open up a wide field of imaginary claims.[38] The law must, therefore, impose arbitrary limitations, such as the requirement that the shock must have resulted from the fear of injury to oneself or, at least, a near relative or witnessing an accident with one's own unaided senses, in order

---

[31] At 502 and 503.
[32] [1990] 2 AC 605.
[33] *Galoo Ltd v Bright Graham Murray* [1994] 1 WLR 1360.
[34] *Chaudry v Prabhakar, The Times,* 8 June 1988.
[35] *Smith v Eric S Bush Ltd* [1989] 2 All ER 514.
[36] *JEB Fasteners Ltd v Marks Bloom and Co* [1983] 1 All ER 583.
[37] *Spring v Guardian Assurance* [1994] 3 All ER 129.
[38] J Fleming, *The Law of Torts* (9th edn, 1998), p 173.

to reduce the potential number of pursuers. As with the case for liability for negligent statements, foreseeability of injury is by itself incapable of providing a solution as to whether the pursuer should recover.

It is usual for the courts to divide victims of nervous shock into primary victims **3.34** and secondary victims. The courts will normally only allow one to recover in respect of psychiatric injury if one has been subjected to a traumatic event such as a road or an industrial accident. The only exception to this is that, in certain circumstances, one can recover in relation to psychiatric injury which is caused by stress at work.[39]

Primary victims

In order that one can recover as a primary victim of nervous shock, one must physically **3.35** participate or be actively involved[40] in the very events which cause the psychiatric injury. It is not sufficient simply to witness the event.[41] A good illustration of a primary victim of nervous shock can be found in *Dooley* v *Cammell Laird Ltd*.[42] In that case the claimant was operating a crane which was being used to unload a ship. The crane rope snapped and the load which was being carried plummeted into the hold of the ship where the claimant's colleagues were working. He sustained nervous shock as a result and successfully sued his employers. *Dooley* is also authority for the proposition that the claimant need not apprehend danger to himself in order to recover.

The leading case on the subject of primary victims of nervous shock is now *Page* v **3.36** *Smith*.[43] In this case the claimant, who was suffering from a condition which was known as chronic fatigue syndrome, was involved in a minor road accident. He was uninjured but his condition became permanent as a result of the accident and he successfully claimed damages in respect of this. The House of Lords refused to draw a distinction between psychiatric injury and physical injury. Essentially, the House of Lords held that notwithstanding the fact that the type of injury which the claimant sustained was not reasonably foreseeable, given the fact that physical injury to the claimant's person was foreseeable, the law should not draw a distinction between these forms of injury as far as liability in negligence was concerned. It sufficed simply that some form of injury was foreseeable.

Secondary victims

What we are looking at here is at a situation where the pursuer suffers nervous shock **3.37** by witnessing some sort of traumatic event.

The leading case on the subject is now *Alcock* v *Chief Constable of South Yorkshire*,[44] **3.38** where the defendant was responsible for the policing of a football match. Overcrowding in part of the stadium was caused by the negligence of the police and 95 people were crushed to death. Many more were seriously injured. Live pictures of the harrowing

---

[39] See, eg, *Fraser* v *State Hospitals Board for Scotland* 2001 SLT 1051.
[40] *Salter* v *UB Frozen and Chilled Foods Ltd* 2003 SLT 1011.
[41] *Robertson* v *Forth Road Bridge Joint Board (No 2)* 1994 SLT 56. See also *Cullin* v *London Fire and Civil Defence Authority* [1999] PIQR 314.
[42] [1951] 1 Lloyd's Rep 271.
[43] [1996] AC 155.
[44] [1991] 4 All ER 907.

event were broadcast on television. The claimants were all related to, or were friends of, the spectators who were involved in the disaster. Some people witnessed the traumatic events from other parts of the stadium. Others saw the events on television. However, all claimants alleged that that they had suffered nervous shock. The House of Lords held that in order to succeed it was necessary for the claimants to show both that the injury which was sustained was reasonably foreseeable and also that the relationship between the claimant and the defendant was sufficiently proximate. As far as the latter was concerned, the relationship between the claimant and the victims had to be one of love and affection. Such a degree of affection would be assumed in certain cases, such as when a parent/child or husband/wife was injured. In other cases, however, the requisite affection would require to be proved. This would be the case in respect of remoter relationships such as cousins. Furthermore, the House of Lords held that the claimant was required to show propinquity (or closeness) in terms of both time and space to the accident or its immediate aftermath. A fairly recent Scottish case in which Alcock was followed was *Keen* v *Tayside Contracts*.[45] In that case the pursuer, a road worker, had been instructed by his supervisor to attend the scene of a road accident. The pursuer witnessed badly crushed and burned bodies. He suffered psychiatric injury as a consequence. He sued his employers, in essence, for having negligently exposed him to such traumatic circumstances. He failed in his action, on the basis that his injury was simply caused by his witnessing a traumatic event. In other words, he ranked in the eye of the law as a secondary victim. He was not related to any of the victims. Therefore, his action failed.

Postscript on nervous shock

3.39   One could argue that in its attempt to reduce the number of unmeritorious claims the law has set too high a ceiling in respect of secondary victims of nervous shock. Indeed, the man in the street, told of both the facts and the outcome of the decisions in *Alcock* and *Keen*, may have been very surprised!

3.40   The Scottish Law Commission has recently compiled a report on the law relating to nervous shock.[46] Among its recommendations is that one should abolish the rule that the injury in question requires to be brought about by a sudden assault on the senses, that is to say, by a traumatic event. The Commission also advocated that the distinction between primary victims and secondary victims should be abolished and that victims' claims should be governed by new rules. Furthermore, the Commission also recommended that the rule in the case of *Page* v *Smith*[47] be abolished. The effect of this would be that there would be no liability for unintentionally inflicted psychiatric injury which was not a reasonably foreseeable consequence of the defender's negligence.

The duty of care and affirmative action

3.41   Before concluding discussion of the subject of duty of care, very brief mention should be made of the duty of care and affirmative action. In short, the question which should be asked here is whether I can be sued under the law of negligence for my

---

[45] 2003 SLT 500.
[46] Scot Law Com No 196, SE/004/129.
[47] [1996] AC 155.

simply failing to take appropriate action in respect of someone who is in need of help. For example, could I be sued in the law of negligence for failing to shout a warning to someone walking towards a dangerous cliff? The general rule is that the law refrains from imposing an affirmative duty on the defender. I can stand idly by and watch a baby to whom I am not related drown in a shallow pool of water.[48] However, there are certain situations where the law does require me to take affirmative action. For example, I am under a duty not to allow my land to become a known source of danger to my neighbours.[49]

(2) THE STANDARD OF CARE

Once one has established that the defender owes a duty of care to the pursuer, it **3.42** is necessary to ascertain whether the duty of care has been breached. Whether the defender is negligent or not is judged objectively. In other words, no account is taken of individual disabilities or idiosyncrasies, except in relation to children who are judged in terms of the standard of children of the age of the defender. The leading case on this point is *Nettleship* v *Weston*.[50] In that case a learner driver was held to be required to attain the same standard of driving as an ordinary competent driver. This approach may seem harsh but one can appreciate that it would be extremely difficult for the courts to take individual circumstances into account and adopt a subjective approach to the standard of care. In the case of learner drivers, for example, how much higher a standard of care should be demanded of a learner driver who had received ten driving lessons than one who had received only five? Again, if one were to take age into account, how much concession in terms of the standard of care should one make in relation to an 85-year-old driver? These questions would pose the courts great difficulty and it is therefore far simpler to adopt an objective approach to the standard of care.

The courts take into account a number of factors in order to decide whether the **3.43** defender has been negligent. These are now discussed.

The state of current knowledge

The leading case here is *Roe* v *Minister of Health*.[51] In that case the claimant went into **3.44** hospital for a minor operation. He was given a spinal injection. The fluid which was used for the injection was kept in an ampoule, that is, a very small glass container, which, in turn, was kept in a phenol solution. At this time it was not known that phenol could seep into the ampoule through invisible cracks. The claimant was paralysed from the waist downwards. He sued the Minister of Health who was responsible for the hospital concerned. His action failed because the defendant's hospital had not breached its standard of care since it had acted in a way in which any other reasonable hospital would have acted in the situation, as the dangers from this type of ampoule were not known at that time.

---

[48] See Eldridge, *Modern Tort Problems*, p 12.
[49] See, eg, *Sedleigh-Denfield* v *O'Callaghan* [1940] AC 880; *Goldman* v *Hargrave* [1967] 1 AC 645; and *Leakey* v *National Trust* [1980] 1 All ER 17.
[50] [1971] 2 QB 691.
[51] [1954] 2 QB 66.

The magnitude of risk

3.45   The greater the risk of injury from the activity which is the subject-matter of the action, the greater the amount of precautions which the defender is required to take. In *Blyth* v *Birmingham Waterworks Co*[52] the defendant water board laid a water main which was 18 inches in depth. One year there was an extremely severe frost which penetrated the ground as far as the water main. The main burst and flooded the claimant's premises. It was held that the water board was not negligent because it had taken reasonable precautions in the circumstances. The modern case on this aspect of the standard of care is *Bolton* v *Stone*.[53] In that case the claimant, while standing in a quiet suburban highway outside her house, was struck by a cricket ball. The claimant was situated 100 yards from the batsman and the ball had cleared a 17-foot fence which was situated 78 yards from him. Similar hits had occurred only about six times in the previous 30 years. The House of Lords held that since the likelihood of injury was small, the claimant had not established that the defendant had broken his duty of care towards the claimant.

The risk of serious harm

3.46   Here, one takes into account not the likelihood that an accident will occur but, rather, the seriousness of the injury should an accident occur. The leading case is *Paris* v *Stepney BC*.[54] There, a one-eyed worker was injured while at work. He claimed that his employers should have provided and also required him to use goggles while he was carrying on work. It was proved that there was no greater a likelihood that an accident would take place to the claimant than to a worker with normal sight. However, the House of Lords held that since the consequences of an injury to the claimant were graver, extra precautions were necessary. The standard of care which the law demanded of the defendant had been breached.

The utility of the defender's activity

3.47   The social utility, or usefulness, of the relevant activity which is the subject-matter of the action is taken into account. The greater the utility, the less likely it is that the court will hold that the relevant standard of care has been breached. The leading case is *Watt* v *Hertfordshire CC*.[55] The claimant was a fireman. One day, his station received a call that a woman was trapped under a heavy lorry as a result of a road accident. A jack was required to lift the vehicle. The lorry which was designed to carry such a device was not available. Two of the claimant's colleagues threw a heavy jack on to a lorry in which they were to travel. The lorry was not designed to carry a jack. During the journey the jack rolled away from its original position and injured the claimant. It was held that the defendants had not been negligent. In reaching its decision the court took into account the social utility of the journey, namely the rescuing of an injured person. However, simply because the defender is involved in an activity which has some social worth does not automatically exonerate him from the need to take

---

[52] (1856) 11 Ex 781.
[53] [1951] AC 850.
[54] [1950] 1 KB 320.
[55] [1954] 1 WLR 835.

care. This point was decided in *Ward* v *London County Council*.[56] There, the driver of a fire engine was held to have been negligent in driving through a red traffic light and injuring the claimant. It was held that the defendant could not use the reason that he was involved in a journey of social worth as an excuse for his breach of duty of care.

The practicality of precautions

The easier it is to take measures to counteract the risk, the more likely it is that the courts **3.48** will hold that the appropriate duty of care has been breached. In *Latimer* v *AEC Ltd*[57] the floor of the defendant's factory was flooded by an exceptionally heavy rainstorm. Oil which was kept in troughs was washed out on to the factory floor. The defendant put sawdust on the floor but there was not enough sawdust to cover the entire factory floor. The claimant, who was working on the floor, slipped and injured himself. He sued the occupier of the factory. It was held that the defendant was not liable since it had taken all appropriate precautions short of closing the factory. However, this decision has been criticised on the ground that commercial profitability was given too much prominence by the court over the personal security of the workers.

Emergency situations

If the defendant is placed in a sudden emergency situation which is not of his own **3.49** creation, his actions must be judged in the light of those circumstances. In *Ng Chun Pui* v *Lee Chuen Tat*[58] it was held that the driver of a coach who had braked, swerved and skidded when another vehicle had cut across his path had acted reasonably in an emergency.

Children

Children are treated as a category apart. In order to ascertain if the defender has been **3.50** negligent, one takes into account what degree of care a child of the particular age of the defender can be expected to take.[59]

It should be briefly mentioned by way of conclusion that the courts have formulated **3.51** special rules to determine whether professional people, such as doctors, have breached the standard of care which the law demands of them.[60]

(3) CAUSATION

Factual causation

Finally, in order to succeed in a negligence claim it is necessary to prove that the **3.52** negligent act in question actually caused the relevant injury or damage which is the subject-matter of the action. There are two main tests which the courts use in order to ascertain whether the defender's conduct caused the loss in question, namely:

---

[56] [1938] 2 All ER 341.
[57] [1953] AC 643.
[58] (1988) 132 SJ 1244.
[59] *Yachuk* v *Oliver Blais Co Ltd* [1949] AC 386; *Gough* v *Thane* [1966] 3 All ER 398.
[60] See F McManus and E Russell, *Delict* (1998), Ch 10.

(a) the "but for" test; and

(b) the "material contribution" test.

The tests are mutually exclusive. It is also difficult to predict which test will be used by the court.

(a) The "but for" test

3.53 The question which the court asks itself here is: but for the negligent act of the defender, would the pursuer have been harmed? The leading case on the subject is *Barnett* v *Chelsea and Kensington Hospital Management Committee*.[61] In that case Barnett, a night-watchman, called early one morning at the defendants' hospital. He had been deliberately poisoned and was complaining of sickness. The doctor in charge refused to see him and suggested that he should consult his GP in the morning. However, Barnett died before he could visit his GP and his widow sued the hospital in negligence. She failed since it was proved that her husband would have died anyway. No form of medical treatment would have saved him at the time he presented himself at the hospital. In other words, the defendant had not caused Barnett's death.

(b) The "material contribution" test

3.54 As far as this test is concerned, the courts are willing to accept that the defender has caused the relevant damage if his negligent act materially contributes to, as opposed to being the sole cause of, the accident. The test is well illustrated in *Wardlaw* v *Bonnington Castings*.[62] In that case the pursuer's illness was caused by an accumulation of dust in his lungs, the dust in question coming from two sources. The defenders (Wardlaw's employers) were not responsible for one of the sources, but they could have prevented (and were therefore negligent concerning) the other. The dust from the latter source (in other words, the "illegal" dust) was not in itself sufficient to cause the disease but the pursuer succeeded because the "illegal" dust had made a material contribution to his injury.[63]

3.55 It is also important to understand that the pursuer requires to prove that the negligent act of the defender caused his injury on a balance of probabilities.[64]

Departure from the "rules"

3.56 In *Fairchild* v *Glenhaven Funeral Services*[65] it was held that in certain circumstances one could depart from the well-established rules governing factual causation. In that case Fairchild had been employed at different times and for different periods by more than one employer. Fairchild's's employers, E1 and E2, had been subject to a duty to take reasonable care or all practicable measures to prevent F from inhaling asbestos dust.

---

[61] [1969] 1 QB 428.
[62] 1956 SC (HL) 26.
[63] See also *McGhee* v *NCB* [1972] 3 All ER 1008.
[64] *Wilsher* v *Essex Area Health Authority* [1988] 1 All ER 871.
[65] [2002] 3 All ER 305.

Both E1 and E2 failed to do so and as a consequence F contracted mesothelioma. On the current limits of scientific knowledge, Fairchild was unable to prove on the balance of probabilities that his condition was the result of inhaling asbestos dust during his employment by one or other or both of E1 and E2. However, the House of Lords held that, in certain special circumstances, the court could depart from the usual test of legal causation and treat a lesser degree of causal connection as sufficient, namely that the defendant's breach of duty had materially contributed to causing the disease by materially increasing the risk that the disease would be contracted. Any injustice that might be involved in imposing liability in such circumstances was heavily outweighed by the injustice of denying redress to the victim. The exception to the rules governing caution which was established in *Fairchild* was extended by the House of Lords in *Barker v Corus UK Ltd*[66] to include a situation where the victim's exposure to asbestos was the result of both tortious (delictual) and non-tortious conduct. Furthermore, the amount of damages which each defendant should pay should be commensurate with the degree of risk to which the defendant exposed the claimant.[67]

Legal causation (remoteness of damage)

The law will not allow the pursuer to recover in relation to injury which is deemed to be too remote. One can illustrate this point by considering the following scenario: I encourage Albert, a young man, to take up rowing. I know that he is short-sighted. Several years later, while he is rowing on a canal, he fails to notice another boat, which is being rowed by Pat, approaching his boat. Albert's boat collides with Pat's boat which is sunk. Pat manages to swim to safety but he is cut by glass which has been dumped by the side of the canal. Could I be sued by Pat for the injury and loss which he has sustained?   **3.57**

It is probably true that the accident would never have taken place had I not encouraged Albert to take up rowing. However, Pat would certainly not be able to sue me successfully in the law of negligence because the type of injury which has been inflicted is too remote. The leading case on this issue is *The Wagon Mound*[68] where it was held that in order for the pursuer to be able to recover for injury or damage he has sustained, that loss must be reasonably foreseeable.   **3.58**

VICARIOUS LIABILITY

Accidents are often caused by those who are carrying out work for others. For example, an employee who performs his duties negligently may injure a fellow worker or a member of the public. Sometimes, however, an accident occurs while someone, who is not an employee of another person, is carrying out work for that person. For example, a taxi driver whom I have commissioned to take me to the railway station may negligently run over a cyclist on his way to the station. The   **3.59**

---

[66] [2006] 2 WLR 1027.
[67] As far a liability for injury which is caused by exposure to asbestos is concerned, s 3 of the Compensation Act 2006 makes defenders jointly and severally liable (or *in solidum*: for the whole) of the injury which is caused. In other cases, proportional liability as established in *Barker* will apply.
[68] [1961] AC 388.

important question one must answer here is whether the injured person, in each of the above cases, can sue the person who is paying the person at the time when the accident took place. In short, subject to several limited exceptions, only an employer can be sued for the delicts (including negligent conduct) which have been committed by his servant (or employee) during the scope of his employment. One who simply pays someone else to carry out work for him on an ad hoc basis cannot normally be sued if that person causes injury or damage. One cannot therefore normally be sued for work which is being carried out by an independent contractor. What the courts thus do is to distinguish between an employee and an independent contractor. An employee is employed under a contract of *service* whereas an independent contractor is employed under a contract for *services*.

3.60   In order to ascertain who is an employee and who is an independent contractor, the courts adopt a variety of tests. The most important are:

(1) To what extent, if any, does the person who pays the other have the right to choose who works for him? The right to choose is more consistent with a contract of service.

(2) Are wages or other forms of remuneration paid to the other? The right to receive wages and remuneration is more consistent with a contract of service.

(3) To what extent can the person who is paying control the manner in which the tasks which the other has to perform are carried out? The greater the degree of control, the more likely that the relevant relationship is that of employer–employee. However, given that employees nowadays are carrying out much more technical and esoteric tasks than in the past, this test is losing some of its currency.

(4) The right to "hire and fire" the other is more consistent with a contract of service.

3.61 It is often said that it is easy to recognise a contract of service when one sees it but it is difficult to say where the distinction lies between that and a contract of services. That being said, examples of those who are employed under a contract of service would include a ship's master, a chauffeur, a reporter on a newspaper and a schoolteacher. A taxi driver and a newspaper contributor would, however, be employed under a contract for services.

FOR WHICH ACTS OF AN EMPLOYEE IS THE EMPLOYER LIABLE?

3.62 An employer is only liable for acts which are done in the course of the servant's employment. An employer will be liable for the conduct of his employees at the relevant place of employment during the hours for which the employee is employed and also as long as the employee is on the premises concerned within reasonable limits of time of the commencement and conclusion of the shift. In *Bell* v *Blackwood, Morton and Sons*[69] a woman in the employment of a firm of carpet manufacturers was jostled by a fellow employee while travelling down a stair, after the hooter had sounded for the end of

---

[69] 1960 SC 11.

the shift. The defenders were held vicariously liable for the conduct of the negligent employee.

"Frolic" on part of employee

There are a number of cases which concern an employee failing to carry out his duties **3.63** in the manner which his employer requires. If the employee has gone on "a frolic of his own", this act takes him outside the course of his employment and the employer is not liable for the acts of his employee. If the frolic consists of the employee going on a journey of his own, if the deviation from the normal journey is substantial then the employer would not be liable. In *Storey* v *Ashton*[70] a cart driver completed his employer's work and then went to visit a relative. During the course of the journey the carter injured the claimant. It was held that the employer was not liable for this tort, on the basis that the employee had gone on a frolic of his own. Again, in *Hilton* v *Burton*,[71] X, H and Y were building workers who were employed at a building site. H drove them to a café seven miles away, in order to buy tea. X was killed by the negligent driving of H. It was held that H was not acting within the scope of his employment. Again, in *Williams* v *Hemphill*[72] a bus driver, while carrying children, made a detour at the request of some of the children. The bus was involved in a collision. A passenger was injured. It was held that the driver was still acting within the scope of his employment notwithstanding that the deviation from the route which the bus driver's employers wished the driver to take was fairly substantial.[73]

Certain other forms of conduct can take an employee outside the scope of his **3.64** employment. Essentially, an employer will be vicariously liable for the conduct of his employee if the employee is carrying out incompetently something which he is authorised to do.[74] This principle is neatly illustrated in *Century Insurance Co Ltd* v *Northern Ireland Transport Board*.[75] Here, the driver of a petrol lorry struck a match while filling a tank at the petrol station. There was an explosion and property was damaged. It was held that the employer was liable since the employee was acting within the scope of his employment. He was doing what he was employed to do, albeit in an incompetent way. One could also say that what the driver did was so reasonably incidental to his work that it did not take him outwith the scope of his employment.

In deciding whether a given act on the part of the employee takes him outwith **3.65** the scope of his employment, the courts have recently displayed a generous approach as to which acts on the part of the employee can be regarded as being within that scope. In *Lister* v *Hesley Hall Ltd*[76] L was resident in a boarding house which was attached to a school which was owned and managed by H. W, a warden of the boarding house, without the knowledge of H, systematically sexually abused L. L claimed damages against H. The House of Lords held that there was a sufficient connection between the work which W had been employed to do and the acts of abuse

---

[70] (1869) LR 4 QB 476.
[71] [1961] 1 All ER 74.
[72] 1966 SC 259.
[73] See also *Smith* v *Stages* [1989] 2 WLR 529.
[74] *Kirby* v *NCB* 1958 SC 514.
[75] [1942] AC 509.
[76] [2001] 2 WLR 1311.

that he had committed for those acts to have been regarded as having been committed within the scope of his employment. H was therefore vicariously liable for the acts of W. Again, in *Mattis v Pollock*[77] the defendant (P) owned a nightclub. He employed X as a doorman. X was expected to act aggressively towards customers. X grabbed a member of a group of people who were about to enter the nightclub. X was struck several times and also hit by a bottle. X then escaped to his flat from which he emerged and stabbed M. It was held that P was vicariously liable for the assault since X's act was so closely connected with what the employer either authorised or expected of X that it was fair, just and reasonable to make P vicariously liable for the assault.

DEFENCES

3.66 Only very brief mention can be made of the defences which are relevant in a negligence action. The most important are those of (1) contributory negligence; (2) consent; and (3) illegality. These will be dealt with in turn.

(1) CONTRIBUTORY NEGLIGENCE

3.67 The law allows me to recover for injury which has been negligently inflicted on me notwith-standing that I am to some extent the author of my own misfortune. For example, if I am cycling along the road and I am knocked over by a car driver who is at fault and receive head injuries, I can still succeed in a negligence action against the driver, notwithstanding the fact that my injuries are more severe by dint of my failure to wear a crash helmet. Under s 1 of the Law Reform (Contributory Negligence) Act 1945 a negligence claim may not be defeated by reason of the fact that the pursuer was negligent. However, the damages which are recoverable fall to be reduced to such extent as the court thinks just and equitable having regard to the claimant's share of responsibility for the damage.

(2) CONSENT

3.68 Briefly, the law provides that no wrong is done to he who has consented. This is expressed in the Latin maxim *"Volenti non fit injuria"*. Where a person consents to run the risk of injury which is caused by another, he cannot thereafter claim damages in respect of the injury. The defence must be specifically pled. The onus of proof that the pursuer consented rests on the defender. The defence operates as a complete defence. In other words, if the defence succeeds, the pursuer's claim fails *in toto*.

(3) ILLEGALITY

3.69 The courts will sometimes prevent the pursuer from recovering damages in respect of the negligent act of another, on the ground that the pursuer has, at the time of the accident, been involved in an illegal act. The defence must be specifically pled.

---

[77] [2003] 1 WLR 2158.

If the defence succeeds it operates as a complete defence, thereby depriving the pursuer of the award of any damages. The defence represents a grey area of the law. It should be stated that it is not every illegal act on the part of the pursuer which will deprive him of the chance of succeeding against the defender. For example, the fact that I am driving my car (in respect of which I do not possess a relevant MOT certificate and which therefore contravenes relevant road traffic legislation) on a public road would not *per se* preclude me from succeeding in a negligence claim against another driver who negligently collided with my car and injured me.

REMEDIES

The main remedies in the law of delict are interdict, declarator and damages. The last mentioned is the most important as far as negligence actions are concerned. Indeed, the award of damages is the normal form of remedy for a delictual wrong. It is said that money is the universal solvent.[78] The purpose of damages is to restore the pursuer, as far as possible, to the position in which he was before the delictual conduct took place. The amount of damages bears no relation to the degree of fault on the part of the defender. Finally, there is no such thing as punitive damages in the law of delict.

3.70

ESSENTIAL FACTS

3.71

NATURE OF LAW OF DELICT

- The law of delict is concerned with civil wrongs.
- The person injured invokes the law of delict to obtain compensation for injury caused to him.

NEGLIGENCE

- In order to recover for damage caused by negligent conduct one must establish that the defender owes the pursuer a duty of care in law, that the standard of care has been breached and that the negligent act caused the requisite injury.

DUTY OF CARE

- The duty of care in the law of negligence is determined by the "neighbour" principle. One is liable if one can reasonably foresee that one's conduct will injure the pursuer.
- It must also be proved that in the very circumstances in which the pursuer was injured the defender owed him a duty of care in law.

---

[78] *Auld* v *Shairp* (1874) 2 R 191.

THE STANDARD OF CARE

- The standard of care which the law demands of the defender is set by the "reasonable man" test.

- In order to determine whether the requisite standard of care has been breached one takes a number of factors into account, including the state of current knowledge, the magnitude of risk, the risk of serious harm, the utility of the defender's conduct and the practicality of precautions.

CAUSATION

- In order to succeed in a negligence claim it is necessary to prove that the negligent act in question actually caused the relevant injury.

- There are two main tests which the courts use in order to ascertain whether the defender's conduct caused the loss in question, namely the "but for" test and the "material contribution" test.

- The law will not allow the pursuer to recover in relation to injury which is too remote.

VICARIOUS LIABILITY

- An employer is vicariously liable for acts done in the course of the servant's employment.

- There is no liability for "frolics" on the part of the employee.

DEFENCES

- Damages which are recoverable fall to be reduced to such extent as the court thinks just and equitable having regard to the pursuer's share of responsibility for the damage.

- No damages are recoverable by a person who has consented to the wrong.

- The courts will sometimes prevent the pursuer from recovering damages if the pursuer has been participating in an illegal act when he was injured.

REMEDIES

- The main remedies in the law of delict are interdict, declarator and damages.

- Damages is the most important as far as negligence actions are concerned.

ESSENTIAL CASES

DUTY OF CARE

3.72

Donoghue v *Stevenson* (1932): "The rule that you are to love your neighbour becomes in law, you must not injure your neighbour; and the lawyer's question, Who is my neighbour? receives a restricted reply. You must take reasonable care to avoid acts or omissions which you can reasonably foresee would be likely to injure your neighbour. Who then is my neighbour? The answer seems to be persons who are so closely and directly affected by my act that I ought reasonably to have them in contemplation as being so affected when I am directing my mind to the acts or omissions which are called into question" (per Lord Atkin at 580).

Caparo v *Dickman* (1990): This case concerned an action in negligence against auditors who had negligently prepared an audit of a company the consequence of which was that the shareholders had purchased shares in reliance on the report and had suffered financially. The House of Lords held that no duty of care was owed by the auditors to the shareholders. A relationship of proximity was required to exist. The court had to consider if it was fair, just and reasonable that the law should impose a duty of a given scope. Foreseeability was a necessary, but not a sufficient, requirement to establish a duty of care in law.

Hill v *Chief Constable of West Yorkshire* (1989): The mother of one of the Yorkshire Ripper's victims sued the Chief Constable for failure to apprehend the Ripper. It was held that no duty of care was owed even though it was reasonably foreseeable that if Sutcliffe, the Ripper, was not apprehended, he would inflict serious injury on members of the public. "A great deal of police time, trouble and expense might be expected to have to be put into the preparation of the defence to the action and attendance of witnesses at the trial. The result would be a significant diversion of police manpower and attention from their most important function, that of suppression of crime" (per Lord Keith at 63).

STANDARD OF CARE

Nettleship v *Weston* (1971): A learner driver was held to be required to attain the same standard of care as an ordinary competent driver.

CAUSATION

Factual causation

Barnett v *Chelsea and Kensington Hospital Management Committee* (1969): Barnett, a night-watchman, called early one morning at the defendants' hospital, complaining of sickness. He had been deliberately poisoned. The doctor in charge refused to see him and told him to consult his GP in the morning. However, Barnett died before he could consult his GP. His widow sued the hospital in negligence. She failed since no form of medical treatment would have saved him at the time he presented himself at the hospital. The defendant's negligence had not caused Barnett's death.

Remoteness of damage

Overseas Tankship v *Morts Dock and Engineeering Co Ltd* (1961): A ship, the *Wagon Mound*, was taking on furnace oil when the appellants' servants negligently allowed oil to spill into the water. Wind and tide carried the oil about 200 yards to the respondents' wharf where servants of the respondents were repairing a vessel by using welding equipment. A piece of metal fell from the wharf and set on fire cotton waste which was floating on the oil which in turn set the oil alight. The wharf was severely burned. The Privy Council held that one should determine whether any given type of injury was too remote by employing the "foreseeability" test. In other words, one asks whether the type of damage which was sustained by the pursuer was reasonably foreseeable.

VICARIOUS LIABILITY

Century Insurance Co Ltd v *Northern Ireland Transport Board* (1942): The driver of a petrol lorry struck a match while filling a tank at the petrol station. There was an explosion and property was damaged. It was held that the employer was liable since the employee was acting within the scope of his employment. He was doing what he was employed to do, albeit in an incompetent way.

Lister v *Hesley Hall* (2001): L was resident in a boarding house which was attached to a school which was owned and managed by H. A warden of the boarding house, without the knowledge of H, systematically sexually abused L. Held that there was a sufficient connection between the work which the warden was employed to do and the acts which he had committed for those acts to be regarded as having been committed within the scope of his employment.

4 CONTRACT

The law of contract is fundamental to society. It is one of the few areas of law in which **4.1** most people are involved on a daily basis. From where we live to what we buy, to how we get to work, there are contracts involved in every stage of daily life and business.

A contract is a voluntary obligation between two or more parties who have reached **4.2** agreement on its terms and who have capacity to contract and intend to create certain legally binding obligations between them. Most contracts are bilateral onerous contracts because they are between two parties, each party has certain obligations under it and each contributes something of value to it. For example, in the purchase of a car, there are two parties, one of whom agrees to buy the car for a certain price and the other who agrees to hand over possession and ownership of the car in exchange for that price. A contract is a voluntary obligation because the parties have to agree to be legally bound by it – the purchaser cannot be forced into buying the car. This contrasts with other legal obligations which are imposed by law, such as the duty imposed on a parent to support a child.

It is important to know when an arrangement falls into the category of "contract" **4.3** because it is legally enforceable as such; if one party does not carry out his part of the deal then the other can take certain measures against him, including court action if necessary. Non-contractual agreements, such as agreeing to meet up for a drink in the pub, cannot be enforced in this way.

It is also possible to have voluntary obligations which are not bilateral onerous **4.4** obligations and which are also enforceable. These are gratuitous contracts and promises. A gratuitous contract is a contract in which the parties agree to something which does not necessarily bestow a benefit on one of them. This is demonstrated by the case of *Morton's Trustees* v *Aged Christian Friend Society of Scotland*[1] in which Mr Morton offered a charitable donation to the Society which was accepted by it. The donation was to be paid by instalments but Mr Morton died before all of them had been paid. The court held that there was a legally enforceable contract between Mr Morton and the Society and that his estate had to pay the remainder. A promise is very similar but, unlike a gratuitous contract, it is not reciprocal in nature: there is no need for the promisee to accept a promise and it can bind only the promisor.

Examples of promise are found in *Littlejohn* v *Hadwen*[2] in which there was the **4.5** promise to keep an offer open for a certain period of time and in *Stone* v *MacDonald*[3] in which there was a grant of an option to buy land which was held to be binding as a promise. Reward cases, in which a reward is offered for information or lost property, are usually categorised as promise in Scots law.

---

[1] (1899) 2 F 82.
[2] (1882) 20 SLR 5.
[3] 1979 SLT 288.

4.6   In studying contract law, there are a number of basic issues to consider:

- Formation: when does a contract come into being?
- Problems: certain problems can affect the validity or enforceability of a contract and it is important to be able to identify these problems and their effect on the contract.
- Breach of contract: what happens when one party does not perform his part of the contract?
- Termination: when does a contract (or the obligations under it) come to an end?

FORMATION

4.7   A contract is formed when an offer is met with an acceptance.

OFFER

4.8   An offer must be clear, capable of acceptance, include the intention to be legally bound and be communicated to the other party. That party may be a particular person or the offer may be made to the general public as in the case of *Carlill* v *Carbolic Smoke Ball Company*[4] in which the offer was made by way of an advert to the world at large. A company offered a £100 reward to anyone who bought and used its smoke ball correctly but who nevertheless came down with flu.[5] Unlike many adverts, this one had the characteristics of an offer as it was specific, had been effectively communicated and, importantly, the company showed the seriousness of its intentions by declaring that it had lodged £1,000 in a bank to fund payouts. In commerce, there are many situations which might look like offers but which, in fact, are not. Thus, an offer can be contrasted with an invitation to treat which happens when one party displays goods in a shop window, as in the case of *Fisher* v *Bell*;[6] on self-service shelves in a shop, as in *Pharmaceutical Society of GB* v *Boots Cash Chemists*;[7] or on a website. An offer is not a willingness to negotiate,[8] an invitation to tender, a quotation[9] or putting something up for auction.[10] An offer can be verbal, written or made by action as in the case of a slot machine.[11]

4.9   An offer can be revoked at any time before acceptance unless a time limit has been placed on it, in which case it cannot be revoked without breaching that promise.[12] An offer will lapse if a time limit set for acceptance passes without the contract being concluded or, if no time limit is set, is not accepted in a reasonable period of time.[13]

---

[4] [1893] 1 QB 256.

[5] Note: *Carlill* is an English case and the judgment refers to the offer of the reward as a "promise". However, promise is not recognised in the same way as in Scots law and, therefore, this is a case of contract in English law, requiring offer and acceptance.

[6] [1961] 1 QB 394.

[7] [1953] 1 QB 401.

[8] *Harvey* v *Facey* [1893] AC 552.

[9] However, a very specific quotation may be enough to amount to an offer: *Jaeger Bros Ltd* v *J & A McMorland* (1902) 10 SLT 63.

[10] Section 57(2) of the Sale of Goods Act 1979 makes clear that the offer is made by the bidder and the acceptance by the auctioneer.

[11] *Thornton* v *Shoe Lane Parking* [1971] 2 QB 163.

[12] *Littlejohn* v *Hadwen* (1882) 20 SLR 5.

[13] *Wylie & Lochhead* v *McElroy & Sons* (1873) 1 R 41.

ACCEPTANCE

Acceptance can be verbal, in writing or made by action. It must usually be **4.10** communicated to the offeror, although the case of *Carlill* shows that this need not always be the case: Mrs Carlill did not advise the Carbolic Smoke Ball Company that she was accepting its offer but her actions amounted to acceptance. The offer may state how acceptance is to be made in order to be valid and the usual rule is that silence from the offeree is not enough. Although these concepts are straightforward, it can be difficult to tell in a real-life situation when an offer or an acceptance has been made. For example, the purchase of a newspaper may take place without verbal or written communication; the seller will not say "I offer to sell this paper". Indeed, while it is on the shelf, there is no offer, merely an invitation to treat. Once the purchaser picks it up and takes it to the checkout, there can be said to be an offer to buy at that stage. That offer can be accepted by the seller simply by accepting the money for it. In more complex commercial situations, such as the purchase of a factory or goods, there may be protracted negotiations and pinpointing when an offer and acceptance have been made can be difficult. In these negotiations, the offeree may make a qualified acceptance (also known as a counter-offer) which accepts the offer subject to certain important changes. The effect of this was discussed in *Wolf & Wolf v Forfar Potato Co Ltd*[14] and it was held that a counter-offer cancels the original offer so that it can no longer be accepted. The ball is then in the original offeror's court to decide whether to accept the counter-offer or not. Until he does so, there is no contract.

Postal rule

A further complication arises if the contract is being made by post. In that case, the **4.11** contract is made as soon as the acceptance is posted. The case of *Dunlop, Wilson & Co v Higgins and Son*[15] held that if a time limit is set on acceptance being made but it is delayed in the post, the postal rule operates to conclude the contract. However, there is Scottish authority to suggest that there is no contract if the letter is not merely delayed but lost.[16] The application of the rule in a case where the letter was incorrectly addressed was considered in *Jacobsen, Sons & Co v Underwood & Son Ltd*[17] and it was held that the rule did apply to conclude the contract, regardless of this mistake. As acceptance concludes the contract, it cannot generally be revoked.[18] An acceptance will conclude the contract.

Once the contract has been formed, it cannot be cancelled except in very limited **4.12** circumstances. For example, there are short "cooling off" periods for some consumer credit contracts and distance selling contracts whereby the consumer can cancel within 14 days but unless there is a legal right to cancel then both parties are bound

---

[14] 1984 SLT 100.
[15] (1848) 6 Bell's App 195.
[16] *Mason v Benhar Coal Co Ltd* (1882) 9 R 883.
[17] (1894) 21 R 654.
[18] This is subject to the interpretation of the case of *Countess of Dunmore v Alexander* (1830) 9 S 190 in which two letters were sent separately but arrived together. Although many academics now consider that the case is an example of an offer of employment being withdrawn, it was thought for some time that the first letter was an acceptance of an offer and that the second was a revocation of acceptance which the court allowed because both letters were delivered together.

to carry out their respective obligations under the contract or face the consequences of not doing so.

CONTRACTUAL TERMS

Written contracts

4.13   Contracts can be concluded in many ways: e-mail,[19] face to face, fax, telephone, post or by the actions of the parties. The vast majority of contracts do not have to be in writing to be valid, other than those listed in the Requirements of Writing (Scotland) Act 1995,[20] but if the parties choose to put the contract in writing then the Contract (Scotland) Act 1997 applies. Under this Act, the written contract is presumed to contain all of the contractual terms and conditions but in cases where the contract does not expressly state this, then evidence from outwith the contract can be examined to find out if there are any other contractual terms.

Incorporation

4.14   The terms of any contract, written or not, will be those incorporated into the contract at the time of formation: contractual terms cannot be incorporated afterwards, except with the consent of both parties. It is important that contractual terms are brought to the attention of the other party. Tickets and notices cause particular problems for incorporation: when does a term on a ticket or a notice form part of the contract? Some tickets are contractual, like rail tickets, and their terms (or terms referred to on them) are contractual. However, incorporation can be prevented by use of tiny print[21] or by referring to terms on the back of the ticket.[22] Other "tickets" can actually be classified as receipts or invoices, issued after the contract has been concluded, and in those cases, the terms on them cannot be contractual.[23] Notices are often not visible until after the contract has been concluded and so any terms on those will not be contractual, as in the case of *Thornton* v *Shoe Lane Parking Ltd* in which the contract to use a car park was concluded at the entry barrier from which the notice denying liability for injury in the car park could not be seen. Similarly, a notice in a hotel room which was seen by the guests only after they had checked in and gone to their room did not form part of the contract in *Olley* v *Marlborough Court Ltd*.[24]

Conditions

4.15   The contractual terms will specify what each party has to do to fulfil his obligations under it and it will also set when these obligations have to be fulfilled. Some obligations will be contingent upon other things happening first: for example, if one party is to pay for goods by instalments then he has an obligation to pay but not until the due dates are reached or goods are delivered.

---

[19] Section 7 of the Electronic Communications Act 2000 makes authenticated electronic signatures admissible in court proceedings to establish the authenticity of the communication.
[20] See below.
[21] *Williamson* v *North of Scotland and Orkney Steam Navigation Co* 1916 SC 554.
[22] *Parker* v *South Eastern Railway Co* (1877) 2 CPD 416: however, in this case, the words "see back" were printed on the front and therefore the terms were incorporated.
[23] *Taylor* v *Glasgow Corporation* 1952 SC 440: receipt for baths was post-contractual.
[24] [1949] 1 KB 532.

PROBLEMS WITH CONTRACTS

Although most contracts are valid and binding as soon as they are formed, there are a **4.16** number of problems which can render the contract void, voidable or unenforceable.

VOID

A contract which is void is so fundamentally flawed that the contract is prevented from **4.17** being formed at all. The parties may have thought that they had formed a contract and, indeed, may have acted on it but the law deems it to be lacking a vital ingredient and so never a real contract at all. If this happens and the parties have already acted on the "contract" (eg bought and sold goods in exchange for money) then the law of unjustified enrichment can be used to "settle up" between the parties: goods and money will be returned where this is still possible. The return of money is called *repetition* and the return of goods is called *restitution*. If one party has benefited from the void contract in some other way then a payment called recompense can be made to cover the other party's loss.

VOIDABLE

A voidable contract, unlike a void contract, is not so flawed as to actually prevent it **4.18** from coming into existence. Instead, the flaw allows one party to challenge the contract which, if accepted by the other party or upheld in court, will result in the contract being set aside ("reduced"). The court will only set aside a contract if the parties can be restored to their pre-contract positions (*restitutio in integrum*) and the parties are not personally barred from seeking to have the contract set aside by having discovered the flaw but affirming the contract anyway.

UNENFORCEABLE

An unenforceable contract is not void or voidable but the courts will not uphold it for **4.19** another reason such as illegality.

SUMMARY

Thus, in establishing that a contract has a flaw, it is necessary to know what the effect **4.20** of that flaw is on the contract: does it render it void, voidable or unenforceable? A contract can be affected by (1) lack of consensus; (2) lack of consent to create legal obligations; (3) lack of capacity; (4) lack of formality; (5) illegality; (6) restrictions on the freedom of contract; and (7) other prejudicial circumstances.

(1) LACK OF CONSENSUS

It is essential that both parties have *consensus in idem*; in other words, both are **4.21** agreeing to the same thing. If they do not agree on the important aspects of the contract then this will prevent the contract from being properly formed at all and it will be void.

4.22   The Scottish courts apply an objective test in deciding if the parties have consensus. An objective test is one which does not take into account what the parties themselves think but which applies a benchmark test to decide whether consensus has been reached.

4.23   Lack of consensus (also known as "dissensus") is illustrated by the case of *Mathieson Gee (Ayrshire) Ltd v Quigley*[25] in which Mathieson offered to supply plant equipment to clear a pond (ie an offer of hire) and Quigley accepted that by confirming his acceptance to an offer to clear the pond (ie accepting an offer to do something else). The court held that, notwithstanding what the parties themselves thought, there was no consensus and so no contract.

Error

4.24   A lack of consensus may arise out of a mistake or misrepresentation (error). In this case the parties or one of them has made a mistake about an important matter to do with the contract.

Unilateral error

4.25   The general rule is that a mistake made by one of the parties (unilateral error) does not affect the contract even if it is an essential error[26] unless it has been induced by something the other party has said or done (induced error).

Essential error

4.26   An essential error is one which goes to the heart or substantials of the contract and traditionally includes, but is not limited to, error as to subject-matter,[27] identity of the parties,[28] price,[29] quantity, quality or nature of the subject-matter of the contract and error as to the nature of the contract.[30]

Induced error

4.27   Inducement can take three forms: innocent misrepresentation; fraudulent misrepresentation; and negligent misrepresentation. The effect of misrepresentation may make the contract void or voidable. If the error is essential and amounts to lack of consensus then the contract will be void but if it is incidental then the contract will be voidable and so the contract will be reduced only if the criteria for reduction are met.

4.28   *Innocent misrepresentation* happens when one of the parties tells the other a fact about a material aspect of the contract (ie an important aspect of the contract but

---

[25] 1952 SC (HL) 38.
[26] This is certainly the case for onerous written contracts, following *Stewart v Kennedy* (1890) 17 R (HL) 25, but may not be the case in other contracts where the error leads to lack of consensus or in gratuitous contracts (*Hunter v Bradford Property Trust* 1970 SLT 173).
[27] *Raffles v Wichelhaus* (1864) 2 H & C 906.
[28] Note, however, that this will only be applicable in contracts where the identity of the parties is crucial, as in *Morrison v Robertson* 1908 SC 332; cf *Macleod v Kerr* 1965 SC 253.
[29] *Wilson v Marquis of Breadalbane* (1859) 21 D 957.
[30] However, this is only likely to affect the contract if induced.

not necessarily falling into the category of essential error) which is wrong and that misleading information induces the other party to enter into the contract.

Fraudulent misrepresentation happens when the mistake is not made innocently but **4.29** is made fraudulently; this can include information which the party putting forward knows to be wrong or which he puts forward recklessly.

The difference between the two is shown in the two cases of *Boyd & Forrest* v *Glasgow* **4.30** *& South Western Railway Co*[31] which arose out of the same situation. Boyd & Forrest contracted with the railway company to do some work for a price based on figures supplied by the railway company. Unfortunately, those figures were wrong because they had been changed by an engineer (a genuine mistake). This meant that the actual cost of the work carried out by Boyd & Forrest was hugely more expensive than the agreed contract price. They claimed fraudulent misrepresentation (1912 action) and, when no fraud was established, they argued innocent misrepresentation (1915 action) but although this was proved, restitution was not possible because the route had been dynamited and could not be restored to its previous state.

If reduction is not possible then there are no further remedies for innocent **4.31** misrepresentation but damages are available for fraudulent misrepresentation under delict.

Negligent misrepresentation can also affect a contract and, in this case, damages are **4.32** available under s 10 of the Law Reform (Miscellaneous Provisions) (Scotland) Act 1985 which allows the innocent party to claim damages if he cannot have the contract reduced and has suffered a loss (provided that he can show that the other party owed him a duty of care).

Bilateral error

If both parties have made a mistake then this is called bilateral error; it can be either **4.33** common or mutual. A common error is where both have made the same mistake and mutual error occurs where they have reached different but wrong opinions on a matter to do with the contract. If the error is essential and amounts to a lack of consensus then the contract is void.

It should be noted that a clerical error in writing down a contract – an error of **4.34** expression – is not enough to amount to lack of consensus and a clerical error can be corrected by application to the court under s 8 of the Law Reform (Miscellaneous Provisions) (Scotland) Act 1985, provided that third parties are not prejudiced by the correction.

(2) LACK OF CONSENT

It is essential that the parties intend to create a binding legal obligation and so it is **4.35** necessary to distinguish between social and domestic arrangements which are presumed not to include this consent and business arrangements which are presumed to include consent to binding legal obligations.

If parties are negotiating a business deal and want to avoid certain pre-contractual **4.36** negotiations becoming binding as contracts, they have to make it very clear that they do

---

[31] 1912 SC (HL) 93 and 1915 SC (HL) 20.

not intend to be legally bound by such an agreement in order to rebut the presumption that these "agreements" are contractual and therefore binding.[32]

4.37   If parties have reached this type of pre-contractual agreement and it is breached then the law becomes more complex. A breach of pre-contractual agreements cannot be dealt with by contract law because there is no contract. This problem arose in *Dawson International plc* v *Coats Paton plc*[33] in which it was held that if one party "breached" this type of pre-contractual agreement then, as a matter of equity, the "innocent party" could claim back any money spent honouring the agreement if the one who pulled out had assured the "innocent party' that there was a contract (even although there was not).

4.38   Family arrangements are presumed not to have this element of consent to create legal obligations, as shown in the case of *Balfour* v *Balfour*,[34] and some other arrangements such as sporting and gaming contracts do not create enforceable legal obligations despite the intentions of the parties because they fall into the category of *sponsiones ludicrae*, a category of illegal contracts.[35] However, the courts have enforced a contract between friends in which one person had agreed to share her bingo winnings with another, in *Robertson* v *Anderson*.[36] However, gambling contracts are now enforceable as s 335 of the Gambling Act 2005 came into force on 1 September 2007.

(3) LACK OF CAPACITY

4.39   Both parties to a contract must have the capacity (legal ability) to enter into that contract. A complete lack of capacity on the part of either party will render the contract void. There are different rules for different legal persons: children and young persons, the insane and businesses.

Children and young persons

4.40   The Age of Legal Capacity (Scotland) Act 1991 applies. The age at which full capacity is reached is now 16. Children below 16 years of age have no capacity as a general rule under s 1, although transactions commonly entered into by children are excluded from the no-capacity rule, provided they are concluded on reasonable terms under s 2. This will mean such things as buying sweets and comics in shops, travel on buses and trains and, as they get closer to 16, it will apply to contracts such as after-school work and holiday jobs and the purchase of more expensive items, such as computing or musical equipment.

4.41   Although full capacity is reached at 16, there are further protections for 16- and 17-year-olds. If a person aged 16 or 17 enters into a contract which is a "prejudicial transaction" as defined by s 3 of the 1991 Act then it may be set aside in certain circumstances. A transaction is prejudicial if it (a) is one which an adult, exercising reasonable prudence, would not have entered into in the circumstances of that young

[32] *Stobo Ltd* v *Morrisons (Gowns) Ltd* 1949 SC 184.
[33] 1988 SLT 854.
[34] [1919] 2 KB 571.
[35] *Kelly* v *Murphy* 1940 SC 96 and *Ferguson* v *Littlewoods Pools Ltd* 1997 SLT 309. See below for a discussion of illegal contracts.
[36] 2003 SLT 235.

person and (b) has caused or is likely to cause substantial prejudice to the young person.

If a young person makes such a contract then he must apply to the court under s 3 **4.42** to have it set aside. He has until the day before he reaches his 21st birthday to do this. There are three important restrictions in relation to contracts. A young person cannot apply to the court to have a prejudicial transaction set aside if:

(1) the transaction was made in the course of his business trade or profession (s 3(2)(f)); or

(2) he lied about his age and this fraudulent misrepresentation induced the other party into entering into the contract with him (s 3(2)(g)); or

(3) he ratified the contract after the age of 18 despite knowing his right to ask for it to be set aside (s 3(2)(h)).

Only the young person has the right to apply to the court; the other party to the **4.43** transaction does not. The result of a successful application is that the contract is set aside and the parties returned to their previous positions, subject to the general law relating to voidable transactions.

A third party worried about this can apply to court to have the contract ratified under **4.44** s 3(3)(j) and the court will decide whether it is reasonable or not.

Adults with incapacity

Many adults suffer from mental health or mental disorder problems such as psychiatric **4.45** problems and dementia. A number of adults are affected by learning difficulties. Under the common law, an "insane" person has no contractual capacity, which can have serious implications for managing his affairs.[37]

The Adults with Incapacity (Scotland) Act 2000 provides a legal framework for managing the affairs of incapax adults, primarily for financial and medical matters.

Intoxicated persons

The level of intoxication through alcohol or drugs or solvent abuse must be very high **4.46** in order to result in a loss of capacity.[38]

Corporate bodies

The capacity of a corporate body will be determined by its constitution and any **4.47** contract which is outwith its powers (*ultra vires*) will be void. However, this rule has been significantly diluted for registered companies. A registered company is a legal person in its own right, separate from the shareholders who own it and the directors who run it. A company has full legal capacity and ss 35, 35A and 35B of

---

[37] Note that s 3(2) of the Sale of Goods Act 1979 provides that persons suffering from mental incapacity must pay a reasonable price for necessaries if sold or delivered to him (necessaries are defined in the Act as goods suitable to the condition in life of the person and to his actual requirements at the time of sale and delivery).

[38] *Taylor v Provan* (1864) 2 M 1226. Section 3(2) of the Sale of Goods Act 1979 also applies for the purchase of "necessaries" by the intoxicated.

the Companies Act 1985 state that a company has full capacity regardless of any restrictions contained in its memorandum. Furthermore, a contract made by the board of directors outwith the company's powers cannot be challenged on grounds of lack of capacity, provided that the third party is in good faith. The third party may not have this protection if he knows that the company's power to agree is restricted by its constitution but the mere fact of knowing this does not automatically mean that he is in bad faith.[39]

Partnerships

4.48 Partnerships (firms) have separate legal personality in Scotland (s 4(2) Partnership Act 1890) which means that the firm can sue and be sued. Contracts can also be entered into by the partners on behalf of the firm which bind the firm, provided that the partner(s) act within the confines of s 5 of the Partnership Act 1890 which sets out their authority.

Unincorporated bodies

4.49 Clubs and associations etc do not have contractual capacity and must contract through their office bearers.

(4) LACK OF FORMALITY

4.50 Most contracts do not have to be in writing but those which do are listed in the Requirements of Writing (Scotland) Act 1995. Section 1 lists, among other things, certain contracts and promises which must be in writing to be valid. These include contracts or unilateral obligations for the creation, transfer, variation or extinction of a real right in land except tenancies or rights to occupy land for less than one year under s 1(7) (unless these are rolling arrangements) and gratuitous unilateral obligations (ie promises) except those undertaken in the course of business. Thus, contracts for buying, selling and leasing property such as houses, farms, factories and offices must be in writing to be valid.

Formal writing

4.51 The writing required is formal writing: the contract must be subscribed by the parties which means that they must sign it at the end of the document. Electronic writing is now valid for the formation of these contracts.[40] The contract or promise can be made probative (self-proving in a court action) by attestation (ie by being witnessed) (s 3) or by endorsement with a court certificate (s 4). Only one witness is required and he must be 16 or over.

---

[39] This has been kept the same under the Companies Act 2006 which is expected to come into force for new companies in October 2007.
[40] The Automated Registration of Title to Land (Electronic Communications) (Scotland) Order 2006 (SSI 2006/755) amended the Requirements of Writing (Scotland) Act 1995 to allow electronic contracts created within the automated Registration of Title ("ARTL") system. There are special authentication rules for these electronic contracts. The change came into force 5 October 2006.

Curing lack of formality

If a contract which should be in writing is not but the parties act on it anyway then the **4.52**
1995 Act makes provision to cure this problem under s 1(3) and (4) which allow the contract
to stand if certain criteria are met. To cure a contract, the following questions need to
be asked:

(a) Is the contract one of those listed in s 1(2) which therefore should be in
    writing?
(b) Has one party with a right under the contract done something (eg started
    ordering bricks for a new house to be built on the land to be bought under it) or
    not done something (eg not renewed the lease on his current rented home as he
    expects to move into the new house soon) in reliance on the contract?
(c) Does the other party know about that?
(d) Has the other party acquiesced (this could be a positive act of consent or he
    could acquiesce by seeing what is going on but not telling the other party to
    stop)?
(e) Has the first party been affected to a material extent by what he has done/not
    done (usually, this means – "is he out of pocket?")?
(f) Would he be affected to a material extent if the other party pulled out now?

If the answer to all of these questions is "yes", then the contract is cured under s 1(3) **4.53**
and (4) and is valid and the parties are personally barred from arguing that it is not.[41]

Notarial execution

People who cannot sign contracts because of blindness, paralysis or other difficulty **4.54**
can use the device of notarial execution to subscribe contracts under s 9 of the 1995
Act whereby a solicitor, JP or other party listed in the section reads the contract to that
person who confirms that they have agreed to its terms and the solicitor then signs
on their behalf. The separate matter of probativity is achieved by witnessing or court
certificate as before.

(5) ILLEGALITY

The general rule is that illegal contracts ("*pacta illicita*") are unenforceable. However, **4.55**
certain contracts which are illegal under statute may be void, voidable or unenforceable,
depending on the wording of the statute. A contract can be illegal in whole or in part.
 There is a difference between contracts concluded for an illegal purpose and **4.56**
contracts which are performed illegally:

Illegal purpose

If the contract is formed for an illegal purpose then it is unenforceable. This can arise **4.57**
in two situations. First, the illegal purpose may be clear from the contract itself. This

---

[41] Note that this is '*personal* bar', so only applies to personal rights and not to real rights: *Advice Centre for
Mortgages* v *McNicoll* 2006 SLT 591.

was demonstrated in the case of *Barr v Crawford*[42] in which the contract was for a bribe to be paid by a pub landlady to members of the licensing board. Secondly, the contract may be for a legitimate purpose on the face of it but the parties know that it is really for an illegal purpose. This is shown in the case of *Pearce v Brooks*[43] in which a contract for the hire of a coach to a prostitute to allow her to ply her trade was held to be illegal.

4.58   As the contract cannot be enforced, it cannot form the basis of any claim between the parties (*ex turpi causa non oritur actio*) and so if one party considers that the other has breached the contract, he cannot sue for breach of contract and the general rule is that the court will not "settle up" between the parties: loss lies where it falls (*ex turpi causa melior est conditio*). However, the court may allow a remedy to one party if it considers that the other party shares more of the blame than him, ie they are not *in pari delicto*.

Illegal performance

4.59   Alternatively, the contract may be concluded for a legitimate purpose but one or both of the parties may perform it in a way which breaches a particular law. This occurred in the case of *Dowling & Rutter v Abacus Frozen Foods Ltd (No 2)*[44] in which two parties had a contract whereby one, the employment agency Dowling & Rutter, supplied labour to the other, Abacus. That is not an illegal contract in itself. However, Dowling & Rutter supplied illegal immigrants to do the work. The way in which this contract was performed therefore breached immigration legislation. However, Dowling & Rutter did not know that the workers were illegal immigrants and the court held that it was entitled to be flexible in the way in which it decided how this form of illegality would affect the contract and the parties. It decided that an equitable remedy would be to allow the party which had performed the contract illegally – Dowling & Rutter – to recover their fees for the supply of labour. This case would probably have been decided differently had Dowling & Rutter known about their breach of legislation. The important point to note is that illegal performance of a contract does not *automatically* render it unenforceable.

Common law illegality

4.60   Common law does not allow contracts which are contrary to public policy to be enforced. The following categories have all been established as being illegal at common law: criminal contracts; contracts which promote sexual immorality; contracts which interfere with the court system (such as bribing witnesses) or which try to bar one party from seeking legitimate redress through the courts; and gaming contracts.

4.61   A very important category of illegal contracts is restrictive covenants which are also known as restraints of trade. These are commonly used in employment contracts, contracts for the sale and purchase of businesses and solus agreements.

---

[42] 1983 SLT 481.
[43] (1866) LR 1 Ex 213.
[44] 2002 SLT 491.

Employment contracts

These clauses are put into contracts of employment by employers to try to prevent **4.62** the employee from working within a certain geographical area or with a competitor of the employer for a designated period of time after the employee leaves the service of the employer. The presumption is that these clauses are unenforceable *unless* three criteria are met by the restriction. The criteria are re-stated in *Bridge* v *Deacons*:[45] the restriction must protect the legitimate business interests of the employer; it must be reasonable; and it must be in the public interest.

If an employee does breach the restrictions placed on him in the contract then **4.63** the employer can go to court and ask for a court order called an interdict which will prohibit the employee from continuing to work for the rival business. The court will take the following matters into account when deciding whether to enforce the restrictive covenant and grant an interdict.

Legitimate business interests. In the case of *Bluebell Apparel Ltd* v *Dickinson*,[46] Bluebell **4.64** manufactured Wrangler jeans and Dickinson, their employee, knew Bluebell's trade secrets and was a manager with them. He left them and went to work for Levi's, a competitor. Bluebell was entitled to protect trade secrets to which Dickinson had been privy during the course of employment with them. The court upheld a restrictive covenant which prohibited him from disclosing the trade secrets to any unauthorised person and from working for any competitor for 2 years after leaving Bluebell's employment. The court will consider the position held by the employee (eg the more senior the employee and the greater access he has to confidential information, the more likely the court is to enforce the restrictive covenant).

Restrictions in geographical area and time limits. The court will look at the location **4.65** of the business and consider whether the geographical limit is reasonable. A business located in a sparsely populated rural area is more likely to get away with stating a larger radius within which the employee should not work than one located in a busy city centre. The cases which demonstrate this are:

Stewart v *Stewart*[47] – a work ban as a photographer within a 20-mile exclusion zone **4.66** around Elgin was reasonable.

Dallas, McMillan & Sinclair v *Simpson*[48] – a restriction prohibiting a former partner **4.67** in a firm from working for 3 years within a 20-mile radius of Glasgow Cross was not reasonable even although the clause actually stated that it was agreed by all of the parties that both the time limit and the geographical limit were reasonable.

The court will look at the type of business and decide if it merits a long ban on **4.68** working for a rival or not. Fast-moving industries prone to technological change and fast-moving markets are unlikely to get away with longer time bans.

Severability. If a contract contains some restrictions which are reasonable and some **4.69** which are not, is the entire restrictive covenant unenforceable? It will depend on

---

[45] [1984] AC 705.
[46] 1978 SC 16.
[47] (1899) 1 F 1158.
[48] 1989 SLT 454.

whether the different elements are severable, ie capable of being separated out from the others and applied separately. This is an issue of how the clauses are drafted and the court will not redraft the clause but will delete unenforceable parts, leaving any reasonable parts which can stand alone.[49] This has led to the standard practice of drafting restrictive covenants which have different elements in them as separate clauses for each restriction rather than lumping them together in one clause.

Sale and purchase of business

4.70 The purchaser of a business will not want the seller to set up a new rival business nearby. The purchaser of a business wants to protect the goodwill of the business which he has bought and will often want to include a restrictive covenant in the contract for the purchase and sale of the business. The same criteria apply in deciding enforceability as they do to employer – employee contracts but the courts are more likely to enforce such business-to-business contracts because of the greater equality in bargaining position and the fact that legitimate business interest in enforcing the clause will be easier to prove.

4.71 The following two cases illustrate how the courts have treated these clauses:

4.72 *Nordenfelt* v *Maxim Nordenfelt Guns and Ammunition Co Ltd*[50] – a worldwide ban on operating in international arms dealing for 25 years was reasonable because of the specialised nature of the business and the fact that purchasers of guns and ammunition were sovereign states and therefore limited in number.

4.73 *Dumbarton Steamboat Co Ltd* v *Macfarlane*[51] – a 10-year UK-wide ban on operating a carrier's business was not reasonable because the business which had been sold had only operated on the west coast of Scotland and not throughout the UK. There were therefore no UK-wide interests to protect.

Solus agreements

4.74 Solus agreements are made between a wholesaler/distributor and a retailer who agrees to stock only that wholesaler/distributor's brand (usually in return for discounts). A solus agreement may or may not be included in another contract between the parties (the most common being if the wholesaler leases the business premises to the retailer too). These can be enforced if reasonable. In the case of *Esso Petroleum Co Ltd* v *Harper's Garages (Stourport) Ltd*[52] a 21-year-long solus agreement was held to be unenforceable. The Competition Act 1998 also prohibits price fixing and cartels.

(6) RESTRICTIONS ON THE FREEDOM OF CONTRACT

4.75 As the category of illegal contracts shows, there are restrictions on what parties can contract to do. Further restrictions on the freedom to agree terms include restrictions on the use of exclusion clauses and restriction on the use of "unfair terms".

---

[49] *Mulvein* v *Murray* 1908 SC 528.
[50] [1894] AC 535.
[51] (1899) 1 F 993.
[52] [1968] AC 269.

Exclusion clauses

An *exclusion* clause is an attempt to exclude an obligation for breach of contract or for **4.76**
negligence. A *limitation* clause attempts to limit liability for such a breach. These will
be looked at very carefully by the courts. Such a clause will be applied *contra proferens*
(against the party trying to rely on that clause) to avoid his trying to escape paying out
for those breaches if it is at all ambiguous.[53] Many of these clauses are now subject to
the statutory controls of the Unfair Contract Terms Act 1977 ("UCTA") and the Unfair
Terms in Consumer Contracts Regulations 1999 (SI 1999/2083).

UCTA applies to a wide range of contracts but not to all contracts nor to all exclusion **4.77**
clauses. It does apply to sale of goods contracts, contracts for services, employment
contracts and contracts which allow others to enter land. It does not apply to insurance
contracts, contracts for formation of companies and partnerships nor to contracts
for real rights in land (eg buying or selling land). It also applies to non-contractual
notices.

UCTA does a number of things: **4.78**

(1) it renders clauses which limit/exclude liability for death or personal injury
arising out of breach of duty void;
(2) it allows clauses which limit/exclude liability for other losses arising out of
breach of duty if they are fair and reasonable;
(3) it allows clauses in standard form or consumer contracts which limit/exclude
liability for breach of contract if they are fair and reasonable;
(4) it allows indemnity clauses (a clause allowing one party to recover monies paid
out by him from another party) in consumer contracts if fair and reasonable
and;
(5) it prohibits sellers of goods from excluding certain implied terms found in
the Sale of Goods Act 1979 in contracts with consumers and only allows such
exclusions in other contracts if fair and reasonable.

Breach of duty

Section 16(1) UCTA states that: **4.79**

"where a term of a contract or a provision of a notice given to persons generally or to
particular persons purports to exclude or restrict liability for breach of duty arising in the
course of any business or from occupation of any premises used for business purposes of
the occupier, that term or provision –

(a) shall be void in any case where such exclusion or restriction is in respect of
death or personal injury:
(b) shall, in any other case [eg in respect of financial loss], have no effect if it was
not fair and reasonable to incorporate the term in the contract [or to put it in the
notice]."

Breach of duty is defined in s 25 as a breach: **4.80**

---

[53] *W & S Pollock* v *Macrae* 1922 SC (HL) 192 and *Smith* v *UMB Chrysler and South Wales Switchgear Ltd* 1978
SLT 21.

"(a) of any obligation, arising from the express or implied terms of a contract, to take reasonable care or exercise reasonable skill in the performance of the contract;

(b) of any common law duty to take reasonable care or exercise reasonable skill (but not any stricter duty);

(c) of the duty of reasonable care imposed by section 2(1) of the Occupier's Liability (Scotland) Act 1960."

4.81   It will therefore include negligence claims.

4.82   The definition of what is fair and reasonable for exclusion clauses which try to avoid financial loss is set out in s 24:

"regard shall be had only to the circumstances which were, or ought reasonably to have been, known to or in the contemplation of the parties to the contract at the time the contract was made"

and in respect of a non-contractual notice "regard shall be had to all the circumstances obtaining when the liability arose".'

Limitation clauses

4.83   Section 24(3) also sets out a reasonableness test for clauses which do not exclude liability but which try to limit liability by capping it at a certain level (eg "we accept liability up to £300"). In this type of contract/notice, the reasonableness test allows the following to be taken into consideration in determining if that amount is "fair and reasonable": (a) the resources which the party seeking to rely on that term could expect to be available to him for the purpose of meeting the liability should it arise; and (b) how far it was open to that party to cover himself by insurance. Section 24(4) places the onus of proving that the term/provision is fair and reasonable on the party trying to rely on the exclusion or limitation.

Breach of consumer or standard form contracts

4.84   Section 17 deals with this type of exclusion or limitation clause which attempts to exclude or limit liability for breach of contract (rather than the other breaches of duty covered by s 16). Breach of contract is dealt with below. Generally, if one party fails to perform his part of the contract, or performs it badly, then he is in breach of that contract and certain remedies can be taken against him, which can include having to pay damages to the other party. However, one party may try to exclude or limit liability for breach of contract by stipulating in the contract that an obligation which would otherwise be imposed on him is excluded or limiting liability for breach or non-performance in some way. In the case of consumer contracts or standard form contracts then s 17 states that such exclusions or limitations must be fair and reasonable.

4.85   "Consumer contract" is defined in s 25 as a contract in which:

"(a) one party to the contract deals, and the other party to the contract ('the consumer') does not deal or hold himself out as dealing, in the course of a business, and (b) in the case of a contract such as is mentioned in s 15(2)(a) of this Act [ie of sale of goods or supply of goods], the goods are of a type ordinarily supplied for private use or consumption".

"Standard form contract" is not defined in UCTA. However, it can include a contract **4.86** which is one which is not individually negotiated between the parties but which has most of its terms pre-printed with some details such as price and names left blank to be completed by the parties before signature. The case of *McCrone* v *Boots Farm Sales Ltd*[54] found that conditions of sale could be covered as a standard form contract under s 17.

Unfair terms

The Unfair Terms in Consumer Contracts Regulations 1999 also apply to exclusion **4.87** clauses but have a much wider application than that. Unlike UCTA, these Regulations apply only to consumer contracts where the seller deals in the course of business and the consumer is a natural person acting outwith his usual trade or profession. Under the Regulations, a contractual term which has not been individually negotiated shall be regarded as unfair if, contrary to the requirement of good faith, it causes significant imbalance in the parties' rights and obligations arising under the contract, to the detriment of the consumer. This means that if a business puts a term into such a contract which is one-sided and favours the business while prejudicing the consumer then it may be considered unfair under the Regulations.

If a contractual term is deemed to be unfair by the Regulations then it is not binding **4.88** on the consumer under reg 8 but the rest of the contract will stand if it can continue in existence without that offending term.

Some exclusion and limitation clauses are included in a list of terms which are **4.89** considered as unfair. However, the Regulations are much broader than UCTA in scope and deem a much wider range of terms to be unfair, including, for example, any term enabling the seller or supplier to alter the terms of the contract unilaterally without a valid reason which is specified in the contract. Anyone involved in drafting standard trading terms and conditions for businesses which deal with consumers must therefore take these Regulations into account.

(7) OTHER PREJUDICIAL CIRCUMSTANCES

There are other circumstances surrounding the formation of a contract which taint it. **4.90** These are to do with the way in which one of the parties behaved in order to get the other to enter into the contract. These circumstances may render the contract void or voidable. The circumstances include:

Facility and circumvention (voidable)

Vulnerable people may retain capacity but be termed "facile" in law and be taken **4.91** advantage of ("circumvention") by the other party in the contract, as in the case of *MacGilvary* v *Gilmartin*[55] in which a recently widowed mother was taken advantage of by her daughter to sign over the title deeds on a house. The court set aside the transfer.

---

[54] 1981 SLT 103.
[55] 1986 SLT 89.

Undue influence (voidable)

4.92   Similarly, a person can abuse their own position of trust, as in a case where a parent influences a child to make a decision which is not in his interest[56] or in cases of professional advisers who abuse their positions of trust to their own advantage. Such contracts are voidable. This happened in a case in which a professional art adviser built up a relationship of trust with his client, only to use that to have her bequeath four valuable paintings to him in her will.[57]

Force and fear (void)

4.93   Consensus cannot exist where one party is threatened with or actually assaulted into agreeing to a contract. This is vividly demonstrated in the case of *Earl of Orkney* v *Vinfra*[58] in which the Earl held a knife to his victim in order to convince him to sign over some property to him. This amounted to a lack of consent and the contract was void.

4.94   More subtle measures such as economic pressure have been discussed in the courts[59] and it has been held that as long as no unlawful means are used to back up such financial pressure then it is acceptable. Of course, one would need to look at the relationship between the parties to establish whether such pressure amounted to circumvention or undue influence.

BREACH OF CONTRACT

4.95   Once the parties have formed their contract, each will expect the other to perform his part of it. However, breach of contract arises where one party refuses to perform (repudiation/anticipatory breach), fails to perform (without actually refusing to do so) or performs his part of it but does so defectively. In those circumstances, the party who is not in breach, the innocent party, needs to consider what remedies are available to him. It should be noted that he cannot claim a remedy if he is also in breach, because of the principle of mutuality of contract.[60] The remedies available for breach of contract are: contractual remedies, damages, action for payment, action for specific implement, action for interdict, rescission, retention and lien. There are also specific remedies and actions which can be taken under the Sale of Goods Act 1979 for breaches of sale of goods contracts. Some remedies have to be sought in the courts but others can be taken without court action.

ANTICIPATORY BREACH

4.96   In the case of anticipatory breach, which occurs when the party in breach issues a refusal to perform his obligations *before* the due date for performance, then there are additional choices for the innocent party to make. He has to decide whether to accept

---

[56] *Gray* v *Binny* (1879) 7 R 332.
[57] *Honeyman's Executors* v *Sharp* 1978 SC 223.
[58] (1606) Mor 1648.
[59] *Allen* v *Flood* [1898] AC 1.
[60] *Graham* v *United Turkey Red Co* 1922 SC 533.

the refusal to perform when it is issued. If he does accept the refusal then the contract is repudiated.[61] The innocent party no longer has to fulfil his obligations under the contract and can sue the party in breach for damages for loss arising out of the breach. Alternatively, the innocent party can wait to see if the party in breach is bluffing and will actually perform the contract on the due date and, indeed, he can go ahead and perform his own obligations under it at the proper time, regardless of what the party in breach does except in very limited circumstances where it can be shown that the innocent party has no legitimate interest in keeping the contract alive.[62] He can ask the court to compel the party in breach to carry out his obligations, using the action of payment, specific implement or interdict as appropriate.

REMEDIES

The remedies are: **4.97**

Contractual remedies

The contract may contain an interest clause for late payment or a liquidated damages clause which sets an agreed level of damages to paid out for breach of contract without having to resort to court action.[63] The contract should also be checked for any enforceable contractual restrictions on remedies such as an exclusion clause or a limitation clause.

Damages

A claim for damages from the party in breach can be raised in court by the innocent   **4.98**
party if he does not want to insist on performance of the contract but wants monetary compensation for losses arising out of the breach of contract instead. The amount of damages which will be awarded by the court is strictly limited. The loss claimed for must be caused by the breach[64] and must not be too remote. A claim will be too remote if the claim does not fall into the category of general damages or special damages, the tests for which are set out in the important case of *Hadley* v *Baxendale*[65] and discussed in more detail in *Victoria Laundry (Windsor) Ltd* v *Newman Industries*.[66] General damages are those which arise naturally in the ordinary course of things and therefore include matters which the parties are imputed (implied) to know. Special damages are those which should have been in the reasonable contemplation of the parties at the time the contract was concluded and include matters which the parties actually knew about. Thus, in *Hadley* v *Baxendale*, profits lost when a broken mill crank shaft was not replaced quickly enough were not found to be general damages because, in the ordinary course of things, mills carried spare parts and so, in the

---

[61] W McBryde, *The Law of Contract in Scotland* (2nd edn, 2001), paras 20–30.
[62] *White and Carter (Councils) Ltd* v *McGregor* 1962 SC (HL) 1.
[63] Note that these will only be enforced if a fair assessment of likely losses arising from breach and dispute can arise if the "innocent party" tries to rescind the contract (ie pull out) and *then* tries to claim interest: *Black* v *McGregor* [2006] CSIH 45. Punitive clauses are not enforceable: *Dingwall* v *Burnett* 1912 SC 1097.
[64] *A/B Karlshamns Oljefabriker* v *Monarch Steamship Co Ltd* 1949 SC (HL) 1.
[65] (1854) 9 Exch 341.
[66] [1949] 2 KB 528.

ordinary course of things, production should not have stopped. They did not fall under special damages because the party in breach had not been told that the crank shaft was needed urgently. In *Victoria Laundry*, there were two losses arising out of the failure to deliver a new boiler on time: anticipated profits from new business which the new boiler could have serviced, and large government contracts. The court held that the lost profits had arisen in the ordinary cause of things and so were recoverable. However, the government contracts did not fall into this category. The court had to decide whether these fell into the category of special damages but as the party in breach did not know about them when the contract was concluded, they did not meet the test for special damages and so could not be recovered. In the case of *Balfour Beatty (Construction) Ltd* v *Scottish Power plc*,[67] the court had to decide how much one business could be expected to know about another as this would determine what fell into the category of "ordinary course of things" and what would require special knowledge of the circumstances. It was held that "It must always be a question of circumstances what one contracting party is presumed to know about the business activities of the other. No doubt, the simpler the activity of the one, the more readily can it be inferred that the other would have reasonable knowledge thereof".[68]

4.99   Quantification of damages may be difficult in some cases. While financial or patrimonial loss may be relatively easy to work out where there is a loss of profits, some breaches may lead to other losses which are not as easy to calculate. For example, if a builder performs a contract to build a house but does not do it properly, then remedial work may be needed to put it right. In this sort of case, the measure of damages will be based either on the cost of putting it right or on the difference in value between the house as it should be if built properly and the actual valuation.[69] In contracts for entertainment or enjoyment such as holiday contracts, there may be no financial loss as a result of the breach of contract but the innocent party has suffered disappointment or inconvenience. In limited circumstances, the courts will award damages for this non-patrimonial loss.[70]

Action for payment

4.100   If the breach is a failure to pay a bill or invoice due under the contract, the innocent party can raise a court action to recover payment of this debt.

Action for specific implement

4.101   If the breach is a failure to do something other than pay money, then the innocent party can raise a court action for specific implement which is a court order compelling the party in breach to carry out his obligations under the contract. It is not available for payment of money nor for contracts which have a strong personal element such as

---

[67] 1994 SC (HL) 20.
[68] Lord Jauncey of Tullichettle at 810F.
[69] However, the court will consider proportionality in making this decision: *McLaren Murdoch & Hamilton Ltd* v *Abercromby Motor Group Ltd* 2002 GWD 38–1242.
[70] *Diesen* v *Samson* 1971 SLT (Sh Ct) 49; *Farley* v *Skinner* [2002] 2 AC 732. Courts used to extend this to a contract for solicitors' services in business in the case of *Siddiqui* v *James & Charles Dodd (A Firm)* [2006] EWHC 1295.

employment or partnership contracts. The court will also consider whether compliance is likely to be very difficult and may refuse to grant it if that is the case. Breach of an order for specific implement is contempt of court and can carry a prison sentence of up to 6 months under the Law Reform (Miscellaneous Provisions) (Scotland) Act 1940.

Action for interdict

In this case, the innocent party is seeking a court order to prevent or stop the party in breach from doing something.   **4.102**

Rescission

If – and only if – the breach is material, then the innocent party can terminate the contract by rescission. This remedy is non-court based and allows the innocent party to walk away from the contract without penalty. He can still claim damages in court from the party in breach if there are any losses. However, the case of *Wade* v *Waldon*[71] shows that this remedy comes with a risk. If the breach is not in fact material, then the innocent party cannot rescind the contract and, by doing so, he becomes the party in breach and is open to action being taken against him.   **4.103**

Retention

This non-court based remedy allows the innocent party to retain payment or withhold performance under the contract until the breach is remedied.   **4.104**

Lien

An innocent party can retain property of the party in breach which he has in his possession until the breach is remedied. This is a non-court based remedy and will be particularly useful for businesses which repair goods which can be retained until the repair bill is paid.   **4.105**

    In deciding which remedy to seek, the innocent party needs to identify the breach and then choose the appropriate remedy.   **4.106**

TERMINATION OF CONTRACT AND OBLIGATIONS

A contract (or the obligations under it) will terminate in certain circumstances: **4.107**

ACCEPTILATION

The innocent party accepts the breach and treats the contract as terminated.   **4.108**

CONFUSION

The debtor and creditor under the same obligation become one and the same person.   **4.109**

---

[71] 1909 SC 571.

COMPENSATION

4.110   If the parties owe each other money, then one debt can be used to cancel out or reduce the other. Thus, if X owes Y £50 and Y owes X £20, then X can pay £30 to Y rather than pay the full £50 and try to recover the outstanding £20 from Y.

FRUSTRATION

4.111   There are certain situations in which the law recognises that a contract cannot be performed and, in those narrow cases, frees the parties from further performance: the contract itself is not terminated but the need to perform it is. This can happen if there is supervening impossibility, supervening illegality or a supervening change in circumstances between the date the contract is made and the date of performance.

Supervening impossibility

4.112   Supervening impossibility can occur if the subject-matter of the contract is destroyed (*rei interitus*). This may be actual or constructive destruction. Actual destruction occurred in *Taylor v Caldwell*[72] in which a music hall which had been hired for a particular date burned down before then. The court held that this frustrated the contract. Constructive destruction is demonstrated in *Mackeson v Boyd*,[73] in which a large house was to be let out under a contract. Unfortunately, war broke out and it was requisitioned for use by the authorities and so not available for use by the tenants.

Supervening illegality

4.113   The law may be changed during the period between the date the contract is made and the due date for performance which makes it illegal. This would happen if war was declared and the contracting parties belonged to enemy states, as in the case of *Fraser & Co Ltd v Denny, Mott & Dickson Ltd*.[74]

Supervening change in circumstances

4.114   A contract may still be frustrated even if it is not impossible or illegal to perform but events take a turn which means that the nature of the contract is changed and it becomes something different from that contemplated by the parties when they made the contract. However, that would not extend to something simply becoming less profitable than hoped for. The application of this type of frustration is demonstrated in the case of *Krell v Henry*:[75] Henry hired a flat in Pall Mall from Krell for two days. It was not stated in the contract that the purpose of the hire was to view the Coronation procession of Edward VII, but the letting was for the two days for which the Coronation was scheduled. The Coronation was postponed because of the King's illness, and Henry tried to cancel his contract with Krell who refused and sued him for the rent. The court held that the contract was for licence to use rooms for a particular purpose (implied condition since it was not express in the contract), and since the Coronation was postponed, the contract was frustrated. This decision was

---

[72] (1863) 122 ER 309.
[73] 1942 SC 56.
[74] 1944 SC (HL) 35.
[75] [1903] 2 KB 740.

based on the court's findings that the whole point of the contract and the reason that it had been entered into by both of the parties was for the purpose of watching the Coronation. However, this case has been treated with reserve in later cases and so this type of frustration is very narrow.

What if the parties have already carried out some of their obligations before the **4.115** contract is frustrated and monies have been paid over in anticipation of the contract being performed? If that has happened then the law of unjustified enrichment may be used to "settle up" between the parties.[76]

NOVATION

One contract will be terminated if the parties to it decide to replace it with a new **4.116** agreement.

PRESCRIPTION (PRESCRIPTION AND LIMITATION (SCOTLAND) ACT 1973)

What happens if a long period of time passes after the contract is concluded without any **4.117** action being taken to perform or enforce it? Does it last forever? The answer is "no" – the Prescription and Limitation (Scotland) Act 1973 places a time limit on how long certain obligations can last if no action is taken on them for a specified period of time. The relevant time period for contracts (unless specifically excluded under the Act) is called the short negative prescription and lasts for 5 years. The effect of prescription means that if a contract is not subject to a "relevant claim" or "relevant acknowledgement" within that 5-year period, the obligations under it are extinguished.

A relevant claim would include one party trying to enforce the contract and a **4.118** relevant acknowledgement would include one party actually performing his obligations or writing to the other party making it clear that the obligations were still "live".

The excepted contracts are: **4.119**

(i) contracts contained or evidenced in a probative writ (except guarantees or those which contain an obligation to pay a periodical sum of money such as rent);
(ii) partnership and agency contracts;
(iii) contracts relating to land (except those requiring a periodical sum of money);
(iv) imprescriptible obligations (this includes real rights of ownership in land and the right to challenge a contract on the grounds of invalidity *ex facie* or forgery).

---

[76] *Cantiere San Rocco* v *Clyde Shipbuilding Co* 1923 SC (HL) 105.

4.120

ESSENTIAL FACTS

INTRODUCTION

- A contract is a voluntary obligation arising out of an agreement between two parties which creates legal obligations between them.

- A promise is a gratuitous unilateral obligation (not requiring the promisee's consent) which can only be enforced by the promisee against the promisor.

FORMATION

- A contract is formed when an offer is met with an acceptance.

- An offer must be capable of acceptance, it must be communicated in clear terms and it must include the intention to be legally bound. Offers do not include: invitations to treat, requests for quotations, tenders and willingness to negotiate.

- Offers lapse if not accepted on time (time limit/reasonable period of time) or if met with a counter-offer. Offers can be revoked at any time before acceptance, unless a time period has been set for acceptance.

- An acceptance cannot be revoked/cancelled as it concludes the contract. The postal rule applies to contracts made by post: a contract is concluded as soon as the acceptance is posted. Once concluded, it cannot be cancelled unless the parties agree or it is a regulated contract such as certain consumer credit contracts.

- Written contracts are subject to the Contract (Scotland) Act 1997 which presumes that the written contract contains all contractual terms.

- The rules of incorporation apply to all contracts: contractual terms must be incorporated into the contract when the contract is made and not after-wards.

PROBLEMS WITH CONTRACTS

- A contract which appears to have been formed by offer and acceptance may have a flaw which renders it void, voidable or unenforceable.

- Void: so fundamentally flawed that it does not amount to a contract at all. Voidable: less flawed but can be challenged by one of the parties and set aside by a court. An unenforceable contract such as an illegal contract is neither void nor voidable but will not be enforced by the courts.

- The main problems which can affect contracts are as follows:

(1) Lack of consensus

- The parties must have consensus (agreement). Lack of consensus may be caused by error if it goes right to the heart of the contract (NB: that is not an *automatic* consequence of essential error).

- Uninduced error: the general rule is that an uninduced unilateral error will not affect the contract. Induced error includes innocent misrepresentation, fraudulent misrepresentation and negligent misrepresentation.
- Bilateral error: an error made by both parties will render the contract void if essential.

(2) Lack of consent

- The parties must intend to create legal obligations. This is not usually found in social, domestic and trivial arrangements such as gaming contracts. See also illegal contracts.

(3) Lack of capacity

- Both parties must have the capacity or legal ability to enter into the contract.
- The capacity of certain groups of persons is restricted in law as follows:
  - *Children and young persons*: capacity is governed by the Age of Legal Capacity (Scotland) Act 1991. Generally, children under 16 have no contractual capacity and young persons aged 16 and over have full capacity. Exceptions: (1) under 16s can enter into contracts of a type normal for their age on reasonable terms; and (2) young persons can apply to the court to have any "prejudicial transaction" made at the ages of 16 or 17 set aside.
  - Insane adults have no capacity at common law.
  - Intoxicated persons: a person has to be very drunk or high on drugs to lose capacity.
  - Registered companies have capacity to contract. This will only be limited if its constitution limits what the directors of the company can do and the third party with whom they are dealing is in bad faith.
  - Partnerships: firms have capacity.
  - Unincorporated bodies: no capacity.

(4) Lack of formality

- Contracts which must be in writing to be valid are listed in the Requirements of Writing (Scotland) Act 1995. These are contracts relating to creation, transfer, variation or extinction of an interest in land (eg buying a house). Promises (except if given in the course of business) must also be in writing.
- A lack of formality can be cured if the circumstances of ss 1(3) and (4) apply.
- If writing is required then it must be written (not electronic) and subscribed under s 2 of the 1995 Act. A contract can be made probative (self-proving) by attestation (witnessing) under s 3 of the 1995 Act or by being endorsed with a court certificate under s 4 of the 1995 Act.

- Notarial execution is permitted under s 9 of the 1995 Act.

(5) Illegality

- A contract formed for an illegal purpose is unenforceable. A contract may also be unenforceable if it is to be performed in an illegal way.
- Contracts illegal at common law include those contrary to public policy (eg criminal/sexual morality/interfering with justice/restrictive covenants).
- Restrictive covenants are found in employment contracts, sale and purchase of business contracts and solus agreements and are unenforceable unless they protect legitimate business interests of the party seeking to enforce the covenant, are reasonable (court will consider geographical limits, time limits, trade secrets etc) and in the public interest.

(6) Restrictions on freedom to contract

- These include common law on exclusion clauses, Unfair Contract Terms Act 1977 (UCTA) and Unfair Terms in Consumer Contracts Regulations 1999.
- Common law and exclusion clauses: courts not keen to enforce attempts to contract to exclude obligations or restrict liability. Such clauses are construed *contra proferens* (against the party seeking to rely on it).
- UCTA applies to many (but not all) contracts. It does five things: (a) it renders clauses which limit/exclude liability for death or personal injury arising out of breach of duty void; (b) it allows clauses which limit/exclude liability for other losses arising out of breach of duty if they are fair and reasonable; (c) it allows clauses in standard form or consumer contracts which limit/exclude liability for breach of contract if they are fair and reasonable; (d) it allows indemnity clauses in consumer contracts if fair and reasonable; and (e) it prohibits sellers of goods from excluding certain implied terms found in the Sale of Goods Act 1979 in contracts with consumers and only allows such exclusions in other contracts if fair and reasonable.
- Unfair Terms in Consumer Contracts Regulations 1999: these apply to certain consumer contracts (if consumer a natural person). Terms deemed unfair (those which are too pro-business and anti-consumer) are not enforceable against the consumer.

(7) Other prejudicial circumstances

- Facility and circumvention (voidable): taking advantage of vulnerable person may render contract voidable.
- Undue influence (voidable): similar but different – position of trust is abused.

- Force and fear: effect depends on level of and nature of methods used. Physical force = void through lack of consensus. Economic pressure = OK unless unlawful means used (eg blackmail).

BREACH OF CONTRACT

- A breach of contract is a failure to perform the contract in whole or in part. This allows the innocent party to take certain action against the party in breach.

- There are three main types of breach: repudiation/anticipatory breach; late (or non-) performance; and defective performance.

- Remedies fall into the following categories: contractual remedies (interest clauses and liquidate damages clauses); damages (raise court action for monetary compensation); action for payment (raise court action to obtain order to get outstanding bill paid); action for specific implement (raise court action to obtain court order telling party in breach to fulfil the contract); action for interdict (raise court action to obtain court order telling party in breach to stop doing something); rescission (self-help remedy – innocent party's right to terminate the contract); retention (self-help remedy – withhold performance until breach remedied); and lien (self-help remedy – keep goods belonging to party in breach until breach remedied). There are for remedies available under sale of goods contracts.

- Damages: most widely available remedy. Must show that the breach has caused the damages claimed for (causation) and that the loss is not too remote (general and special damages).

TERMINATION OF CONTRACT AND OBLIGATIONS

- Contracts can be terminated by acceptilation, confusion, compensation, novation and prescription. The parties may also be freed from their obligations if the contract is frustrated.

- Frustration happens when there is supervening impossibility: destruction of the subject-matter; supervening illegality; or a supervening change in the circumstances.

- Prescription is regulated by the Prescription and Limitation (Scotland) Act 1973.

ESSENTIAL CASES

4.121

INTRODUCTION

Morton's Trustees v *Aged Christian Friend Society of Scotland* (1899): gratuitous contract;

Littlejohn v *Hadwen* (1882): promise in business (keeping an offer open);

Stone v *MacDonald* (1979): promise in business (option granted over land in favour of another).

FORMATION

Thornton v *Shoe Lane Parking Ltd* (1971): offer and acceptance by action (slot machine);

Fisher v *Bell* (1961): flick-knife case – shop window display is invitation to treat;

Pharmaceutical Society of GB v *Boots* (1953): medicines case – display did not amount to offer;

Carlill v *Carbolic Smoke Ball Co* (1893): an advert by a company was an offer. The customer accepted by action;

Jaeger Bros Ltd v *J & A McMorland* (1902): a detailed quotation can amount to offer;

Harvey v *Facey* (1893): expressing willingness to negotiate is not an offer;

Littlejohn v *Hadwen* (1882): offer cannot be revoked during period specified for acceptance;

Wylie & Lochhead v *McElroy & Sons* (1873): offer lapses if not accepted within a reasonable period of time;

Wolf & Wolf v *Forfar Potato Co Ltd* (1984): counter-offer causes original offer to lapse;

Dunlop, Wilson & Co v *Higgins and Son* (1848): established postal rule;

Mason v *Benhar* (1882): not a firm decision but indicates that Scots courts would treat acceptance lost in the post as not concluding the contract;

Jacobsen, Sons & Co v *Underwood & Son Ltd* (1894): postal rule – incorrectly addressed letter still concluded contract;

Countess of Dunmore v *Alexander* (1830): controversial postal rule case;

Williamson v *North of Scotland and Orkney Steam Navigation Co* (1916): tiny print can prevent incorporation of terms;

Parker v *South Eastern Railway Co* (1877): "see back" printed on front of ticket incorporated those terms into the contract;

Taylor v *Glasgow Corporation* (1952): receipt for baths could not contain contractual terms;

Olley v *Marlborough Court Ltd* (1949): post-contractual notice in bedroom case.

PROBLEMS WITH CONTRACTS

(1) Lack of consensus

Mathieson Gee (Ayrshire) Ltd v *Quigley* (1952): parties agreed to different things. No consensus so no contract;

Stewart v *Kennedy* (1890): an essential error, provided it is not induced by the other party, does not invalidate a written onerous contract;

Hunter v *Bradford Property Trust* (1970): errors in gratuitous contracts are more likely to adversely affect the contract;

Boyd & Forrest v *Glasgow & South Western Railway Co* (1912, 1915): a genuine mistake in figures = innocent misrepresentation;

Raffles v *Wichelhaus* (1864): each party had a different ship in mind when forming contract to transport cargo – contract void through lack of consensus;

Morrison v *Robertson* (1908): error about the identity of the other party: contract void. Contrast with *Macleod* v *Kerr* (1965);

Macleod v *Kerr* (1965): the error was not essential here because the seller of the car entered into contract with a purchaser – it didn't matter to him who the purchaser was. Contract was only voidable;

Wilson v *Marquis of Breadalbane* (1859): error as to price not always essential.

(2) Lack of consent

Stobo Ltd v *Morrisons (Gowns) Ltd* (1949): pre-contractual negotiations in business;

Dawson International plc v *Coats Paton plc* (1988): breach of pre-contractual agreement;

Balfour v *Balfour* (1919): domestic arrangement did not imply consent to be legally bound;

Kelly v *Murphy* (1940) and *Ferguson* v *Littlewoods Pools Ltd* (1997): gaming contracts are *sponsiones ludicrae*;

Robertson v *Anderson* (2003): an agreement to share bingo winnings was enforceable.

(3) Lack of capacity, (4) Lack of formality and (5) Illegality

Barr v *Crawford* (1983): a contract of bribery in exchange for liquor licence renewal was illegal and unenforceable;

Dowling & Rutter v *Abacus Frozen Foods Ltd (No 2)* (2002): supply of labour contract performed illegally because it breached immigration legislation. However, court allowed it to be enforced (lack of knowledge a factor);

Bridge v *Deacons* (1984): criteria for enforceability of restrictive covenants;

Bluebell Apparel Ltd v *Dickinson* (1978): restrictive covenant case – wide ban on working for rival jeans company upheld to protect trade secrets;

Stewart v *Stewart* (1899): restrictive covenant – 20-mile restriction around Elgin was enforceable;

Dallas, McMillan & Sinclair v *Simpson* (1989): restrictive covenant – 20-mile radius around Glasgow Cross not enforceable;

Mulvein v *Murray* (1908): severable clauses can be saved if some reasonable but others not – court will delete unreasonable parts;

Nordenfelt v *Maxim Nordenfelt Guns and Ammunition Co Ltd* (1894): the ultimate restraint – 25 years, worldwide but still enforceable in the circumstances;

Dumbarton Steamboat Co Ltd v *Macfarlane* (1899): the purchaser of a business operating on the west coast of Scotland only could not impose a UK-wide ban on its seller;

Esso Petroleum Co Ltd v *Harper's Garages (Stourport) Ltd* (1968): 21-year solus agreement too long.

(6) Restrictions on freedom to contract and (7) Other prejudicial circumstances

MacGilvary v *Gilmartin* (1986): facility and circumvention case – contract entered into by widowed mother with daughter was set aside;

Gray v *Binny* (1879): undue influence case – mother influenced son to make a bad bargain over his inheritance;

Honeyman's Executors v *Sharp* (1978): undue influence case involving professional adviser;

Earl of Orkney v *Vinfra* (1606): force and fear case – sign contract or be stabbed: void;

Allen v *Flood* (1898): economic pressure not force and fear unless unlawful.

BREACH OF CONTRACT

Dingwall v *Burnett* (1912): liquidate damages clauses will only be enforced if they are a fair assessment of likely losses;

Graham & Co v *United Turkey Red Co* (1922): a party cannot seek a remedy for breach of contract by the other party if he is also in breach of the contract;

Wade v *Waldon* (1909): note rescission only available if breach material;

White & Carter (Councils) Ltd v *McGregor* (1962): in a case of anticipatory breach, the innocent party is not obliged to accept it and can therefore go on with his part of the contract;

Hadley v *Baxendale* (1854): established two-part test for remoteness of damages: loss naturally arising as a consequence of breach and loss for special circumstances if party in breach knew about them when contract made;

Victoria Laundry (Windsor) Ltd v *Newman Industries* (1949): loss naturally arising includes things known about in the ordinary course of things but special circumstances must actually be known and not implied;

Balfour Beatty Construction (Scotland) Ltd v *Scottish Power plc* (1994): "ordinary course of things" did not include detailed knowledge of concrete pouring procedures;

McLaren Murdoch & Hamilton Ltd v *Abercromby Motor Group Ltd* (2002): courts will look at proportionality in assessing pursuer's claim for damages in defective performance of building contracts;

Diesen v *Samson* (1971): wedding photos ruined – damages awarded for non-patrimonial loss (in this case, disappointment);

Farley v *Skinner* (2002): country house valued correctly but client had asked for "peaceful" retreat and it was ruined by flight path – damages could be awarded for non-patrimonial loss (in this case, loss of amenity) although no actual financial loss.

TERMINATION OF CONTRACT AND OBLIGATIONS

Taylor v *Caldwell* (1863): music hall case. Contract for hire of hall frustrated when it was burned down;

Mackeson v *Boyd* (1942): tenancy frustrated when country house requisitioned in the war (constructive destruction of subject-matter);

Fraser & Co Ltd v *Denny, Mott & Dickson* (1944): supervening illegality caused by declaration of war;

Krell v *Henry* (1903): Coronation case – purpose of contract thwarted when Coronation postponed.

5 AGENCY

WHAT IS AGENCY?

It is a commonplace in business for one person (the principal) to engage another (the 5.1
agent) to carry out certain duties on the first person's behalf. There are many reasons
for this. The principal may not have the experience, knowledge, resources or time to
attend to the task himself. Perhaps the agent is geographically better located to carry
out the tasks. Maybe the principal requires to absent himself for a time, say by being
out of the country on business or on holiday.

There are well-recognised categories of agent: factors, brokers, solicitors, estate 5.2
agents, bankers, partners of a business, directors of a company, and so on. Business
would come to a halt without agents.

The law divides up the class of agents into two recognised categories: general and 5.3
special agents. General agents have authority to act for the principal in a wide range
of diverse actions limited only by the professional or employment competence of the
agent. For example, a solicitor is expected to deal with all the legal aspects of a client's
affairs. A company director is expected to further the company's business. A special
agent, on the other hand, is authorised to act for the principal only in a very limited
manner: say, to conduct a particular transaction. It follows that authority given to a
special agent, at the time of the creation of the agency relationship, will be very specific.
A general agent's authority may be given in very general terms or simply implied by
the nature of the agent's profession or employment.

What is common to all agents is that each and every one of them is an authorised 5.4
representative of the principal and is expected to act on their behalf for as long as the
relationship continues.

The law of agency sets a framework for the creation and termination of the 5.5
relationship of agency, for the liabilities of the principal to the agent and of the agent
to the principal, for the safeguarding of third parties dealing with agents and, more
indirectly, for the liability of persons who hold themselves out as agents with an
ostensible authority when in fact they do not have such authority. In the following
sections we shall examine each of these areas in turn. We shall also look at the
characteristics of certain particular types of agent.

CREATION OF THE AGENCY RELATIONSHIP

The relationship of agency is created by contract. Therefore, there must be agreement 5.6
between the principal and the agent as to the instructions. This can come about in a
variety of ways.

EXPRESS AGREEMENT

5.7   The usual form of agency is created by express agreement either verbally or in writing. The agreement will occur prior to, or at the latest contemporaneously with, the tasks to be carried out. In the case of a general agent (by far the commonest form of agency) the instructions to the agent will be unspecific on the details and the agent will be expected to use his discretion to fulfil the delegated task or tasks. But with a special agent, where the instructions are limited to a particular transaction, the instructions will be the most specific and the discretion, if any, of the agent will be minimal. The principal may dictate precisely how a task is to be performed, or may dictate what the outcome is to be, or with whom the agent is to deal. Such specific instructions are most likely to be given in writing, since this will enable proof of the terms of the appointment. In practice many general agents will acknowledge their instructions by the issue of letters of engagement (for example, solicitors and accountants). Since the agency relationship is one of contract, both principal and agent must clearly understand what is expected of them and of the other. It is this which dictates how the agency will be created. In matters of importance or intricacy, writing will be used. There is no set form of document and the contract can be constructed from a series of letters or acknowledgments.

5.8   An example of agency constituted by verbal agreement alone is given in the case of *Picken* v *Hawkes*.[1] Picken entered into an oral contract with Hawkes whereby he would act as sole agent for Hawkes in Scotland for 3 years. The contract included clauses setting remuneration and commission. Six months later, Hawkes informed Picken that he was no longer in his employment. Picken sued for breach of contract. Hawkes argued that Picken was engaged under a contract of service (employment) and that, in accordance with the rules of evidence which applied at the time, proof had to exclude the verbal evidence of Picken. Picken argued that the contract was one of agency and therefore no restriction should be placed on the manner of proof. In deciding this issue, Lord Craighill said "service, undoubtedly, in a certain sense is involved, but agency is the fundamental characteristic".

IMPLICATION

5.9   The relationship may also be created by implication and so not expressly stated. This is most likely to occur where the relationship arises by way of the agent's employment. For example, a shop manager, by virtue of employment as such, is the agent of the shop by implication and the manager has the ostensible authority to enter into contracts with the shop's suppliers and customers unless restricted by the employers. Implication can also occur by the building up of a continuing trade practice. For example, where there is a history of trading facilitated by the agent, that relationship, even where originating in express agreement, will be deemed to continue after the initial term by implication until it is revoked. There is no express agreement for the continuing agency, but the agent continues to act for as long as required by the principal, and third parties dealing with the agent will regard the agent as having authority to act. In the case of implied agency, the principal is bound on the basis of the legal principle of personal bar. For example, the shop would be barred from refusing to acknowledge the

---

[1] (1875) 5 R 676.

manager's authority for as long as the manager remained in that employment. Agents whose authority is implied may be held by third parties with whom they deal to have "apparent" or "ostensible" authority – but we shall deal with that further below.

An example of implied agency is found in *Barnetson v Petersen Brothers*.[2] Petersen **5.10** Brothers owned a steamship which, with its Master (an agent for Petersen Brothers), was chartered by a third party. While in port in Methil, the third party instructed Barnetson, a shipbroker, to carry out necessary works. Barnetson sought recovery of outlays and commission from Petersen Brothers as owners of the ship. The court held that the master of the ship had accepted the services, and as Petersen Brothers had had the benefit of the services they were directly liable to Barnetson. Lord Trayner said:

> "The defenders' vessel, the 'Rocklands', arrived in Methil in January 1900, there to load a cargo of coal. The services of a shipbroker were necessary, and the services were rendered by the pursuer. He did the ship's business at the Custom-House and elsewhere, and made all the necessary disbursements. He advanced money to the captain, paid the pilotage, towage, and dock dues, and the other sums enumerated in his account. ... *Prima facie* the defenders are liable for the pursuer's account, as they took the benefit of the pursuer's services and are *lucrati* to the extent to which he made advances on the ship's account."

Statutory implication

A refinement on implication occurs when an agent is created by statutory implication. **5.11** The clearest example of this is the position of a partner in a partnership, since s 5 of the Partnership Act 1890 states that "every partner is an agent of the firm". A company director has authority to act as agent for the company since a company has no powers to act other than through its directors. However, the appointment is not strictly one of statutory implication since the powers of the directors will be authorised by its memorandum and articles of association.

NECESSITY

In some jurisdictions (such as in England) a relationship of agency may arise from **5.12** necessity, so that, where a person with no authority acts for another in an emergency, he may recover the expenses of doing so from the benefited party. It is, however, necessary that the agent in this situation has been unable to communicate with the benefited party and has acted in good faith and within reasonable constraints. In Scotland this concept is included under the doctrine of *negotiorum gestio* and is of a very limited nature. It will be noted that prior or contemporaneous agreement could not have been obtained and the concept relies on the idea that the principal will ratify (that is, approve of) the actions of the agent retrospectively.

RATIFICATION

Agency can be created by retrospective acts of ratification, even in situations where **5.13** there is no emergency. The agent strictly has no prior authority to act and the situation is remedied by the ratification which deems the prior unauthorised acts to be approved

---

[2] (1902) 5 F 86.

and will make the principal liable to the agent and to third parties as though the agency had existed from the outset. Such a situation is likely to occur where a duly authorised agent has exceeded his authority out of considerations of expediency, in the expectation that the principal will approve of the actions in due course.

5.14   There are, however, conditions on such ratification. The chief of these are that the principal must exist at the time of the agent's actings; the principal must have the necessary legal capacity; and the ratification must be timeous.

5.15   In the case of *Tinnevelly Sugar Refining Co Ltd v Mirrlees Watson and Yaryan Co Ltd*,[3] promoters of a company bought defective machinery *prior* to Tinnevelly being formed and as a result the company was held not to be entitled to sue under the contract of purchase.

5.16   In *Goodall* v *Bilsland*,[4] a wine and spirit merchant in Glasgow applied to the licensing court for renewal of his public house licence. Objectors employed a solicitor to lodge objections with the court. The licence was granted but the solicitor for the objectors appealed. The appeal court sustained the appeal. The merchant sought to reduce the decision of the appeal court. He claimed that the solicitor had no authority to appeal to the licensing court because he had no instructions to do so, had therefore exceeded his authority, and had not obtained ratification from his clients timeously which he could have done had he done so within the 10 days allowed for marking the appeal. The appeal was therefore an entirely unauthorised act. Lord Dunedin said:

> "it is said, and it was argued very strenuously, that although Mr. Kyle [the solicitor] had no authority when he lodged the appeal his proceedings were homologated afterwards. ... Homologation in this case means that, after the whole thing was over and when this case of reduction was raised, then the parties in whose names the appeal was taken are asked, in the action of reduction, whether they approved of everything that Mr. Kyle did, and they said, 'Oh, certainly we do.' Well, that is homologation of a very easy character ... it is homologation after you perfectly well know that the case has been decided in your favour ... it seems to me that the gentleman here who got his licence was entitled to hold that licence unless within the ten days a note of appeal was lodged by a person authorised to lodge that note of appeal; that no such person was here in this case; and that consequently the whole proceedings were *funditus* null and void."

5.17   Provided an agent acts within the authority expressly or by implication given by the principal, the principal will be liable to third parties by the actions of the agent. If, however, the agent acts beyond the authority then the principal may not be liable to third parties. The nature of the authority and instructions are therefore of great importance in determining who is liable to whom and for what.

TERMINATION OF THE AGENCY RELATIONSHIP

MUTUAL CONSENT

5.18   An agency agreement, like any contract, can be terminated by the parties to it. This will often be achieved by mutual agreement. In some cases, in order to bring the agent's ostensible authority to an end, notice will require to be given to third parties.

---

[3] (1894) 21 R 1009.
[4] 1909 SC 1152.

UNILATERAL TERMINATION BY PRINCIPAL

5.19 Difficulties can be encountered where the principal attempts to terminate the agreement without the agent's consent. This is because the agent may be liable to third parties with whom he has entered into legal relations on the principal's behalf. Termination will then not be possible until notice has been given to these third parties. The notice serves to ensure that the principal is not held further liable on the basis of his agent's ostensible authority.

5.20 In some cases an agency agreement envisages that the agent will pursue not only his principal's interests but also his own. Such an agent is said to have "a procuratory *in rem suam*" (a power for his own benefit). It follows that the agent has to have the opportunity to conclude his interests. This situation is illustrated in *Premier Briquette Co Ltd* v *Gray*.[5] The principal may remain liable to the agent for losses or damages until the final termination.

5.21 An example of an attempt by a principal to revoke agency is given in *Galbraith & Moorhead* v *The Arethusa Ship Co Ltd*.[6] Galbraith & Moorhead agreed with the Arethusa Ship Co to take shares in the company provided that Galbraith & Moorhead would be the sole chartering brokers for the *Arethusa*. After a number of years, Galbraith & Moorhead discovered that the sole brokerage contract had been breached. They sued for damages. The court held that the agency agreement was one which continued for as long as the company remained in business. It was therefore not an agreement which could be terminated at the will of the company.

RENUNCIATION BY AGENT

5.22 An agent may renounce his agency, but in some situations he may remain liable to the principal for damages as a result of breach of the contract.

FULFILMENT OF PURPOSE

5.23 Where an agency agreement is created in order to achieve a particular result or is declared to last for a specified term, the performance of that result or the expiry of the term will bring the agreement to a natural close.

5.24 In *Brenan* v *Campbell's Tr*,[7] the pursuer, a civil engineer and architect in Oban, was employed by the defendants as factor on their estate for a period of 4 years from Martinmas 1890. He was allowed and did continue to practise as an engineer and architect in Oban. In October 1894 he was informed that his contract would terminate after Martinmas 1894. He raised an action against the defendants, claiming 6 months' pay in lieu of notice. The court held that he was not entitled to payment in lieu of notice as he was engaged for a definite period.

DISCONTINUANCE OF PRINCIPAL'S BUSINESS

5.25 Agency also ceases where the principal discontinues a business in which the agent is employed. The agent may be entitled to damages for breach of contract only where

---

[5] 1922 SC 329
[6] (1896) 23 R 1011.
[7] (1898) 25 R 423.

it is proved that the business should have continued to a later termination date. In *Patmore & Co v B Cannon & Co Ltd*,[8] the pursuers agreed to act as agents for the defenders for a period of 5 years. Three months later, the defenders discontinued their fancy leather trade which was the area of business relating to the agency. The court held that the pursuers were not entitled to damages for breach of contract as the defenders had not agreed in the agency agreement to bind itself to carry on its business, or any part of it, for the 5 years purely for the benefit of the pursuers. The agency existed to serve the business but the business did not exist to serve the agency.

5.26   Once an agency is terminated, the agent is entitled to receive a discharge.

TERMINATION BY OPERATION OF LAW

5.27   Agency can also be terminated by the operation of law as a result of death, bankruptcy or insanity of the principal or agent.

Death

5.28   The death of either principal or agent will bring the agency to an end. However, the agent's actions continue to be valid until he has notice of the death of the principal. Even then, it appears, the agent may conclude any business which is ongoing at the time of death. In *Campbell v Anderson*,[9] the agent continued acting in the *bona fide* belief that the principal was still alive. He was held to have bound the principal and not to be personally liable. Where the agent dies, his representatives on death are not entitled to continue the agency.

Bankruptcy

5.29   Agency is terminated by the bankruptcy of the principal. This is because the principal has lost the capacity to act. In the case of *McKenzie v Campbell*,[10] a solicitor received £285 from a client, with instructions to defend that client from charges of forgery. A few days later the client was sequestrated and his trustee in bankruptcy thereafter sought to recover the money from the solicitor. The court held that the solicitor's agency had been terminated by the sequestration and the solicitor was under a duty to account to the trustee for the funds.

Insanity

5.30   Insanity will also terminate an agency agreement since the principal has lost the capacity to act. However, if the insanity is only temporary then the agency will not terminate and an agent will be entitled to remuneration or relief for anything done by him during the period of incapacity. In *Wink v Mortimer*,[11] the court held that a period of temporary insanity did not terminate the agency. Lord Fullerton said:

> "the confinement was temporary and lasted only a few weeks. There was no pretence for stating that the business was not done, or was not done beneficially for the employer; and it

---

[8] (1892) 19 R 1004.
[9] (1829) 3 W & S 384.
[10] (1894) 21 R 904.
[11] (1849) 11 D 995.

would be of the most injurious consequences to hold that in such circumstances, an agent was bound to withhold his services during his employer's temporary disability, until he obtained some regular judicial authority for the continuance of his acting. I think in the circumstances of this case, there can be no doubt that the currency of the account was not interrupted by the very short illness of the employer".

Since it is not always clear whether insanity is temporary or permanent, there is **5.31** a blurred line at which the agent's authority will cease. This is the meaning of the reference to obtaining "judicial authority" in the above case. In recent years this difficulty has been addressed by statutory provisions, for example s 71 of the Law Reform (Miscellaneous Provisions) (Scotland) Act 1990 and more recently the provisions of the Adults with Incapacity (Scotland) Act 2000 which allows for continuing powers of attorney even where insanity is permanent.

DUTIES OF AGENT TO PRINCIPAL

Given that the relationship of agency derives from a contract between principal and **5.32** agent, it follows that the agent is under a duty personally to fulfil the instructions given in so far as this is possible.

PRECISE PERFORMANCE

Where instructions are specific, then they must be performed precisely. In the case **5.33** of *Gilmour* v *Clark*[12] an agent was instructed to deliver goods and load them onto a named ship. The goods were loaded onto another ship which sank and the goods were lost. The agent was held liable for the value of the goods since he had not fulfilled his specific instructions. In addition to being liable for loss and damage caused by failure to fulfil instructions, such an agent is not entitled to remuneration for actions while in breach of the contract of agency.

PERSONAL PERFORMANCE

The general rule is that agency instructions must be performed personally. The **5.34** Scots law principle is *delegatus non potest delegare* which means that an agent may not further delegate his duties to someone else. But there are many exceptions to this principle. Delegation may be common in particular trades or professions or may be necessitated by circumstances. But the principle will be strictly adhered to where the agency agreement expressly prohibits delegation or where the expertise, speciality or knowledge of the agent is of particular relevance and importance for the fulfilment of the instructions. Such a situation is known as *delectus personae* and indicates that the principal has chosen a particular delegate and no other to fulfil the instructions. In situations where delegation is allowed, it is normal for an agent to remain liable to the principal for the actions of the sub-agent who performed the work.

An example of where delegation was allowed is given in *Black* v *Cornelius*[13] where **5.35** an architect was engaged in connection with building work. The architect instructed

---

[12] (1853) 15 D 478.
[13] (1879) 6 R 581.

a surveyor to carry out measurements and prepare plans. The building work was not proceeded with and the architect sought recovery of fees and outlays including the surveyor's fees. The client argued that he was not liable for the surveyor's fees since he had not instructed him. Lord Ormidale observed: "I have no doubt that an architect employed in the ordinary way has authority to employ a surveyor, and that the surveyor, if not otherwise paid, has a good claim against the person who employs the architect."

DUTY OF CARE AND SKILL

5.36   An agent must exercise due skill and care in the performance of the instructions. If the agent fails to exercise due skill and care then he will be liable to the principal for any loss or damage which results from such failure. The standard of care for agents of ordinary competence is described in Bell's *Commentaries*, I, 516 as the standard of skill and care of an ordinary prudent man managing his own affairs. A breach of this standard occurs where no ordinary prudent man would have acted in the way the agent did in the circumstances. A professional agent is required to fulfil a higher standard of care. This was described in the case of *Hunter* v *Hanley*[14] as that standard of care which an ordinarily competent professional would have brought to bear in the performance of the instructions. A breach of this standard occurs where the act is one that "no professional man of ordinary skill would have taken if he had been acting with ordinary care".

GOOD FAITH

5.37   An agent must act in good faith and so only for the benefit of the principal. The agent must therefore not allow any conflict to occur between his duties to the principal and the agent's own self-interest or the interest of any other person.

DUTY TO ACCOUNT

5.38   The agent also has a duty to account to the principal for all actions done on the principal's behalf. This duty is not limited to accounting for financial actions but should be understood as the duty to keep the principal fully informed of the progress or otherwise in performing the agent's duties and of the results of that performance.

5.39   The duty to account is illustrated in *Tyler* v *Logan*[15] where the owner of the shoe business appointed Logan as manager of one of his shops. Goods were marked with selling prices and sent to the shop and Logan signed receipts for the goods received. During a stocktaking carried out on behalf of the owner, a deficit was discovered and the owner brought an action against Logan for payment. Even though there was no proof of dishonesty or negligence, Logan was held liable to the owner in the sum claimed.

---

[14] 1955 SC 200.
[15] (1904) 7 F 123.

OTHER FIDUCIARY DUTIES

The agent also has a number of fiduciary duties. That is to say that the principal must   **5.40**
be able to rely absolutely on the agent fulfilling the essential purposes of the agency.
Any conflicts of interest must be avoided. Such conflicts may arise in three areas. First,
an agent should avoid a conflict between his principal's interest and his own personal
interest. In *Cunningham* v *Lee*,[16] a solicitor bought shares on behalf of a client. On the
settlement date, when the price required to be paid, the client failed to produce the
price. The solicitor should have sold the shares, which had fallen in value, and claimed
the loss from the client. Instead, he retained the shares and sold them without loss
sometime later, when the price had risen. The solicitor claimed the "loss" from the
client but retained the profit. The court held that "no agent can buy the property of
his principal in any case, except when he is specially authorised to do so. But here
there was no authority or consent … his actings were quite against the settled rule
of law". Equally, an agent cannot sell his own property to the principal. Second, an
agent must not take a secret profit for himself but must account to the principal for
any discount, commission or other profit received. In *Ronaldson* v *Drummond & Reid*,[17]
a solicitor received a commission from an auctioneer for selling clients' furniture. The
court held that the solicitor was bound to account to the clients for the commission.
Third, any information which an agent receives concerning his principal's business
must be regarded as confidential. In *Liverpool Victoria Legal Friendly Society* v *Houston*,[18]
an agent who had worked for the plaintiffs, and who had in the course of the agency
received lists of persons insured by them, offered the lists to a rival insurer following
the termination of the agency. The court held that the information was confidential
and the defendant was not entitled to use them to the detriment of the plaintiffs. He
was also held liable to them for damages.

RIGHTS OF AGENT AGAINST PRINCIPAL

REMUNERATION

Perhaps the most important result of the agency agreement from the point of view   **5.41**
of the agent is the right to remuneration. A principal is obliged to pay the agent
remuneration either at the rate provided for expressly in the agreement or alternatively
quantum meruit ("as much as has been earned") being at a rate which is appropriate to
the type of agency undertaken, which may be fixed by a scale of fees, or which may
be due according to professional or trade custom. It is common for disputes to arise
in this area. In *Walker, Fraser & Steele* v *Fraser's Trs*,[19] estate agents were instructed by a
landowner to sell an estate. The instructions specified a minimum price. Over a period
of 3 years the estate agents negotiated with a potential purchaser. The negotiations
failed. A year later, the landowner contacted the potential purchaser directly and this
resulted in the sale of the estate at a price substantially less than that specified in the

---

[16] (1874) 2 R 83.
[17] (1881) 8 R 956.
[18] (1900) 3 F 42.
[19] 1910 SC 222.

agency agreement as the minimum. The court held that the estate agents were entitled to a reasonable commission because they had introduced the purchaser to the estate and contributed in a substantial degree to the sale.

REIMBURSEMENT OF EXPENSES, RELIEF

5.42 An agent is also entitled to be reimbursed all expenses properly incurred in performance of his duties. He is also entitled to be relieved of any liabilities incurred in such performance. In *Stevenson & Sons* v *Duncan*,[20] stockbrokers were instructed by the defender to sell a holding of shares. It turned out that the defender did not own the shares. The stockbrokers were found liable in damages to the purchaser and accordingly they raised an action of relief against the defender. The court held that the defender was bound to relieve them of the damages.

GENERAL LIEN

5.43 To secure the payment of remuneration or any other sums due by the principal, the agent is entitled to a general lien over any of the principal's property in his possession. The property may be retained in security until such sums have been paid but the agent is not entitled to sell or dispose of the property in question unless this has been agreed with the principal.

5.44   In *Sibbald* v *Gibson and Clark*,[21] the pursuer instructed the defenders to purchase a large quantity of Irish oats. The defenders held these in store. The oats were sold and dispatched to various parts of the country. There was some dispute about the rate of commission. Subsequently the pursuer sent a quantity of beans to the defenders for them to sell. They did so but when they remitted the net proceeds they deducted the commission in respect of the oats. The pursuer sought to recover the balance of the price of the beans, claiming that the defenders were not entitled to retain their commission from the proceeds of the sale. Lord Cockburn said:

> "a factor has a right of retention not only on each individual transaction, but that he is entitled to retain on subsequent consignments, in payment of prior unsettled transactions … the retention of a factor covers his right to commission, not only in the goods in his hands, but on prior consignments, unless some special agreement can be shown as to the way in which he was to account for the goods, which would have the effect of preventing his retaining his commission, or the two transactions were separated by such a distance in point of time as to show an abandonment of it".

PROTECTIONS FOR THIRD PARTIES

HOLDING OUT

5.45 Very often the purpose behind the creation of an agency relationship will be to allow the agent to negotiate and bind the principal in contracts with third parties. In these

---

[20] (1842) 5 D 167.
[21] (1852) 15 D 217.

circumstances, it is normal and correct practice for the agent to declare the existence of the agency and to name the principal. The contract will then be between the principal and the third party.

We have seen that an agent's actual authority derives from his express or implied **5.47** appointment. Third parties, however, are unlikely to have any knowledge of the actual terms of the relationship existing between the principal and agent. What is important for third parties is the authority which the agent appears or is presumed to have. This is known as "apparent" or "ostensible" authority and is inferred from the actions and statements of the principal and agent. It is clear that there is scope for a principal or an agent to misrepresent the agent's authority.

In such circumstances, an agent may have been held out as having a greater **5.48** authority than he actually holds and so when he enters into a contractual relationship with a third party innocent of the misrepresentation, the principal will be bound to perform the obligations undertaken with the third party. The principal is held to be personally barred from arguing that the represented agency does not exist. This situation commonly occurs where a principal has withdrawn or limited an agent's authority but has not sufficiently notified third parties.

In *Hayman* v *American Cotton Oil Co*,[22] the defenders held out by newspaper **5.49** advertisement and in letters to customers that the firm of McNairn & Co were their exclusive Scottish agents and announced that all offers to purchase oil had to be made through their agents. A customer agreed with the agents to buy 100 barrels of oil which had been shipped to Glasgow. McNairn & Co were paid in advance of final delivery to the customer. McNairn & Co went bankrupt and there were then competing claims for the barrels. The defenders claimed that the barrels were theirs and that McNairn & Co had only been distributing agents. Lord Justice-Clerk MacDonald opined:

> "it seems to me plain that McNairn & Company were held out as being the American Company's agents in quite distinct terms, and without any qualification whatever. … In any ordinary sale McNairn & Company must be held to be selling for the American Cotton Oil Company by delegated authority, binding that company as if they themselves had directly made the contract of sale".

AGENT LIABLE TO THIRD PARTY

The normal rule, as we have seen, is that the parties bound to a contract negotiated **5.50** by the agent will be the principal and the third party. The agent will "drop out" of the contractual obligations. But there are circumstances where an agent will be held to remain liable to the third party. Sometimes an agent will be held to have assumed personal responsibility for a contract. For example, in *Stewart* v *Shannessy*,[23] the sales manager of the cycle company, who was also the manager for a tyre company, wrote to the pursuer appointing him as representative and stating the terms for payment of commission. The letter was signed by the sales manager, using his personal name only. There was no reference to the manager's roles in the two companies. Sometime later, the pursuer raised an action against the sales manager, seeking payment of commission. The court held that the sales manager was personally liable to the pursuer as he had

[22] (1907) 45 SLR 207.
[23] (1900) 2 F 1288.

signed the letter in his own name and without indicating that he was merely doing so in his capacity as agent for the two companies.

5.50   Liability of an agent may sometimes arise as a result of a custom of trade. In *Livesey* v *Purdom & Son*,[24] a Scottish solicitor instructed an English solicitor to raise an action in the English courts on behalf of a client. The English solicitor later sought payment from the Scottish solicitor and relied on the English custom by which, where one solicitor employs another to conduct a client's affairs, the first solicitor is personally liable for costs unless he expressly disclaims such liability. The Scottish court held that the English solicitor had failed to prove that this custom of trade extended to Scotland, to the situation where an English solicitor was employed by a Scottish solicitor. While this case proves that this particular custom of trade did not exist in Scotland at the time, it establishes the principle that a custom of trade can give rise to an agent's personal liability (at the time this custom was limited to the English jurisdiction). However, the practice in Scotland has now changed and a solicitor who employs another solicitor on behalf of a client, whether or not he discloses the client, is liable to the other solicitor for fees and outlays unless he disclaims liability at the outset.

5.51   An agent will be personally liable where he acts for a principal who is not a legal person and cannot be sued. This rule is exemplified by s 36(c) of the Companies Act 1985 which provides that an agent is personally liable where he acts for a company that is not yet registered.

UNDISLOSED PRINCIPAL

5.52   Sometimes an agent enters into negotiations with a third party and discloses the fact that he is an agent but does not identify the principal. In such circumstances, the third party is unable to sue the agent. In *Matthews* v *Auld & Guild*,[25] a merchant instructed a Dundee stockbroker to sell securities and purchase others. The Dundee stockbroker in turn instructed a Glasgow firm of stockbrokers to carry out the instructions. He told them he was acting on behalf of a client but did not disclose the client's identity. Once the instructions had been fulfilled, the Glasgow stockbrokers held a balance due to the client of £83 and 13 shillings. The Dundee stockbroker absconded, owing a substantial sum to the Glasgow stockbrokers. The merchant contacted the Glasgow stockbrokers, requesting payment of the sum due to him, but they responded by saying that they were entitled to set off this sum as part compensation of the debt due to them by the Dundee stockbroker. The court observed: "if a person buys goods of another, whom he knows to be acting as an agent for another, though he does not know who the principal is, he cannot set off a debt due to him by the agent in an action by the principal for the price of the goods".

5.53   The position is different where an agent refuses to disclose the identity of the principal since this prevents the third party from suing the principal. In these circumstances the court may hold an agent to be personally liable to the third party. In *Gibb* v *Cunningham & Robertson*,[26] Gibb agreed to sell shares and a dwelling house to an undisclosed principal for whom Cunningham & Robertson were acting. Only part of the

[24] (1894) 21 R 911.
[25] (1873) 1 R 1224.
[26] 1925 SLT 608.

price was paid. Cunningham & Robertson were formally asked to disclose the identity of the undisclosed principal. They made no reply. Gibb raised an action against them seeking implement of the bargain, failing which, payment of damages. Cunningham & Robertson pleaded that they had only contracted as agents and not as principals and should therefore be assoilzied (absolved). The court held that Cunningham & Robertson, having failed to answer Gibb's request for who their principals were, were personally liable to the pursuer for the fulfilment of the contract.

When an agent fails to disclose both the name and the existence of a principal, **5.54** the third party is wholly unaware of the existence of any agency and the agent is likely to be held liable to the third party under the contract. If at a late stage the agent reveals the principal's identity, the third party must elect whether to sue the agent or the principal. Such election is final.

SPECIAL TYPES OF AGENT

SOLICITORS

Solicitors, formerly called "law-agents", can be either general or special agents, **5.55** depending on the extent of the authority required to fulfil the client's instructions. The relationship between a solicitor and the client is of a particularly fiduciary and confidential nature. Where a solicitor is instructed in a court matter, there is an implied authority to instruct counsel and a local agent and to take all steps which are necessary to pursue the client's claim.

ADVOCATES

Advocates are usually special agents entrusted to carry out a specific task. Where an **5.56** advocate is instructed in a court matter, the advocate has a wide measure of discretion in carrying out the client's instructions but must act in good faith. The advocate owes a duty both to his client and also to the court.

MERCANTILE AGENTS

A mercantile agent is defined by s 1(1) of the Factors (Scotland) Act 1890 as a person **5.57** "having in the customary course of his business as such agent, authority either to sell goods or consign goods for the purpose of sale, or to buy goods, or to raise money on the security of goods". Mercantile agents may be either factors or brokers. A factor has possession of his principal's goods and is entitled to sell them in his own name. A broker does not have possession of the principal's goods and is simply an arranger or middleman in respect of those goods. A factor has a lien over the goods, whereas a broker has none. To tell whether a mercantile agent is a factor or a broker, it is necessary to look at the nature of the transaction being undertaken. In *Glendinning* v *Hope & Co*,[27] Glendinning instructed Hope & Co, a firm of stockbrokers, to purchase 100 shares in a company. He paid the price of the shares. Later he instructed them to purchase 200 further shares in the company. Glendinning then instructed a second firm of

---

[27] 1911 SC (HL) 73.

stockbrokers to complete the latter purchase. Hope & Co sought payment of their expenses. They claimed they were entitled to refuse to transfer the initial 100 shares to Glendinning until the debt was paid. Glendinning raised an action against Hope & Co, seeking delivery of the transfer. The court held that Hope & Co were entitled to retain the transfer until payment of the second transaction had been made. Lord Kinnear said that "for the balance which may arise on his general account the factor has a right of retention or lien over all the goods and effects of the principal which, coming into his hands in his character of factor, may be in his actual or civil possession at the time when the demand against him is made".

5.58   An auctioneer is a good example of a factor since he has the client's goods in his possession for the purpose of selling them. Usually, a stockbroker is not regarded as a factor but a broker since he does not normally have possession of his client's shares but merely facilitates a contract between the client and a third party.

DEL CREDERE AGENTS

5.59   *Del credere* agents are mercantile agents who, for a fee, act as guarantors of the solvency of third parties. They will indemnify the principal if the third party fails to pay what is due. *Del credere* agents were of importance when a principal wished to sell goods abroad but did not wish to undertake the risk of not being paid. Their use has to a great extent been rendered obsolete by credit guarantee schemes and modern payment methods.

COMMERCIAL AGENTS

5.60   A commercial agent is defined in the Commercial Agents (Council Directive) Regulations 1993 (as amended) as a "self-employed intermediary who has continuing authority to negotiate the sale or purchase of goods on behalf of another person (the 'principal'), or to negotiate and conclude the sale or purchase of goods on behalf of and in the name of that principal". As a result of this definition, the regulations do not apply to many people who would normally be regarded as agents in Scots law. They do not apply to employed persons or to partners representing their businesses. But they can apply to companies. The regulations govern continuing agency relationships (and so do not apply to one-off transactions) and contain detailed provisions that oblige both principal and agent to act dutifully towards each other and in good faith, and that specify the manner and times of payment, indemnity, termination and compensation.

ESSENTIAL FACTS

5.61   • Agency is a contractual relationship between a principal, who gives instructions, and an agent, who performs the instructions. Agents are all around us in the business environment and include factors, brokers, solicitors, estate agents, bankers, partners of a business, directors of a company, and so on. Agents can be general (engaged for general business) or special (engaged in relation to a particular transaction).

- Because agency is a contractual relationship, it is strongly dependent on the underlying law of contract. This dictates how the relationship comes into existence or is extinguished, and the extent of liability between the principal and agent, and with third parties.

- An agent cannot have more capacity than that of his principal. As a result, where a principal dies or loses capacity, the agency is terminated.

- Agency may be created by *express* agreement (whether in writing or verbally); or by *implication* (from the nature of employment (as a manager, say), by the building up of a trade practice, by statutory implication (as with partners in a partnership)); or occasionally by reason of *necessity*.

- A person who acts without a valid appointment may have his unauthorised acts ratified by the person for whom he was acting. Ratification must be timeous and the principal must have capacity.

- Agency may end by mutual agreement; by unilateral termination by the principal (except where the agent has been authorised to act in his own interests as well as those of his principal); by renunciation by the agent; by fulfilment of the particular purposes of a special agency; or when a principal ceases a business which has incidentally be served by an agency. In addition, because of contract law, an agency is terminated on the death, insanity or bankruptcy of the principal, or the death of the agent.

- Again as a result of contract law, an agent is obliged personally, precisely and completely to perform the instructions given by the principal. The agent must act in good faith and apply the appropriate standard of skill and care to the delegated tasks. The agent must account to the principal for his performance.

- The principal is obliged to remunerate the agent with the agreed remuneration or to pay the amount that the work is worth (*"quantum meruit"*). The agent is entitled to reimbursement of expenses incurred and is entitled to a general lien over the principal's property in his possession.

- An agent is usually engaged to bind the principal into contracts with third parties. An agent may appear to third parties to have an "apparent" or "ostensible" authority to bind the principal. This may exceed the agent's actual authority in some circumstances. In these circumstances the principal will still be held bound to the third parties.

- In some circumstances an agent may remain personally liable to a third party where there is a trade practice or custom to this effect, or where the agent has failed to make clear to the third party that he is acting as agent, or has refused to identify the principal. An agent will remain liable when he acts for a principal who is not a legal person and cannot be sued by the third party.

ESSENTIAL CASES

5.62

CONSTITUTION OF AGENCY

Picken v *Hawkes* (1875): here, an agency relationship, including agreement on the 3-year length of the agency, the remuneration and commission rates, were agreed verbally. There was no written agreement. After 6 months Hawke tried to terminate the agreement, saying it was one of employment ("service") only and so could be terminated within the 3 years. Picken sued for breach of contract. The judge held that agency was the fundamental characteristic of the verbal agreement.

Barnetson v *Petersen Brothers* (1902): this involved agency constituted by implication. A chartered steamship required work and put into port. The shipbroker engaged by the Master sought recovery of outlays and commission from the owners of the ship. The court held that the master of the ship had accepted the services as agent for the owners who were therefore liable.

Tinnevelly Sugar Refining Co Ltd v *Mirrlees Watson and Yaryan Co Ltd* (1894): this case involved ratification by a company of a contract made by its promoters who bought defective machinery for the company. But contracts can only be ratified by an agent who was in existence at the time the contract was made and who acts timeously. The company had not been in existence at the time of the original contract of purchase of the machinery and so it could not ratify the contract and sue for damages under it.

Goodall v *Bilsland* (1909): objections to the grant of a public house licence were held as invalid on appeal because the solicitor for the objectors had not been instructed timeously to act in the appeal. The objectors had 10 days to mark the appeal. Their solicitor should have obtained instructions within this time and then marked the appeal. But he did not obtain instructions within the 10 days. The appeal was therefore an entirely unauthorised act.

TERMINATION OF AGENCY

Premier Briquette Co Ltd v *Gray* (1922): an agent had a procuratory *in rem suam* (a power for his own benefit). It was held that the agency could not be terminated by the principal's unilateral act. The agent had to have the opportunity to benefit from the agency agreement which he would not have undertaken had this potential benefit not been available.

Brenan v *Campbell's Trustees* (1898): this case involved a fixed-term agency which was to exist for 4 years. At the end of the term the agent raised an action against the principals, claiming 6 months' pay in lieu of notice. The court held that the agent was not entitled to payment as the agency agreement was for a fixed term only and it was not envisaged that it would be extendable.

Patmore & Co v *B Cannon & Co Ltd* (1892): the pursuers agreed to act as agents for the defenders for a period of 5 years. The intention was to service the defenders' business interests. But 3 months later, the defenders discontinued this business. The court held that the defenders had not agreed to bind themselves to carry on their business, or any part of it, for the full 5 years purely for the benefit of the pursuers. The agency existed to serve the business but the business did not exist to serve the agency. The pursuers were therefore unable to obtain damages.

In *Campbell* v *Anderson* (1829): the usual rule is that agency terminates on death (subject to the winding-up of ongoing transactions). But in this case the agent continued acting for some time, as he believed that the principal was still alive. As a result, the court held that he was not personally liable but had bound the deceased principal's estate.

McKenzie v *Campbell* (1894): a solicitor received £285 from a client, with instructions to defend that client from charges of forgery. When the client was sequestrated, his trustee in bankruptcy was able to recover the money from the solicitor.

Wink v *Mortimer* (1849): while insanity terminates agency, the court held that a period of temporary insanity did not terminate it. One important factor is that the effect of suspending an agency immediately can cause a principal to suffer losses.

DUTIES OF AGENT TO PRINCIPAL

Duty to perfom the instructions precisely

Gilmour v *Clark* (1853): an agent must perform the delegated task precisely as instructed. In this case the agent loaded goods onto a ship other than that which the principal had named. The agent had not fulfilled his instructions and so was held liable for the value of the goods which were lost when the ship carrying them sank.

Duty not to delegate

Black v *Cornelius* (1879): an agent may not delegate the task delegated to him. But there are exceptions. This case concerned an architect who was engaged in connection with building work. The architect instructed a surveyor to carry out measurements and prepare plans and sought recovery from the principal of the surveyor's fees. The court held that the architect had authority to employ the surveyor and so could recover the fees. This exception extends to other professions where there is a need to obtain specialist skills in order to complete the instructions.

Duty to account

Tyler v *Logan* (1904): during a stocktaking carried out on behalf of the owner of a shoe business, a deficit was discovered and the owner brought an action against the manager for payment. Even though there was no proof of dishonesty or negligence, the manager was held liable to the owner in the sum claimed.

Other fiduciary duties

Cunningham v *Lee* (1874): a solicitor bought shares on behalf of a client. On the settlement date, when the price required to be paid, the client failed to produce the price. The solicitor should have sold the shares, which had fallen in value, and claimed the loss from the client. Instead, the solicitor kept the shares and sold them later, when the price had risen. Instead of accounting to the client for the "profit", the solicitor kept it for himself; he claimed the notional "loss" from the client and retained the profit. In effect, he was suggesting that he had bought the shares from the client on the settlement date, thus incurring a loss for the client, and had made the profit for himself from the shares as he owned them after the settlement date up to the time of the final sale. The court held that "no agent can buy the property of his principal in any case, except when he is specially authorised to do so". The solicitor had no such authority.

Ronaldson v *Drummond & Reid* (1881): a solicitor received a commission from an auctioneer for selling clients' furniture and should have accounted to his clients for the commission received.

Liverpool Victoria Legal Friendly Society v *Houston* (1900): a former agent for the plaintiffs offered the lists of persons insured to a rival insurance company. The court held that the information was confidential and so the agent was liable to the plaintiffs in damages.

RIGHTS OF AGENT AGAINST PRINCIPAL

Remuneration

Walker, Fraser & Steele v *Fraser's Trustees* (1910): estate agents were instructed by a landowner to sell an estate and the agents unsuccessfully negotiated with a potential purchaser over a period of years. A year later, the landowner contacted the potential purchaser directly and sold the estate to him at a much lower price. The court held that the estate agents were entitled to a reasonable commission because they had introduced the purchaser to the estate and contributed to the sale.

Reimbursement of expenses; relief

Stevenson & Sons v *Duncan* (1842): stockbrokers were instructed by the defender to sell a holding of shares. But the defender did not own the shares. The stockbrokers therefore had to pay damages to the purchaser and accordingly they claimed relief against the defender. The court held that the defender was bound to relieve them of the losses they incurred.

Security; lien

Sibbald v *Gibson and Clark* (1852): the pursuer instructed the defenders to sell a quantity of beans. The defenders did so but deducted from the proceeds commission which they calculated was due on previous transactions involving oats. The court held that "a factor has a right of retention not only on each individual transaction, but that he is entitled to retain on subsequent consignments, in payment of prior unsettled transactions ... the retention of a factor covers his right to commission, not only in the goods in his hands, but on prior consignments, unless some special agreement can be shown as to the way in which he was to account for the goods, which would have the effect of preventing his retaining his commission, or the two transactions were separated by such a distance in point of time as to show an abandonment of it".

PROTECTIONS FOR THIRD PARTIES

Holding out

Hayman v *American Cotton Oil Co* (1907): the defenders held out that McNairn & Co were their exclusive Scottish agents. A hundred barrels of oil were shipped to Glasgow and held by McNairn & Co who then went bankrupt. There were competing claims for the barrels. The pursuer claimed that McNairn & Co, as agents for the defenders, had bound the defenders in a sale of the barrels to the pursuer. The barrels therefore belonged to the pursuer. The defenders claimed that the barrels were theirs as McNairn & Co had only been distributing agents and could not bind them into a sale. Therefore they should get their barrels back. The court held that the defenders had instructed McNairn & Co as their agents in quite distinct terms, and without any qualification whatever, and that they were not merely distributors. The pursuer as entitled to the barrels.

Agent liable personally to a third party

Stewart v *Shannessy* (1900): the court held that the sales manager of both a cycle company and a tyre company was personally liable to the pursuer who he had appointed as an agent, as he had signed the letter of appointment in his own name without indicating that he was merely doing so in his capacity as agent for the companies.

Undislosed principal

Matthews v *Auld & Guild* (1873): a Dundee stockbroker instructed a Glasgow firm of stockbrokers to carry out sales of stock. He told them he was acting on behalf of a client but did not disclose the client's identity. Once the instructions had been fulfilled, the Glasgow stockbrokers held a balance due to the client of £83 and 13 shillings. The Dundee stockbroker absconded, owing a substantial sum to the Glasgow stockbrokers. The owner of the stock contacted the Glasgow stockbrokers, requesting payment of the sum due to him, but they said that they were entitled to set off this sum as part compensation of the debt due to them by the Dundee stockbroker. The court observed: "if a person buys goods of another, whom he knows to be acting as an agent for another, though he does not know who the principal is, he cannot set off a debt due to him by the agent in an action by the principal for the price of the goods".

Gibb v *Cunningham & Robertson* (1925): in this case Gibb agreed to sell shares and a dwellinghouse to an undisclosed principal for whom Cunningham & Robertson were acting. Only part of the price was paid. Cunningham & Robertson were formally asked to disclose the identity of the undisclosed principal. They made no reply. The court held that Cunningham & Robertson, having failed to answer Gibb's request for who their principals were, were personally liable to the pursuer for the fulfilment of the contract.

6 FAMILY LAW

Family law is concerned with regulating relations between family members. The **6.1**
boundaries of family law change over time because what society views as a family
unit constantly evolves. In particular, Scottish family law has undergone a period
of extensive reform in the last two decades. While marriage was traditionally at the
centre of Scots family law, more recent developments have focused on heterosexual
cohabitees and same-sex relationships since these have increasingly formed part of
private life. Family law also regulates the care and upbringing of children, which
includes private relations within families as well as relations between children, their
families and the State. An overview of Scots family law, concerning both adults and
children, is given in this chapter, although child law is such a significant part of Scots
law that many consider it to be a legal field within its own right.

LEGAL PERSONALITY

The law recognises only persons who have legal personality. Until a person possesses **6.2**
legal personality, that person holds no legal rights or responsibilities. Legal persons
may be either artificial (eg a company or other juristic person) or natural. The general
rule is that human beings, who are natural persons, acquire legal personality at birth.
Prior to birth, a foetus or unborn child possesses no legal personality. This position
has been consistently upheld in Scottish courts and, more recently, in the European
Court of Human Rights.[1] However, in certain circumstances, the law will backdate legal
personality if to do so would benefit a child who is born alive. This is known as the
nasciturus principle: a Roman law rule which traditionally allowed posthumous children
to obtain a share in a deceased parent's estate. The principle has been developed and
extended in case law and statute throughout recent decades. For example, the *nasciturus*
principle now allows a child born after the death of a parent who died in a car crash to
sue for damages as a "relative" in terms of the Damages (Scotland) Act 1976.[2]

THE CHILD'S LEGAL CAPACITY

Although children acquire legal personality at birth, they do not automatically **6.3**
possess the full legal rights and responsibilities enjoyed by adults. A person's age
and ability determine their legal status and, as children grow and develop, the
law accords them greater powers and duties. There is no particular age in Scotland

---

[1] *Kelly* v *Kelly* 1997 SLT 896; *Paton* v *UK* (1981) 3 EHHR 408; *Vo* v *France* (2004) 79 BMLR 71.
[2] *Elliot* v *Joicey* 1935 SC (HL) 57; *Cohen* v *Shaw* 1992 SLT 1022; Damages (Scotland) Act 1976, s 1.

upon which a person moves from childhood to adulthood. Historically, Roman law principles divided the development between childhood, youth and adulthood into three distinct legal stages. "Pupils" were girls under the age of 12 and boys under the age of 14. Girls between 12 and 18 were known as "minors", as were boys between the ages of 14 and 18. At 18, both sexes attained "majority". Pupils possessed very limited legal capacity, and minors slightly more, while the person who had reached majority was generally recognised as an adult with full adult capacity.[3] The provisions of the Age of Legal Capacity (Scotland) Act 1991 have now largely replaced the Roman law system and although the concepts of pupillarity and minority still exist in Scots law, their modern impact on legal capacity is very limited. In addition, a wide range of legislation also specifies particular ages at which individuals are considered mature enough to participate in various activities.[4]

6.4   The Age of Legal Capacity (Scotland) Act 1991 regulates the general legal capacity of children and young people where there is no specific statutory provision concerning age. Section 1 of the 1991 Act does this by creating a general rule in two parts. The first part of the rule states that a person under the age of 16 has *no* legal capacity. However, the 1991 Act then lists a series of exceptions to this part of the general rule. The exceptions are found in s 2 of the Act which provides that:

- A person under 16 may enter into transactions of a kind commonly entered into by those of his age and circumstances. This would, for example, allow a child to buy a packet of sweets from a newsagent or a cinema ticket.

- A person under 12 may draft his own will or instruct a legal representative to do so on his behalf.

- A person over 12 has the capacity to consent or refuse to consent to his own adoption. This does not mean that a child under the age of 12 should have his views ignored, as will be noted in the following exception.

- A person under 16 is competent to instruct his own solicitor in connection with any civil matter, always provided that he has a general understanding of what it means to do so. The Act goes on to state that a person of 12 years or older will be presumed to be of sufficient age and maturity to have such a general understanding. The existence of this presumption means that, while an average person over the age of 12 will be competent to instruct a solicitor, a person under that age may also instruct a solicitor provided he can demonstrate sufficient understanding and maturity. The 1991 Act does not affect the age of criminal responsibility (at present 8 years) nor the age at which a person accused of a crime may instruct a solicitor to defend himself.

- A person under the age of 16 can consent on his own behalf to any surgical, medical or dental procedure or treatment where, in the opinion of a qualified medical practitioner attending him, he is capable of understanding the nature and possible consequences of the procedure or treatment. This exception, in particular, causes difficulty since there is no universal agreement among the medical or legal profession about how full an understanding of the consequences

---

[3] Erskine, i, 7, 1; the Age of Majority (Scotland) Act 1969, s 1 reduced the age of majority, which was initially 25, to 18 years.
[4] See, eg, Road Traffic Act 1988, s 101; Child Support Act 1991, s 55; Licensing (Scotland) Act 1976.

of any treatments need be, or whether the capacity to consent to treatment also carries with it the capacity to refuse to consent.[5]

The second part of the general rule in s 1 of the 1991 Act concerning legal capacity **6.5** provides that a person attains *full* legal capacity at the age of 16. Unless another statute specifically limits the capacity of a person over 16, he may act as an adult in all legal transactions, subject to the provisions of ss 3 and 4 of the 1991 Act. Those sections allow a limited exception (or, rather, protection) by providing that a person under the age of 21 may apply to the court to set aside a "prejudicial transaction" which he entered into while he was between the ages of 16 and 18. A prejudicial transaction might include, for example, a transaction in which a 17-year-old takes out a high-interest loan. If it can be shown that a prudent adult would not have done so then the court may set the transaction aside. Transactions entered into in the course of a young person's work cannot be set aside, nor can transactions in which a young person has lied about his age.[6] There is also provision in the Act for transactions between adults and persons between the ages of 16 and 18 to be approved by the court.[7] Approved transactions may not subsequently be set aside.

There are other provisions within Scots law which affect the general legal capacity **6.6** of children and young people[8] but these are outwith the scope of the present chapter on family law.

CHILDREN'S RIGHTS

"Children's rights" means different things to different people but the legal significance **6.7** of these rights, however they are perceived, has grown throughout the second half of the 20th century. Until the 1990s, any rights Scottish children and young people possessed were generally exercised by adults on their behalf. In December 1991 the UK Government ratified the UN Convention on the Rights of the Child[9] and domestic law began to reflect the internationally recognised rights prescribed by the Convention. These comprise a broad range of detailed rights to protection (eg from child labour, and sexual exploitation), provision (eg educational, and health care) and participation (eg making decisions and expressing opinions). Unlike the European Convention on Human Rights,[10] the UN Convention does not automatically override incompatible statutes or court rulings in the UK. The Convention is, however, increasingly referred to in legislation, and decisions of Scottish courts and tribunals

---

[5] See, eg, Report on *Legal Capacity and Responsibility of Minors and Pupils* (Scot Law Com No 110, 1987); *Houston, Applicant* 1996 SCLR 943, per Sheriff McGowan. For an alternative English approach, see *Gillick* v *West Norfolk and Wisbech AHA* [1986] 1 AC 112 and the more recent case of *R (on the application of Axon)* v *Secretary of State for Health* [2006] QB 539.

[6] 1991 Act, s 3(3) and (4).

[7] 1991 Act, s 4(1) and (2).

[8] See, eg, 1991 Act, s 1(3)(c) and Erskine, i, 7, 63; *McKinnell* v *White* 1971 SLT (Notes) 61; Vulnerable Witnesses (Scotland) Act 2004; Criminal Law (Consolidation) (Scotland) Act 1995, s 5.

[9] For the full text of the Convention, see the Unicef website: http://www.unicef.org/crc/. Key articles, such as Art 12 which accords children the right to express a view, are now reflected in domestic legislation: see the Children (Scotland) Act 1995, ss 6 and 11(7)(a) and (b). All countries, save the USA and Somalia, have ratified the UN Convention on the Rights of the Child.

[10] See the Human Rights Act 1998.

have been successfully challenged on the grounds that children's rights have been violated or overlooked.[11]

CHILDREN AND PARENTS: RESPONSIBILITIES AND RIGHTS

LEGAL PARENTHOOD

6.8   The first legal relationship a child has is with his parents. This means that determining who will be considered, in law, to be the parent of a child is particularly important. There are three situations in which identifying and providing for the parent–child relationship can give rise to legal complexities. The first concerns paternity of children and the issue of "legitimacy"; the second concerns the more modern difficulties arising from assisted reproduction; and the third relates to the adoption of children.

Paternity and "legitimacy"

6.9   Where a child is born as a result of sexual intercourse between a woman and a man, the law provides that the mother is whichever woman carried and gave birth to that child.[12] Paternity is determined in law by reference to a series of presumptions, contained in s 5 of the Law Reform (Parent and Child) (Scotland) Act 1986. A man will be presumed to be a child's father if he is either married to the mother (at any time between conception and birth) or if he is registered on the birth certificate as father and generally acknowledged as such. If a mother is unmarried and no-one is registered as the child's father then no person will be presumed to be the child's father. A presumption of paternity may be established or rebutted by proof on a balance of probabilities, and blood or DNA test results are regularly sought in actions concerning paternity.

6.10   Scots law historically discouraged the birth and rearing of children born as a result of any relationship other than that of husband and wife. Children born to parents who were married at the time of their birth, or subsequently, were known as "legitimate" children. Such children were fully recognised in law, as was their relationship with both parents. Children who had unmarried parents were termed "illegitimate" and, for centuries, faced legal obstacles in their personal and professional lives.[13] Although these obstacles were substantially reduced as a result of piecemeal legislative provisions throughout the 20th century,[14] it was not until the Family Law (Scotland) Act 2006 was passed that a general equality between children came about. Prior to the

---

[11] See, eg, *Dosoo* v *Dosoo (No 1)* 1999 SCLR 905; *Shields* v *Shields* 2002 SLT 579.

[12] See also the Human Fertilisation and Embryology Act 1990, s 27.

[13] For example, illegitimate children could not historically inherit from either parent, draft wills, take up certain respectable professions etc. See Stair, *Institutions*, III, 3, 4; *Corrie* v *Adair* (1860) 22 D 897; *Beaton* v *Beaton's Trs* 1935 SC 187; and piecemeal statutory reform beginning with the Bastards (Scotland) Act 1836. The driving force behind recent reform is the Scottish Law Commission Report on *Family Law* (Scot Law Com No 135, 1992).

[14] Prior to the 2006 Act, the most recent significant statute in the area was the Law Reform (Parent and Child (Scotland) Act 1986 but s 9 of the 1986 Act preserved the status of illegitimacy. The 2006 Act, s 21, abolishes the status within very limited exceptions relating to inheritance of coats of arms and other hereditary titles.

2006 Act, the children of unmarried fathers had no recognised legal relationship with their father who could only obtain parental responsibilities and rights by signing a formal agreement with the child's mother or by going to court.[15] The 2006 Act gives unmarried fathers who are registered as a child's father after 4 May 2006 the same automatic parental responsibilities and rights as married fathers. Since the provisions of the Act are not retrospective, they do not affect children whose parentage is registered before this date.

Assisted reproduction

A small but growing proportion of children are born as a result of infertility treatment, **6.11** such as *in vitro* fertilisation, artificial insemination and embryo implantation. The Human Fertilisation and Embryology Act 1990 regulates licensed infertility services throughout the UK and makes legal provision about this artificial means of creating the parent–child relationship. Once a man or woman has been deemed to be the parent of a child in terms of the 1990 Act, a permanent legal fiction has been created and the Act makes no provision for challenging the imposed parental status.

When a child is born as a result of infertility treatment, the "mother" is whichever **6.12** woman carried and gave birth to that child, even if she has no genetic link with the child.[16] There are several provisions concerning the imposition of legal fatherhood where infertility treatment gives rise to the birth of a child. Where the "mother" of the child is married, the law will deem her husband to be the father of the child, even if donor sperm is used, unless it can be shown that her husband did not consent to the treatment through which the child was born. Where the "mother" has a male partner to whom she is not married, that man will also be deemed to be the father of the child as long as there is evidence that the treatment was provided jointly to the couple in a licensed facility. There is also limited provision in the 1990 Act for a deceased husband or partner to be deemed the "father" of an artificially conceived child, even where the child is born some years after the "father's" death and as a result of stored sperm or embryos from a donor.[17] Where assisted reproductive treatment is not provided by a licensed facility (ie "do-it-yourself" insemination) the legal mother of the child remains the woman who carries the child and gives birth and the legal father is the man who has provided the sperm.[18]

A parent–child relationship can also be created where a child is born as a result of **6.13** a surrogacy arrangement. The 1990 Act allows the court to impose a parental order on the couple who have commissioned the surrogate mother if they apply for the order within 6 months of the child's birth and do so with the surrogate's agreement.[19] If

---

[15] The formal agreement is known as a "s 4 agreement", in terms of the Children (Scotland) Act 1995. Such agreements can still be entered into between mothers and unmarried fathers of children who are not registered as the father of a child after 4 May 2006.

[16] Eg the "mother'" may give birth because she has been implanted with a donated egg or embryo: see s 27 of the 1990 Act.

[17] Provisions about paternity are found in s 28 of the 1990 Act. See, in particular, s 28(2) and (3). Donors are generally anonymous, although there is some provision for children born as a result of donor gametes to find out information about their genetic parents: *Evans* v *Amicus Healthcare Ltd* [2004] EWCA Civ 727; Human Fertilisation and Embryology Authority (Disclosure of Donor Information) Regulations 2004 (SI 2004/1511).

[18] See *X* v *Y* 2002 Fam LR 58.

[19] Section 30 of the 1990 Act. See also *C* v *S* 1996 SLT 1387.

the commissioning couple cannot satisfy the conditions for a parental order the court may, alternatively, grant an adoption order in their favour in terms of the Adoption (Scotland) Act 1978.[20] Adoption is discussed below.

Adoption

6.14   Courts have the power to create the parent–child relationship through the making of an adoption order. When such an order is made between a child and his adoptive parents, a legal fiction is created whereby the relationship between the birth parents and the child is severed and the child becomes, for all purposes, the lawful child of the adoptive parents. Any unmarried person under the age of 18 may be adopted.[21] The Adoption (Scotland) Act 1978, the provisions of which will soon be replaced by those of the new Adoption and Children (Scotland) Act 2007, regulates Scottish adoptions. At present, only married couples and single people can adopt, although the provisions of the 2007 Act, when it comes into force, will allow civil partners and unmarried couples of both sexes to adopt children together.[22]

6.15   Since adoption severs the relationship between birth parents and their child, the court may make an order allowing the adoption only if the birth parents agree to it or if their consent is dispensed with on one of four statutory grounds found in s 16 of the 1978 Act. These are that:

- the parent is not known, cannot be found or is incapable of agreeing;
- the parent is withholding consent unreasonably;
- the parent has persistently failed to fulfil parental responsibilities;
- the parent has seriously ill-treated the child.

6.16   The 2007 Act creates new grounds which are broadly similar to those found in s 16 of the 1978 Act and creates a new "catch-all" ground which allows the court to dispense with parental consent where the welfare of the child requires it. It is anticipated that this new ground will make it easier to progress the adoption process in difficult cases.[23] Since the provisions of the 2007 Act will not be retrospective, the existing grounds will remain relevant for some time to come.

6.17   Once an adoption order is made, the relationship between the birth parents and the child is permanently severed and the adoption order is irrevocable in all but the most exceptional circumstances.[24] All parental responsibilities and rights in respect of the child concerned are conferred on the adoptive parents. It is possible, although unusual, for adopted children to maintain face-to-face contact with their birth families. The majority of those currently adopted in Scotland are not babies but children and young people who have been looked after by the State. Growing concern over severing

---

[20] Sections 16 and 18 of the 1978 Act. It should be noted that the Adoption and Children (Scotland) Act 2007 is expected to come into force during 2008 and will change Scottish adoption law considerably.

[21] Adoption (Scotland) Act 1978, s 12. The 2007 Act makes important changes to adoption policy and procedure but will not affect the legal status of the adoptive parent–child relationship, once created, in Scots law.

[22] See *T, Petitioner* 1997 SLT 724 and the new s 29 of the 2007 Act.

[23] See s 31 of the 2007 Act. See also *AB v CB* 1990 SCLR 809; *West Lothian Council v M* 2002 SLT 1155; *Lothian Regional Council v A* 1992 SLT 858; *Johansen v Norway* (1997) 23 EHRR 33.

[24] *J v C's Tutor* 1945 SLT 479; *Cameron v MacIntyre's Executors* 2004 SLT 79. Adoption orders may be revocable, for example, where the order has been granted incompetently or as a result of fraud.

enduring ties with a birth family in such circumstances led to the creation of a new order, called a permanency order, in Part 2 of the 2007 Act. Permanency orders are designed to be flexible and, as such, will allow a child to be looked after in a new, permanent, family setting while maintaining links with his birth family.[25]

GENERAL LEGAL EFFECTS OF PARENTHOOD

6.18 Two principal legal consequences flow from parentage. The first and most significant consequence is that parents legally hold general parental responsibilities and rights in respect of their children. These varied responsibilities and rights will be considered below. Second, parents owe certain specified legal duties to their children.

Parental responsibilities and rights

6.19 In Scotland, and in Scottish law, it has long been understood that parents have the right to determine how they wish to raise their own children. The European Convention on Human Rights and the UN Convention on the Rights of the Child, both of which give children and parents the right to respect for family life, reinforce this.[26] However, bringing up children properly entails various responsibilities and the law lays down certain standards parents are expected to meet. Society, Parliament and our courts have acknowledged that meeting these standards is a necessary part of functional family life. A broad overview of what the law expects of parents can now be found in Part 1 of the Children (Scotland) Act 1995.

6.20 "Children" are defined, for the majority of the provisions of the 1995 Act, as being persons under the age of 16, although, for specific purposes, childhood is extended in the Act to include persons under the age of 18.[27] "Parents' are defined in the 1995 Act to include only those whom the law recognises to be parents. For the purposes of the 1995 Act, "parents" includes mothers and married fathers. Unmarried fathers who have obtained parental responsibilities and rights either by court order, by signing a formal agreement with the child's mother or who have been registered as father after 4 May 2006 also fall within the definition of "parent".[28] A parent's parental responsibilities and rights continue after parental separation. Section 1 of the 1995 Act sets out the general responsibilities parents owe to their children. These responsibilities are:

- to safeguard and promote the child's health, development and welfare;
- to provide the child with direction and guidance. The responsibility to provide guidance, unlike all other responsibilities which end when a child reaches 16, continues until a child is 18 years old;[29]

---

[25] Permanency orders, found in ss 80–88 of the 2007 Act, will replace the existing parental responsibilities orders (s 86 of the Children (Scotland) Act 1995) which are rarely used.

[26] Article 8 of the ECHR and, eg, Arts 7 and 9 of the UN Convention on the Rights of the Child.

[27] Section 15 defines the terms used, including "child", in Pt 1 of the 1995 Act. In Pt 2, s 93, "child", for example, is defined to include those who are over 16 but under 18 and subject to a supervision requirement made through the children's hearing system.

[28] Part 1 of the 1995 Act, as amended by the Family Law (Scotland) Act 2006. In terms of s 7 of the 1995 Act, guardians (parent substitutes appointed after death of a parent) are also "parents" within the terms of the Act.

[29] There is also a difference between guidance, direction and discipline. See *Peebles v McPhail* 1990 SLT 245. The boundaries of physical punishment can be found in Criminal Justice (Scotland) Act 2003, s 51.

- to maintain personal relations and direct contact with the child, if the parent and the child are not living together;
- to act as the child's legal representative.

6.21   In order to fulfil these responsibilities, parents are also empowered by the 1995 Act. Section 2 provides that parents hold the following rights in respect of their children:

- to determine where the child is to reside;
- to control, direct and guide the child;
- to maintain personal relations and direct contact with the child if not living with the child;
- to act as the child's legal representative.

6.22   The rights relate directly to the responsibilities. The broad definitions allow for flexibility of family circumstances. Through exercising parental responsibilities and rights, parents can make decisions about their child's education, health and general living arrangements. Although it is normally the case that two parents will share these responsibilities and rights, the 1995 Act permits parents to act without the consent of the other in all matters save the removal of a child from the United Kingdom.[30]

6.23   The overarching responsibility to safeguard and promote the child's health, development and welfare in all decisions is very broad and leaves scope for parental disagreement. Where parents disagree, either may apply to the court for a determination of what course of action best suits the child's welfare. Importantly, s 6 of the 1995 Act requires parents, courts or any other person reaching a major decision about a child to have regard to the expressed views of the child, taking account of the child's age and maturity. What constitutes a "major decision" is not defined in statute but it is thought to include education, health and other matters of significance.[31] Where parents agree on a course of action then, unless visibly detrimental to the child's welfare, that decision will determine what happens.

Other specified legal duties parents owe to their children

6.24   In addition to the broad parental responsibilities and rights contained in the 1995 Act, parents owe other statutory obligations towards their children. Two significant duties are:

- *Financial maintenance*: irrespective of whether parents hold parental responsibilities and rights, they must ensure that their children are financially supported. In reality, disputes over child maintenance arise only where parents separate. There are two broad legal frameworks in force to ensure that parents pay for their children. The first framework is one of child maintenance and is governed by the Child Support Act 1991. The overwhelming majority of financial child maintenance cases are dealt with in terms of this Act which gives the Child Support Agency the power to determine, with reference to a

---

[30] The decision to retain a child outside the UK is also one which must be taken by both parents: s 2(6). Child abduction is a specialised field of the law and is outwith the scope of this chapter.
[31] See, eg, *Fourman* v *Fourman* 1998 Fam LR 98, where the views of three siblings were sought in respect of a proposed move to Australia.

prescribed maintenance formula, the amount of maintenance an absent parent should pay.[32] The second framework is found in the Family Law (Scotland) Act 1985. The 1985 Act provides that parents owe a duty of "aliment" towards their children and empowers courts to make aliment awards which are reasonable having regard to the families' circumstances. Applications can be made to court in terms of the 1985 Act in respect of children who are between the ages of 16 and 25 and at university or college or in other limited situations where the Child Support Agency does not have jurisdiction.[33]

- *Education*: in terms of the Education (Scotland) Act 1980 and the Standards in Scotland's Schools etc Act 2000, children have a right to education and parents have a duty to ensure they receive adequate and efficient education which is directed towards developing their talents and abilities. "Parents" are defined widely in respect of educational duties and include anyone with care and control of a child or with a legal duty to maintain a child financially.[34]

COURT ORDERS RELATING TO CHILDREN

It is sometimes necessary in private family life to seek a court order to regulate a child's upbringing. There are several orders a court might be asked to make and orders concerning parental responsibilities and rights and these are found in s 11 of the 1995 Act. It is not just parents who can seek s 11 orders. On the application of any person who has parental responsibilities and rights or any person "claiming an interest" in the child concerned, either the Court of Session or the sheriff court can make such orders.[35] Those claiming an interest in a child might include, for example, step-parents, wider relatives or family friends. Local authorities, for whom provision is made elsewhere in the 1995 Act, and persons who have had their parental responsibilities and rights removed by adoption or any other public law process, cannot seek s 11 orders. However, a child himself may ask the court to grant a s 11 order as long as he has a general understanding of what it means to instruct a solicitor.[36]

6.25

Section 11 orders

The range of orders a court may make when private individuals seek orders to regulate an aspect of a child's care and upbringing are listed in s 11(2)(a)–(h) of the 1995 Act. They are:

6.26

- An order depriving a person of some or all of his parental responsibilities and rights. Such an order is generally hard to justify. In order to ensure that a person who holds parental responsibilities and rights may no longer insist on exercising them (even where that individual has not seen a child for some time), a legal order formally depriving of parental responsibilities and rights would be necessary.

---

[32] 1991 Act, ss 1–9.
[33] 1985 Act, ss 1–7.
[34] Education (Scotland) Act 1980, ss 1–5 and 135.
[35] Section 11(3) and (4).
[36] See *D* v *H* 2004 Fam LR 94 and *E* v *E* 2004 Fam LR 115; Age of Legal Capacity (Scotland) Act 1991, s 2(4A).

- An order imposing parental responsibilities and rights. This order might be made in respect of, eg, an unmarried father who does not already hold parental responsibilities and rights, or grandparents with whom the child is living.

- An order regulating arrangements with whom a child is to live. This is known as a "residence order" and the court may make an order which specifies that the child is to reside with each parent for a proportion of his time.

- An order regulating arrangements for maintaining personal relations and direct contact between the child and a person with whom he is not living. This is known as a "contact order". Although, as with all s 11 orders, any person claiming an interest may seek the order, it is principally sought by fathers after parents separate. Courts have a wide discretion and it is not unusual for contact orders to contain provisions about holidays, recreational activities and telephone and e-mail contact.

- Orders regulating any "specific issue" which has arisen. This order is intended to be flexible and has been used, among other things, to resolve disputes over education, health and holiday arrangements.

- An interdict to prevent a person acting in a manner which the court is persuaded would be contrary to the child's welfare. This might include, for example, an interdict to prevent a parent from removing a child from the care of the other parent, a school or even outwith the country.

- An order appointing a judicial factor to manage the property of the child. Judicial factors are officers appointed by the court in situations where there is no other appropriate person to manage property or finances.

- An order appointing or removing a guardian. Guardians are parent-substitutes, usually appointed by a parent to look after the child in the event of parental death. If it is shown that the appointment of such a guardian is contrary to the child's welfare then the court can remove the guardian. The court is also empowered by s 11 to appoint guardians.

6.27   The "welfare test"

When a court is reaching a decision about whether to make a s 11 order in favour of the applicant, it is bound by a three-fold statutory test. This is known as the "welfare test" and the court can make an order only when what are often termed the "overarching principles" of the test are satisfied. The test is found in s 11(7) and provides that:

- The court must have regard to the welfare of the child as its "paramount consideration". This is known as the "welfare principle" and there has been much deliberation over what this means[37] but courts have, over time, established a range of factors which are considered relevant to establishing what best meets a child's needs. These include providing for a child's material,[38]

---

[37] Section 11(7)(a). See, in particular, *J* v *C* [1970] AC 668, per Lord McDermott at 672.
[38] However, in *Sloss* v *Taylor* 1989 SCLR 407, an unemployed father was preferred as the residential parent to a working mother because he had more time to devote to the child.

spiritual,[39] emotional,[40] health care,[41] personal[42] and educational[43] needs. Most recently, the Family Law (Scotland) Act 2006 has added to this list by providing specifically that the court must have regard to protecting the child from the risk of domestic abuse or damaging parental disharmony.[44]

- The court should make no order unless satisfied that it is better for the child that the order be made than that no order is made at all. This is known as the "non-intervention principle" and is designed to prevent unnecessary orders being made about children where an informal, and perhaps more flexible, arrangement might better serve a child's needs. Although this principle has been noted to be less significant than the "welfare principle", its import is nonetheless strengthened by Art 8 of the European Convention on Human Rights which provides for the right to respect for privacy and non-interference in family life.[45]

- The court is to give the child the opportunity to indicate whether he wishes to express a view on the matter in dispute *and*, if the child does wish to express a view, give the opportunity to do so and have regard to any view expressed. When having regard to a child's view, the court's duty is to have regard to the child's view so far as is practicable, taking into account the child's age and maturity. This obligation derives from Art 12 of the UN Convention on the Rights of the Child which provides that children should be given the right to express a view in matters concerning them. The right to express a view does not equate with the right to decide. Although s 11 provides that a child of 12 or over shall be presumed to have sufficient maturity to express a view, there are conflicting decisions about the minimum age at which a child may be deemed sufficiently mature to express a view worthy of judicial regard.[46]

If the court is satisfied that the three principles of the "welfare test" are met then it will make an order about the child. Since the court is empowered to grant orders *ex proprio motu*, it may do so regardless of whether the parties have sought the order.[47] The court may also grant interim (temporary) orders to regulate living arrangements until such

---

[39] In the past, atheists and homosexuals have been deemed to be inappropriate full-time carers (and occasionally this has caused problems with contact) of children: *Early* v *Early* 1989 SLT 114; *Meredith* v *Meredith* 1994 GWD 19–1150; *McClements* v *McClements* 1958 SC 286. The present position is that neither religion (or lack of it) nor sexual orientation is perceived in itself to be detrimental to a child's welfare unless there are additional elements of parental behaviour which give the court concern: *McKechnie* v *McKechnie* 1990 SLT (Sh Ct) 75; *Da Silva Mouta* v *Portugal* 2001 Fam LR 2.

[40] Violent or irrational behaviour, aggression or drunkenness are obviously not conducive to welfare: *Geddes* v *Geddes* 1987 GWD 11–349; *Shearer* v *Shearer* 2004 GWD 38–773; *Shishodia* v *Shishodia* 1995 GWD 17–926.

[41] See *Houston, Applicant* 1996 SCLR 943; *Finlayson, Petitioner* 1989 SCLR 601.

[42] There is recent evidence to suggest that the perception of women being better carers for babies and younger children persists (this is often referred to as the "doctrine of tender years": *Brixey* v *Lynas* 1996 SLT 908; *Sanderson* v *McManus* 1997 SLT 629.

[43] Normally the residential parent will assume responsibility for day-to-day educational decisions: *Clayton* v *Clayton* 1995 GWD 18–1000.

[44] New s 11(7A)–(7E), inserted by s 24 of the 2006 Act.

[45] Section 11(7)(a). It has been argued, even before this principle was committed to statute, that it created an unfair power imbalance in favour of the residential parent (usually the mother), making it more difficult for fathers to obtain court awards in their favour: *Porchetta* v *Porchetta* 1986 SLT 105. In more recent case law the significance of this principle has been reduced: *White* v *White* 2001 SLT 485, *J* v *J* 2004 Fam LR 20.

[46] Section 11(7)(b): See *Shields* v *Shields* 2002 SLT 579 and *C* v *McM* 2005 Fam LR 21.

[47] This means that the court may make any order it thinks fit, even where the parties have not specifically asked for that order to be granted: s 11(2).

time as final living arrangements are settled. If there is a change of circumstances in the child's life then the court can recall an existing s 11 order and make a different one.

PUBLIC LAW AND THE FAMILY

6.28 Scots law generally permits parents and others who hold parental responsibilities and rights freedom to determine how their children are raised. In doing this the State complies with Art 8 of the European Convention on Human Rights and Arts 7 and 9 of the UN Convention on the Rights of the Child. However, the State is also obliged morally, and in terms of these Conventions, to ensure that children are not victims of abuse, neglect or other inhumane and degrading treatments in public or in private life. The State is accordingly empowered to act against parents through a number of legal provisions. The most significant provisions in respect of child protection within the family setting are found in Part 2 of the Children (Scotland) Act 1995.[48]

LOCAL AUTHORITY DUTIES: CHILD PROTECTION

6.29 Part 2 of the 1995 Act is begins by outlining the general State support available for children and their families through local authorities. For example, local authorities are required to provide education, health care and day care to children living in their area. They also have duties to provide more specific assistance to children who are vulnerable and they are obliged, where possible, to make every effort to preserve the family unit when providing this assistance.[49] To that end, even where children are "looked after" by a local authority, there is still an onus to return children to their families wherever possible.[50] However, where there are serious concerns about parental behaviour, it is not always judicious that children remain within their own family.

6.30   Removing a child from his family unit is an interference with both the child's and the parents' right to respect for private and family life. The interference will be justifiable in terms of Art 8 of the European Convention on Human Rights only if it is both necessary and in proportion to the concerns about the child's welfare. Unlike Part 1 of the 1995 Act, the basic provisions of Part 2 extend beyond "parents" with parental responsibilities and rights, to a broader category of adults termed "relevant persons". Relevant persons include, in addition to parents and others who hold

---

[48] There are also many other important statutes, both civil and criminal, which exist to protect children, eg the Children and Young Persons (Scotland) Act 1937; the Matrimonial Homes (Family Protection) (Scotland) Act 1981; the Protection of Children (Scotland) Act 2003; and the Criminal Procedure (Scotland) Act 1995.

[49] See, eg, *Sloan* v *B* 1991 SLT 530, in which nine children were removed from their homes in Orkney by social workers, only to be returned several months later with no further action being taken against their parents. Vulnerable children are likely to fall within the definition in s 93(2) of the 1995 Act of a "child in need". This includes children disadvantaged for personal, educational, health, family, financial or other reasons and imposes additional duties in respect of such children on local authorities. There is also a statutory duty in s 16(2) of the 1995 Act, providing that local authorities must take account of children's expressed views.

[50] "Looked after" is the current statutory term, found in s 17(6) of the 1995 Act, replacing "in care". It applies to children who are in local authority accommodation and who are subject to a supervision requirement made by the children's panel (see below).

parental responsibilities and rights, adults who have charge or control of a child.[51] In terms of Part 2 of the 1995 Act there are three short-term orders local authorities can seek in respect of children they believe to be at risk. They are:

- A *child protection order*: this emergency order can be obtained within a matter of hours. Once granted, it allows children to be removed from their home and taken to a place of safety (eg a police station, hospital, social work centre etc) without parental agreement. It is the only order which "any person", not just local authorities, may seek in respect of a child in danger. This provision would allow, for example, the police, a charity or even a neighbour to apply for the order. There are a number of stringent legal conditions which must be met by the applicant before a child protection order will be granted.[52] In addition, the period throughout which a child protection order may remain in force is strictly regulated by the 1995 Act and relevant persons have the opportunity to seek variation or recall of the order at various stages in the process.[53]
- A *child assessment order*: this can be sought by a local authority where there are concerns about the health or welfare of a child and the relevant persons refuse to consent to an examination (medical, psychological or otherwise). Child assessment orders cannot remain in force for more than 7 days and, due to the short timescale, no provision is made for variation or recall.[54]
- *Exclusion orders*: where a local authority believes it is more appropriate that an abuser, or potential abuser, be removed from the family home than the child, it can seek this order. Before the court grants such an order it must be satisfied that the order is necessary and reasonable and that an appropriate person will remain in the family home to care for the child. Exclusion orders are a temporary remedy: they cannot remain in force for more than 6 months and are not renewable.[55] As with child protection orders, an application may be made to vary or recall the terms of an exclusion order.[56]

Local authorities and courts making decisions about emergency orders must also take **6.31** into account the expressed views of any child, having regard to age and maturity. The only exception to this general rule is in the early stages of the procedure governing child protection orders and this is because there might not be time to seek a child's views.[57] After emergency protective orders have been obtained, local authorities must look to the general welfare of the child. This may involve allowing contact between the child and any relevant persons[58] and the possibility of reintegrating the child into his family. Children cannot remain the subject of emergency protective orders indefinitely. Where children are unable to return home then various longer-term options, such as foster care and adoption, must be explored.

---

[51] Adults with care or control might include, for example, grandparents or wider relatives: s 93(2).
[52] In particular, the order must be deemed necessary for the child's protection by the court: ss 57 and 63–68. The procedures governing child protection orders are very complex.
[53] Section 60 of the Act allows for applications to recall, vary or discharge the child protection order.
[54] Section 55(1) and (2).
[55] Sections 76–80. For duration, see s 79.
[56] Section 79(3).
[57] Section 16(4).
[58] Section 58, for example, provides that the court must consider whether it is appropriate for a child subject to a child protection order to have contact with any relevant person.

THE CHILDREN'S HEARING SYSTEM

6.32   The children's hearing system is a unique feature of our Scottish legal system and was established in 1970 following the Kilbrandon Committee report into child and juvenile crime and abuse.[59] Before 1970, juvenile offenders were largely dealt with in the adult court system which was almost universally acknowledged to be an inappropriate setting for young people. Fundamental to the ethos of the hearing system is the belief that young people who have committed a criminal offence and those who are victims of abuse or neglect are all children for whom the normal process of growing up has failed. Accordingly, the hearing system was established to ensure that the majority of young victims and offenders should be dealt with in a similar manner through the non-judicial process.[60] This process is principally focused on the child's welfare rather than punishment for wrongful behaviour, of either children or adults. In serious cases, disciplinary steps may well be in the child's best interests and criminal authorities will also prosecute adults who offend against children. The aim of the children's hearing system is, however, to address the underlying causes of detrimental behaviour and provide compulsory State assistance if at all possible within the family unit, with the co-operation and involvement of all relevant persons.[61]

6.33   The children's hearing system operates through the children's panel and each panel comprises three panel members (one of whom sits as chair). Panel members are volunteers trained by the Children's Panel Advisory Committee and thereafter supported by the children's reporter.[62] The children's reporter is the central figure in the panel system. He receives information (from, eg, schools, the police, family members or neighbours) about children in difficulty, investigates the matter and convenes a children's hearing in cases where he believes one or more of the statutory grounds for referral to the hearing system is satisfied and compulsory steps are required. There are 13 grounds and all are listed in s 52(2) of the 1995 Act. Some of the grounds most frequently used are that the child is suffering through lack of parental care, has failed to attend school, has committed a criminal offence or has himself been the victim of a criminal offence. Normally the child and all relevant persons will be invited to attend the hearing.[63] In certain cases (eg where there are complex factual matters or where there is a possibility that the child may be deprived of his liberty as a result of the panel's decision) legal aid may be granted to the child for legal representation.[64]

6.34   At the hearing, the panel will listen to the views of the child and any relevant persons, read relevant police statements, local authority reports and other available

---

[59] The Report of the Committee on Children and Young Persons (Cmnd 2306, 1964). The Social Work (Scotland) Act 1968 translated almost all Kilbrandon recommendations into law. The main provisions of the 1968 Act have now been replaced by Pt 2 of the 1995 Act.

[60] The children's hearing system has jurisdiction in respect of children and young people under 16 and those between 16 and 18 years who are already the subject of a supervision requirement made by the children's hearing: s 93(2)(b). In cases where young people (over the age of 8) have committed very serious crimes they may still be prosecuted within the criminal justice system: Criminal Procedure (Scotland) Act 1995, s 41: *Walker v C (No 2)* 2003 SLT 293.

[61] "Relevant persons" is defined to include parents, those with parental responsibilities and rights and those who have charge of, or control over, a child: s 93(2).

[62] 1995 Act, Sch 1, paras 1 and 3.

[63] Section 45: the child has a right and a duty to attend while relevant persons have a duty to attend and may be excluded if their presence at the hearing is distressing to the child.

[64] The blanket refusal to grant legal aid to children was held in the leading decision of *S v Millar* 2001 SLT 531 to be in breach of Art 6(1) of the European Convention on Human Rights.

information and decide whether it believes the statutory ground for referral to the hearing system to be established. The panel is not a court of law and it may only dispose of a case where the child and all relevant persons agree with the ground of referral. If not, the case must be referred to the sheriff court where a hearing will take place to establish the grounds.[65] If the grounds are proved, the case is referred back to the hearing who may then make a supervision requirement which will impose conditions upon the child and relevant persons. The supervision requirement is binding and courts should not generally make s 11 orders inconsistent with it.[66] The conditions in a supervision requirement might include, for example, supervision by a social worker or in more serious cases the requirement that a child be looked after by the local authority or (very rarely) detained in a secure unit. The 1995 Act makes provision for supervision requirements to be reviewed regularly and relevant persons and children[67] can appeal to the sheriff court against the decision of a children's hearing with which they disagree.

More recently, the powers of the State to intervene in situations where young people   **6.35** exhibit antisocial behaviour have been increased by the Antisocial Behaviour etc (Scotland) Act 2004, the provisions of which enable courts to grant antisocial behaviour orders ("ASBOs") and parenting orders. Since a child or young person subject to an ASBO can be referred to the children's panel, future developments concerning the 2004 Act are likely to impact on the children's hearing system.[68]

REGULATION OF ADULT RELATIONSHIPS

Adult relationships take many forms in Scotland. Not all personal adult relationships   **6.36** are defined or regulated in law, although Parliament has increasingly legislated to broaden the variety of personal relationships which are legally recognised and bear legal consequences. Accordingly, the entrance into and the exit from heterosexual marriage, heterosexual cohabitation, civil partnerships and same-sex cohabitation are all now regulated in law.

MARRIAGE

Although various recent statutes have given greater recognition to alternative forms   **6.37** of adult relationship, marriage remains an important institution. Marriage is a quasi-contractual relationship which involves two adults – a male and a female – agreeing to be married and to enter into the legal consequences which follow. The Marriage (Scotland) Act 1977 sets down the requirements on parties to a marriage. They must give the district registrar notice of their intention to be married. Once the registrar is

---

[65] Section 68. The circumstances surrounding the grounds of referral will be heard by the sheriff who will decide, on a balance of probabilities, whether they are established in law. If a relevant person does not appear at a hearing it is not necessary that he accepts the grounds.
[66] For s 11 orders, see above. See also *P* v *P* 2000 SLT 781.
[67] See ss 51 and 73.
[68] The granting of an ASBO in respect of a child forms a ground of referral to the children's hearing system: s 52(2)(m).

satisfied that the parties are eligible and have the capacity to marry, he will issue a schedule allowing the parties to proceed. If, for example, one or either of the parties is already married, is under the age of 16 or is subject to any other legal incapacity, no schedule will be issued.[69] A marriage ceremony can be conducted either by the district registrar or by a minister of the Church of Scotland or a religious celebrant from another approved organisation. The ceremony itself must be witnessed by two witnesses professing to be over the age of 16, the parties must exchange consent to be husband and wife and the marriage schedule must then be registered with the district registrar. Marriage creates a new legal status, carrying with it a number of rights and obligations the most significant of which are noted below.

NAME, NATIONALITY, DOMICILE AND CITIZENSHIP

6.38   There is no legal requirement that a wife assume the surname of her husband, although this is common practice in Scotland. Often, both maiden and married names are referred to in formal legal documents. Marriage no longer has a significant impact on nationality which is instead acquired through a process of naturalisation based on residence within the UK,[70] although the period of naturalisation for spouses is reduced. Marriage does not carry with it an automatic right to enter or remain in the UK, although it is likely that a spouse would be treated more favourably than others if a dispute over residence arose. Wives no longer have a domicile of dependence on their husbands and husbands are no longer accorded the sole legal right to decide where both spouses reside.[71]

SUCCESSION

6.39   Spouses hold succession rights in the estate of the other and if one spouse dies without a will the remaining spouse is entitled to claim both prior rights and legal rights. These rights enable the surviving spouse to claim a proportion of the deceased spouse's heritable and moveable estate.[72] Even if the deceased spouse does have a will, the surviving spouse is still entitled to claim prior rights which would provide a third (and in some cases a half) of the moveable property of the deceased. When spouses separate or a marriage ends in divorce, prior wills in which spouses have bequeathed money or property to each other are not automatically revoked.

ALIMENT

6.40   Spouses have a legal obligation to support each other financially during the marriage, irrespective of whether they are living together. The legal duty is defined in the Family Law (Scotland) Act 1985 as one to pay such support as is reasonable in the circumstances, having regard to the parties' needs, resources, earning capacities and all relevant circumstances.[73] Parties can agree privately on the amount of

---

[69] 1977 Act, ss 1–8.
[70] See *Ahmed* v *Secretary of State for the Home Department* 2001 SC 705 and Immigration Police Statement DP3–96.
[71] See *Marsh* v *Marsh* 2002 SLT (Sh Ct) 87.
[72] See the Succession (Scotland) Act 1964; Prior Rights of Surviving Spouse (Scotland) Order 1999 (SI 1999/455)
[73] 1981 Act, ss 1–7.

financial support to be paid. Where a spouse makes an application to court, the court can grant an award of aliment, which will take the form of a periodical payment in his favour.

CONTRACT AND DELICT

6.41 Marriage does not affect the contractual capacity of either spouse, although a spouse may, either impliedly or expressly, appoint the other to act as his agent. Spouses may sue each other in contract or delict and neither is liable automatically jointly and severally for the debts of the other.[74]

RIGHTS TO PROTECTION AND OCCUPATION OF THE MATRIMONIAL HOME

6.42 In terms of the Matrimonial Homes (Family Protection) (Scotland) Act 1981, spouses have the right to occupy the matrimonial home, regardless of whether the other spouse is sole owner or tenant (termed the "entitled spouse" in the Act). This right generally endures as long as the marriage does and cannot generally be defeated through the other spouse selling the property to a third party. If both spouses own the matrimonial home then each is an "entitled spouse" in terms of the 1981 Act and each has a right to occupy the property.

6.43 In the event of domestic violence, one spouse can seek an interdict, with a power of arrest attached, against the other. The 1981 Act also allows one spouse to seek an exclusion order, excluding the other from the matrimonial home or any part of it.[75] Before a court grants an exclusion order it must be satisfied that the order is necessary to protect the applicant spouse, or any child of the family, from threatened, reasonably apprehended or ongoing conduct which would be injurious to the physical or mental health of the applicant or child. This is a high legal test and courts are generally reluctant to grant exclusion orders without unambiguous supporting evidence.[76]

BANKRUPTCY AND TAX

6.44 In general, marriage does not affect ownership of property or liability for debt, although the Family Law (Scotland) Act 1985 does create a presumption that household goods are jointly owned.[77] If one spouse becomes bankrupt, the other does not bear liability for the debts but creditors are entitled to challenge any transfers made from the bankrupt spouse throughout the preceding 5 years.[78] It is accordingly possible that gifts or any other payments made within this period to the solvent spouse could be clawed back by the bankrupt spouse's creditors. Since 2000, when married person's allowance and tax relief were abolished, there are no tax benefits generated by being married save the ability to pass property on death to a spouse without incurring inheritance tax.

---

[74] It should be noted, however, that many spouses hold joint assets and liabilities and joint and several liability arises in respect of these.

[75] 1981 Act, ss 3, 4, 14 and 15.

[76] 1981 Act, s 4; *Bell* v *Bell* 1983 SLT 224; *Smith* v Smith 1983 SLT 275; and more recently *Pryde* v *Pryde* 1996 SLT (Sh Ct) 26.

[77] 1985 Act, s 25.

[78] Bankruptcy (Scotland) Act 1985, s 34.

CHILDREN

6.45 Historically, children of unmarried parents were deemed "illegitimate", an inferior legal status which impacted negatively on both social and family relationships. However, legislation has gradually reduced the impact of illegitimacy and its remaining significance in Scots law relates to succession to titles of honour and coats of arms.[79] Section 23 of the Family Law (Scotland) Act 2006 now gives unmarried fathers who register as father of their child after 4 May 2006 the same parental responsibilities and rights as married fathers and, in effect, will render negligible the distinction between married and unmarried fathers in future.

GIVING EVIDENCE IN COURT

6.46 In all court proceedings, whether criminal or civil, spouses are both competent witnesses. This means that either may give evidence for, or against, the other. "Marital communications" are protected by privilege and so neither spouse can be compelled to give evidence in court on private matters which have passed between them. In criminal proceedings, a spouse is not compellable at the instance of either a co-accused or the prosecution. This means that a spouse may not give evidence in criminal proceedings against the other if the accused spouse does not consent.

GROUNDS OF DIVORCE

6.47 Marriage ends on either death or divorce. Although it is possible for spouses to remain separated permanently, most choose to end their relationship formally in divorce. The Divorce (Scotland) Act 1976 provides two grounds for divorce in Scotland. The first ground is that the marriage has broken down irretrievably, and this can be proved in one of four ways. The second ground, recently inserted by the Gender Recognition Act 2004, is that an interim gender recognition certificate has been issued to either spouse.[80] A divorce will be granted on any ground only once evidence of that ground has been satisfactorily provided to the court.

IRRETRIEVABLE BREAKDOWN

Adultery of the defender

6.48 Irretrievable breakdown of the marriage may be proved if one of the parties has committed adultery. "Adultery" is defined in the 1976 Act as voluntary sexual intercourse between a spouse and a third party of the opposite sex since the date of the marriage.[81] The intercourse need take place on only one occasion and may occur after parties have formally separated. The pursuer's encouragement or condonation of

---

[79] Law Reform (Parent and Child) (Scotland) Act 1986, s 9(1), as amended by the Family Law (Scotland) Act 2006.
[80] 1976 Act, s 1(1)(b).
[81] Section 1(2). If a spouse is raped she does not commit adultery; neither does a spouse who conceives a child through artificial insemination: *McLennan* v *McLennan* 1958 SC 105.

the adultery is a defence to the action.[82] A sexual liaison with a member of the same sex will not amount to adultery, although it may well form the basis for a divorce on the ground of behaviour.

Behaviour of the defender

If one of the parties has, since the date of the marriage, behaved in either a passive or **6.49** an active manner in such a way that the other spouse cannot reasonably cohabit with that spouse, then irretrievable breakdown of the marriage may be established.[83] Very serious behaviour need not be repeated and a physical condition is not behaviour. Behaviour has been held to include excessive working, neglect, cruelty, inappropriate relations with members of the same and the opposite sex, drunkenness and assault.[84]

Separation: 1 year with consent and 2 years without consent

Parties may obtain a divorce if they have not lived together as husband and wife **6.50** for either 1 or 2 years. In the case of separation for 1 year, both parties must consent to the action and consent can be withdrawn at any time before decree of divorce is granted.[85] If the divorce is sought on the ground that the parties have been separated for 2 years, the defender need not consent. Parties can be separated while living in the same house. All that is required is that they cease to cohabit as a "normal" husband and wife.[86]

In order to encourage reconciliation, the 1976 Act allows the parties to cohabit as **6.51** spouses for a number of months without breaking the separation period, although these months will not count towards the required period of separation.[87] Collusion, the situation where spouses put forward false grounds to obtain a divorce, is no longer a bar to divorce or a ground on which the decree may later be reduced.[88]

CIVIL PARTNERSHIP

The Civil Partnership Act 2004 allows for registration of civil partnerships between **6.52** same-sex couples. Civil partnership confers broadly similar legal rights and obligations to marriage throughout its duration. As with marriage, civil partnership may be formed only between those over the age of 16 who are not already party to a civil partnership or a marriage. Unlike marriage, civil partnerships may be carried out only by a district registrar, although a similar process to that of entering into marriage is followed. Parties must submit a notice of intention to enter into the civil partnership and obtain a civil partnership schedule from the district registrar. The ceremony must be witnessed

---

[82] Section 1(3) and s 2. See also *Stewart v Stewart* 1914 SLT 310; *Sands v Sands* 1964 SLT 80; *Gallacher v Gallacher* 1928 SC 586.
[83] 1976 Act, s 1(2)(b). See also *White v White* 1966 SLT (Notes) 52; and *Meikle v Meikle* 1987 GWD 26–1005.
[84] See *Graham v Graham* 1992 GWD 38–2263; *Hastie v Hastie* 1985 SLT 146; and *Stewart v Stewart* 1987 SLT (Sh Ct) 48.
[85] Sections 1(2)(d) and (e), and 2 of the 1976 Act. See also cases under the previous provision for 2 and 5 years' separation, the broad procedures of which remain the same: *Taylor v Taylor* 1988 SCLR 60.
[86] For a discussion of this, see L Edwards and A Griffiths, *Family Law* (2nd edn, 2006), Chapter 14.
[87] 1976 Act, s 2.
[88] Family Law (Scotland) Act 2006, s 14.

by two witnesses who are over the age of 16 and the parties must exchange consent to enter into the civil partnership.[89]

6.53   Since many of the consequences which flow from marriage also flow from civil partnership, much of the legislation applicable to spouses has been amended to include parallel provisions for civil partners. Civil partners owe a duty of financial support (aliment) to each other, they are entitled in the same way as spouses to prior and legal rights on the death of their partner and they have a right to occupy the matrimonial home and seek protective orders.[90] Civil partnerships end on death or dissolution.

GROUNDS OF DISSOLUTION

6.54   A civil partnership can be dissolved on the same grounds as marriage. These are, first, that there has been irretrievable breakdown and, second, through the grant of a gender recognition certificate.[91] Irretrievable breakdown of a civil partnership can be established in three of the four ways in which irretrievable breakdown of a marriage is established. The grounds are:

- unreasonable behaviour;
- separation for 1 year with consent; and
- separation for 2 years without consent.[92]

6.55   Although voluntary sexual activity between a civil partner and a third party might well be the basis of a dissolution on the grounds of unreasonable behaviour, adultery (sexual intercourse with a member of the opposite sex) is not a ground of dissolution. As with divorce, the law encourages reconciliation and periods of cohabitation throughout the parties' separation will not break the separation, although such periods of cohabitation will not count towards the separation period.[93]

ANNULMENT

6.56   If a party to either a marriage or a civil partnership satisfies the court that the relationship has never been legally valid then he may be granted an annulment. It is not possible to found on minor irregularities in either the marriage or civil partnership ceremony but if it is shown that a party is under the age of 16, is already party to a subsisting marriage or civil partnership or has not understood the nature of the ceremony then the marriage or civil partnership in question is invalid.[94] Where parties

---

[89] Sections 1 and 86–114 of the 2004 Act.
[90] See, eg, Family Law (Scotland) Act 1985, ss 1–7; Matrimonial Homes (Family Protection) (Scotland) Act 1981; and Civil Partnership Act 2004, Schs 10 and 24.
[91] 2004 Act, s 117.
[92] 2004 Act, s 117(3).
[93] 2004 Act, ss 118 and 119.
[94] Marriage (Scotland) Act 1977, ss 1 and 23A; Civil Partnership Act 2004, ss 86–114; *Long* v *Long* 1950 SLT (Notes) 52.

are related to a degree which renders them unable in law to enter into a marriage or civil partnership (eg blood relatives, adoptive children and parents etc[95]) there will be a fatal invalidity. Similarly, the marriage or civil partnership will be invalid where, as with forced marriages, one of the parties did not genuinely consent to entering into the relationship.[96] Finally, where "spouses" are shown to be of the same sex, or "civil partners" are shown to be of the opposite sex, the marriage or civil partnership in question will be invalid.[97]

FINANCIAL PROVISION ON DIVORCE AND DISSOLUTION

When spouses divorce or civil partnerships are dissolved, the parties may agree a **6.57** private financial settlement. If not, an application can be made to court, and the court will have regard to a set of statutory rules and principles contained in the Family Law (Scotland) Act 1985 when deciding how to divide up the parties' property. A substantial body of case law has amassed in recent decades concerning financial provision on divorce. Although the Civil Partnership Act 2004 and the Family Law (Scotland) Act 2006 extend the provisions of the 1985 Act to civil partners, there is, as yet, little available case law. Since the provisions applicable to civil partners are almost identical to those applicable to spouses, it can be assumed that many important judgments concerning financial provision on divorce will apply to the dissolution of civil partnerships.

THE LEGAL FRAMEWORK

The Family Law (Scotland) Act 1985 sets out the orders courts may make on divorce **6.58** and dissolution of a civil partnership. The underlying philosophy of the 1985 Act is that there should be a "clean break" when marriages and civil partnerships end and so a financial award made should, wherever possible, be final, ending any ongoing dependence between parties. The orders a court may make are:

- The *payment of a capital sum*. The sum can be paid on divorce or at another time appointed by the court. It is possible to pay a capital sum in instalments, even over a period of years.[98]

- An *order transferring property* (eg the family home from one spouse or partner to another).[99]

- An *order relating to pension benefits*: either a capital sum in exchange for a claim on a pension or a pension sharing order whereby pension funds are themselves

---

[95] 1977 Act, s 2 and Sch 1, as most recently amended by the Family Law (Scotland) Act 2006, s 1.
[96] See *Buckland* v *Buckland* [1968] P 296; *Mahmood* v *Mahmood* 1993 SLT 589; and *Mahmud* v *Mahmud* 1994 SLT 599.
[97] Although the Gender Recognition Act 2004 allows for what might be termed a confidential "sex change" upon the issuing of a gender recognition certificate, without such a certificate individuals remain classified according to their birth sex. See *Corbett* v *Corbett* [1971] 2 All ER 33; *Bellinger* v *Bellinger* [2003] UKHL 21; and *Goodwin* v *UK* (2002) 35 EHRR 18.
[98] 1985 Act, s 8(1)(a).
[99] 1985 Act, s 8(1)(aa).

transferred.[100] Since pensions, as accruing future benefits, are notoriously hard to value, the 1985 Act provides a formula for valuing the "cash equivalent transfer value" (CETV). This means, unless the policy is particularly unusual and requires further investigation, that all pensions can be valued in the same manner at a date specified by the court (usually the date the parties separate).

- A *periodical allowance*. The court will make an award for an ongoing allowance (similar to aliment between spouses and civil partners) only if both a capital sum and transfer of property are insufficient in the circumstances to meet the claim for financial provision.[101] A periodical allowance can be awarded for a fixed period, an indefinite period or until a specified future date and the court has the power to recall the award at a later stage.[102]

- *Incidental orders* and *anti-avoidance orders*: these confer on the court the general power to enable any order orders to take effect. For example, the court might grant an incidental order authorising the sale or valuation of property or furniture.[103]

SECTION 9 PRINCIPLES

6.59   Section 9 of the 1985 Act gives the court what might be termed "controlled discretion" when it makes an award for financial provision. In other words, the section sets down a number of circumstances to which the court should have regard when determining an award which is reasonable and justified in the circumstances.[104] The principles are as follows:

- *Section 9(1)(a): the net value of the matrimonial/partnership property should be shared fairly between the parties*

This is the dominant principle and the terminology used is defined in s 10 of the 1985 Act. "Net value" means that all debts (eg mortgages, bank loans etc) should be deducted from the matrimonial/partnership property before a division takes place. "Shared fairly" creates a presumption that the overall property should be divided equally between the parties unless any of the other s 9 principles justifies an unequal sharing. "Matrimonial/partnership property" is defined as all property belonging to either or both spouse(s)/partner(s) at a date sanctioned by the court and it includes everything accumulated throughout the marriage or civil partnership. It generally includes rights and interests under a life policy or pension scheme.[105] It also includes property acquired before the marriage or partnership if it was acquired for use as the home or as furniture and plenishings for the home. Most other property acquired before the marriage or after the court-sanctioned date will not form part of the matrimonial/partnership property.[106] Any property inherited from, or gifted by, a third party to either spouse or partner will not form part of the matrimonial/partnership property.

---

[100] 1985 Act, ss 8(1)(ba), 12A and 12A(1).
[101] 1985 Act, s 8(1)(b). See also *Cunniff* v *Cunniff* 1999 SC 537; and *MacDonell* v *MacDonell* 2001 SLT 757.
[102] 1985 Act, s 13(4).
[103] 1985 Act, s 8(1)(c). See also *Demarco* v *Demarco* 1990 SCLR 635.
[104] 1985 Act, s 8(2)(a) and (b).
[105] *Little* v *Little* 1990 SLT 230; but see also *Dibie* v *Dibie* 1997 SC 134.
[106] *Skarpaas* v *Skarpaas* 1991 SLT (Sh Ct) 15; *Tyrell* v *Tyrell* 1990 SLT 406. See *Sweeney* v *Sweeney* 2005 SLT 1141 regarding tax payable on disposals of matrimonial property.

The date sanctioned by the court is the date at which the matrimonial/partnership property is valued. This date may be the "relevant date" or the "appropriate valuation date". Although it is normally the date at which the parties separated (the "relevant date"), another, appropriate, date can nominated if this would avoid an unfair financial outcome. For example, where a family home has increased in value considerably since the date of separation, it would be unfair if the court could not take this increase into account in calculating what resources should be shared between the parties.[107] "Sharing fairly" means, unless any special circumstances exist, sharing equally. The special circumstances are defined in s 10(6) of the 1985 Act and, if proved, allow the court to depart from the presumption that fair sharing means an equal division of the matrimonial/partnership property. For example, where the parties have already agreed how the property should be divided, where one party has been largely responsible for good financial fortune or where one party has destroyed or damaged property, unequal division of property might be fair.

- *Section 9(1)(b): fair account should be taken of any economic advantage derived by either party from the contributions by the other, and of any economic disadvantage suffered by either party in the interests of the other party or of the family*

Typically, this principle has allowed for the contributions of a "stay at home" spouse who has raised children to be acknowledged and recompensed in a financial division. Section 9(1)(b) has also been used to recompense mortgage payments made by one spouse over the family home after the date of separation.[108]

- *Section 9(1)(c): any economic burden of child care, after the divorce/dissolution, should be shared in respect of children under the age of 16*

A "child" means a child of the marriage or any child accepted into the family. The award in terms of s 9(1)(c) should not be confused with aliment or child support and is intended to redress the balance a little for the spouse/partner who will bear the long-term day-to-day financial responsibility for any child. The court can order a lump-sum payment, transfer of property or a periodical allowance.[109]

- *Section 9(1)(d): dependence to a substantial degree by one spouse/partner on the financial support of the other party*

In such a situation, the court has the power to award such financial provision as is reasonable to enable the dependent spouse/partner to adjust, over a period of time of not more than 3 years, to the loss of support. The court may award a periodical allowance only where a capital sum or property transfer order is insufficient. The court can take into account earnings and future earning capacity of both spouses/partners.[110]

---

[107] Section 16 of the Family Law (Scotland) Act 2006 creates a new s 10(3A) of the Family Law (Scotland) Act 1985 which allows the court to substitute an "appropriate evaluation date" in such circumstances. See *Wallis* v *Wallis* 1993 SC (HL) 49; and *Jacques* v *Jacques* 1995 SLT 963.

[108] *Coyle* v *Coyle* 2004 Fam LB 67–7; *Louden* v *Louden* 1994 SLT 381; *Quinn* v *Quinn* 2003 SLT (Sh Ct) 5; *Banks* v *Banks* 2005 Fam LR 116.

[109] 1985 Act, ss 8(1) and 13(2).

[110] *Wilson* v *Wilson* 1999 SLT 249; *Sherett* v *Sherett* 1990 SCLR 799.

- *Section 9(1)(e): a party who seems likely to suffer serious financial hardship as a result of the divorce/dissolution should be awarded reasonable financial provision to relieve him*

This principle, which allows for a period allowance to be granted "over a reasonable period", has been invoked in respect of long-standing marriages where the spouses are older and the likelihood of re-training or re-marrying seems unlikely. It is most often used where a spouse suffers ill health. The court may also grant a capital sum or a property transfer and any periodical allowance can subsist until remarriage or death.[111]

COHABITING COUPLES: HETEROSEXUAL AND SAME SEX

6.60 Cohabitees have, for some time, been afforded limited rights of occupancy in the family home and access to various protective remedies in terms of the Matrimonial Homes (Family Protection) (Scotland) Act 1981.[112] A cohabitee could also claim, as a relative, if his partner's death occurred as a result of negligence.[113] However, prior to the Family Law (Scotland) Act 2006, the status of both heterosexual and same-sex cohabitees was largely unaffected in family law.[114] The 2006 Act significantly alters the position of both same-sex cohabitees who live together in the same manner as civil partners and heterosexual cohabitees who live together in the same manner as spouses. The Act introduces the following rights for such cohabitees:

- Rights in *household goods, money and property*: it is presumed that cohabitees have an equal share in household goods acquired during the period of cohabitation unless these were received from a third party.[115]
- *Financial provision* when cohabitation ends: although the court's powers are not as extensive as when it makes financial provision on divorce or dissolution of civil partnership, the court is empowered to make two broad types of financial provision orders. The first is an order requiring one party to pay a capital sum to the other and the second (which may be made as an alternative or in addition to the first) is an order to pay for the economic burden of caring for a child of the relationship.[116]
- *Succession rights*: if one cohabitee dies without a will, the court has the discretion to award a capital sum to the surviving cohabitee from the deceased's estate.[117] Difficulties are predicted in this area where one cohabitee is still married to a

---

[111] See *Haughan* v *Haughan* 2002 SLT 1349.
[112] In terms of s 18 of the 1981 Act, cohabitees can apply for occupancy rights which will last for no more than 6 months. Since the Protection from Abuse (Scotland) Act 2001 has enabled the court to attach a power of arrest to any interdict granted, the need for a matrimonial interdict to afford cohabitees a power of arrest has become less significant.
[113] Damages (Scotland) Act 1976, s 1 and Sch 1, para 1.
[114] See various attempts made by UK courts to provide recompense or benefit to cohabitees on separation/death: *Shilliday* v *Smith* 1998 SLT 976; *Fitzpatrick* v *Sterling HA* [1999] 4 All ER 707; and *Armour* v *Anderson* 1994 SLT 1127.
[115] 2006 Act, s 19.
[116] 2006 Act, s 21. A "child of the relationship" includes children accepted into the family and does not depend on any biological relationship between the carers and the child.
[117] 2006 Act, s 22.

third party who then claims prior and legal rights. Since the surviving cohabitee does not possess a legal right to benefit from the deceased's estate, the prior and legal rights must be taken before any award made in favour of the surviving cohabitee is considered.

Before any of the rights contained in the 2006 Act can be claimed by cohabitees, it must be demonstrated that they are in fact living together either "as husband and wife" or "as civil partners". In order to determine this the court will have regard to a number of factors, listed in s 25(2) of the 2006 Act, which include the nature of the relationship, the length of time the parties have lived together and the nature of any financial arrangements between them.   **6.61**

6.62

ESSENTIAL FACTS

LEGAL PERSONALITY, CAPACITY, AND STATUS OF FAMILY MEMBERS

- Family law is concerned with regulating relations between family members and each other, and between family members and the State.

- The law recognises only persons who have legal personality. The general rule is that human beings acquire legal personality at birth. Prior to birth a foetus or unborn child possesses no legal personality but in certain circumstances the law will backdate legal personality if to do so would benefit a child who is born alive.

- A person's age and ability determine their legal status and, as children grow, the law accords them greater powers and duties. The Age of Legal Capacity (Scotland) Act 1991 regulates the general legal capacity of children and young people and provides that a person under the age of 16 has no legal capacity while a person over 16 has full legal capacity. The 1991 Act then lists a series of exceptions to the general rule which allows children to buy sweets, consent to medical treatment, instruct solicitors and so on.

- The Human Fertilisation and Embryology Act 1990 makes legal provision for the parent–child relationship where children are born as a result of reproductive technologies. Once a man or woman has been deemed to be the parent of a child in terms of the 1990 Act, a permanent legal fiction has been created.

- Where a child is born as a result of normal sexual intercourse, paternity is determined in law by reference to a series of presumptions, contained in s 5 of the Law Reform (Parent and Child) (Scotland) Act 1986. A man will be presumed to be a child's father either if he is married to the mother (at any time between conception and birth) or if he is registered on the birth certificate as father and acknowledged as such. If a mother is unmarried and no-one is registered as the child's father then no person will be presumed to be the child's father.

PARENTAL RESPONSIBILITIES AND RIGHTS

- A broad overview of what the law expects of parents is found in the Children (Scotland) Act 1995. "Parents" are defined in Pt 1 of the 1995 Act to include only those whom the law recognises to be parents. "Parents" include mothers and married fathers.

- Unmarried fathers who have obtained parental responsibilities and rights either by court order, by signing a formal agreement with the child's mother or by being registered as father after 4 May 2006 also fall within the definition of "parents".

- Section 1 of the 1995 Act sets out the general responsibilities parents owe to their children. In order to fulfil these responsibilities, parents are also empowered by s 2 of the 1995 Act.

- Sections 1 and 2 of the 1995 Act allow parents to decide on the day-to-day care of their children, where they live and who they spend time with. Parents are also able, in terms of the 1995 Act, to provide discipline and guidance and to act as legal representative on their child's behalf. Parents also have duties to ensure that their children are educated and supported financially.

- The range of orders a court may make when private individuals seek orders to regulate an aspect of a child's care and upbringing are listed in Pt 1, s 11(2)(a)–(h) of the 1995 Act. These include, eg, residence orders, contact orders and specific issue orders.

- When a court is reaching a decision about whether to make a s 11 order in favour of the applicant it is bound by a three-fold statutory test known as the "welfare test". This provides that (i) the welfare of the child is the paramount consideration; (ii) the court must not intervene in family life unless it is better for the child that an order is made than no order at all; and (iii) regard must be had to any expressed views of the child.

ADOPTION, CHILD PROTECTION AND THE CHILDREN'S HEARING SYSTEM

- Courts have the power to create the parent–child relationship through the making of an adoption order. When such an order is made, the relationship between the birth parents and the child is severed and the child becomes, for all purposes, the lawful child of the adoptive parents.

- The Adoption (Scotland) Act 1978, the provisions of which will be replaced by those of the new Adoption and Children (Scotland) Act 2007, regulates Scottish adoptions. At present, only married couples and single people can adopt, although the provisions of the 2007 Act, when it comes into force, will allow civil partners and unmarried couples of both sexes to adopt children together.

- The court can make an order allowing the adoption only if the birth parents agree to it or if their consent is dispensed with on one of four statutory grounds found in s 16 of the 1978 Act. These grounds are that the parent (i) is not known, cannot be found or is incapable of agreeing; (ii) is withholding consent unreasonably; (iii) has persistently failed to fulfil parental responsibilities; or (iv) has seriously ill-treated the child.

- The State is obliged to ensure that children are not victims of abuse, neglect or other inhumane and degrading treatments in public or in private life. The State is empowered to act against parents through a number of legal provisions. Some of the most significant provisions in respect of child protection within the family setting are found in Pt 2 of the Children (Scotland) Act 1995.

- Unlike Pt 1 of the 1995 Act, the basic provisions of Pt 2 extend beyond "parents" with parental responsibilities and rights to a broader category of adults termed "relevant persons". Relevant persons include, in addition to parents and others who hold parental responsibilities and rights, adults who have charge or control of a child.

- In terms of Pt 2 of the 1995 Act there are three short-term orders local authorities can seek in respect of children they believe to be at risk: (i) child protection orders; (ii) child assessment orders; and (iii) exclusion orders. Courts will only grant these orders if satisfied they are necessary to protect a child from immediate danger. There is tight statutory regulation governing the granting of these orders and the ability of relevant persons to challenge them.

- The children's hearing system is a unique feature of our Scottish legal system. The system operates through children's panels on which three volunteer panel members sit to make decisions about children who require compulsory State assistance. The aim of the children's hearing system is to provide support if at all possible within the family unit with the co-operation and involvement of all "relevant persons".

- There are 13 grounds of referral to the children's hearing system and all are listed in s 52(2) of the 1995 Act. Some of the grounds most frequently used are that the child is suffering through lack of parental care, has failed to attend school, has committed a criminal offence or has himself been the victim of a criminal offence.

- If the hearing finds the ground of referral established it can make a supervision requirement which will impose conditions upon the child and relevant persons.

REGULATION OF ADULT RELATIONSHIPS

- Adult relationships take many forms in Scotland. Not all personal adult relationships are defined or regulated in law, although Parliament has increasingly legislated to broaden the variety of personal relationships which are legally recognised and bear legal consequences.

- Marriage is a quasi-contractual relationship involving two adults – a male and a female – who have agreed to be married and to enter into the legal consequences which follow. The Marriage (Scotland) Act 1977 governs the requirements for entry into marriage.

- Spouses hold succession rights to the estates of the other, have a duty to aliment each other in terms of the Family Law (Scotland) Act 1985 and hold rights to protection and occupation in the family home. The latter rights are governed by the Matrimonial Homes (Family Protection) (Scotland) Act 1981.

- The Civil Partnership Act 2004 allows for registration of civil partnerships between same-sex couples. Civil partnership confers broadly similar legal rights and obligations to marriage throughout its duration. As with marriage, civil partnership may only be formed between those over the age of 16 who are not already party to a civil partnership or a marriage.

GROUNDS OF DIVORCE/DISSOLUTION/ANNULMENT

- The Divorce (Scotland) Act 1976 provides two grounds for divorce in Scotland. The first ground is that the marriage has broken down irretrievably and this can be proved in one of four ways: adultery; unreasonable behaviour; separation for 1 year (with consent of both spouses); and separation for 2 years. The second ground, recently inserted by the Gender Recognition Act 2004, is that an interim gender recognition certificate has been issued to either spouse.

- Civil partnerships can also be dissolved on two grounds found in the Civil Partnership Act 2004: irretrievable breakdown and on the grant of a gender recognition certificate.

- Irretrievable breakdown of a civil partnership can be established in three of the four ways in which irretrievable breakdown of a marriage is established. The grounds are unreasonable behaviour; separation for 1 year (with consent of both spouses); and separation for 2 years.

- If a party to either a marriage or a civil partnership satisfies the court that the relationship has never been legally valid then he may be granted an annulment.

FINANCIAL PROVISION ON DIVORCE/DISSOLUTION

- When spouses divorce or civil partnerships are dissolved the court has regard to a set of statutory rules and principles contained in the Family Law (Scotland) Act 1985 when deciding how to divide up the parties' property.

- The underlying philosophy of the 1985 Act is that there should be a "clean break" when marriages and civil partnerships end and so any financial award made should, wherever possible, be final, ending any ongoing dependence between parties.

- The financial orders a court may make on divorce/dissolution are (i) payment of a capital sum; (ii) an order transferring property; (iii) an order relating to pension benefits; (iv) a periodical allowance; and (v) incidental orders.

- Section 9 of the 1985 Act sets down a number of circumstances to which the court should have regard when determining an award which is reasonable and justified in the circumstances. These principles are further defined in s 10 of the 1985 Act.

- Courts should ensure, in terms of s 9(1) of the 1985 Act, that the net value of the matrimonial/partnership property is shared fairly between the parties at the relevant/appropriate date.

- When making a financial order the court should also have regard to any economic advantage or disadvantage, the economic burden of child care after divorce, any degree of dependence by one spouse on the other throughout the relationship and the possibility of serious financial hardship resulting from the divorce.

COHABITATION

- The 2006 Act significantly alters the legal position both of same-sex cohabitees who live together in the same manner as civil partners and of heterosexual cohabitees who live together in the same manner as spouses, by according them access to financial provision on termination of the relationship.

- Before any of the rights contained in the 2006 Act can be claimed by cohabitees it must be demonstrated to the court that they are in fact living together either "as husband and wife" or "as civil partners".

ESSENTIAL CASES

6.63

- *Kelly* v *Kelly* (1997): a husband and wife separated while the wife was pregnant. The husband sought an interdict (preventive order) to stop the wife terminating the pregnancy. The court held that the foetus had no right to exist within the mother's womb and that the father had no right to prevent a termination.

- *Gillick* v *West Norfolk and Wisbech AHA* (1986): Mrs Gillick had five daughters under the age of 16. She sought a guarantee from the health authority that it would not provide any of her daughters with access to sexual health care (eg contraceptive treatment, termination of pregnancy) while they were under the age of 16 without her knowledge and consent. When the health authority refused, she took it to court. The House of Lords decided (under English law) that children under 16 had the right to seek sexual health care advice and treatment without parental knowledge or consent as long as they understood the nature of that treatment. In Scotland, the position is now regulated by the Age of Legal Capacity (Scotland) Act 1991.

- *Shields* v *Shields* (2002): this case concerned a child, D, who was aged 7 at the time parental court proceedings began over his upbringing when his parents separated. Throughout the course of the action his mother asked to grant a specific issue order to allow her to take D to Australia with her to live. D's views were not taken at the time the court made the decision allowing his mother to take him outwith Scotland. He was by that time 9 years old. On appeal to the Court of Session it was held that the sheriff court had erred in failing in its continuing duty to offer a child the opportunity to express a view throughout the duration of ongoing proceedings.

- *C* v *S* (1996): Mr and Mrs C asked a surrogate, S, to carry and give birth to a child on their behalf. They paid her £8,000 "loss of earnings" to cover the period during which she was pregnant. The surrogate was artificially inseminated with Mr C's sperm. When the child was born she refused to consent to asking the court for a parental order, in terms of the Human Fertilisation and Embryology Act 1990, in favour of Mr and Mrs C. Mr and Mrs C went to court and the sheriff granted them a residence order in relation to the child. Both parties appealed. The Court of Session granted Mr and Mrs C an adoption order rather than a parental order because the payment of £8,000 had contravened the 1990 Act and the surrogate had refused consent.

- *Johansen* v *Norway* (1997): a baby was removed from her mother at birth by the State and placed with foster carers. The mother was mentally unstable, was addicted to drugs and unable to care for the child permanently. She argued that the removal of her child and refusal of contact was a breach of Art 8 of the ECHR. The court held that the removal of the child from her care did not breach Art 8 but the refusal to allow the mother contact to her child did. The refusal of contact was not a proportionate response in terms of the ECHR.

- *Brixey* v *Lynas* (1996): unmarried parents separated after the mother had given birth to a little girl. Both parties wanted residence and the father raised an action to resolve the dispute. The father lost residence because the court decided that young children, particularly girls, were better cared for by their mothers. The House of Lords upheld this decision, placing emphasis on "maternal preference".

- *Sanderson* v *McManus* (1997): Mr Sanderson raised proceedings for paternity of, and to pursue a relationship with, a child born during his relationship with Ms McManus. The case began before the Children (Scotland) Act 1995 came into force, so he sought "access", the forerunner to contact. Ms McManus did not dispute paternity but argued that Mr Sanderson's action was based on merely a parental "right" to see his son and showed no clear benefit that his son would derive from the contact. The child made allegations that Mr Sanderson had hit him during a contact visit and although the allegations were never properly tested in court, it was decided that the child was deriving no benefit from contact which the father sought as a question of "right". Mr Sanderson's action was eventually refused by the House of Lords.

- *White* v *White* (2001): Mr and Mrs White separated and their two children remained with Mrs White while Mr White had contact with his children. Following an argument, Mrs White prevented contact. When Mr White raised court proceedings for contact there was a dispute over who bore the legal onus about the contact order being sought. Mrs White argued that, because of the non-intervention principle found in s 11(7) of the 1995 Act, Mr White had to prove that contact was beneficial for the children. The court held on appeal that no-one bore the onus since the non-intervention principle did not exist to give one party an unfair advantage over the other but rather to indicate that parents should not ask for unnecessary court orders to regulate their child's upbringing. If, however, parents could not reach agreement then the court could intervene and make whatever orders it thought best.

- *S* v *Millar* (2001): a child (S) was referred to the children's hearing system on the ground of his involvement in a violent incident which resulted in death. The hearing authorised S's detention in secure accommodation and S's lawyers challenged the decision on the ground that S's human rights were breached, among other things, because he was not provided with a solicitor. The court held that a blanket ban on legal aid for children's hearings was a contravention of Art 6 of the ECHR. It was particularly important that children were provided with legal advice in a hearing which might deprived them of their liberty.

- *McLennan* v *McLennan* (1958): Mrs McLennan left her Scottish husband and went to the USA for some months. When she returned to Scotland she was pregnant with a child conceived as a result of infertility treatment. Mr McLennan raised proceedings for divorce on the ground of her adultery and the court held that artificial insemination did not amount to adultery since adultery required that a spouse engage in voluntary sexual intercourse.

- *Corbett* v *Corbett* (1971): George Jamieson became April Ashley after undergoing a "sex change" operation. April Ashley then went through a marriage ceremony with Arthur Corbett. Shortly after the ceremony, the relationship broke down and Arthur Corbett was successful in his application to have the "marriage" annulled. The court held that April Ashley was not female since her operation had not changed her true male sex (as registered on her birth certificate) and she remained male. As such, she could only marry a female. The Gender Recognition Act 2004 now provides that someone in Ms Ashley's position may seek a gender recognition certificate to become known legally as a woman and so this situation would be unlikely to arise today.

- *Shilliday* v *Smith* (1998): this case, which predates the Family Law (Scotland) Act 2006, concerned heterosexual cohabitees. During the relationship they purchased a house, intending to live there after they were married. Title to the house was taken in the sole name of Mr Smith. When the couple separated Ms Shilliday sought recompense for the renovations she had paid for in his house. The court held that the money should be repaid on the principle of "unjust enrichment".

- *Cunniff* v *Cunniff* (1999): this complex case involved wealthy spouses who were separating. The wife sought financial provision on divorce and the court ordered the transfer of the family home from joint names into her sole name (as a home for her and the children of the marriage). This was held to be justified on appeal even although the house represented almost all of the realisable (available at the time) matrimonial property. The Inner House of the Court of Session held that the husband had a very large pension entitlement and a high-earning position. The wife required to look after the children for the foreseeable future and the significant award in her favour was upheld.

7 SUCCESSION LAW

The purpose of the law of succession is to regulate the way in which property passes **7.1** from the dead to the living. When a person dies, title to the deceased's property is passed to his successors. It is the law of succession which determines who is to succeed to that property.

It is a common mistake to think that succession is only concerned with wills. Indeed, many people die without having made a will. There are therefore two situations where the law of succession applies. The first is where the deceased made a will, and this is called *testate* succession. The person making the will is called the testator. The second situation is where there is no will or other testamentary writing, and this is known as *intestate* succession. There is a third possibility, and that is *partial intestacy*. This is where a will exists it but doesn't dispose of the deceased's whole estate. Testate succession applies to the part of the estate disposed of by the will and intestate succession to the other part.

THE OPERATION OF THE LAW OF SUCCESSION

Before the law of succession can operate, there must be evidence that (first) the person **7.2** has actually died (second) those entitled to succeed have survived and (third) any debts due by the deceased have been paid.

PROOF OF DEATH

In succession there must be proof of death. A doctor must complete a certificate of **7.3** death and this must then be registered within 8 days with the Registrar of Births, Deaths and Marriages. The Registrar can then issue an extract of the death certificate from the Register of Deaths.

Section 41 of the Registration of Births, Deaths and Marriages (Scotland) Act 1965 provides that such an extract "shall be sufficient proof of death". Note that this is not conclusive proof and can be challenged, for example where there is a question of mistaken identity

If the death is suspicious then the procurator fiscal can order a post-mortem examination.

Missing persons

A person may go missing by simply disappearing. Alternatively, there may be **7.4** particular circumstances surrounding the disappearance where it is highly probable that the person has died but a body has not been found. Such a situation could arise where a pilot is flying solo and crashes into the sea; the wreckage of the plane is found but not the body of the pilot. In either case the courts can issue a decree of declarator of death under the Presumption of Death (Scotland) Act 1977. Where the person has simply disappeared, the court will grant decree only after a period of 7 years from the time the person went missing. Proof of death is always on the balance of probabilities.

7.5   The decree dissolves any marriage, and this remains the case even if the missing person turns out to be alive. It has no effect on criminal liability. The Act also covers the possibility of mistake. The most obvious case is the re-appearance of the missing person after he had been declared dead. Section 4 of the Act allows for the decree to be recalled or varied by the same court that granted it. The rights of third parties are not affected by the variation or recall of the decree.

SURVIVORSHIP

7.6   Survivorship is essential to succession. As long as there is survivorship, even for part of a second, this is sufficient to allow for succession to take place. In the vast majority of cases it is quite clear whether or not someone has survived the death of a testator.

Common calamity

7.7   Difficulties arise where there is common calamity and proof of survival is impossible. A common calamity is where two or more persons die at the same time and have an entitlement to each other's estate.

7.8   Under the old common law there was no presumption as to survival in cases of common calamity. This could result in unfairness where relatives of the deceased were unable to inherit or the wishes of the deceased were defeated.[1] A change in the law was brought about by s 31 of the Succession (Scotland) Act 1964. This provides that for all purposes of succession, where there is no proof as to survival in a common calamity the younger person is deemed to have survived the elder. There are two exceptions to this rule:

1. Under s 31(1)(a) of the Succession (Scotland) Act 1964 in a common calamity involving a husband and wife, the rule is that neither is to be regarded as having survived the other. This is a repetition of the common law position and means that neither spouse can succeed to the estate of the other.
2. Under s 31(2) of the Succession (Scotland) Act 1964, where the calamity does not involve a husband and wife the general rule that the younger survived the elder does not apply if:

    (a) the elder left a will containing a provision in favour of the younger, whom failing to a third party, and

    (b) the younger died intestate.

    In such cases the rule is that the elder survived the younger.

---

[1] See *Drummond's JF v Lord Advocate* 1994 SC 298; *Ross's JF v Martin* 1955 SC (HL) 56; *Mitchell's Exrx v Gordon* 1953 SC 176.

DISQUALIFICATION OF BENEFICIARIES AND ENTITLEMENT TO SUCCEED

Unworthy heir

Where there is a culpable killing of a person by someone entitled to inherit from the 7.9 victim's estate, the killer is often referred to as an "unworthy heir". The law, which is partly statutory and partly common law, acts to prevent the unworthy heir from reaping the benefits of the crime.

In Scotland the Parricide Act 1594 disinherited any person convicted of murdering 7.10 their parents or grandparents. Although never repealed, this ancient Act is probably no longer in force.

The common law in Scotland has followed that of England.[2] Under the common 7.11 law there is a public policy rule, which can apply whether or not there has been a conviction,[3] that a person cannot benefit from his own crime. In cases of murder there is an automatic forfeiture of the right to inherit. In cases of culpable homicide, in theory, the rule is not absolute[4] but in practice there has been only one case in England where the forfeiture rule was not applied.[5] The rule is therefore a fairly strict one. In some cases it could be viewed as being too harsh, especially where there are valid mitigating circumstances such as a history of violence and abuse on the part of the victim towards the offender.

The Forfeiture Act 1982 gives the court a discretionary power to modify the common 7.12 law rule and allows at least partial, if not total, relief from the rule.[6]

Section 2(2) of the 1982 Act sets out the grounds on which the court may modify the 7.13 rule, as follows: "that having regard to the conduct of the offender and of the deceased and to such other circumstances as appears to the court to be material, the justice of the case requires the effect of the rule to be modified". The Act specifically rules out modification in cases where there has been a conviction for murder.

Children

As the law now stands, all children have rights in succession apart from step-children. 7.14 The Law Reform (Parent and Child) (Scotland) Act 1986 abolished the distinction between legitimate and illegitimate children for the purposes of succession and s 21 of the Family Law (Scotland) Act 2006 abolished the status of illegitimacy altogether.

Adopted children cannot claim on their natural parents' estates and cannot inherit 7.15 titles, coats of arms, honours or dignity "transmissible on the death of the holder".[7]

Where a child is born posthumously, that is after the death of a parent, that child is 7.16 entitled to succeed as long as it is born alive and gains a direct benefit. A child who is still *in utero* is considered to be born for the purposes of succession

---

[2] *Smith, Petr* 1979 SLT (Sh Ct) 35.
[3] *Gray* v *Barr* [1971] 2 QB 554.
[4] *Gray* v *Barr* [1971] 2 QB 554 at 587.
[5] *Re H (Deceased)* [1990] 1 FLR 441 (contrast this case with *Jones* v *Roberts* 1995 2 FLR 422 where the forfeiture rule was applied even although the applicant was suffering from paranoid schizophrenia when he murdered his parents).
[6] Forfeiture Act 1982, s 2(4)(a); see also *Cross, Petr* 1987 SLT 384.
[7] Succession (Scotland) Act 1964, s 37(1).

Cohabitees

7.17   Historically, two persons cohabiting had no rights in the succession to a deceased partner's estate, and that situation remains the same today. The position of cohabitees has, however, improved to some extent.

7.18   Section 29 of the Family Law (Scotland) Act 2006 now permits an application to the court by a cohabitee for discretionary provision where the partner has died intestate. Any order by the court must not exceed the amount to which the survivor would have been entitled had the survivor been a spouse or civil partner.[8]

PAYMENT OF DEBTS AND THE ROLE OF AN EXECUTOR

Payment of debts

7.19   In all cases any debts due by the estate of the deceased have to be paid before the executors can distribute the remaining estate. The order in which debts have to be paid is contained in s 51 of the Bankruptcy (Scotland) Act 1985:

1. expenses of sequestration if the estate is insolvent;
2. funeral expenses;
3. secured debts;
4. preferred debts (taxes and employees' wages);
5. ordinary debts.

Note that inheritance tax has to be paid before confirmation is granted and is thus paid first. If the executor is of the opinion that there are insufficient funds to pay the debts, a judicial factor or a trustee in bankruptcy may have to be appointed and the expenses incurred as a result of insolvency take precedence over any other debts.

Executors

7.20   There are two types of executor whose role it is to wind up an estate. Where the deceased has left a valid will this will normally contain a clause appointing the person or persons whom the deceased has entrusted to ingather and distribute the estate. This type of executor is called an *executor-nominate*. Where the deceased died intestate, the court has to appoint one. This type of executor, usually a close relative, is called an *executor-dative*.

7.21   Both types of executor have the same rights and duties. An executor is in a position of trust and must therefore keep his own personal affairs totally separate from those of the executry estate. He may be personally liable for any breach of his fiduciary duties as he acts as trustee for the deceased.

Confirmation

7.22   The main job of an executor is to ingather and distribute the estate but this can only be accomplished once confirmation has been obtained from the sheriff court. Confirmation gives the executor the legal right and title to wind up the estate. The executor obtains confirmation by completing an inventory of the estate which is also used for the calculation of inheritance tax. This is lodged along with any supporting documents, including the will, with the commissary office of the sheriff court. The executor has to swear an oath that what is contained in the inventory and any other documents is correct. Once confirmation has been granted the executor can start to ingather the estate. He can then pay any debts and distribute the estate to those entitled to it.

LEGAL RIGHTS

7.23 The aim of legal rights is to provide a basic safety net for the immediate family of the deceased by giving them a claim on the estate whether the deceased left a will or not. They can only be claimed from the moveable part of the estate and therefore any heritable property, such as a house, is unaffected.

7.24 Legal rights can be claimed by a surviving spouse, civil partner[9] or any children of the deceased.

7.25 The right of a surviving spouse is called either the *ius relictae* (widow's right) or *ius relicti* (widower's right) and the entitlement is to one-half or one-third of the net moveable estate, depending on whether there are any children surviving. The right of children or their descendants is known as *legitim* or *bairn's part* and the entitlement is again to a one-half or one-third of the net moveable estate, depending on whether there is a surviving spouse or civil partner.

LEGAL RIGHTS IN INTESTATE SUCCESSION

7.26 Legal rights in intestacy are only paid after any prior rights of a surviving spouse or civil partner. Where there is partial intestacy, legal rights are available from both the testate and intestate parts of the estate

LEGAL RIGHTS IN TESTATE SUCCESSION

7.27 In testate succession, legal rights constitute a restriction on the ability of a testator to dispose of the moveable part of his estate, as they cannot be defeated by testamentary provision. There are ways round this, by ensuring, for example, that the estate is predominantly heritable or by simply distributing it prior to death.

7.28 The part of the net moveable estate over which there is no claim for legal rights is often called the *dead's part*. The size of the dead's part will vary according to whether or not legal rights are being claimed.

7.29 There is an entitlement to legal rights whether or not provision has been made in a will for a spouse or children or both. Where there is provision, a decision has to be made whether to accept it and take a legacy under the will or to reject it and claim legal rights. This will normally depend on whether claiming legal rights will be more financially beneficial than claiming under the will.

APPROBATE AND REPROBATE

7.30 It is important to remember that claiming legal rights prevents benefiting under a will and vice versa.[10] This is an example of the principle of approbate and reprobate and means that a person cannot accept the provisions of a will and at the same time reject

---

[8] Family Law (Scotland) Act 2006, s 29(4).
[9] Civil Partnership Act 2004, s 131.
[10] Succession (Scotland) Act 1964, s 13.

them. A choice or election must be made to take one or the other, as the claimant cannot benefit from both. Legal rights are often not claimed, either because there is adequate provision in the will or because those eligible do not wish to make a claim.

PAYMENT OF LEGAL RIGHTS

7.31 Legal rights can only be settled after payment of all proper debts and expenses but before any legacies or bequest are settled in terms of the will. This can mean that there may be insufficient funds to pay legacies either in full or at all. Interest is due from date of death.

LEGITIM

7.32 This is the right of children to claim a one-half or one-third share of the net moveable estate of a deceased parent. This right is subject to the principles of representation and collation.

Representation

7.33 Section 11(1) of the Succession (Scotland) Act 1964 introduced the principle of infinite representation in legitim. Under this principle, grandchildren and great-grandchildren of the deceased can represent a dead parent and claim legitim. For example, if A dies leaving a child, B, who predeceases A, any children of B can claim A's entitlement to legitim.

Division of the legitim fund

7.34 The principle of representation can affect how the legitim fund is divided. Under s 11(2) of the Succession (Scotland) Act 1964, division may be either *per capita* (by head) or *per stirpes* (by branch).

7.35 *Per capita* division is where all those entitled to claim legitim are related to the deceased in the same degree. Therefore where all the claimants are children there will be *per capita* division and each child will receive an equal share. Where they are of different degrees of relationship to the deceased, for example grandchildren and children, then the division will be *per stirpes*. This means that any children of a predeceasing parent divide up the their parent's share between them.

7.36 **Example of *per capita* division**

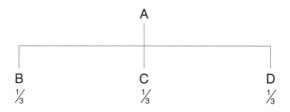

B, C, and D are all children of the deceased A and therefore of the same degree of relationship to A. Each child would receive a one-third share of the legitim fund.

Example of *per stirpes* division 7.37

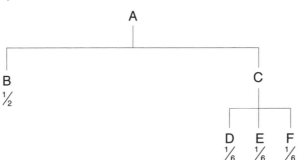

A is the deceased, with two children, B and C. C died before his parent, A, leaving three children, D, E and F, who are the grandchildren of A. The persons entitled to claim legitim are B, who is a child of A, and A's grandchildren, D, E and F, who represent their dead parent. As the claimants are of different degrees of relationship to A, there is *per stirpes* division. B is entitled to a one-half share and D, E and F to a one-third share each of their parent's one-half share, giving each a one-sixth share.

COLLATION[11]

Where there is more than one claimant for legitim, the amount payable may have to be 7.38 adjusted where any of the children claiming has already received an advance from the deceased. This is on the common law principle of *collatio bonorum inter libros*, the aim of which is to place all claimants on an equal footing so that no one claimant obtains an advantage. The principle does not apply to every type of advance and does not include an outright gift. Provision of a house or a loan is not collatable; neither are payments made by a parent for a child's maintenance or education. However, where money has been provided to one child to help set up a business or to buy a house, and this was not intended as a gift, the advance will have to be collated if that child claims on the legitim fund. Collation also applies to a claim by grandchildren under the principle of representation.

Example of collation

A receives a collatable advance of £10,000 from his father, to buy a house. A has a 7.39 brother, B, and when their father dies both make a claim on the legitim fund. The fund amounts to £20,000. The £10,000 advance has to be collated by adding it to the £20,000 fund, making £30,000. This is then divided by two, giving each brother £15,000. The collatable advance of £10,000 is then deducted from A's share, leaving A with a claim of £5,000 and B with a claim of £15,000.

DISCHARGE OF LEGAL RIGHTS

The right to claim legal rights is automatically discharged under s 13 of the Succession 7.40 (Scotland) Act 1964 where the claimant decides to take a legacy under a will. However, any election to discharge legal rights may be reduced where proper independent legal

---

[11] Succession (Scotland) Act 1964, s 11(3).

advice has not been given, or insufficient information has been supplied, or the claimant lacked capacity. An election by a child under 16 is automatically void, although the parents can make an election on behalf of the child. Children between the ages of 16 and 18 can make an election, but this is subject to a right to have this set aside where it is shown to be prejudicial

EFFECT OF A DISCHARGE ON THE LEGITIM FUND

7.41   If the right is discharged prior to the death of the parent, the fund is increased by the amount of that person's share and is available to the other claimants.[12] If it is discharged after the death then the right is forfeited and the fund is not increased. The share then goes to the free estate under intestacy or to the dead's part where there is a will. In the latter case, where the discharge is after death, other claimants will not therefore benefit from the discharge.

INTESTATE SUCCESSION

7.42   An intestate is defined as "a person who has died leaving undisposed of by testamentary disposition the whole or part of his estate".[13]

Intestate succession therefore usually arises where the deceased has not left any valid testamentary writing, which in most cases is a will. Occasionally, however, there is an existing will or other form of testamentary writing which for some reason is invalid and therefore the estate or part of it will fall into intestacy.

7.43   There are three stages in the administration of an intestate estate after payment of debts and funeral expenses. They are:

1. prior rights;
2. legal rights;
3. free estate.

1. PRIOR RIGHTS

7.44   Where the deceased is survived by a spouse or civil partner,[14] the Succession (Scotland) Act 1964 sets out certain rights to which the spouse or partner is entitled in the deceased's estate. These rights are called prior rights because they rank before the rights of anybody else, including any children of the deceased, and must be paid first. They only apply in intestacy, as opposed to legal rights, which are available in both testate and intestate succession. There are three rights which are set out in ss 8 and 9 of the 1964 Act.

Dwellinghouse

Relevant interest

7.45   Sections 8(1) and (2) of the Succession (Scotland) Act 1964 deal with the right of the surviving spouse or civil partner to what the Act refers to as the "relevant interest" in

---

[12] *Hog* v *Hog* (1791) Mor 8193.
[13] Succession (Scotland) Act 1964, s 36(1).
[14] Civil Partnership Act 2004, s 131.

a dwellinghouse in which the spouse or partner was ordinarily resident. The relevant interest is the value of the deceased's interest in the house and the entitlement is to that value and not necessarily the house itself.

Spouses or civil partners may have owned the house together and the title is then **7.46** held in common. This means that each spouse or partner owned a one-half *pro indiviso* or undivided share. If one of the spouses died intestate then it is the one half-share that belonged to the deceased which is the relevant interest.

The term "dwellinghouse" includes a part of a building, for example a flat in a **7.47** tenement, and any ground or garden attached which is necessary for the amenity and use of the property. Where there is more than one house in which the survivor was ordinarily resident, a choice has to be made between them within 6 months of the death.

Tenancies

The relevant interest can be that of owner or tenant. In theory, therefore, a relevant **7.48** interest applies to tenancies.[15] In practice, as far as residential tenancies are concerned, the rules governing succession are contained in the relevant legislation applying to the type of tenancy concerned.[16] Succession to farms that are leased is governed by the Agricultural Holdings (Scotland) Act 1991.

Current value of the relevant interest

The value of the relevant interest cannot currently exceed £300,000 and is subject to **7.49** any heritable security (loan) secured over the property.[17] Thus, a dwellinghouse valued at £200,000 wholly owned by the deceased, in which the surviving spouse or civil partner was ordinarily resident and which is subject to a mortgage of £50,000, will result in a relevant interest of £150,000 being available to the surviving spouse or civil partner.

Where the relevant interest is equivalent to or less than £300,000 then the surviving **7.50** spouse is only entitled to that amount. Usually this will mean that the spouse will simply take the house and not the money. Where the interest is more than £300,000 there is only an entitlement to the cash value and the spouse will have to pay the difference into the estate in order to keep the house.

Special destinations

In some cases the title of the dwellinghouse is subject to what is called a special **7.51** destination. The title is held equally between the parties and to the survivor of them. The result is that the one-half share that belonged to the deceased goes directly to the surviving spouse, and does not form part of the intestate estate for the purpose of confirmation. As the house will already be fully owned by the surviving spouse, it is not subject to a claim for the deceased's relevant interest.

---

[15] Succession (Scotland) Act 1964, s 8(6)(d).
[16] Eg assured tenancies.
[17] Succession (Scotland) Act 1964, s 8(6)(d).

Furniture and plenishings

7.52 A surviving spouse or civil partner is also entitled under s 8(3) of the Succession (Scotland) Act 1964 to furniture and plenishings (other household items) up to a value of (currently) £24,000. This applies to any house in which the spouse or civil partner was ordinarily resident. If there is more than one such house then the right can only be exercised over one of them and a choice between them must be made within 6 months.[18] The right does not include anything that was used for business purposes, cash or heirlooms, but otherwise includes all other household items such as furniture, paintings, books and other common household articles.[19] Note that where the house is subject to a special destination, as described above, this does not affect the right to furniture and plenishings.

Financial provision

7.53 Under s 9(1) of the Succession (Scotland) Act 1964 the surviving spouse or civil partner is entitled to financial provision of up to £42,000 where there is issue, that is, children or grandchildren. The amount is increased to £75,000 where there is no issue. The financial provision is only payable to the surviving spouse after satisfaction of the previous two prior rights.[20]

Where the intestate estate is large enough and there is heritable and moveable estate remaining after satisfaction of the previous two prior rights, the financial provision is not just taken from the moveable estate but is taken rateably from both the moveable and the heritable estate.[21] This is to increase the amount available for legal rights, which comes from the moveable estate only, and is payable after satisfaction of prior rights. So, for example, where there is remaining estate of £100,000 comprising heritable estate of £60,000 and moveable estate of £40,000, the ratio is 60:40. The financial provision of, say, £42,000 will therefore be made up of £25,200 from the heritable part and £16,800 from the moveable part.

7.54 Finally, where there is partial intestacy and the surviving spouse has received a legacy, this must be set off against the financial provision. However, if the legacy is a house[22] or furniture and plenishings in a house in which the surviving spouse or civil partner was ordinarily resident then there is no set-off and no deduction from the financial provision.[23]

2. LEGAL RIGHTS

7.55 The legal rights of any surviving spouse, civil partner or children are payable after satisfaction of prior rights from any remaining moveable estate.[24]

---

[18] Succession (Scotland) Act 1964, s 8(3).
[19] Succession (Scotland) Act 1964, s 8(6)(d).
[20] Succession (Scotland) Act 1964, s 9(6)(a).
[21] Succession (Scotland) Act 1964, s 9(3).
[22] Where a house was subject to a special destination this is treated as a legacy under s 36(1) of the Succession (Scotland) Act 1964. However, if the house is one to which s 8 of the 1964 Act applies, there is no deduction under s 9(1).
[23] Succession (Scotland) Act 1964, s 9(1).
[24] Succession (Scotland) Act 1964, s 10(2).

3. FREE ESTATE

7.56 The free estate is what remains of the intestate's heritable and moveable property after satisfaction of prior and legal rights.

7.57 Succession to the free estate is regulated by s 2 of the Succession (Scotland) Act 1964 which sets out in order of preference the various classes of person entitled to inherit. Each class must be exhausted before moving on to the next one. If there are no blood relations surviving then the crown inherits as *ultimus haeres*.

Descendants, collaterals, spouse and ancestors

7.58 The persons entitled to inherit the free estate are divided into descendants, collaterals, spouse and ancestors.

- *Descendants* are children or grandchildren of the deceased.
- *Collaterals* are brothers and sisters, or aunts and uncles, or brothers and sisters of a grandparent of the deceased. A collateral can be of the "whole blood", where they have the same parents, or of the "half blood", where they share only one parent. It does not matter whether the shared relationship is through the mother or the father. Under s 3 of the 1964 Act, collaterals of the whole blood are preferred to those of the half blood. Brothers are thus preferred to half-brothers.
- A surviving *spouse* is given a fairly low ranking when it comes to the free estate. This is because provision has already been made under prior and legal rights.
- *Ancestors* are the parents, grandparents etc of the deceased.

Representation

7.59 Representation applies except for a surviving spouse or parents.[25] This means, for example, that nephews or nieces can inherit by representing a predeceasing brother or sister of the deceased. Representation is not allowed in the case of a spouse to prevent any claim by surviving step-children who have no right to inherit as there is no blood relationship with the deceased. In the case of parents it prevents half-brothers or sisters, where there is only one common parent, from inheriting along with brothers and sisters of the full blood. However, half-brothers or sisters can inherit where there are no brothers and sisters of the full blood surviving.[26]

Division of the free estate

7.60 The free estate is divided either *per capita* or *per stirpes*, depending on the degree of relationship of those entitled with the deceased. If they are all of the same degree, for example all children, then it will be *per capita* and if of different degrees, for example children and grandchildren, it will be *per stirpes*.

Order of succession

7.61 The order of succession is thus:

---

[25] Succession (Scotland) Act 1964, s 5(1).

(a) children (descendants);

(b) parents one-half share (ascendants): brothers and sisters (collaterals) one-half share;

(c) brothers and sisters (where no parents);

(d) parents (where no brothers and sisters);

(e) spouse;

(f) aunts and uncles (collaterals);

(g) grandparents (ascendants);

(h) great-uncles and great-aunts (collaterals);

(i) remoter ancestors;

(j) the Crown as *ultimus haeres.*

ARTIFICIAL INTESTACY

7.62   It is possible to create intestacy on purpose. In *Kerr, Petr*[27] the deceased had left all his moveable estate to his wife. The moveable estate was valued at around £2,500. The deceased had a daughter who was of course entitled to claim her legal right to one-third of the moveable estate. The daughter did claim legitim and the spouse then renounced her claim under the will. The reason she did this was because under the rules of intestacy she was entitled to the whole of the moveable estate and this defeated the daughter's claim.

Alternatively, intestacy can be created unintentionally. An example of this would be if the will or part of it is so unclear that it cannot be implemented.

TESTATE SUCCESSION

TYPES OF TESTAMENTARY WRITINGS

Wills

7.63   A will does not have to be in any particular form as long as it demonstrates the final testamentary intention of the writer. In most cases a will is prepared by a lawyer but there is no requirement for this to be done and there are many examples of wills written by the testator in letter, note or other form.

7.64   Sometimes it may be difficult to distinguish between final intentions and mere instructions to draw up a will. In *Jamieson's Exr v Fyvie*[28] the testator, Miss Jamieson, had made a valid will. When she died, there was found in her desk at her home a note which was addressed to her solicitor. It was written in her own hand and was signed and dated. The note expressed the wish of Miss Jamieson to double the amount of two legacies contained in her will and there were further instructions regarding the

---

[26] Succession (Scotland Act 1964, s 3. (This section applies not only to brothers and sisters but also ancestors ie aunts and uncles, great-aunts and great-uncles.)

[27] 1968 SLT (Sh Ct) 61.

[28] 1982 SLT 198. See also *Barker's Exrs v Scottish Rights of Way Society* 1996 SLT 1319.

residue of the estate. The note concluded: "I hope this can be done." The court looked at the actual language used by Miss Jamieson in the note and concluded that it did not contain a final testamentary intention and was no more than an *aide-memoire* for discussion with the lawyer.

Will substitutes

There are situations where a document other than a will disposes of the deceased's **7.65** estate. An example of this is a joint life assurance policy. If the policy states that the proceeds are to go to the survivor on the death of the first party then those proceeds do not form part of the deceased's estate. The testator has no power under a will to alter the terms of the document and it becomes a will substitute.

Another example of a will substitute is a special destination in the title to a **7.66** house.

Trust disposition and settlement

A trust disposition and settlement is similar to a will but instead of a legacy going **7.67** straight to the beneficiary the will creates a trust which continues until the trust purposes have been fulfilled. A common example of this is where provision is made for a child and the testator instructs the executors to hold the legacy in trust until the child reaches the age of majority.

Codicil

Sometimes a testator wishes to change the provisions of an existing will. It may be to **7.68** increase a legacy or include another legatee or to revoke an existing legacy. Instead of completing a new will the testator will usually add a codicil to the main will. There may be several codicils and the usual practice is, where possible, to add any codicil at the end of the existing will.

Informal writings

Many wills include a clause directing the executors to give effect to what are known **7.69** as informal writings. This could be a letter or a note giving further instructions to the testator's executors. Such writings give the testator a certain amount of flexibility and allow amendments to be made without the need to add a codicil or indeed make a new will. They can of course give rise to difficulties where the validity or interpretation of the informal writing is in doubt.

FORMAL VALIDITY

Before the executors nominated in a will can proceed to wind up an estate, confirmation **7.70** has to be obtained from the court. A court will not grant confirmation until it is as certain as it possibly can be that the will is not a forgery and contains the true intentions of the testator; in other words, that it is valid. It is only when the court is satisfied that a will is properly signed, witnessed and dated that it will grant confirmation and allow the executors to deal with the estate.

7.71   There are rules that must be followed before a testamentary writing will be considered formally valid. If a court does not accept a will because of some lack of formality, although this can sometimes be rectified,[29] it will not grant confirmation and the estate will fall into intestacy.

7.72   The original rules governing the authentication of particular types of documents, including wills and other types of testamentary writing, were changed by the Requirements of Writing (Scotland) Act 1995. Many wills were of course executed prior to 1 August 1995, when the Act came into force. As a result, one set of rules applies to wills executed before 1 August 1995 and another set to those executed after that date.

Wills executed pre-1995

7.73   The law relating to the execution and authentication of documents prior to 1995 is contained in various statutory rules and court decisions. There were two basic types of testamentary writing that were acceptable to the courts as being valid under the old rules. They were probative and privileged writings. The latter were subject to a further process of validation by the court under s 21 of the Succession (Scotland) Act 1964. Legacies which were not in writing and had a value of not more than £100 Scots were also valid. These were called verbal nuncupative legacies. However, verbal legacies probably became obsolete many years ago.

Probative wills

7.74   A will that is probative has been subscribed, ie signed below the text, by the testator on each page. The signature on the last page was witnessed by two witnesses who had to be at least 16 years old and of sound mind. They were required either to see the testator sign the will or to have the testator acknowledge to them that the signature was his. Where a will is probative the court accepts it as valid and will grant confirmation.

Holograph writings

7.75   A holograph will is one that is written entirely in the handwriting of the testator and signed at the bottom of the last page. Such a will is not probative and therefore confirmation will not be granted by the court unless there is sufficient evidence that the handwriting and signature were those of the testator. Evidence is by way of the affidavits of at least two persons. An affidavit is evidence in the form of a written statement sworn before a notary public.

7.76   There is a second form of a holograph will. This is where the will is not in the testator's own handwriting and is usually typewritten or printed. It is then adopted as his writing by adding the words "adopted as holograph" at the end and then signed underneath. Where a typewritten will is not adopted as holograph it will be invalid even if it has been subscribed by the testator.

7.77   As with a fully holograph will, evidence as to the signature is required.

---

[29] Certain minor defects, such as not including the full name and addresses of a witness, could be cured under s 39 of the Conveyancing (Scotland) Act 1874 and for wills post-1 August 1995 under s 4 of the Requirements of Writing (Scotland) Act 1995.

Standard form wills

Problems arose with standard form wills which are partly printed and partly in **7.78** the writing of the testator who fills in the blank parts. If the will was not properly signed and witnessed, making it probative, the typewritten parts had to be adopted as holograph. A simple signature was sufficient for the handwritten parts but not for those that were printed. The court then had to decide if the handwritten part amounted to a testamentary writing.[30]

Informal writings

It was, and still is, a common practice for wills to contain a clause instructing executors **7.79** to give effect to any informal writing by the testator. This means that a simple note or letter of instruction, even in some cases those without a signature, could have testamentary effect. This is because if the will itself is formally valid it can then adopt the informal writing as being valid too.

The principle of adoption has been taken in some cases to an extreme, as in **7.80** *Davidson* v *Convy*.[31] Here, an unsigned holograph will was found in an unsealed envelope. On the envelope were written the words "my will" and underneath these words was the signature of the testator. The court held that the words and signature were sufficient to adopt the unsigned will as a valid testamentary writing.

Wills executed post-1 August 1995

Self-proving wills

The rules of formal validity were changed by the Requirements of Writing (Scotland) **7.81** Act 1995. Probative and privileged writings were dispensed with and replaced with a new, self-proving status. To be self-proving for the purpose of confirmation, a will still has to be subscribed on every page but there is now a requirement for only one witness.[32] The will must also state the full name and address of the witness and the testator must sign the will in the presence of the witness or acknowledge his signature, as was the case for witnesses prior to 1995.

Holograph wills

Although privileged writings, which included holograph wills, are no longer recognised **7.82** as having any status under the new rules, a subscribed holograph writing is still a valid way of making a will. This is because under s 2(1) of the Requirements of Writing Act (Scotland) 1995 subscription of the will is sufficient to make it a valid writing.

Where the will is not witnessed it cannot be accepted by the court for confirmation. **7.83** Under the new provisions[33] a court certificate can be granted where there is evidence that the signature is that of the testator. Confirmation can then be granted. As with

---

[30] *Carmichael's Exrs* v *Carmichael* 1909 SC 1387.
[31] 2003 SC 420.
[32] Requirements of Writing (Scotland) Act 1995, s 3.
[33] Requirements of Writing (Scotland) Act 1995, s 4.

holograph wills under the previous rules, evidence of the validity of the signature is by way of affidavit evidence.

7.84   One of the benefits of the new rules is that the problems associated with standard form wills have disappeared. This is because the Requirements of Writing (Scotland) Act 1995 simply requires writing and subscription for the will to be valid.

Informal writings

7.85   Under the new rules informal testamentary writings have to be subscribed, which was not always necessarily the case under the old ones. Thus, even if a will is formally valid and makes provision for future informal writings, this fact is probably now not sufficient to validate an unsubscribed letter, note or other document.

Subscription of a testator who is blind or cannot write

7.86   Under the rules prior to 1 August 1995 the execution of a will by someone on behalf of a person who was blind or unable to write was called notarial execution. Only certain persons such as a solicitor or minister of religion was permitted to do so. Under s 9(3) of the Requirements of Writing (Scotland) Act 1995, subscription can now be effected only by a "relevant person", ie a solicitor, advocate, justice of the peace or sheriff clerk.

7.87   The will is read over to the blind person in the presence of a witness who must then give authority to subscribe. The will is then signed and witnessed. The person signing must have no interest in the will and any benefit obtained can be struck down by the court.

ESSENTIAL VALIDITY

7.88   A will can be challenged on the ground that it lacks formality. There can also be a challenge on the ground that the will may not represent the true intentions of the testator.

7.89   There are basically two situations in which the essential validity of a will can be challenged.

1. Lack of capacity

7.90   In the first situation the testator is said to be unable to form a proper testamentary intention because of lack of age or mental capacity. Children under the age of 12 do not have testamentary capacity and any estate is dealt with under the rules of intestate succession.[34]

7.91   People who are generally insane are considered incapable of making a will. However, where a person has lucid periods or suffers from some sort of delusion there is a presumption against insanity unless the person has been certified as insane. In such cases the court has to be satisfied that the delusion or mental illness actually affected the making of the will. For example, in *Smith* v *Smith's Trs*[35] it was alleged that

---

[34] Age of Legal Capacity (Scotland) Act 1991, s 2(2).
[35] 1972 SLT (Notes) 80.

the testator suffered from a delusion that his dead wife had returned to him. There was, however, no evidence that this affected the making of the will and the action for reduction of the will failed.

A will made by a person under the influence of drugs or alcohol is valid as long the **7.92** testator was capable of forming testamentary intention.

2. Undue influence and facility and circumvention

Where the testator has come under improper pressure or has been taken advantage of **7.93** in some way, the will, or a provision of the will, can be declared invalid.

In Scotland a will can be declared invalid where there has been either undue **7.94** influence or facility and circumvention.

Undue influence

Undue influence and facility and circumvention are both fairly similar. The main **7.95** difference is that in cases of undue influence there is a relationship of trust. Persons holding a position of trust include lawyers, doctors, accountants and ministers of religion as well as members of the family. The position of trust can allow self-interest to deflect the advice or guidance given to the testator, thereby influencing him to act in a way he might otherwise not have done. Undue influence need not necessarily involve any actual fraud.

Facility and circumvention

Facility occurs where the testator is easily manipulated but it does not mean that the **7.96** person is in any way insane. Very often persons of advanced years are more susceptible to the malign influence of others and many cases of facility and circumvention involve older people. However, the term "facility" has a wider application than just old age and includes persons suffering from illness, alcoholism, bereavement and downright fear.

Circumvention means getting round the testator by putting pressure on him in **7.97** a dishonest way. A third factor must also be present in that there must be actual harm to the testator's interest. This is called lesion. When considering cases involving facility and circumvention the courts have to take all these factors into consideration together.

A good example of facility and circumvention can be seen in the recent case of **7.98** *Horne* v *Whyte*[36] where a retired colonel was persuaded to leave a legacy of £50,000 to his housekeeper in a codicil to his will. The legacy was held to be invalid on the ground that the colonel was in a state of facility at the time of making the legacy and had come under the influence of the housekeeper upon whom he relied totally. He was terrified that she would leave and had become obsessed with keeping her happy. The housekeeper had then used her influence to pressurise the colonel into changing the will in her favour. The codicil was also reduced on the ground of undue influence as the housekeeper had been in a position of trust, especially as the colonel had not received any independent advice prior to making the legacy.

---

[36] [2005] CSOH 115.

REVOCATION OF A WILL

7.99   Where someone has made a valid will, is it possible for that person to change his mind by making a new will or changing provisions in the existing one? The answer is that a testator can change or alter a will at any time up until death, as a will has no effect until the death of the testator.

7.100   There is an exception to this general rule and that is where there is a contractual obligation involved. In *Paterson* v *Paterson*[37] a son lent his mother money in return for the mother's agreement that she would make him the beneficiary of her will. This was done by way of a formal agreement and a will which was declared irrevocable. The mother made a later will revoking the first one in which the son was the beneficiary. The court held that the first will could not be revoked because the testator had bound herself in a separate agreement. Contractual obligations are also found in mutual wills where more than one party, usually husband and wife, have their wills made in one document rather than two separate ones. Sometimes the terms of this type of will are contractual and cannot be revoked.

Validity of the revoking will

7.101   The will itself of course has to be a valid one or the revocation will not be effective. This may result in a previous will being revived. In *Bruce's Judicial Factor* v *Lord Advocate*[38] the testator executed a will in 1945 which was retained by the solicitor. A new will was made in 1949 revoking all prior wills and this will was kept by the testator herself. After she died the second will could not be found and it was presumed to have been intentionally destroyed by her. It was held that the previous 1945 will should be revived and given effect.

Methods of revocation

7.102   There is a general rule that since testamentary writings are the last will of the testator, earlier wills are revoked by later ones.

Express revocation

7.103   Many wills contain an express clause making it clear that any prior testamentary writing is revoked. Sometimes the wording of such a clause can lead to difficulties. For example, in *Clark's Trs* v *Clark's Exrs*[39] the words "I cancel all wills previously executed by me" was not sufficient to revoke a legacy of a stamp collection made by the testator in a separate letter.

Implied revocation

7.104   Where the revocation of previous wills is not expressly stated it can be implied where there are contradictory provisions in a later will. If there is a complete new universal

---

[37] (1893) 20 R 484.
[38] 1969 SLT 337.
[39] 1925 SC 431.

settlement, where the whole estate is disposed of, then any previous will is revoked. Where there is only partial revocation by a subsequent will or testamentary writing (where only part of the estate is disposed of) then both documents will be looked at together and there will be revocation of the previous provision where there is any inconsistency between the two.

Revocation by alteration

It is possible to revoke provisions of a will by simply altering them. For example, the **7.105** testator might score out or delete a particular provision, thereby revoking it. There has to be proof that it was the testator who made the alteration intentionally. The intention to alter the will is known as *animus revocandi*. There must therefore be evidence to show that it was the testator and not some other person who altered the will. The signature of the testator is obviously the best way of providing such evidence.

Destruction

A more drastic way of revoking a will is to physically destroy it. However, simply **7.106** tearing a will up may not be enough. The destruction must be intentional. If there is sufficient proof that the testator was drunk, or the will was torn up by mistake, or some other person destroyed it without permission, there is no revocation as there is not the required intention.

There is, however, a presumption that the testator will have intentionally destroyed **7.107** the will where it was known to have been in his possession and cannot be found after his death.[40]

Actual destruction of the will itself is not always necessary. In *Thomson's Trs* v **7.108** *Bowhill Baptist Church*[41] the testatrix had cut out certain clauses in a copy of the will and had written on the copy the reason for this having been done and had signed the statement. This was held in the circumstances to be sufficient proof of intention and the clauses were revoked.

Conditio si testator sine liberis decesserit

This is a rarely used method of revocation. It applies where a child is born after a **7.109** parent's will has been executed and there is no provision for that child in the will. Where the parent then dies there is a presumption that the parent would not have intended to disinherit such a child and the whole will is consequently revoked.

The presumption can of course be challenged where there is evidence that it was **7.110** indeed the intention of the testator to exclude the child. An example of this would be if provision for the child has been made elsewhere. The condition will still apply even after a period of years has elapsed in which the parent could have altered the will for the benefit of the child.

The estate will fall into intestacy where the condition is applied and this may still **7.111** result in the child receiving nothing, as the prior rights of an existing spouse can easily

---

[40] *Clyde* v *Clyde* 1958 SC 343; and see also *Bruce's JF* v *Lord Advocate* 1969 SC 269.
[41] 1956 SLT 302.

use up the whole estate. It may therefore be preferable for the child to claim legal rights from the estate rather than to have the will revoked.

THE INTERPRETATION OF WILLS

7.112 There is a general rule that a court will interpret a will intrinsically, by looking at what the testator has actually written. Any evidence that is extrinsic or outwith the actual writing is not admitted.[42] The court is therefore only interested in interpreting what is to be found in the document and not with conjecture as to what the testator was thinking about or what influenced any decisions when the will was being made. How, then, do the courts construe a testator's intentions from the language used in the will? There are some general rules. First, the will should be construed to avoid where possible intestacy; second, it should be read as a whole; third, words should be given their ordinary meaning; and fourth, conflicting intentions should be reconciled where possible.

7.113 Despite the general rule that extrinsic evidence is not allowed, there are limited circumstances in which such evidence is admitted. These circumstances can be summarised as follows: (1) when looking at questions of capacity or intention to make or revoke a will; (2) translating or decoding a will; (3) finding out whether the testator was aware of the ownership of particular property; (4) identifying the subject of a bequest or the person who is the beneficiary; (5) ascertaining the meaning of a word where there is more than one ordinary meaning; and (6) where a testator has made a provision for a beneficiary more than once in the will, to decide whether this was the intention of the testator, as there is a presumption against making a double provision.

LEGACIES

7.114 In testate succession the testator may bequeath his estate in a single legacy of the whole estate (often this is to the surviving spouse) or by several legacies to a variety of people which may include friends, relations and very often charities.

7.115 Any legacy can be made the subject of a condition whereby the legacy will not be paid until the condition is fulfilled. The condition may, however, be struck down where it is, for example, immoral, illegal or impossible to perform.

CLASSIFICATION OF LEGACIES

Special legacies

7.116 A special legacy is one where the subject-matter of the legacy is a particular item. This may be a painting or a clock or a stamp collection. It does not have to be moveable and the legacy of a house or the share of a house is still a special legacy.

---

[42] Section 8 of the Law Reform (Miscellaneous Provisions) (Scotland) Act 1985 provides a general rule that extrinsic evidence is excluded in the interpretation of formal documents such as wills.

Demonstrative legacy

7.117 A demonstrative legacy is similar to a special one except that the legacy is taken from a particular source specified by the testator; for example, a legacy of £1,000 from a particular bank account or a set of chairs to be taken from a particular house

General legacy

7.118 A general legacy differs from the two preceding types of legacy in that it is not a legacy of a particular item and there are no directions as to the source of the legacy. General legacies are usually sums of money which can be paid from the general fund of money that belonged to the testator.

Residual legacies

7.119 A legacy of the residue of an estate comprises what is left after payment of legal rights and other legacies. This can amount to almost the whole estate or to a very little if the other legacies have disposed of a large part of the estate. It is always important to ensure that there is a residual legatee because if any other legacy fails for some reason it will become part of the residue and will not fall into intestacy

ABATEMENT OF LEGACIES

7.120 An important reason for classifying legacies is to regulate the order of the settlement or payment for each type of legacy. Abatement means that some types of legacy are reduced before other categories where there are insufficient funds to pay all of them.

7.121 A situation can arise where the estate has to pay off a lot of debt and all the legacies cannot be paid in full. Where this happens there are rules which set out which type of legacy must bear the burden of the debt first. Under theses rules a residual legacy will abate or be reduced first. Thus, a residual legatee may receive nothing while the other legatees are paid in full.

If there are still insufficient funds general legacies are abated after residual ones and only then are demonstrative and special legacies abated. Residual, general and demonstrative legacies are abated *pari passu* which means proportionately. For example, where there is one legacy of £10,000 to John and another of £4,000 to Jim, but there is only £7,000 left in the estate, John would receive £5,000 and Jim £2,000.

ADEMPTION

7.122 One of the most disappointing experiences faced by any beneficiary is to discover that a much longed-for legacy no longer exists. This often occurs where the deceased has already sold the subject of the legacy. There is nothing the beneficiary can do about this, as the legacy is subject to ademption, which means cancellation, and it no longer forms part of the testator's estate.

LEGATUM REI ALIENAE

7.123 There is an exception and that is where the subject of the legacy was never in the ownership of the testator. It is therefore not subject to the principle of ademption. This is called *legatum rei alienae* which means a legacy of something you have never owned. If it can be proved that the testator was fully aware that that he was never the owner of the item then this can be interpreted as an instruction to the executors to purchase it for the beneficiary

LEGACIES AGAINST PUBLIC INTEREST

7.124   Testators sometimes become carried away when deciding how they are going to dispose of their property and the courts may decide that a bequest benefits nobody, or that it is against public policy or is illegal. Good examples of this can be seen in the cases of *McCaig v Glasgow University*[43] and *Aitken's Trs v Aitken*.[44] In the first case the testator directed his trustees to erect statues and towers of himself and his family on his estate in Oban. This meant that his sister, who would have been the sole beneficiary under the rules of intestacy, received nothing. The court declared the legacy to be invalid as it benefited nobody. In *Aitken's Trs v Aitken* the testator belonged to a family with a strong connection with Musselburgh. In his will he instructed his trustees to erect a bronze statue of himself in the town. The Town Council did not want this and the legacy was declared invalid as there was no personal or public benefit.

DESTINATIONS OVER

7.125   If a beneficiary is to inherit a legacy then he must survive the death of the testator. Where the beneficiary does not survive then the legacy will either fall into intestacy or become part of the residue. The testator may not wish this to happen, in which case he must make provision for some other chosen person to take the legacy. This could be called a second choice.

7.126   The main device for doing this is a destination over, where the legacy is bequeathed to "A whom failing B", so that B inherits if A does not survive.

7.127   In the law of succession A is called the institute and B may be either the conditional institute or the substitute. The difference between a conditional institute and a substitute is this. Taking the above example, if B is a conditional institute and A survives the testator then B's right to the legacy fails and A inherits. Where B is a substitute and A survives the testator, A will inherit but B will retain an interest in the legacy. B will become entitled to the legacy when A dies, as long as A has not disposed of it prior to his death.

7.128   Where a will does not make it clear, there is a presumption that a legacy including moveable estate will result in conditional institution.
    Substitution is presumed if the legacy is of heritable property, such as a house.

7.129   There is a condition called the *conditio si institutis sine liberis decesserit* which may in certain circumstances replace the conditional institute in the will with somebody else who must be closely related to the testator. Thus, if a father leaves a legacy to his son, whom failing to a friend, and the son predeceases the father, any grandchildren can inherit where the condition is applied, replacing the friend as conditional institute.

---

[43] 1907 SC 231.
[44] 1927 SC 374.

ACCRETION

Not all legacies are bequeathed to individuals. A legacy may be left to more than one **7.130** person or to a whole class of persons. For example, where there is a legacy to "Harry and Bob" or to "all my nephews", what happens if Bob or one of the nephews has died before the testator? The answer is that the principle of accretion applies and the entitlement of those who have predeceased the testator accresces to any survivor. The principle underlying this is that the legacy is a joint one to all the parties. A joint legacy indicates that testator wishes survivors to take the whole legacy. If there is an indication that the legacy is not a joint one and that each person is to have a separate interest, then accretion does not apply. Thus, if the testator uses what are called words of severance, such as "equally between them", this is a direction that each person is only entitled to his own share and no more. However, in cases of legacies to a class of persons, such as "all my nieces", accretion will always apply even if there are words of severance.

VESTING

Vesting is a subject of considerable complexity but the basic principle is that where **7.131** property vests in someone it becomes that person's property. However, this does not mean that there is an immediate right to take actual possession of the property.

In succession, no property can vest in the beneficiaries until the testator dies and **7.132** there is always a presumption in favour of early vesting. However, vesting may take place at a later time where this is the testator's intention. Indeed, it is possible to have a vested right in property and die before actually enjoying possession of it. In some cases vesting takes place immediately, as with legal rights, or where the legacy is unconditional. In other cases vesting may be suspended where the testator stipulates a condition such as surviving for a particular period of time. There is no guarantee that the beneficiary will actually survive the given period; the legacy cannot vest in the beneficiary until he actually does survive it.

Where it is certain that an event will take place, such as a death, vesting takes place **7.133** immediately. A common example of this is a liferent where the beneficiary cannot take possession of the property until the death of the liferenter but it vests in the fiar on the death of the testator.

In some cases a condition attached to a legacy creates the possibility that the legacy **7.134** may be defeated if a particular event takes place, such as the birth of a child. The vesting of such a legacy is immediate but will be defeated on the occurrence of the particular event. This is known as vesting subject to defeasance.

ESSENTIAL FACTS

INTRODUCTION

7.135

- The law of succession regulates how a person's property is transferred after his death.
- *Testate* succession applies where the deceased has left some form of valid testamentary writing.
- *Intestate* succession applies where there is no valid testamentary writing.

OPERATION OF THE LAW OF SUCCESSION

Proof of death

- There must be proof of death before succession can operate. A death certificate is normally sufficient.
- Where someone is missing the court can grant a decree of declarator of death under the Presumption of Death (Scotland) Act 1977. Decree can be granted either after a period of 7 years or, where no body has been found, there is sufficient evidence that the person has died.

Survivorship and entitlement to succeed

- Where two or more persons die simultaneously in a common calamity, the rules under s 31 of the Succession (Scotland) Act 1964 will apply. There is a general presumption that the younger survived the elder. This presumption does not apply to spouses or where the elder has left a legacy to the younger whom failing to a third party and the younger dies intestate.
- Under the common law forfeiture rule, a person cannot generally benefit from an unlawful killing. The rule can be modified by application to the court under the Forfeiture Act 1982 but the Act does not apply to cases of murder.
- All children now have rights in succession, except step-children. Adopted children cannot inherit titles or coats of arms.
- Cohabitees have no rights in succession but can apply under s 29 of the Family Law (Scotland) Act 2006 for discretionary provision.

Payment of debts and the role of the executor

- All debts owed by the deceased must be paid prior to distribution of the estate. The order of priority for payment is contained in s 51 of the Bankruptcy (Scotland) Act 1985.

- Executors are responsible for the winding-up of the deceased's estate. An executor can be appointed under the will of the deceased and is called an *executor-nominate*. In cases of intestacy the court appoints the executor, who is called an *executor-dative*.

LEGAL RIGHTS

- Legal rights provide a safety net for the immediate family of the deceased.
- Legal rights can be claimed in both testate and intestate succession.
- The right of the surviving widow is called the *ius relictae*, and that of a widower the *ius relicti*. The right of any child is called legitim. Civil partners can also now claim legal rights
- The entitlement is to either one-half or one-third of the *moveable* estate.
- Legal rights cannot be defeated by testamentary provision. They can be defeated by, for example, leaving only heritable property.
- In intestate succession, legal rights are payable only after payment of prior rights.
- In testate succession, where there is provision under the will the spouse, civil partner or child must elect either to take the provision or to claim legal rights. They cannot have both. This is under the principle of approbate and reprobate.
- Legitim is subject to the principles of representation and collation.
- Under the principle of representation, grandchildren, for example, can claim legitim in the place of the parent, ie the child of the deceased, where the parent has not survived.
- Where the claimants are related in different degrees to the deceased, eg children and grandchildren, the division of the legitim fund is *per stirpes*. Where they are of the same degree the division is *per capita*.
- Under the principle of collation, certain types of payment made to one child during the lifetime of the deceased may have to be taken into account when calculating the amount of legitim where there is more than one claimant. This is to ensure that the child who received the payment does not benefit twice, to the disadvantage of other children.
- Legal rights can be discharged before or after the death of the parent. Under s 13 of the Succession (Scotland) Act 1964, any legal right is automatically discharged where the claimant takes a legacy under the will of the deceased.

INTESTATE SUCCESSION

- The rules regulating the distribution of an intestate estate are mainly contained in the Succession (Scotland) Act 1964.

- There are three stages in the distribution of an intestate estate. First, payment of the prior rights of the surviving spouse or civil partner; second, payment of legal rights; and third, distribution of any remaining estate (called the free estate).

- There are three prior rights set out under ss 8 and 9 of the Succession (Scotland) Act 1964. First, there is the right to the relevant interest (ie the deceased's interest) in a dwellinghouse in which the surviving spouse was ordinarily resident, up to a value of £300,000. Second, the right to any furniture and plenishings, up to a value of £24,000 in any dwellinghouse in which the surviving spouse was ordinarily resident. Third, a right to a financial provision of up to £42,000 where there are surviving children and £75,000 where there are no children. This is only paid after the first two rights have been satisfied.

- Legal rights are paid after prior rights.

- Any free estate is distributed in terms of s 2 of the Succession (Scotland) Act 1964.

TESTATE SUCCESSION

- There are various types of testamentary writing. These include wills, trust dispositions and settlements, codicils and informal writings.

Formal validity

- Any testamentary writing has to be formally valid. If it is not then the estate will fall into intestacy.

- Wills executed prior to 1 August 1995 had to be either probative or privileged writings.

- Wills executed on or after 1 August 1995 have to conform to the provisions of the Requirements of Writing (Scotland) Act 1995.

- Rules for the execution of wills by persons who are blind or unable to write are contained in s 9(3) of the Requirements of Writing (Scotland) Act 1995.

Essential validity

- Essential validity concerns the capability of the testator to make a will. This may be because the testator lacks capacity in some way or is unfairly influenced through the pressure of others.

- A person can lack capacity to make a will because of mental illness or because he is too young.

- The essential validity of a will may also be challenged where the testator has been subject to undue influence from a person who is in a position of trust.

- Where the testator is easily influenced and somebody takes advantage of this for their own benefit, the will can be challenged. This is known as facility and circumvention.

Revocation of a will

- A will can be revoked or altered at any time up until the death of the testator. The only exception is where there is a contractual obligation.
- A will may be revoked expressly in writing or impliedly by the making of a subsequent will.
- The will may be altered at any time, although there must be evidence of intention to do so.
- A will may be physically destroyed. The destruction must be intentional.
- Where a will cannot be found after the testator's death, there is a presumption that it was destroyed intentionally if it had been in the possession of the testator.
- A will may be revoked by the *conditio si testator sine liberis decesserit*.

Interpretation of wills

- The general rule is that extrinsic evidence is not admissible in the interpretation of a will. It must be interpreted from the words actually used.
- Extrinsic evidence can be admitted in certain limited circumstances, such as identifying the subject of a bequest.

Legacies

- There are several types of legacies. The main categories are special legacies; demonstrative legacies; general legacies; and residual legacies.
- The main purpose of the classification of legacies is to regulate the order in which they abate.
- Abatement of legacies arises where there are insufficient funds to pay all of them.
- Legacies are subject to ademption or cancellation where the legacy does not form part of the testator's estate.
- A legacy can be made subject to a condition which must be fulfilled before it is paid, unless the condition is immoral, illegal or impossible to perform.
- A legacy may be rendered invalid if it serves no purpose or is against public policy.
- A destination over is where a testator provides for a substitute legatee in the event of the prior death of the original one.

- Where a legacy is left to more than one person then the principle of accretion will apply in the event of the death of one of the beneficiaries if the legacy is a joint one. The legacy will then pass to the other joint beneficiaries.

- Where the testator uses words of severance then accretion will not take place.

- Legacies to classes of persons such as "nephews" are always joint and accretion will apply.

ESSENTIAL CASES

7.136

Smith, Petitioner (1979): this is an example of the very strict application of the forfeiture rule under the common law. A woman was convicted of the culpable homicide of her husband. In view of the compelling mitigating circumstances involved in the killing, she only received a 2-year suspended sentence. Despite this, she was barred from inheriting her late husband's estate.

Hog v *Hog* (1791): this concerned the effect of the discharge of legal rights prior to the death of the deceased. The testator was survived by six children, five of whom had discharged their claim to the legitim fund prior to the death of their father. The wife of the testator had also predeceased him. The question was whether the remaining child was entitled to half of the moveable estate and thus entitled to claim the shares of all the other children. It was held that where a *lifetime* discharge is made by a child, then that child's share of the legitim fund goes or accresces to any other child or children claiming legal rights. The child who had not renounced the claim to legitim was therefore entitled to the other children's shares. Note, however, that where a child discharges his legal rights after death, any other children claiming legal rights are not entitled to claim that share.

Smith v *Smith's Trs* (1972): this involved a challenge to a will based on its essential validity. The question for the court was whether or not the testator had the mental capacity to make a will. The testator suffered from depression and this involved the delusion that his dead wife had returned to him. The court held that this did not affect the ability of the testator to make a valid will.

Horne v *Whyte* (2005): this is another case involving essential validity. An aged retired colonel had become reliant on his housekeeper. As a result of improper pressure by the housekeeper, the colonel added a codicil to his will, bequeathing the housekeeper £50,000. The codicil was held to be invalid on the grounds of facility and circumvention.

Paterson v *Paterson* (1893): the general rule with regard to the revocation of a will is that the testator can revoke his will at any time up until his death, unless he is contractually obliged not to do so. In this case, a son made various payments to his mother and entered into an agreement that in return for the payments she would bequeath him her whole estate. Having made a will in his favour, she subsequently revoked that will and disposed of the estate to another party. The second will was reduced on the ground that the mother was contractually bound to leave her estate to her son.

Clark's Trustees v *Clark's Executors* (1925): this illustrates the point that even although a testator may revoke all previous wills, such a clause may not revoke a separate bequest made in a different document. The testator had bequeathed his stamp collection in a letter to a friend. Two years later, he made a will bequeathing his whole estate to another party. The revocation clause in this will only referred to other wills and the court held that this did not revoke other testamentary writings such as the letter to his friend. It was also held that the fact that the letter had been delivered did not make the bequest irrevocable.

Thomson's Trs v *Bowhill Baptist Church* (1956): the destruction of a will is one way of revoking it, as long as it can be shown that this was intentional. However, the destruction of the will is not always necessary. In this case the testatrix had cut out certain clauses in a copy of her will and explained her reasons for doing this on the copy. This was held to be sufficient proof of intention and the clauses were revoked.

McCaig v *Glasgow University* (1907): where a testator abuses his power in disposing of his estate, the courts may step in to prevent the abuse. In this case the testator directed his trustees to erect towers and statues of himself and his family on his estate, for the purpose of encouraging Scottish artists. This provision was held to be invalid on the basis that his sister had been disinherited without any benefit being conferred on anybody else.

8 CONSTITUTIONAL LAW

Every civilised country in the world has a constitution, a set of rules which govern **8.1** the structure and functions of government and the relationships between the State and its citizens. Constitutional law is concerned with the study of these rules. In the case of most countries, the constitution takes the form of a written document which contains the most important rules. Such constitutions tend to have a higher status than ordinary laws and are usually more difficult to amend than ordinary laws. A law which contravenes the constitution can be declared invalid. The constitution of the United Kingdom, however, is very unusual in that it is not contained in a single document, easily accessible to the citizens of this country.

Scotland is not a separate state, but it has its own legal system and, since 1999, it has **8.2** had its own Parliament. Constitutional law in Scotland differs in some respects from that of the UK as a whole and is dealt with in a separate section.

WHERE TO FIND CONSTITUTIONAL LAW

ACTS OF PARLIAMENT

There are several sources of constitutional law in the UK. The first of these is *Acts of* **8.3** *Parliament* or *statute law*. Acts which are of constitutional significance have no special status and are passed in the normal way. Examples of constitutional statutes include the Acts of Union 1706 and 1707 which abolished the separate Parliaments of England and Scotland and created the Parliament of Great Britain. More modern examples include the Scotland Act 1998, which re-established a Scottish Parliament, and the Human Rights Act 1998 which enshrines our citizens' right in law.

COMMON LAW OR CASE LAW

The second source is *common law* or *case law*. This is law which is made by the judges, **8.4** either by filling gaps in the law where no statute exists, or by interpreting the words of a statute where the meaning is not entirely clear.

An example of the former is the case of *Burmah Oil Co v Lord Advocate*.[1] The Burmah **8.5** Oil Company's oil installations in Singapore had been destroyed in 1942 by the British forces, to prevent them falling into the hands of the Japanese. When the war was over, the company sued for compensation which the Government did not want to pay. The judges decided that the company had a right at common law to compensation. (This

---

[1] 1964 SC (HL) 117.

case illustrates the sovereignty of Parliament – see below – as Parliament passed the War Damage Act 1965 which *retrospectively* removed the right to compensation where property had been damaged in such cases.) An example of the interpretation of statute law is *Fox* v *Stirk*[2] which involved the meaning of "resident" in the Representation of the People Act 1969. Fox was a student who wanted to be able to vote in the constituency where his hall of residence was situated, rather than in the one where his family home was. The court agreed that the intention of Parliament in passing the Act was to include students as "residents" at their university addresses.

THE ROYAL PREROGATIVE

8.6 Special mention should be made here of the *Royal Prerogative* which is derived from the common law. It has been described as "the residue of discretionary power which at any given time is legally left in the hands of the Crown". It dates back to the time when the monarch held absolute power and could do whatever he wished. Nowadays, however, "the Crown" normally means the Government Ministers rather than the Queen, although the Queen still exercises some prerogative powers, such as choosing the Prime Minister and dissolving Parliament. Examples of Ministers' use of prerogative power include declaring war, making treaties and pardoning convicted criminals. The destruction of the Burmah Oil Company's installations described above was carried out under prerogative powers.

EUROPEAN COMMUNITY LAW

8.7 Since the UK joined the European Community in 1973, after the passing of the European Communities Act 1972, European Community law has become a source of UK constitutional law. EC law includes Treaties, Regulations, Directives and Decisions. As long as the UK remains a member of the EC, EC law has primacy. This means that where a UK law is in conflict with EC law, EC law prevails.

CONVENTIONS

8.8 Conventions are rules of political behaviour which are regarded as binding by those who administer the constitution. They are, however, "non-legal" rules, as the courts will not enforce them although they recognise their existence. They are not written down in any formal sense but evolve over a period of time. They are obeyed by those involved out of political self-interest, because, of the political repercussions and damaging publicity which would result from a breach.

8.9 An example of a convention is that the Queen will not refuse to grant Royal Assent to a Bill, although in law she has the power to do so. Another convention is that a Government which loses a vote of confidence in the House of Commons is expected to resign and ask the Queen for a General Election to be held.

8.10 The Cabinet and the office of Prime Minister are based on convention, as they were not established by Act of Parliament but evolved over the centuries.

---

[2] [1970] 2 QB 463.

THE LAW AND CUSTOM OF PARLIAMENT

Parliament has the right to regulate its own procedures and a body of law and custom   **8.11**
has grown up over the centuries of Parliament's existence. Its rules are contained in
its Standing Orders, in various resolutions passed by either the House of Commons
or the House of Lords and in rulings by the Speaker who presides over the House of
Commons.

AUTHORITATIVE WRITINGS

Where there is no relevant statute or case law, the judges may resort to authoritative   **8.12**
writings, books and articles by leading constitutional lawyers, historians or political
scientists. Examples of these are the works of Walter Bagehot and A v Dicey, two
19th-century constitutional lawyers both of whom are mentioned below. These are, of
course, not legally binding, as they are not law.

CHARACTERISTICS OF THE UK CONSTITUTION

Since there is no single document called "the constitution", the UK constitution   **8.13**
is sometimes described as "unwritten". However, this is inaccurate. Much of the
constitution is indeed found in written documents and thus it is better to describe the
constitution as *"uncodified"*.

    The UK constitution is also very *flexible* in that Parliament can change any law by a   **8.14**
simple majority vote.

    All law-making power stems from the Parliament of the UK and thus the UK   **8.15**
constitution is described as *unitary*, as opposed to federal, where law-making power is
divided between central government and state or provincial governments. Although
the UK Parliament has devolved some law-making powers to the Scottish Parliament,
the Northern Ireland Assembly and the Welsh Assembly, the doctrine of the sovereignty
of Parliament (see below) means that a subsequent UK Parliament could take these
powers back. This is not the case in federal states where the powers of the states or
provinces are protected by the written constitution.

    In the UK, the Head of State is the Queen, not an elected president, and thus the   **8.16**
constitution is *"monarchical"* as opposed to "republican" or "presidential".

THE PRINCIPAL ORGANS OF GOVERNMENT

The principal organs of government in any state are the legislature, the executive and   **8.17**
the judiciary.

    For the UK, the *legislature* is the body which settles policy and makes law and   **8.18**
consists of the Members of Parliament, ie Members of the House of Commons and
Members of the House of Lords.

    The *executive* is the body which directs general policy and executes the laws made   **8.19**
by the legislature. However, if the executive is strong and the legislature weak, the
executive has a powerful role in making policy which the legislature passes into law. In
the UK the executive consists of the Prime Minister, the Cabinet, the other Government

Ministers and civil servants. Included in the executive are police officers, members of the armed forces and members of public bodies established by the Government, such as quangos, executive agencies and service authorities.

8.20   The *judiciary* is the body of professional judges whose function is to settle disputes by interpreting and applying the law.

8.21   The Queen is Head of State and technically is head of each of the three organs of government.

DOCTRINES OF THE CONSTITUTION

THE RULE OF LAW

8.22   The Rule of Law is a rather nebulous concept which does not have any readily definable content. Basically, it means that matters should be regulated not by force but by law and by certain fundamental principles such as justice, morality, fairness and due process. The powers of the state are conferred by law and do not include a general power to act outside the law in the interest of the state. The Government is not above the law.

8.23   The classic case on the Rule of Law is the case of *Entick* v *Carrington*.[3] In this case, the court ruled that a general warrant executed by a Secretary of State for entry into Entick's house and the seizure of his books and private papers was contrary to law and amounted to trespass. The court did not accept the Secretary of State's argument that the power of seizure was essential to government.

THE SEPARATION OF POWERS

8.24   In its pure form, the doctrine of the Separation of Powers means that the powers of the organs of government, legislative, executive and judicial, should be exercised by separate institutions. There should be no overlap of membership or function and one organ should not seek to dominate the others. The reason for this is to avoid the concentration of power in too few hands, as this could lead to tyranny.

8.25   However, the doctrine is not strictly observed in the UK. For example, in terms of membership overlap, the Prime Minister and Ministers who are key members of the executive are also members of the legislature, either in the House of Commons or in the House of Lords. Also, although the two Houses of Parliament together form the supreme law-making body in the UK, the judges make law when they decide cases, either by interpreting Acts of Parliament or by "filling the gaps" where no relevant Act exists. Government Ministers can also make law in the form of statutory instruments.

8.26   However, the separation of the judiciary from the executive and the legislature is fairly strictly observed in the UK and there are a number of rules which aim to ensure their independence. So, for example, members of the judiciary are disqualified by the House of Commons Disqualification Act 1975 from standing for election as members of the House of Commons.

8.27   In addition, they hold office during "good behaviour" and it is extremely difficult to sack a judge. In England, there is a complicated procedure to be followed, involving

---

[3] [1765] 19 State Tr 1029.

both houses of Parliament. This is to protect them from being dismissed for political reasons.

However, the judges who sit in the Appellate Committee in the House of Lords **8.28** (the Law Lords) take part in the law-making business of Parliament. This breaches the doctrine of the Separation of Powers in terms of membership overlap. Another major breach of the doctrine has been the office of Lord Chancellor. He was head of the judiciary in England and Wales, a senior member of the Cabinet and a member of the House of Lords. Thus he was a member of each of the three organs of government. This anomaly was rectified by the Constitutional Reform Act 2005. This Act removes the Law Lords from the House of Lords and appoints them to a new Supreme Court, separate from the Houses of Parliament. This will come into effect, probably in 2009. The role of the Lord Chancellor in relation to the judiciary is modified and a new office of Secretary of State for Constitutional Affairs has been established.

THE SOVEREIGNTY OF THE UK PARLIAMENT

A very important doctrine of the constitution and one which differentiates the UK **8.29** from most other states is the sovereignty or supremacy of Parliament. This means that Parliament has no *legal* restrictions on what laws it can pass. In other states the written constitution sets legal limits on what laws the legislature can pass and if the legislature oversteps these limits, a court can declare its laws to be invalid.

The most famous definition of parliamentary sovereignty is that of a 19th-century **8.30** constitutional lawyer called A v Dicey. In his view:

(1) Parliament is the supreme law-making body and can make or unmake laws on any subject;

(2) no Parliament can be bound by the laws passed by its predecessors, nor can any Parliament bind its successors as to the form or content of future legislation;

(3) no person or body, including a court of law, can successfully challenge the validity of an Act of Parliament.

Examples of point (1) above include: **8.31**

- the Parliament Acts of 1911 and 1949 which reduced the powers of the House of Lords over legislative proposals of the House of Commons from veto to delay;

- the War Damage Act 1965 which had *retrospective* effect and overturned the award of compensation made by a court to the Burmah Oil Company whose property had been destroyed by British forces to prevent it falling into enemy hands during the Second World War;

- the Abdication Act 1936 which removed King Edward VIII from the throne and changed the line of succession to that of his brother who became King George VI, the father of Queen Elizabeth II.

However, there are *practical* and *political limits* on what laws Parliament can pass. For example, it is inconceivable that Parliament would pass a law which stated that all blue-eyed babies were to be strangled at birth. In addition, Parliament can make effective laws only for the territory it controls (although it can make a law whereby a person committing a particular offence abroad may be tried in the UK courts).

8.32   In relation to point (2), if provisions of a later Act of Parliament contradict provisions of an earlier Act, the later Act prevails and is taken to repeal the contradictory provisions in the earlier Act. In the case of *Ellen Street Estates Ltd* v *Minister of Health*,[4] the court decided that it was impossible for Parliament to enact in the Housing Act 1919 that its provisions in relation to compensation for property which had been compulsorily purchased could prevail over contradictory provisions in the Housing Act 1925. This is called the doctrine of implied repeal.

8.33   However, again, there are practical and political limits to this rule. The UK Parliament has passed many Acts granting independence to former colonies. No one expects Parliament to pass Acts to take back the independence, on the basis that, once freedom is conferred, it cannot be revoked.

8.34   However, occasionally, Parliament will insert a section into an Act which seems to be intended to bind a future Parliament. For example, s 1 of the Northern Ireland Act 1998 states that Northern Ireland shall not cease to be part of the UK without the consent of the people of Northern Ireland voting in a poll held for that purpose. Because of the sovereignty of Parliament, this cannot prevent a future Parliament from passing an Act without holding such a poll. However, it might be political suicide to do so.

8.35   An example of point (3) above is the case of *British Railways Board* v *Pickin*.[5] Pickin alleged that Parliament had been misled when considering a Private Bill promoted by British Railways Board and had used the wrong procedure in passing the Act. The court rejected Pickin's challenge, stating that if errors in procedure had occurred, it was for Parliament alone to correct them. The court could not question the validity of any Act.

Parliamentary sovereignty and European Community law

8.36 The UK joined the European Community (EC) in 1973, after passing the European Communities Act 1972. The laws of the EC are binding on all the Member States. This means that EC law prevails over inconsistent UK law. There is no problem in the case of Acts inconsistent with EC law passed before 1973, as the doctrine of implied repeal, discussed above, means that the European Communities Act 1972 repeals the earlier inconsistent Acts.

8.37   The difficulty occurs when an Act passed *after* the UK joined the EC is inconsistent with EC law. The UK courts will try to interpret the Act as widely as possible, to avoid inconsistency. If this cannot be achieved, EC law must be applied, rather than the UK Act. This principle was made clear by the House of Lords in the case of *R* v *Secretary of State for Transport, ex p Factortame*[6] when it set aside provisions of the Merchant Shipping Act 1995 as being incompatible with the EC Common Fisheries Policy.

8.38   The only way to reconcile this with the doctrine of parliamentary sovereignty is to say that the limitation on legal sovereignty has been undertaken voluntarily by the UK and remains only so long as the UK decides to remain a member of the EC.

---

[4] [1934] 1 KB 590.
[5] [1974] AC 765.
[6] [1991] AC 603.

THE UNITED KINGDOM PARLIAMENT

Parliament consists of three elements: 8.39

- the monarch;
- the House of Lords (an unelected body);
- the House of Commons (an elected body).

THE MONARCH

The Queen plays a formal role in the work of Parliament. By convention, she must 8.40
give Royal Assent to Bills which have been passed by the House of Commons and the
House of Lords to enable them to become Acts and therefore law. She also summons
Parliament after each General Election and dissolves it at the end of its term of up
to 5 years. Each term is divided into sessions lasting approximately a year and the
Queen opens each session, normally in November, by making a formal speech from
the throne in which she indicates the Government's programme of laws for the
forthcoming session. The speech is written for her by Government Ministers.

THE HOUSE OF LORDS

Until 1999, the majority of members were hereditary peers (about 750) who had 8.41
inherited their peerages from (normally) their fathers. Under the House of Lords Act
1999, most of the hereditary peers lost the right to sit in the House of Lords.

The composition of the House of Lords now is: 8.42

- 92 hereditary peers;
- around 600 life peers appointed by the Queen on the advice of the Prime Minister
  under the Life Peerages Act 1958;
- 26 spiritual peers who are the senior archbishops and bishops of the Church of
  England;
- 12 Law Lords. These are senior judges and they will lose the right to sit in the
  House of Lords when the new Supreme Court comes into being in 2009.

Powers and functions of the House of Lords

Members of the House of Lords have an important role to play in the law-making 8.43
process. Normally, an Act of Parliament must be passed by both the House of Lords
and the House of Commons and receive the Royal Assent.

Until 1911, the law-making powers of the Lords were equal to those of the Commons, 8.44
although the Lords accepted that they should not initiate or amend Bills relating to
finance, as that was the prerogative of the elected House. However, they claimed the
power to *reject* financial legislation. Attempts to reject the then Government's Finance
Bill led to the Lords' power of veto being reduced to one of delay for a period of 2 years
under the Parliament Act 1911. This was reduced to a period of 1 year by the Parliament
Act of 1949. This means that certain Acts of Parliament can be passed without the
consent of the House of Lords. A recent example is the Hunting Act 2004. However, the
consent of the Lords is still required for a Bill to prolong the length of a parliamentary

term beyond 5 years, for Private Bills, subordinate legislation and for Bills which start in the House of Lords.

8.45   The House of Lords also has the following functions:

- the provision of a forum for debate in matters of public interest;
- the revision of Bills sent up by the House of Commons;
- the initiation of some Bills;
- the consideration of subordinate legislation;
- scrutiny of the work of the executive;
- Select Committee work;
- the final court of appeal for all civil cases in the UK and for criminal cases in England and Wales. This function will transfer to the new Supreme Court in 2009.

REFORM OF THE HOUSE OF LORDS

8.46   The Government has recently published a White Paper entitled *The House of Lords: Reform* (2007). In the Government's view, it is difficult in a modern democracy to justify a second chamber where there is no elected element. The White Paper therefore proposes that a reformed House should be a hybrid House, ie partially appointed and elected. At the time of writing, a free vote in the House of Commons has led to the proposal that the reformed Upper Chamber should be 80 per cent elected. It is likely that a draft Bill will be introduced to Parliament during the course of 2007.

THE HOUSE OF COMMONS

8.47   The House of Commons consists of 646 men and women known as Members of Parliament or MPs. They are elected by the system known as "first past the post" under which the person who secures the largest number of votes is the winner, even if the majority of the voters have voted for other candidates. General Elections are normally held every 4 or 5 years. The maximum life of a Parliament is 5 years.

The right to vote in a parliamentary election

8.48   People entitled to vote are residents of the UK who are:

- British citizens;
- commonwealth citizens;
- citizens of the Irish Republic;
- 18 years of age or over;
- registered in the register of parliamentary elections.

8.49   People who are not entitled to vote are:

- aliens (generally, foreigners);
- minors (under 18);
- members of the House of Lords;

- prisoners;
- offenders detained in a mental hospital;
- undischarged bankrupts
- persons guilty of certain electoral offences.

Disqualification from membership of the UK Parliament

The following are not entitled to sit as Members of Parliament: **8.50**

- aliens;
- people under 21;
- members of the House of Lords;
- people suffering from a mental illness;
- undischarged bankrupts;
- persons guilty of certain electoral offences;
- people sentenced to a term of imprisonment of more than a year;
- persons guilty of treason;
- members of foreign legislatures outside the Commonwealth (excluding the European Parliament and Ireland);
- holders of certain public office, eg judges, members of the armed forces or the police, civil servants, members of certain public bodies and tribunals.

Functions of the House of Commons

The two main functions of the House of Commons are to pass Acts of Parliament **8.51** and to scrutinise the work of the executive (the Government) and hold Ministers to account.

Passing Acts of Parliament

A proposal for an Act is called a Bill. There are three types of Bill. The most common **8.52** is a *Public Bill* which applies to members of the public generally. Most Public Bills are initiated by the Government but some may be initiated by backbench MPs. The latter are called Private Members' Bills. These should not be confused with *Private Bills* which apply to a particular area or, less commonly, to particular persons and which are normally initiated by local authorities or public bodies. A *Hybrid Bill* is one which affects particular persons but also the public generally. An example of a Hybrid Bill was the Channel Tunnel Bill which applied to certain landowners in the south-east of England, but which also enabled the construction of the Channel Tunnel which is a public route. For the various parliamentary stages of Bills, see para 1.17.

Parliamentary questions

Ministers are expected to answer questions from MPs on a rota basis for about an hour **8.53** every day, from Mondays to Thursdays. Prime Minister's Question Time takes place every Wednesday and lasts for 30 minutes. The questions are put down in advance by backbench MPs.

8.54   The main purpose of Question Time should be to extract information or to press for action. However, questions are also used to embarrass the Government, by airing a sensitive matter, to publicise a national or local issue, or to score a political point. Sometimes a question is "planted" by a Minister with a backbencher of the same party, to enable the Minister to make an announcement. Question Time has become something of a ritual and is not a very effective method of scrutinising the work of the Government.

8.55   MPs may also put down questions for written answer. These are generally more serious attempts to gain information.

Debates

8.56   There are various opportunities for MPs to take part in debates. The general debate at the Second Reading of a Bill has already been mentioned in Chapter 1. In addition, the Opposition parties are allocated certain times for debates on subjects of their own choosing.

8.57   Also, at the end of each parliamentary day, there is a short debate, called an adjournment debate. Backbench MPs who wish to use this opportunity take part in a ballot and choose the subject to be debated.

8.58   There is also a procedure called an Early Day Motion. This is a written motion which may be tabled by any MP, requesting a debate on virtually any subject "at an early day".

8.59   Finally, there are Emergency Debates. Any MP may apply to the Speaker (the Chairman) of the House to raise an urgent matter for debate. One successful example was the debate on the deployment of British soldiers in Afghanistan.

Select Committees

8.60   Some Select Committees relate to the running of the House of Commons or to the procedures employed. Others are departmental Select Committees whose task is to investigate and report on the working of a government department and their associated public bodies and agencies. These Select Committees offer the best opportunity for MPs to scrutinise the work of the Government.

8.61   The Committees have the power to send for persons, papers and records, to sit despite the House being adjourned, to meet in different places and to appoint specialist advisers.

8.62   There are too many Select Committees to list here, however, the current list can be accessed via the House of Commons website.[7] The Select Committees are established for an entire parliamentary term and members can develop considerable expertise in the subject-matter of their committees. Their reports have increased the amount of publicly available information about the workings of government. Members, to some extent, put aside their party-political ties and unite to scrutinise the work of Ministers and civil servants, though if their reports are debated by the full House of Commons, these ties may reassert themselves.

---

[7] http://www.parliament.uk/parliamentary_committees/parliamentary_committees16.cfm

Control of financial matters

Constitutionally, Parliament has control over taxation and expenditure. Taxation and **8.63** expenditure policies originate in the Treasury and the Chancellor of the Exchequer presents his Budget to the House of Commons, usually in the spring each year. Parliament must pass an annual Finance Act following the Budget but changes in the rates of taxes can become effective as soon as the House of Commons passes a resolution to that effect. Expenditure plans require to be approved in an annual Appropriation Act.

Scrutiny of public expenditure is carried out by the Public Accounts Select **8.64** Committee which examines reports of audits carried out by an officer of the House of Commons, the Comptroller and Auditor General, head of the National Audit Office. The Committee is chaired by a member of the Opposition and the members generally act in a non-partisan manner. The reports of this Committee are very influential.

THE GOVERNMENT OF THE UNITED KINGDOM

The Government of the UK consists of the monarch, the Prime Minister, the Cabinet **8.65** and other Ministers of the Crown. The Queen is the titular head of the Government and all Government acts are carried out in her name but her role is largely a formal one.

THE MONARCH

Britain has a constitutional monarchy, a king or queen whose role is constrained by **8.66** rules of the constitution. Succession to the throne is governed by the Act of Settlement 1700. The monarch must be a Protestant; Roman Catholics and those married to Roman Catholics are disqualified. Succession is also governed by the rule of male primogeniture. This means that the first-born male child will succeed in preference to an older daughter. When the monarch dies, succession is automatic. If the monarch is under 18, or becomes too ill to carry out his constitutional duties, a regent must be appointed under the Regency Acts 1937–53. This will normally be the adult who is next in line to the throne.

The monarch may adopt whatever title he wishes. The title adopted by the present **8.67** Queen, Elizabeth II, when she became Queen in 1952 was challenged by some Scots on the ground that she was not the second Queen Elizabeth of Scotland (*MacCormick* v *Lord Advocate*[8]) but the challenge was unsuccessful.

The monarch and certain members of his family are funded from the Civil List, a **8.68** fund provided by Parliament.

According to Walter Bagehot, a 19th-century constitutional lawyer, the monarch **8.69** has the right to be consulted by his Ministers and the right to encourage and to warn them. The Queen is kept fully informed of the business of government and meets the Prime Minister on a regular basis. Since she has been on the throne since 1952, she has accumulated vast experience of political matters but she remains above party politics.

---

[8] [1953] SC 396.

8.70   The monarch is said to have a number of "personal prerogatives" or powers. These are:

- the appointment of a Prime Minister, normally the leader of the party which has won the largest number of seats at a General Election;
- the dissolution of Parliament, on the advice of the Prime Minister;
- the dismissal of Ministers (this has not happened in the UK since 1835);
- giving the Royal Assent to Bills (a formality);
- the conferring of various honours, such as the Order of the Thistle.

The extent to which the monarch exercises his own discretion in these matters (apart from the conferring of certain honours) is a matter for debate.

THE PRIME MINISTER AND THE CABINET

8.71   The office of Prime Minister has developed by convention rather than by Act of Parliament. The Prime Minister is the most powerful member of the Government. He is appointed by the Queen who invites the leader of the political party which wins the largest number of seats at a General Election to form a Government. Although in the past there have been Prime Ministers who were members of the House of Lords, nowadays the Prime Minister must, by convention, be a member of the democratically elected House of Commons.

8.72   The Prime Minister chairs the Cabinet which consists of around 20 of the most senior Ministers. In theory, the Prime Minister is "first among equals" but a strong individual can dominate the Cabinet. The Prime Minister effectively appoints members of the Cabinet and all other Ministers. He can ask them to resign or move them to other posts.

8.73   The Prime Minister controls the machinery of government and decides on the distribution of work between departments.

8.74   Members of the Cabinet are drawn mainly from the House of Commons but some come from the House of Lords. Each member holds a major government post. By convention, the Chancellor of the Exchequer, the Home Secretary, the Foreign Secretary and the Defence Secretary are always included in membership.

8.75   The main functions of the Cabinet are the determination of government policy, the general scope of legislation to be enacted by Parliament, control of the executive and the co-ordination of the activities of government departments.

Ministerial responsibility

8.76   The term "ministerial responsibility" has two aspects – individual responsibility and collective responsibility. "Responsible" here means answerable to Parliament. Individual responsibility means that a Minister is responsible for the acts and omissions of his department. So a Minister is required to come before the House of Parliament of which he is a member to answer questions and explain the actions taken within his department. The departments of modern government are huge and it is impossible for any Minister personally to oversee the work of every civil servant in the department. Even so, Ministers should not attempt to put the blame for any act or omission on to a civil servant unless the civil servant has acted contrary to the Minister's wishes.

The acceptance of responsibility by a Minister does not mean that he must inevitably resign over a failure in his department. Resignation will depend on how the Minister is viewed by the Prime Minister and by his colleagues in Parliament.

Collective responsibility means that Ministers, whether members of the Cabinet 8.77 or not, are expected to support the policies of the Government, at least in public. If a Minister cannot publicly support a particular policy, he is expected to resign. Thus, expressions of differing opinions within the Cabinet should be kept private. However, leaks about controversial issues happen frequently and nowadays there is pressure for the workings of government to be made more open.

THE SCOTTISH PARLIAMENT

BACKGROUND

Prior to 1707, Scotland was a separate state from England and had its own Parliament. 8.78 For various reasons, mainly economic, the Parliaments of England and Scotland were united into the Parliament of Great Britain by the Acts of Union of 1706 and 1707. The union was never very popular with the Scottish people and during the 19th and 20th centuries demand grew for some form of Scottish Home Rule.

A Scottish Constitutional Convention was formed in 1989 which published various 8.79 documents culminating in 1995 in *Scotland's Parliament: Scotland's Right* which advocated a Scottish Parliament with legislative powers over a wide range of domestic issues.

The Labour and Liberal Democrat Parties both strongly supported the work of 8.80 the Scottish Constitutional Convention and when the Labour Party won the General Election in May 1997, the new Government announced its plans to establish a Scottish Parliament with legislative and limited tax-raising powers. These plans were endorsed by the Scottish people in a referendum held in September 1997 and the UK Parliament passed the Scotland Act in 1998.

The form of government which the Scotland Act established is known as legislative 8.81 devolution. This means that the UK Parliament has voluntarily transferred some of its law-making powers to the Scottish Parliament without relinquishing its own sovereignty.

ELECTING THE SCOTTISH PARLIAMENT

There are 129 Members of the Scottish Parliament, known as MSPs. They are elected 8.82 by the form of proportional representation known as the Additional Member System. This combines the traditional "first past the post" system, involving single-member constituencies, with an additional element which tops up political parties' representation by allocating regional seats on the basis of a second vote cast not for an individual but for a political party. It is also possible for individuals without any political affiliation to stand as candidates. At each General Election, 73 constituency members and 56 regional MSPs are elected, the latter divided equally among eight regions. The way the regional list works enables representatives of the smaller political parties, such as the Green Party and the Scottish Socialist Party, to win seats.

The two categories of MSPs have equal status in law. 8.83

8.84   The rules regarding the right to vote in Scottish Parliament elections are similar to those for the UK Parliament, but extended to include members of the House of Lords and to citizens of the European Union who are resident in Scotland.

8.85   The rules regarding membership of the Scottish Parliament are also similar to the rules for the UK Parliament, again extended to members of the House of Lords and to European citizens resident in the UK.

8.86   Unlike the UK Parliament, which has a maximum term of 5 years, the Scottish Parliament has a fixed term of 4 years and ordinary General Elections are held on the first Thursday of May.

THE POWERS OF THE SCOTTISH PARLIAMENT

8.87   In passing the Scotland Act 1998, the UK Parliament voluntarily transferred certain law-making powers to the Scottish Parliament without relinquishing its sovereignty. This means that the Scottish Parliament is not independent and is not free to make law in any area it chooses.

8.88   In any system of government where law-making powers are divided between two levels, the powers of each level must be set out in a written document, to minimise the possibility of one level trespassing into the territory of the other. The UK Parliament chose to adopt the *retaining* model and thus the powers which the UK Parliament retains or reserves to itself are listed in the Scotland Act. These are called "reserved matters". It is therefore to be understood that everything not listed is within the powers of the Scottish Parliament and these are called "devolved matters".

8.89   The UK Parliament retains the power to legislate on devolved matters but a convention has arisen that it will not do so without the consent of the Scottish Parliament.

Reserved matters

8.90   The lists of reserved matters are contained in Sch 5 to the Scotland Act 1998. There are several general reservations. These include:

- succession to the Crown;
- the union of the Kingdoms of Scotland and England;
- the UK Parliament;
- international affairs;
- defence and the armed forces;
- the civil service.

8.91   Specific reservations include:

- taxation (except local taxes) and control of UK public expenditure;
- immigration and nationality;
- aspects of trade and industry;
- electricity, nuclear energy and most aspects of coal and gas;
- some aspects of transport;
- social security;
- regulation of the professions;

- employment rights and duties;
- abortion, embryology, surrogacy, genetics and medicines;
- regulation of TV and radio broadcasting;
- equal opportunities;
- miscellaneous matters, including weapons of mass destruction; regulation of activities in outer space; timescales and time zones.

Devolved matters

Broadly speaking, devolved matters include: **8.92**

- overall responsibility for the NHS in Scotland;
- education and training;
- local government, social work and housing;
- aspects of economic development and transport;
- most aspects of criminal and civil law; the court system; prisons;
- police and fire services;
- protection of animals;
- environmental protection;
- agriculture, forestry and fishing;
- sport and the arts.

In addition to its law-making powers, the Scottish Parliament has the power to increase or decrease the basic rate of income tax paid by Scottish taxpayers by a maximum of 3 pence in the pound. This power has not been used since the Parliament came into being in 1999.

HOW THE SCOTTISH PARLIAMENT WORKS

The Scottish Parliament is given a relatively free hand by the Scotland Act 1998 in **8.93** deciding how it should work. It operates within a comprehensive framework of Standing Orders adopted initially in 1999.

The Parliament normally sits in Edinburgh from Monday afternoon to Friday lunch- **8.94** time. Its recesses take account of the school holidays in Scotland.

The Parliament can meet in plenary session, ie all the MSPs together, or in com- **8.95** mittees. In plenary sessions MSPs have opportunities to debate issues and to question Ministers in much the same way as happens at Westminster.

However, in most of the world's parliaments, much of the detailed work is dealt **8.96** with in committees rather than in plenary session and in the Scottish Parliament the committees play a significant role in proceedings.

Committees

The committees of the Scottish Parliament combine the roles of the Standing and Select **8.97** Committees found in the UK Parliament, with broad remits covering the consideration and scrutiny of both policy and legislation. There are two types of committee: Mandatory Committees and Subject Committees.

8.98   Mandatory Committees must be set up by the Parliament soon after a General Election and they remain in existence for the entire parliamentary session. The Mandatory Committees are:

- Procedures Committee;
- Standards Committee;
- Finance Committee;
- Audit Committee;
- European and External Relations Committee;
- Equal Opportunities Committee;
- Public Petitions Committee; and
- Subordinate Legislation Committee.

Subject Committees are established to deal with a specific subject or group of related subjects. The Subject Committees in existence in 2006 are:

- Communities;
- Education;
- Enterprise and Culture;
- Justice (two committees established because of the workload);
- Environment and Rural Development;
- Health;
- Local Government and Transport.

Each committee has a membership of between five and 15 members, including the convener and vice-convener. Places are allocated to reflect the balance of seats held by the different political parties in the Parliament. Committees may appoint external advisers to assist them in their work. They normally meet in public and although committees may sit anywhere in Scotland, the vast majority of committee meetings are held in the Parliament's headquarters in Edinburgh.

8.99   The Committees have been described as the Parliament's powerhouse. They play a very active role in the Parliament's business, gathering information, scrutinising policy, holding inquiries and scrutinising proposals for legislation. Committees can and have made important changes to Bills and can, themselves, initiate Bills.

The Parliamentary Bureau

8.100   The Parliamentary Bureau consists of the Presiding Officer, who chairs plenary meetings of the Parliament, and a representative of each party with five or more MSPs. Parties with fewer than five MSPs and independent members can combine to form a group for the purpose of appointing a representative to the Bureau. The main function of the Bureau is to recommend the Parliament's business programme. It also recommends the establishment, remit, membership and duration of committees and sub-committees.

THE LAW-MAKING POWERS OF THE SCOTTISH PARLIAMENT

8.101   Section 28 of the Scotland Act 1998 gives the Scottish Parliament its power to make laws. The procedure followed shows some similarities to the procedure used by the UK

Parliament. A proposal for legislation, a Bill, is normally considered by a committee and by the full Parliament. At the end of the process a Bill must receive the Royal Assent and then becomes an Act of the Scottish Parliament (an "asp").

However, there are some important differences. First, the Scottish Parliament has no second chamber, equivalent to the House of Lords, to scrutinise and amend Bills. Second, s 29 of the Scotland Act sets limits on the Scottish Parliament's legislative powers or "legislative competence". **8.102**

The limits are as follows. The Scottish Parliament cannot pass a valid law which would: **8.103**

- form part of the law of any country other than Scotland;
- be incompatible with the European Convention on Human Rights or European Community law;
- relate to reserved matters;
- modify any of the protected enactments set out in Sch 4 to the Scotland Act 1998, such as the Acts of Union of 1706 and 1707;
- remove the Lord Advocate from his position as head of the system of criminal prosecution and investigation of deaths in Scotland.

The provisions of any Bill thus have to be scrutinised very carefully to make sure that they are within the legislative competence of the Scottish Parliament. Consultation with interested parties will normally take place before a Bill is introduced. On introduction, both the Presiding Officer and the MSP who is in charge of the Bill must each provide a written statement that they consider the Bill to be within the Parliament's powers.

Within 4 weeks of the Bill passing through the parliamentary process, the Lord Advocate, the Attorney-General and the Advocate General for Scotland (Law Officers of the Scottish and UK Parliaments), may refer the Bill to the Judicial Committee of the Privy Council to decide whether the Bill is within the legislative competence of the Scottish Parliament. If they do so, the Presiding Officer cannot submit the Bill for Royal Assent until this has been decided. In addition, Secretaries of State in the UK Parliament may make an order prohibiting the Presiding Officer from submitting a Bill for Royal Assent if they think that any provision is outwith the powers of the Scottish Parliament. **8.104**

BILLS IN THE SCOTTISH PARLIAMENT

There are three types of Public Bills, namely Executive Bills; Committee Bills; and Members' Bills. The Scottish Parliament may also pass Private Bills but these are relatively uncommon. For the procedures for passing Bills, see para 1.17. **8.105**

THE SCOTTISH GOVERNMENT

The Government of Scotland is generally known as the Scottish Executive. It consists of the First Minister, Scottish Ministers and the Scottish Law Officers (the Lord Advocate **8.106** and the Solicitor-General). The main rules relating to the appointment of the Scottish Executive are contained in the Scotland Act 1998.

8.107 The First Minister is normally the leader of the party able to command the support of a majority of MSPs. The Additional Member System used to elect the Members of the Scottish Parliament does not usually result in one political party having an overall majority, so a candidate for the post of First Minister must have the support of MSPs of more than one party. The post must be filled within 28 days of a General Election.

8.108 The First Minister nominates a team of Ministers and Junior Ministers from among the MSPs but, unlike at Westminster, the team must be approved by the Parliament before the names are submitted to the Queen for appointment. They may be removed from office by the First Minister and must resign if they lose the confidence of the Parliament. The Ministers, about ten in number, but not the Junior Ministers, are members of the Scottish Cabinet.

RELATIONS BETWEEN THE SCOTTISH AND UK PARLIAMENTS

The Sewel Convention

8.109 As we have seen, the Parliament retains the power to legislate in the areas devolved to the Scottish Parliament. It was always envisaged that there might be occasions when it would be more convenient all round for the UK Parliament to do so. However, the UK Government made it clear from the outset that it expected that a convention would arise that this would only happen with the consent of the Scottish Parliament. The convention is known as the Sewel Convention, after a Government Minister in the House of Lords called Lord Sewel, and the motions put to the Scottish Parliament seeking agreement for the UK Parliament to legislate became known as Sewel Motions. (These have recently been renamed Legislative Consent Motions.) In fact, Sewel Motions have been passed much more frequently than was originally envisaged. This has aroused criticism that the decision-making powers of the Scottish Parliament are being undermined.

Liaison arrangements

8.110 The UK Government and the Scottish Ministers have entered into a memorandum of agreement which sets out how the two should work together at both political and official levels. This agreement is not legally binding and cannot be enforced in the courts. It is a statement of principles, binding in honour only. However, it is of great practical significance. There are also concordats which set out detailed working arrangements between the two administrations. In addition, there are bilateral concordats between the Scottish Executive and the individual UK government departments.

8.111 There is also a Joint Ministerial Committee made up of the Prime Minister, the Scottish and Northern Irish First Ministers, the First Secretary of the Welsh Assembly and the Secretaries of State for Scotland, Northern Ireland and Wales.

The office of the Secretary of State for Scotland

8.112 The office of the Secretary of State for Scotland has a long history, dating back to the time before the Union of the Scottish and English Parliaments in 1707. The government department of the Scottish Office was established in 1885 and was responsible for the administration of government policies in Scotland until the modern Scottish Parliament was elected in 1999. The Secretary of State for Scotland had a seat in the Cabinet.

When the Scottish Parliament assumed its powers in 1999, most of the powers of **8.113** the Secretary of State were transferred to the Scottish Executive and the role of the Secretary of State was diminished. The Scottish Office was renamed the Scotland Office. In 2003, the role of the Secretary of State was altered significantly. Although the post remained, it was added to the responsibilities of another member of the Cabinet who represents a Scottish constituency. In 2003, the Scotland Office was abolished as a separate department and taken under the umbrella of a new Department of Constitutional Affairs headed by its own Secretary of State.

THE SCOTTISH PARLIAMENT AND THE COURTS

As we have seen, the doctrine of the sovereignty of the UK Parliament means that **8.114** no Act of Parliament can be declared invalid by the courts. The Scottish Parliament, however, is a creation of the UK Parliament and is not a sovereign body. This means that its Acts may be successfully challenged in the courts as being *ultra vires* or beyond the powers of the Scottish Parliament. Similarly, actions of the Scottish Executive can be challenged as being beyond the authority granted to the Executive by the Scotland Act 1998.

These challenges are called "devolution issues" and can arise in any court or **8.115** tribunal, in civil or criminal cases. Schedule 6 to the Scotland Act sets out in great detail how such issues are to be handled.

Most of the cases in which devolution issues have been raised so far have been **8.116** criminal cases where it has been alleged that the Lord Advocate has brought a prosecution which is in some way incompatible with the European Convention on Human Rights.

One such case which had significant repercussions is *Starrs v Ruxton*.[9] Starrs was **8.117** being tried before one of the temporary sheriffs appointed by the Lord Advocate on year-long contracts. Article 6(1) of the ECHR guarantees "a fair and public hearing ... before an independent and impartial tribunal established by law". It was successfully argued for Starrs that a temporary sheriff on a short-term contract might not be independent and impartial as he could be influenced in his decision-making by the desire to avoid unpopularity with the Lord Advocate. The decision in this case led to the removal of temporary sheriffs from the Bench in Scotland.

A few cases have involved challenges to the validity of provisions of Acts of the **8.118** Scottish Parliament.

An early case concerned the very first Act passed by the Scottish Parliament. This **8.119** was *Anderson v Scottish Ministers*.[10] After Anderson was convicted of culpable homicide, he was kept under a restriction order in the State Mental Hospital under the Mental Health (Public Safety and Appeals) (Scotland) Act 1999. He argued that s 1 of the Act was incompatible with Art 5 of the ECHR (which concerns the right to liberty) and was therefore outside the legislative competence of the Scottish Parliament. However, the

---

[9] [2000] SLT 42.
[10] [2003] AC 602.

Privy Council, which is the highest court of appeal in devolution issues, held that the Act was not incompatible with Art 5 of the ECHR as it contains exceptions which allow for the detention of people of unsound mind.

8.120   Another case was *Adams* v *Scottish Ministers*.[11] The Act which was being challenged was the Protection of Wild Mammals (Scotland) Act 2002 which made fox hunting with dogs illegal. Adams was a manager of foxhounds. He, along with others who participated in fox hunting, argued that the ban on fox hunting breached Art 8 of the ECHR (respect for private and family life) and Art 11 (right to freedom of peaceful assembly and association with others). If these were breaches then provisions of the Act were outside the legislative competence of the Scottish Parliament and therefore invalid. The court was not convinced of these arguments and held that the Act was valid.

8.121   So far, there has not been a successful challenge to the validity of an Act of the Scottish Parliament.

8.122

ESSENTIAL FACTS

THE UK PARLIAMENT

- The constitution of the UK is to be found in Acts of Parliament; decisions of judges; Royal prerogative powers; European Community law; conventions; the law and custom of Parliament; and authoritative writings.

- The constitution of the UK is uncodified (not found in a single written document); unitary, not federal; flexible, and monarchical.

- The principal organs of government are the legislature, the executive and the judiciary.

- The doctrine of the separation of powers means that the powers of the organs of government, legislative, executive and judicial, should be exercised by separate institutions. However, the doctrine is not strictly observed in the UK except in relation to the independence of the judiciary.

- The sovereignty of Parliament means that the UK Parliament has no legal restrictions on what laws it can pass (except those imposed by membership of the EC).

- No UK Parliament can be bound by the laws passed by its predecessors nor can any UK Parliament bind its successors as to the form or content of future legislation.

- No Act of the UK Parliament can be successfully challenged in the courts.

---

[11] [2004] SC 665.

- Since the UK joined the European Community, EC law prevails over inconsistent UK law but only as long as the UK remains a member of the EC.

- The UK Parliament consists of the monarch; the House of Lords and the House of Commons. The maximum life of a UK Parliament is 5 years.

- An Act of Parliament normally requires the consent of the House of Commons and the House of Lords and the assent of the Queen.

- Most residents of the UK aged 18 years or over are entitled to vote in UK elections and most aged 21 years or over are also entitled to stand for election. Members of the UK Parliament are elected by the system known as "first past the post".

- Important functions of Parliament are the scrutiny of the executive and the control of taxation and expenditure.

- The Government of the UK consists of the monarch, the Prime Minister, the Cabinet and other Ministers of the Crown.

- The Prime Minister is appointed by the Queen and is normally the leader of the party which has won the largest number of seats in a general election. The Prime Minister is the most powerful member of the Government and, by convention, is a member of the House of Commons.

- Ministerial responsibility means that Government Ministers must be answerable to Parliament for the actions of their departments.

THE SCOTTISH PARLIAMENT

- The Scottish Parliament was established in 1999 by the Scotland Act 1998.

- The Scottish Parliament is elected by the form of proportional representation known as the Additional Member System.

- The rules relating to the right to vote and to stand for election to the Scottish Parliament are similar to those for the UK Parliament but include members of the House of Lords and EU citizens resident in Scotland.

- The UK Parliament has devolved certain law-making powers to the Scottish Parliament, but the Scottish Parliament cannot make law in the areas which the UK Parliament has reserved to itself.

- The Scottish Parliament has the power to increase or decrease the basic rate of income tax paid by Scottish taxpayers by a maximum of 3 pence in the pound.

- The role of committees in the Scottish Parliament is more significant than the role of committees in the UK Parliament.

- The main function of the Scottish Parliamentary Bureau is to recommend the Parliament's business programme.

- The Government of Scotland is generally known as the Scottish Executive and consists of the First Minister, Scottish Ministers and the Scottish Law Officers.

- The First Minister is normally the leader of the party able to command the support of a majority of MSPs.

- The Sewell Convention means that the UK Parliament will not make law in devolved areas without the consent of the Scottish Parliament.

- Various liaison arrangements, which are not legally binding, govern relationships between the UK Parliament and the Scottish Parliament.

- The powers of the office of the Secretary of State for Scotland have been diminished since the Scottish Parliament was established.

- The validity of Acts of the Scottish Parliament may be challenged in the courts.

ESSENTIAL CASES

8.123

UK CASES

Burmah Oil Co v *Lord Advocate* (1964): illustration of the sovereignty of Parliament. The War Damage Act 1965 had retrospective effect and overturned the award of compensation made by a court to the Burmah Oil Co whose property had been destroyed by British forces to prevent it falling into enemy hands during the Second World War.

Entick v *Carrington* (1795): classic ruling expounding the rule of law. A general warrant executed by a Secretary of State for entry and seizure of books and private papers was contrary to law and amounted to trespass.

Ellen Street Estates v *Minister of Health* (1934): if provisions of a later Act of Parliament contradict provisions of an earlier Act, the later Act prevails and is taken to repeal the contradictory provisions in the earlier Act.

British Railways Board v *Pickin* (1974): if errors in the procedure of passing a Bill have occurred, it is for Parliament alone to correct them. The court cannot question the validity of any Act of Parliament.

R v *Secretary of State for Transport, ex p Factortame* (1991): in effect confirms the practical limitations placed upon parliamentary sovereignty by EU membership. The European Communities Act 1972 Act allows European legislation to take precedence over that of the UK.

SCOTTISH CASES

Starrs v *Ruxton* (2000): the removal of temporary sheriffs from the Bench in Scotland. Article 6(1) of the ECHR guarantees "a fair and public hearing ... before an independent and impartial tribunal established by law". A temporary sheriff on a short-term contract was not independent or impartial as he could be influenced in his decision-making by the desire to avoid unpopularity with the Lord Advocate.

Anderson v *Scottish Ministers* (2003): an unsuccessful challenge that s 1 of the Mental Health (Public Safety and Appeals) (Scotland) Act 1999 was incompatible with Art 5 of the ECHR (which concerns the right to liberty) and was therefore outside the legislative competence of the Scottish Parliament.

Adams v *Scottish Ministers* (2004): an unsuccessful challenge that the Protection of Wild Mammals (Scotland) Act 2002 breached Art 8 of the ECHR (respect for private and family life) and Art 11 (right to freedom of peaceful assembly and association with others), and was therefore outside the legislative competence of the Scottish Parliament.

9 ADMINISTRATIVE LAW

Administrative law is one of the most interesting areas of constitutional law and one which can potentially affect all of us. So, what is it all about? A definition can make it sound quite dry and boring. For example, "Administrative law is the body of principles and rules governing the functions and powers of all the agencies of government, including government ministers, who are concerned with the application and administration of government policy". In real life, we are all affected by the work of "agencies of government". Most children in Scotland are educated in schools run by local councils; we all drink water provided by Scottish Water; most of us use the National Health Service at some point in our lives. These are just a few of the administrative bodies that we take for granted. **9.1**

But what happens when an administrative body takes a decision or acts (or fails to act) in some way that affects one of us adversely? That is where administrative law comes into play. It can enable individuals who have been aggrieved by the activities of such bodies to seek redress and to enforce duties. Sometimes this will involve going to the Court of Session to seek what is called judicial review but, at other times, another body such as an ombudsman or a tribunal may provide the solution. The purpose of the following chapter is to give the reader an introductory overview of the key areas of administrative law. **9.2**

JUDICIAL REVIEW

A cornerstone of administrative law in Scotland is the inherent common law power of the Court of Session to review or supervise acts or omissions of administrative bodies. This is known as the supervisory jurisdiction of the Court of Session, or "judicial review", and the court has had this power since it was first established in 1532. The supervisory jurisdiction was fully expounded by Lord Shaw in *Moss Empires* v *Assessor for Glasgow*:[1] **9.3**

> "It is within the jurisdiction of the Court of Session to keep inferior judicatories and administrative bodies right, in the sense of compelling them to keep within the limits of their statutory powers ... but it is not within the power or function of the Court of Session itself to do the work set by the legislator to be performed by those administrative bodies or inferior judicatories themselves."

Thus, the Court of Session has the power to ensure that administrative and other bodies act *lawfully*. But since Parliament has entrusted the administrative bodies to carry out **9.4**

---

[1] 1917 SC (HL) 1.

certain functions, the court cannot intervene just because a *wrong* decision has been made, or one that the court would not have made. The judicial review process is confined to whether the administrative body's decision was wrong in *law*, not with the *merits* of the decision, as in *Guthrie v Miller*,[2] where, under a local Police Act, commissioners of police were entrusted with the discretion to provide lighting in public streets. Guthrie claimed in the Court of Session that the commissioners were failing in their duty. The question at issue was whether a lamp-post was necessary at a particular spot. The court refused to become involved in the question, on the ground that this would involve deciding whether lamp-posts should be on every street corner. That was a question of *fact* to be decided by the local authority and there was no question of *law* to be judicially reviewed by the court.

SCOPE OF JUDICIAL REVIEW

9.5   Unlike the same concept in England and Wales, judicial review in Scotland does not favour a strict public/private law approach. Lord Hope in the leading decision of *West v Secretary of State for Scotland* said:[3]

> "The Court of Session has power, in the exercise of its supervisory jurisdiction, to regulate the process by which decisions are taken by any person or body to whom a jurisdiction, power or authority has been delegated or entrusted by statute, agreement or any other instrument ... The competency of the application does not depend upon any distinction between public law and private law, nor is it confined to those cases which English law has accepted as amenable to judicial review, nor is it correct in regard to issues about competency to describe judicial review ... as a public law remedy."

9.6   This is significantly different from the approach taken by the English courts, where the decision on the competency of a review petition is often based upon whether the issue has a sufficient public law element (*O'Reilly v Mackman*).[4] However, in Scotland, review is not confined to the statutory powers of administrative bodies. It is clear from authority that the supervisory jurisdiction may also extend to the actions and omissions of bodies which are clearly "private" in nature, for example, in *McDonald v Burns*[5] where the Church expelled two nuns from a convent, and in *St Johnstone FC v Scottish Football Association*[6] where the SFA fined St Johnstone Football Club. The common characteristic in such cases is not the nature of the body, but the entrusting to it of a decision-making power or duty.

SUBSTANTIVE GROUNDS OF CHALLENGE

9.7   The law relating to the grounds of challenge for judicial review is ever evolving. This is due to the law being based almost wholly upon precedent, with very little legislative input. This has allowed the law to develop in a flexible manner, dealing with each case, based upon its own unique circumstances. The grounds of challenge have been developed by the courts over many years, however, the most modern authoritative statement on the grounds can be found in the decision of *Council of Civil Service Unions v Minister for Civil*

---

[2] (1827) 5 S 711.
[3] 1992 SC 385.
[4] [1983] 2 AC 237.
[5] 1940 SC 376.
[6] 1965 SLT 171

Service.[7] In that case, Lord Diplock set out his famous catalogue of grounds of challenge: "one can conveniently classify under three heads the grounds on which administrative action is subject to control by judicial review. The first ground I would call 'illegality', the second 'irrationality', and the third 'procedural impropriety'."

In creating these categories, Lord Diplock did not intend them to be interpreted rigidly. He stated that they would be subject to future expansion and, indeed, he already spoke at this stage about the introduction of a possible fourth ground of challenge in the European principle of "proportionality".

Illegality

Almost all the powers and duties which public bodies possess are statutory, conferred **9.8** by Act of Parliament or statutory instrument. So the limits of public powers and the extent of public duties are those which statute imposes or grants. Illegality is a central principle of administrative law and can be stated quite simply – a person or body acting under statutory powers can do only those things which statute permits. If a public body exercises its powers without statutory authorisation, then that action will be illegal or *ultra vires* (beyond the powers). The *ultra vires* doctrine is clearly illustrated in *McColl v Strathclyde Regional Council*[8] where the council was held to have acted *ultra vires* in attempting to add fluoride to the public water supply. The statutory powers of the council in this area came from the Water (Scotland) Act 1980 which allowed local authorities to provide a "wholesome" water supply. Since the fluoride was to be added to improve dental health, and not for wholesomeness, the actions were illegal.

There are a number of other aspects of illegality which are different from the **9.9** simple application of *ultra vires*. These include error of law, taking account of irrelevant considerations, and the use of a power for an improper purpose. Readers who seek a detailed account of such aspects of illegality should consult *Scottish Administrative Law Essentials* by McFadzean and McFadden (DUP, 2006).

Irrationality and proportionality

Irrationality, as Lord Diplock expressed in the *Council of Civil Service Unions* case, **9.10** is to be understood as *Wednesbury* unreasonableness. The concept of *Wednesbury* unreasonableness emanates from the celebrated case of *Associated Provincial Picture Houses Ltd v Wednesbury Corporation*[9] which did not purport to create new law, but consolidated some already established points. In *Wednesbury*, the corporation had a statutory power to permit Sunday openings of cinemas "subject to such conditions as the authority thinks fit to impose". Wednesbury gave the plaintiff permission to open, subject to the condition that no children under the age of 15 should be admitted, even if accompanied by an adult. The plaintiff sought a declaration from the court that the condition was *ultra vires*. In his judgment, Lord Greene emphasised two points: that the statute had given local authorities an unlimited power to impose conditions, and that it did not provide an appeal from the authority's decision on any ground. He then went on to consider to what extent the decision might be said to be "unreasonable":

---

[7] [1985] AC 374.
[8] 1983 SC 225.
[9] [1948] 1 KB 223.

"there may be something so absurd that no sensible person could ever dream that it lay within the powers of the authority. Warrington LJ in *Short* v *Poole Corporation* gave the example of the red-haired teacher, dismissed because she had red hair. That is unreasonable in one sense. In another sense it is taking into consideration extraneous matters. It is so unreasonable that it might almost be described as being done in bad faith; and in fact all these things run into one another".

9.11 In *Wednesbury*, it was quite clear that the subject matter dealt with by the condition was a matter a reasonable authority would be justified in considering when deciding what condition to attach to the licence. Indeed, the plaintiff did not argue that the council had taken an irrelevant matter into account, but that the decision was unreasonable, treating that as an independent ground of challenge. Lord Greene said that even where an authority has observed the relevancy rules, a decision may still be unreasonable when the authority has come to a conclusion so unreasonable that no reasonable decision-maker could ever come to it. However, the threshold of unreasonableness necessary to warrant judicial intervention was, and still is to some extent, pitched at an exceptionally high level. Thus, in returning to the facts before him, Lord Greene said that to prove a case of that kind would require something overwhelming and, in the case of *Wednesbury*, the facts did not come anywhere near the threshold level.

9.12   This unusually high threshold reflects the traditional reluctance of the courts to involve themselves in questioning the merits of discretionary decision-making. Indeed, given the constitutional position of the courts, a judge is on dangerous ground in striking down as unreasonable the decision of a statutory authority on a matter given to it for decision by Act of Parliament. However, with the arrival of the Human Rights Act 1998, the concept of unreasonableness has undergone a degree of adjustment. In the *Council of Civil Service Unions* case, Lord Diplock referred to the possible acceptance of proportionality into UK law. At this time, proportionality was well established in the jurisprudence of mainland Europe and although absent as a separate ground of challenge under judicial review in the UK, elements of it could be traced in many decisions (*Roberts* v *Hopwood*;[10] *R* v *Barnsley Metropolitan Borough Council, ex parte Hook*).[11] Thus, the European principle of proportionality has begun to alter the way in which unreasonableness is dealt with by the courts. The introduction of proportionality provides a more rigorous approach to judicial review and involves the court examining the relationship between administrative means and ends. It must examine the level of weight attached by the decision-maker to specific rights and considerations and assess whether the correct balance has been struck. In essence, proportionality is a much less subjective test that that of unreasonableness and attempts to soften the high threshold.

9.13   Proportionality should, however, be viewed with caution since it has not replaced the *Wednesbury* standard of unreasonableness but has merely resulted in an adjustment to the law. The test of proportionality is only engaged in cases where convention and fundamental rights are involved – in all other circumstances, the domestic law remains the same (*R (Association of British Civilian Internees – Far Eastern Region)* v *Secretary of State for Defence*).[12] Thus the concept of proportionality has been incorporated into *Wednesbury* unreasonableness, but for the time being has not replaced it.

---

[10] [1925] AC 578.
[11] [1976] 1 WLR 1052.
[12] [2003] QB 1397.

Procedural impropriety

In its strict sense, this is a different aspect of *ultra vires* and involves situations where **9.14** there has been a failure to follow prescribed procedures. This is known as procedural *ultra vires*. However, in a broader sense, procedural impropriety also incorporates the rules of natural justice, ie the rule against bias, and the right to a fair hearing. When there has been breach of the rules of natural justice then the courts may interfere with a decision based upon procedural impropriety. The scope of this chapter does not allow for a detailed consideration of the rules of natural justice, therefore this section is restricted to an examination of procedural *ultra vires*.

Legislation relating to the activities of public bodies specifies a great number of **9.15** procedural requirements. It covers such things as time limits for the service of notices, rights of appeal, and the giving of reasons for decisions. Where statute lays down statutory requirements, it does not generally specify the consequences that follow from non-compliance, ie it does not generally say whether failure to comply with the legislative procedures invalidates the action or not. Thus, it is almost entirely up to the courts in each case to decide on the issue. However, the courts have shown themselves reluctant to lay down firm rules on this matter and consequently the law has become somewhat fragmented. For example, the fact that a statute uses the word "shall" in relation to certain statutory requirements does not necessarily mean that failure to follow procedure necessarily invalidates the action. Broadly, the courts have to decide whether the requirements are *mandatory* and must be followed, otherwise the action will be invalidated; or *directive*, where failure to follow does not automatically invalidate.

However, this distinction has not been without difficulty and in *London and* **9.16** *Clydeside Estates* v *Aberdeen District Council*,[13] the distinction was held to be too prescriptive by Lord Hailsham who stressed the importance of dealing with each procedural requirement on a case by case basis. Consequently, it is difficult to forecast how the courts will treat a particular requirement, but a few generalisations may be made:

(1) if an administrative requirement imposes some financial burden on a citizen, it is likely that the requirement is mandatory and has to be strictly complied with (*Moss Empires* v *Assessor for Glasgow*);[14]

(2) if a failure in procedure has an adverse effect on a person's property rights, it is likely that the adherence to the procedure is mandatory (*Eldon Garages Ltd* v *Kingston-upon-Hull County Borough Council*);[15]

(3) a failure to comply with a requirement to make an investigation or to carry out a consultation before making a decision that may affect a citizen is likely to invalidate any decision (*Grunwick Processing Laboratories Ltd* v *ACAS*);[16]

(4) where there is a duty to consult, a failure to give those consulted an adequate opportunity to express their views is likely to invalidate a decision (*Lee* v *Secretary of State for Education and Science*);[17] and

---

[13] [1980] 1 WLR 182.
[14] 1917 SC (HL) 1.
[15] [1974] 1 WLR 276.
[16] [1978] AC 655.
[17] (1968) 66 LGR 211.

(5) where a statute gives a right of appeal against a decision, procedures for informing citizens of that right are likely to be mandatory (*London and Clydeside Estates* v *Aberdeen District Council*).[18]

PARLIAMENTARY OMBUDSMEN

CONSTITUTION, APPOINTMENT AND TENURE

9.17   The Parliamentary Commissioner for Administration Act 1967 establishes the office of Parliamentary Commissioner for Administration (PCA), commonly known as the "Westminster Ombudsman". The independence of the PCA from the Executive is protected and the 1967 Act affords a degree of security of tenure. The PCA is appointed by the Crown on the advice of the Prime Minister and holds office during good behaviour, subject to a power of removal on address from both Houses of Parliament. Thus the tenure is similar to that of a High Court judge. The PCA also has a salary fixed by statute and which is chargeable to the Consolidated Fund and carries its own staff subject to Treasury approval as to numbers and conditions of service.

JURISDICTION

9.18   The primary function of the PCA is to investigate complaints by private citizens that they have suffered injustice as a result of maladministration by government departments, agencies, and non-departmental bodies. The full list of bodies subject to the jurisdiction of the PCA is listed in Sch 2 to the 1967 Act and includes all major government departments as well as other non-departmental bodies such as the Arts Council and the Equal Opportunities Commission. As regards those departments subject to investigation, the PCA cannot investigate complaints relating to the exercise of legislative functions, such as the preparation or creation of delegated legislation, although he can investigate complaints into the way in which a scheme set up by way of delegated legislation was actually being administered.

9.19   There are also a number of areas which are outwith the Ombudsman's jurisdiction. These can be found in Sch 3 to the 1967 Act and include, *inter alia*, matters certified by a Secretary of State to affect relations between the UK Government and any other Government or international organisation; the commencement of civil or criminal proceedings before any court of law in the UK; action taken in matters relating to contractual or other commercial transactions of Government; and action taken in respect of any personnel matters. The Act also states that the PCA may not investigate a matter where the citizen generally has a right of redress before any tribunal or court.

9.20   As mentioned above, the Ombudsman can only investigate instances of maladministration causing injustice. However, the term "maladministration" is not defined anywhere within the 1967 Act. This has often been criticised by observers of the system. However, this was a deliberate act of the legislature and has allowed the concept to develop unrestricted on a case-by-case basis. In the Second Reading

---

[18] [1980] 1 WLR 182.

debate on the Bill, Richard Crossman MP famously catalogued possible examples of maladministration as bias, neglect, inattention, delay, incompetence, ineptitude, perversity, turpitude and arbitrariness. This definition is wide, however, it does not generally include the merits of a decision and there must always be an element of injustice present.

MAKING A COMPLAINT

The PCA cannot instigate an investigation personally but can only respond to **9.21** complaints received from members of the public. Currently, the PCA is only entitled to investigate complaints made in writing by a Member of the House of Commons at the instance of a member of the public. The public have no direct access to the PCA and must first approach an MP and request that the complaint be forwarded in writing to the Commissioner. The MP may, of course, refuse. This is known as the "MP filter" and is intended to serve three functions. First, it acknowledges the status of the Commissioner as a servant of Parliament; second, it provides the MP with an opportunity to deal with the complaint as they see fit; and finally, it allows inappropriate and vexatious complaints to be rejected before reaching the PCA, thus reducing workload.

INVESTIGATIONS

If a complaint does fall within the jurisdiction of the Commissioner then an investigation **9.22** may be conducted. At this primary stage, the PCA should try to promote an amicable settlement between the individual and the department or body concerned. However, if this is not possible then an investigation will proceed in accordance with the 1967 Act. All investigations are conducted in private, and the department or body complained of must be given an opportunity to comment on any allegations contained in the complaint. The PCA has powers similar to those of a High Court judge for securing the presence of witnesses and the production of documents, and Crown privilege or public interest immunity cannot be used to exempt information from investigation by the Commissioner.

The PCA is protected in the conduct investigations by the laws relating to contempt **9.23** of court and so any wilful obstruction of an investigation may be punished as if it were a contempt. Complainants and witnesses who have spent time in assisting an investigation are entitled to claim reasonable expenses.

REPORTS

On completing an investigation, the PCA must report the findings to the MP who **9.24** originally referred the complaint, and to the department or body against whom the complaint was made. If the Commissioner finds that injustice was caused by maladministration and this has not been rectified then he may lay a special report before both Houses of Parliament. The Commissioner may also make other special reports as are necessary and must make an annual report to Parliament. The reports of the Commissioner and certain other information relating to investigations are absolutely privileged in the law of defamation.

ENFORCEMENT

9.25 The PCA cannot have any recommendations or reports enforced by law. The Commissioner has no executive power and cannot alter decisions made or order payment of compensation. If, after conducting an investigation, the Commissioner considers that an injustice has not or will not be remedied then he may lay before each House of Parliament a special report on the case, recommending remedial action. That is, however, the extent of the PCA's powers. The issue must then be left to the doctrine of ministerial responsibility, the assumption being that pressure will be put upon the Minister concerned to take remedial action. This may not seem a particularly strong method of enforcement, however, in reality there is strong pressure on the Government to comply with the PCA's findings. Such special powers are often not necessary, since an agreed settlement involving, for example, an apology or compensation, may be reached between the aggrieved individual and the government department concerned.

SCOTTISH PUBLIC SERVICES OMBUDSMAN

INTRODUCTION

9.26 Ombudsman reform within Scotland has been a modern success story. Section 91 of the Scotland Act 1998 placed an obligation upon the Scottish Parliament to create an Ombudsman (or to make alternative arrangements) to deal with any complaints of maladministration in devolved areas. Thus, from July 1999 until 2002, complaints against the Scottish Executive, the Scottish Administration and other public bodies in Scotland were handled by the Westminster Ombudsman in his role as Scottish Parliamentary Commissioner for Administration. This interim period allowed the Scottish Parliament to hold a series of consultations in order to canvass opinion as to the best mechanism for handling complaints within Scotland.

9.27 The result of this consultation was the Scottish Public Services Ombudsman Act 2002 which has established a modern collegiate approach to complaint handling in Scotland. Under the 2002 Act, the various Scottish public-sector Ombudsmen have been amalgamated into one centralised body, allowing for ease of use and simplicity. Although the strengths of the separate Ombudsmen were widely recognised, the disparity between each office was frequently confusing for members of the public. The new "one-stop-shop" approach allows the Ombudsman system to become more co-ordinated and centralised.

CONSTITUTION, APPOINTMENT AND TENURE

9.28 Under the 2002 Act, the new Scottish Ombudsman has assumed the jurisdiction of the transitional post held by the PCA, although the PCA may still investigate maladministration within reserved areas of government. The Scottish Ombudsman has also assumed the jurisdiction of other pre-existing ombudsmen in Scotland, namely the Commissioner for Local Administration in Scotland, the Health Service Commissioner for Scotland, the Housing Association Ombudsman for Scotland, the

External Adjudicators for Scottish Enterprise and Highlands and Islands Enterprise, and the Mental Welfare Commission.

The Scottish Ombudsman is appointed by the Queen on the nomination of the **9.29** Scottish Parliament, and is assisted by three Deputy Ombudsmen who are similarly appointed. The Deputy Ombudsmen are intended to reflect the expertise held by former office holders and to this end the current deputies are drawn from the fields of health, housing and local government.

The Ombudsman and any Deputy Ombudsman may hold office for a period not **9.30** exceeding 5 years, subject to a power of removal in pursuance of a resolution of the Scottish Parliament. Office holders are eligible for reappointment but may not serve a third consecutive term unless through special circumstances it is in the public interest for them to do so. In any event, any office holder who attains the age of 65 must vacate office on 31 December of that year.

The Ombudsman and any Deputy Ombudsman have a salary fixed by the **9.31** Parliamentary Corporation and the office also carries its own staff subject to approval as to numbers and conditions of service.

JURISDICTION

The primary role of the Scottish Ombudsman is to investigate complaints from members **9.32** of the public who claim to have suffered injustice or hardship as a consequence of maladministration by the Scottish Government, agencies and other non-departmental bodies. Schedule 2 to the 2002 Act provides a full list of bodies subject to the jurisdiction of the Ombudsman and is split into two Parts. Part 1 contains a list of authorities which cannot be amended and includes members of the Scottish Executive, health service bodies, local authorities, and the police. Part 2 contains a list of Scottish public authorities and cross-border public authorities such as Scottish Enterprise, the Scottish Legal Aid Board and the National Consumer Council. This list may be amended in the future by Order in Council.

With regard to those bodies subject to investigation, there are a number of **9.33** restrictions placed upon the jurisdiction of the Ombudsman. Schedule 4 to the 2002 Act excludes 15 categories of investigation; these include action taken for the prevention of crime, any civil or criminal legal proceedings, action taken which relates to contractual or commercial matters, and any decision made in a judicial capacity. Furthermore, the Ombudsman may not question the merits of discretionary decisions unless there has clearly been maladministration nor may any matter be investigated where the complainant has an alternative remedy available, for example a right of appeal.

As with the PCA, the concept of maladministration has no direct statutory **9.34** definition in order to allow flexibility. But there have been criticisms of the Scottish Ombudsman in that s 5 of the 2002 Act includes alongside maladministration the right to investigate "service failures" and "any action" (where the action is taken by a registered social landlord, or a health or family care provider). Thus, s 5 essentially provides additional grounds of investigation which are exercisable only in very specific circumstances. This is somewhat at odds with the centralised ethos of the 2002 Act and may add unwarranted confusion for users of the system. In response, the Scottish Parliament has defended the disparities, claiming that they are necessary to reflect the procedural nuances of the pre-existing Ombudsmen.

MAKING A COMPLAINT

9.35 An innovation of the 2002 Act can be found in the removal of the "MP filter" concept resulting in the absence of an "MSP filter" for Scotland. Thus, in keeping with the spirit of a collegiate approach, citizens may complain directly to the Scottish Ombudsman. It is also possible to have a complaint lodged on a person's behalf by any authorised person, for example an MSP or a local councillor. As with the PCA, complaints must be made within 12 months of the date on which the citizen first had notice of the issue complained of, subject to a discretionary power to allow late applications in extraordinary circumstances.

9.36   Complaints may be submitted either in writing or electronically. This is a key difference from the procedure followed by the PCA where all complaints must be submitted in writing. Although the vast majority of complaints are generally written, there is a growing sector of the public who prefer to deal with issues via the Internet. As a result, citizens may submit complaints using an electronic submission form available on the Ombudsman's website. The Ombudsman also has a discretionary power to accept oral complaints in extraordinary circumstances.

INVESTIGATIONS

9.37 If a complaint falls within the jurisdiction of the Ombudsman then an investigation may be conducted. The procedure for investigation is very similar to that of the PCA and is in fact modelled closely upon the 1967 Act. Investigations are conducted in private, and the department or body complained of must be given an opportunity to comment on any allegations contained in the complaint. The Ombudsman may compel the production of any information or documents required and has similar powers to that of a Court of Session judge for securing the presence and examination of witnesses. Crown privilege or public interest immunity claims cannot be used in relation to documents subject to investigation by the Ombudsman.

REPORTS

9.38 On completing an investigation, the Ombudsman must report the findings to the complainant, the department, body or person against whom the complaint was made, and the Scottish Ministers. Furthermore, a report must be laid before the Scottish Parliament which must not identify any person other than the department, body or person complained of. If the Ombudsman finds that hardship or injustice has been caused by maladministration and this has not been rectified then a special report may be laid before the Parliament. In addition, the Ombudsman must also present an annual report to the Parliament.

ENFORCEMENT

9.39 As with the PCA, the Scottish Ombudsman cannot have any recommendations or reports enforced by law. The Ombudsman has no executive power and cannot alter decisions made or order payment of compensation. If, after conducting an investigation, the Ombudsman considers that an injustice has not or will not be remedied then a special report on the case is the strongest form of action. Enforcement is left up to ministerial responsibility and the assumption that pressure will be put upon the government to take remedial action. This may not seem like a particularly strong method of enforcement for a modern Ombudsman system. However, the Scottish Executive identified that keeping enforcement powers to a minimum would in fact aid co-operation between bodies and the Scottish Ombudsman, whereas investing draconian powers of intervention would be likely to hinder investigations. To date, the Scottish Executive appears to have been correct and many cases have been settled through apology, compensation or remedial action stemming from the Ombudsman's comments.

TRIBUNALS

INTRODUCTION

From the Second World War onwards, the size and complexity of the Welfare State in the UK have grown tremendously. Consequently, the State has become involved in more areas of everyday life than ever before. This has led to a marked increase in the number of complaints and disputes which arise from the application of rules and regulations by various organs of the State. These disputes could be settled using the existing courts, however, the court system already struggles to cope with ever-increasing litigation in other areas. As a result, Parliament decided to create special bodies, known as "tribunals", for resolving certain categories of dispute between citizens and the State. It also created a number of tribunals with jurisdiction over disputes between citizens, for example in the area of employment law.

9.40

As with many other features of administrative law in the UK, tribunals have emerged in a patchwork fashion, with little real thought being given to their theory or general principles. The essential feature of tribunals is that they are bodies which are distinctly separate from the court structure, and are independent of government departments. Most tribunals are set up by statute and the powers and scope of the tribunal are contained either within the statute or in regulations issued under its authority. They have a limited scope of authority to deal with administrative-type issues, which are often, but not necessarily, disputes between public authorities and citizens. There are many types of tribunal in the UK today and they cover a wide range of disputes including immigration appeals, employment tribunals, disability living allowance tribunals, benefit appeals, and criminal injuries compensation.

9.41

The position of tribunals within the justice system was clarified in 1958 following the Franks Committee (*Report of the Committee on Administrative Tribunals and Inquiries* (1957)) and the recommendations of the Committee were embodied in the Tribunals and Inquiries Act 1958, now consolidated in the Tribunals and Inquiries Act 1992. The Franks Report was instrumental in the development of the modern tribunal system and stated that all tribunals should be open, fair and impartial, meaning that they should be free from government interference, have clear and consistent procedures and should be held publicly, giving clear and reasoned decisions.

9.42

WHY USE TRIBUNALS?

9.43 Obviously, the types of issues dealt with by tribunals could alternatively be decided by a Government Minister or department, or by the courts. However, there are a number of key reasons why tribunals are used:

(1) Tribunals are preferable to a ministerial decision since they are not influenced by policy in the same way that a Minister would be. Tribunals have a body of statutory rules and codes which they must follow and their task is generally to decide whether, in terms of the rules, an individual making a claim is entitled to succeed. In this way, the tribunal system resembles that of the courts in that they are concerned with the application of statutory rules and not policy. The fact that decisions are made by a separate body leads to increased public confidence.

(2) Tribunals are preferable to courts because of their cheapness and speed. Courts are generally slow and expensive and are inappropriate for many types of administrative disputes. The ordinary courts are in essence a "jack-of-all-trades" and have a very wide jurisdiction. For example, Court of Session judges can be dealing with divorce one day and contractual disputes the next. Consequently, it is unrealistic to expect judges, who are in effect general practitioners, to have the necessary expertise and familiarity to deal with the complex issues of tribunals. Many of the statutory schemes which tribunals have to interpret are very complex and decision-makers can become expert only by intensive specialisation.

Thus, tribunals, which only handle cases of one particular type, can easily become expert in specific areas and recruit members who have specialist knowledge. An example of this can be found in the Lands Tribunal for Scotland, which decides questions of compensation for land which is the subject of compulsory purchase orders. In dealing with such issues, difficult legal and valuation questions frequently arise. The chair of the Lands Tribunal must be a lawyer but always sits with at least one other member, who will be an expert valuer or surveyor who can handle any technical questions that arise. The system works so well that no decision of the Lands Tribunal has been overturned by the Court of Session.

(3) If all disputes were dealt with by the courts, there would have to be an enormous increase in the number of judges, since the court system is already overburdened. The Franks Committee suggested that this would inevitably lower the quality of judges and concluded that the system of administrative tribunals had, in this way, positively contributed to the preservation of the ordinary judicial system.

(4) Tribunals are more user-friendly than the courts. The court system is designed by lawyers for use by lawyers and as such is very formal. Ordinary citizens are often intimidated by the adversarial approach of courts and do not feel at ease in them. Rules of procedure and evidence are complex and as a result many feel the need to employ a lawyer to conduct their case. Tribunals, on the other hand, are generally more informal, and do not operate the same rigid

procedural rules. Tribunals are generally inquisitorial in procedure and the informality allows an individual to represent themselves.

(5) Tribunals can be more aware of the social implications of the statutory scheme which they have to operate. Many judges take a strict, literal approach to statutory interpretation, and are as a result reluctant to consider the underlying purpose of the legislation. Tribunal members, on the other hand, may well take a more sympathetic approach.

(6) Tribunals can allow a greater degree of flexibility than the courts. There is often an overwhelming desire for certainty on the part of the courts, as they strive to adhere to the rules of precedent. Although there is much to be said for this, rigid legal rules can often develop. However, tribunals are free from the restrictions of the courts and often take a much more flexible approach. As a result, they have a lesser tendency to lay out hard and fast legal rules.

COUNCIL ON TRIBUNALS

One of the most important recommendations of the Franks Committee was that a **9.44** Council on Tribunals should be established, to act as a supervisory body for the tribunal system. Franks suggested that there should be two separate Councils on Tribunals one for England and Wales and one for Scotland. However, the Government ultimately set up only one, albeit with a separate Scottish Committee. The Council consists of 10–15 members and a salaried chair appointed by the Lord Chancellor and the Lord Advocate. The Scottish Committee has two or three members of the full Council plus three or four non-members of the Council appointed by the Lord Advocate. The Council has a number of key functions:

(1) to keep under review the constitution and workings of the tribunals;
(2) to make recommendations to the appropriate Minister about the appointment of members of tribunals;
(3) to be consulted by the Minister on procedural rules for tribunals;
(4) to be consulted by Ministers prior to a decision to exempt a tribunal from the duty to give reasons; and
(5) to consider and report on such matters as are referred to it by the Lord Chancellor or Scottish Ministers with regard to tribunals.

The Council is merely an advisory and consultative body, with no decision-making **9.45** functions. It has no power to investigate complaints from members of the public and is unable to initiate investigations unless they relate to the constitution and working of tribunals. Council members pay occasional visits to tribunals and observe and report on their operation. Members' reports are confidential and not made open to the tribunals.

The Council is often criticised as being ineffective, but this is almost wholly due **9.46** to underfunding, understaffing and a relatively poor political position. It must be consulted by government departments before procedural rules are made for tribunals, but its advice need not be taken or even referred to.

CONSTITUTION OF TRIBUNALS

MEMBERS

9.47 Traditional tribunals have a panel consisting of three members, namely a legally qualified chair and two "wing" members. The wing members generally consist of an expert and a layperson with relevant experience (eg in mental health or disability). They will tend to be biased towards their own side but bring invaluable knowledge and experience to the tribunal. Many steps have been taken over the years to ensure the independence of tribunal members. Traditionally, tribunals have been set up under the auspices of government departments and so Ministers have regularly been directly involved in the appointment of members. The Franks Committee recommended that this practice should have been replaced whereby the Lord Chancellor (or the Lord Advocate in Scotland) and the Council on Tribunals would directly appoint all members. However, this has not been reflected in subsequent legislation and under the Tribunals and Inquiries Act 1992 both the Lord Chancellor and the relevant Minister may formally appoint members while the Council may only make recommendations.

PROCEDURE

9.48 Prior to the Franks Report, there were striking differences between the procedures followed in different tribunals. There were no generally applicable rules to such things as legal representation, openness of hearings and the giving of reasons. Franks highlighted the need for consistency among tribunals and many of his recommendations can now be seen in the 1992 Act.

Pre-hearing

9.49 With regard to procedure prior to a hearing, Franks insisted that legal advice should be made available under an official scheme. This would allow citizens to know in advance the nature of the case they would have to meet. This is standard practice today, and is covered by individual tribunals' rules. It is not an overly formalised procedure and often involves the citizen receiving a document setting out the main points of the other side's case beforehand.

Procedural rules

9.50 In relation to the procedure used during hearings, the Franks Committee thought it important to preserve informality while at the same time maintaining an orderly procedure. Franks thought procedure was of the utmost importance, and should be clearly laid down in statute or statutory instruments. However, since tribunals are so diverse in their subject-matter, it would not be appropriate to rely on a single procedural code or small number of procedural codes covering all tribunals. As such, tribunals have a discretion in producing their own rules of procedure. They may vary procedures where it seems necessary in the interests of justice but all tribunal rules must be produced in consultation with the Council on Tribunals, which can advise on best practice. Despite the existence of such rules, actual procedure is largely at the discretion of the chair.

Openness

It is a fundamental principle of tribunals that hearings be heard in public, since one of **9.51**
the Franks Committee's fundamental principles was openness. Most hearings today
are held in public, although there are a few exceptions, for example where there are
considerations of national security, where intimate personal or financial details might
be disclosed, or where a medical examination is involved. Openness is a key factor in
achieving public confidence and trust in the impartiality of the system.

Legal representation

Prior to the Franks Committee, it was common for tribunals to have a ban on legal **9.52**
representation. Today, there is now only one important tribunal where the ban exists:
tribunals appointed to investigate complaints against NHS practitioners. This may well
be justified in that it would almost inevitably be the case that a practitioner complained
of would take advantage of the right to legal representation and the prospect of being
subjected to hostile cross-examination by the lawyer might be off-putting for claimants.
There is, however, widespread debate on the question of legal representation. Without it,
procedures are simplified, less technical and cheaper, thus reflecting the user-friendly
values of the tribunal. Conversely, when legal representation is allowed, procedures
become more complex and expensive. This is a pattern which has arisen rapidly in
modern tribunals and has led to the judicialisation of procedures in many tribunals
dealing with complex issues such as employment and immigration.

Legal aid

Legal aid is a closely related issue to the right of legal representation. Under the **9.53**
current law, legal aid is not available for legal representation before tribunals, with
the exception of the Lands Tribunal for Scotland, and the Employment Appeals
Tribunal. Otherwise, a party who qualifies can receive advice under the statutory
scheme ABWOR (Advice By Way of Representation). This normally involves advice
being given before the hearing. However, the legal adviser is entitled to go into the
tribunal and advise a client, as long as he takes no part in the formal proceedings
(otherwise it would be a fraud on the legal aid scheme). The Franks Committee
recommended that legal aid should be ultimately extended to all tribunals, however,
to date, this has not been achieved. The concept of extending legal aid has also been
frequently highlighted by the Council on Tribunals. In 1973, the Lord Chancellor
set up a committee to consider extension to all statutory tribunals but ultimately
rejected the idea.

Yet, the issue of legal aid and representation continues to be important. Research in **9.54**
the former Supplementary Benefit Appeal Tribunals showed a 30 per cent success rate
for represented claimants, as opposed to 6 per cent for unrepresented ones. Similar
statistics can be found before other tribunals and seriously place doubt upon the
usefulness of the current system. But critics continue to argue that the introduction of
legal aid will result in lawyers becoming commonplace in the tribunal system, leading
to ever-increasing formality. They also recognise that lawyers do not always possess the
necessary expertise for certain tribunals, such as the Mental Health Review Tribunals,
and that non-lawyers with relevant experience are often more skilled. Furthermore,
tribunal work is not popular or financially attractive, and there may be a tendency

for young, inexperienced lawyers to appear, who are not as experienced as some non-lawyers.

Inquisitorial

9.55 Tribunal procedures are intended to be run on an inquisitorial basis, ie the chairman could call and examine witnesses himself. The advantages of this are that it keeps costs down and maintains an air of informality. It also redresses the imbalance in that a relevant government department will be represented by an official who is an expert in the branch of the law in question, and so has an advantage over an unrepresented claimant or even a solicitor.

Giving of reasons

9.56 Another key recommendation of the Franks Committee was that full reasons should always be given for any decision. This reflects the principles of natural justice and is embodied within the right to a fair hearing – *audi alteram partem*. A decision is apt to be better if the reasons have to be set out in writing, since it is more likely to be better thought out. Also, if there is to be an appeal, then a reasoned decision is essential in order that an appellant can assess the grounds for appeal. The duty to give reasons was implemented by the Tribunals and Inquiries Act 1958 and is now contained in s 10 of the 1992 Act, which provides that it is the duty of a tribunal to furnish a statement, either written or oral, of the reasons for a decision. The only grounds for refusal to give reasons are where it would be contrary to the interests of national security, or contrary to the interests of the individual concerned. Some tribunals may also be exempted by the Lord Chancellor or the Lord Advocate from the duty to give reasons, but the Council on Tribunals must be consulted first on any such proposal.

9.57 A useful authority on giving reasons can be found in *Re Poyser & Mills' Arbitration*[19] where an arbiter failed to give adequate reasons to an agricultural tenant concerning a notice to quit which had been served by his landlord. Megaw J said that the duty to give reasons must be read as meaning that proper, adequate reasons must be given. They must also be intelligible and deal with the substantial points that have been raised.

Expenses

9.58 The courts principle, ie that an unsuccessful party pays the other's expenses, does not apply to tribunals, even where the hearing is between two private parties. The only exception can be found in the Scottish and English Lands Tribunals. The Franks Committee also recommended that a successful party should be given a reasonable allowance to cover travel, subsistence and attendance of witnesses. Some tribunals, but by no means all, now have such discretionary powers.

APPEALS FROM A TRIBUNAL

9.59 Appeals from tribunals differ according to the governing legislation for each one. There are no hard and fast rules as to the routes of appeal, however, in the case of

---

[19] [1963] 2 WLR 1309.

Scotland, many statutes convey a right of appeal to the sheriff court and thence to the Inner House of the Court of Session. Where a right of appeal is given to a sheriff and the statute gives no indication about review of the sheriff's decision then it is presumed that the sheriff's decision is final. However, in almost all cases there is a right of appeal on a point of law to the Court of Session. Sometimes there is an appeal on fact or law to a higher tribunal, and usually from there to the Court of Session. Where there is no appeal, there is the possibility of judicial review.

The appeals system has been much criticised since it has no real consistency for **9.60** citizens and reflects the refusal of the legal profession to accept the separation of tribunals from the ordinary courts. The Franks Committee considered the suggestion of creating an Administrative Appeal Tribunal which would be distinctly separate from the ordinary courts. However, this idea was rejected for a number of reasons including the fact that a body of law might build up which would conflict with the ordinary law, and that such a body would need unsustainable levels of staff to cope with its wide jurisdiction. On the other hand, Franks did think that there should always be a right of appeal to a higher tribunal before going to the courts, such as the relationship between employment tribunals and the Employment Appeal Tribunal. This recommendation has not been universally applied.

REFORM

In May 2000, Sir Andrew Leggat was appointed to undertake a fundamental review **9.61** of the tribunal system in the UK. His report, *Tribunals for Users: One System, One Service*, was published in August 2001 and was highly critical of the current system. Leggat felt that tribunals had developed in an *ad hoc* manner, had inadequate appeal procedures, and generally had no real independence. In order to deal with these issues, he felt that tribunals should be brought together into a single system with a common administrative service and a clear appeals procedure.

Government response to Leggat was at first slow, however, in July 2004 the **9.62** Department for Constitutional Affairs (DCA) published a White Paper, *Transforming Public Services: Complaints, Redress and Tribunals*. This paper sought views on the Leggat proposals and has led to the introduction of the Tribunals, Courts and Enforcement Bill. The Bill contains a number of important innovations. Foremost, it is intended that most existing tribunals will be unified under a single body known as the Tribunals Service which will provide common administrative support. This non-statutory body has already been set up within the DCA in anticipation of the new legislation. It has responsibility for 16 of the largest tribunals including the Employment Tribunals Service, and the Appeals Service, with more to be added by 2008.

The Bill will also introduce a simplified two-tier structure for tribunals. A lower tier **9.63** will consist of tribunals hearing appeals as normal while an upper tier, in the form of an Administrative Appeals Tribunal, will be established to deal with appeals against decisions from the lower tier. There will also be a right of appeal via statutory review from the upper tier to a single Court of Appeal judge. It is expected that the scope of the Bill will only extend to non-devolved, central government tribunals, although many of these have a UK-wide jurisdiction and thus the provisions will also have some effect in Scotland and Wales.

ESSENTIAL FACTS

9.64

- Judicial review is an inherent common law power of the Court of Session in Scotland.

- The competency of an application for review in Scotland does not depend upon any distinction between public law and private law.

- The substantive grounds of challenge under judicial review are illegality, irrationality (or unreasonableness), procedural impropriety and, more recently, proportionality.

- The Parliamentary Commissioner for Administration (PCA) was created by the Parliamentary Commissioner for Administration Act 1967 which lays out the composition, jurisdiction and powers of the PCA. The remit of the PCA extends to England and Wales, as well as any reserved matters for Scotland.

- The primary role of the PCA is to investigate complaints by private citizens who have suffered injustice as a result of maladministration by government departments, agencies and non-departmental bodies.

- The Scottish Public Services Ombudsman (SPSO) was created by the Scottish Public Services Ombudsmen Act 2002 which lays out the composition, jurisdiction and powers of the SPSO.

- The SPSO is a collegiate body and also incorporates the jurisdiction of pre-existing ombudsmen in Scotland, namely the Commissioner for Local Administration in Scotland, the Health Service Commissioner for Scotland, the Housing Association Ombudsman for Scotland, the External Adjudicators for Scottish Enterprise and Highlands and Islands Enterprise, and the Mental Welfare Commission.

- The primary role of the SPSO is to investigate complaints from members of the public who have suffered injustice or hardship as a consequence of maladministration. Complaints may be made directly to the Ombudsman since there is no "MSP-filter".

- On completion of an investigation, the PCA must produce a report containing findings and recommendations and may lay a special report before Parliament where no remedial action is taken in light of the report. The SPSO must act similarly, with a special report being laid ultimately before the Scottish Parliament.

- Neither the PCA nor the SPSO has any legal powers of enforcement. They cannot coerce action to be taken in light of their recommendations. Instead, they rely upon co-operation from bodies complained of through ministerial responsibility and Government pressure.

- Tribunals have a limited scope of authority to deal with administrative-type issues, which are often, but not necessarily, disputes between public authorities and citizens. They can be either statutory or non-statutory but most are set up by statute and their powers and scope are contained either within the statute or in regulations issued under its authority.

- Tribunals should be open, fair, and impartial, meaning that they should be free from Government interference, have clear and consistent procedures, and should be held publicly, giving clear and reasoned decisions.

- The key advantages of tribunals are speed, cheapness, accessibility, informality, expertise and flexibility.

- Legal aid is unavailable for tribunals except the Lands Tribunal for Scotland and the Employment Appeals Tribunal.

- Tribunal proceedings are subject to the principles of natural justice and their decisions may be subject to appeal or review.

- Tribunals and public inquiries are scrutinised by the Council on Tribunals which is a statutory body with a consultative and advisory role relating to the constitution and operation of tribunals and inquiries.

ESSENTIAL CASES

Moss Empires v *Assessor for Glasgow* (1917): definition of the supervisory jurisdiction.   **9.65**

Guthrie v *Miller* (1827): the distinction between law, facts and merits.

West v *Secretary of State for Scotland* (1992): the scope of judicial review; clarification of public/private law distinction.

Council of Civil Service Unions v *Minister for Civil Service* (1985): an outline of the substantive grounds of challenge under judicial review; the Diplock catalogue.

McColl v *Strathclyde Regional Council* (1983): an example of an action of an administrative body being declared *ultra vires*.

Associated Provincial Picture Houses Ltd v *Wednesbury Corporation* (1948): an explanation of "unreasonableness" and the creation of the high-threshold *Wednesbury* style unreasonableness.

10 CRIMINAL LAW

Criminal law is a subject that provokes great interest, and often controversy, among **10.1** people, whether they are qualified in law or not. To be brief and practical, a crime can be defined as an act – or, in some instances, a failure to act – that may be the subject of a prosecution, where a person who is found guilty is convicted and then punished by means of a sentence. Scots criminal law is concerned with the substantive matters relating to the crimes recognised in Scotland. However, it is only reasonable to go further in introducing this area of law. In order to do this effectively, the arguable aims and competing theories regarding the role of law will be considered. Thereafter, the relationship between criminal law and other areas of law will receive broad consideration.

Thoughts about aims beg the question "What is the criminal law trying to do?". **10.2** Commentators in this area have produced a range of answers. One, apparently contradictory, view is that the criminal law aims to cause crime,[1] since no crime can exist unless it is part of the criminal law. Others have taken this theme and extended the explanation by stating that the law aims to criminalise acts and omissions that are deemed to be harmful, even if many people would disagree with this.[2] Likewise, the criminal law can be said to tell people what will happen to them if they do not behave, rather than striving to achieve anything more positive.[3]

Theories about the moral principles that should inform the development of **10.3** criminal law are just as wide ranging. Those with a more conservative viewpoint state that the criminal law should uphold the views of the "moral majority".[4] Others have written of the need to use the criminal law to prevent people and institutions from causing harm, so as to allow society to function properly.[5] However, the more liberal viewpoint is quite different: this states that the criminal law ought to be used only to prevent harm to others. This theory is quite definite that it should not be used to protect persons from themselves.[6] The study of criminal law will reveal that these competing theories can be viewed in the ways in which the law has developed and will develop; however, no theory can be said to support all of the criminal law.

Returning to practical concerns about what the criminal law actually is, its main **10.4** characteristics can be identified. It belongs to those areas of law categorised as "public law", where the law is concerned with the relationship between the State and persons

---

[1] J Michael and M Adler, *"Crime, Law and Social Science"* (1993).
[2] M R Cohen, *"Reason and Law"* (1950).
[3] Lord Devlin, *"The Enforcement of Morals"* (1965).
[4] HLA Hart, "Social Solidarity and the Enforcement of Morality" (1967) 35 U Chicago LR 1.
[5] Lord Devlin, *The Enforcement of Morals* (1965), p. 22.
[6] J S Mill, *On Liberty* (1859), Chap 1, para 9.

living within the State. Principally, this is a reference to the State's position as the prosecutor of crimes. (NB: while "private" prosecutions are possible, they are extremely rare.) And so, a prosecution will proceed only where there is sufficient evidence to justify this and where doing so is in the public interest.

10.5   The criminal law exists in order to allow those who have acted inappropriately to be punished. While some would argue that modern sentencing does not always appear to involve punishment, this aspect of criminal law is still quite different from the role of the civil law, which is involved in establishing liability and, if this has been done, granting remedies.

10.6   Unlike many of the world's jurisdictions – for example, the federal state and the individual states in America – the UK's jurisdictions do not have criminal codes where all of the relevant law is collected in one document or a series of documents. Instead, Scots criminal law is dependent upon a variety of sources for its existence.

10.7   The main source, given the UK's constitutional arrangements, is the law that is enacted by Parliament. Examples of criminal law arising from "primary" legislation can be found in the Misuse of Drugs Act 1971 and the Criminal Law (Consolidation) (Scotland) Act 1995, while "secondary" legislation is also used, as with the Traffic Regulations 1956, reg 52(1) and the Misuse of Drugs Regulations 1985.

10.8   Since devolution,[7] there have been two Parliaments with influence over Scots criminal law: the UK Parliament at Westminster and the devolved Scottish Parliament in Edinburgh. The Scottish Parliament has the power to legislate in relation to most aspects of the criminal law. Accordingly, the Scottish Parliament is the main source for any new legislation affecting criminal law and criminal procedure. The Westminster legislation that was passed for Scotland prior to devolution continues to affect Scotland; otherwise, Westminster has retained legislative authority in "reserved" areas. In relation to the criminal law, these areas include health and safety law and consumer law, for example.

10.9   However, legislation has not created criminal law in every area. In those areas that have not been legislated upon, the relevant law is derived from the "common law". This includes a number of different possibilities:

- *The declaratory power of the High Court of Justiciary*: this is sometimes referred to as "judicial legislation". In fact, it refers to the High Court's power to declare the common law of crime where it is felt that something is a significant corruption of morals and harm is being caused to society. This power has not been used in recent times. It is unlikely that it will be used in the future, given the argument that it ignores democracy in the creation of law.

- *Precedent*, which may also be called "case law": this is the law that emerges from decisions that have been made by superior courts. More specifically, in Scotland, it is the law emanating from decisions of the High Court of Justiciary in appeal cases. The rules concerning the creation and use of precedent are quite technical and are beyond this introduction to the law.

- *Institutional writers*: these are respected academics whose writings are still referred to in relation to areas where Parliament or the High Court has not marked out the law. The main writers still referred to are:

---

[7] Scotland Act 1998.

Baron Hume   *Commentaries* (1797)
Alison   *Principles of the Criminal Law of Scotland* (1832)
Macdonald   *Practical Treatise of the Criminal Law of Scotland* (1948)

- *Custom*: this concerns the practices that have emerged over a lengthy period of time without reference to any of the previously noted sources. It is, in effect, the way things have always been done. If the law has not been found by referring to the earlier sources, the court will look to the established practice as a guide to how its decision ought to be reached.
- *Equity*: ultimately, if no law has been found elsewhere, equity involves the court in ruling in a manner that appears, objectively, to be fair.

Much of the modern criminal law of Scotland is still sourced from the common law. **10.10** Accordingly, that law is subject to continual re-interpretation and evolution, as opposed to a situation where the courts are concerned with the relatively direct practice of interpreting and applying legislation.

The substantive criminal law must now be noted and explained. This will be done **10.11** by considering the following:

- the basic components of a crime;
- the different doctrines concerned with establishing criminal liability;
- the defences that are recognised in relation to criminal law;
- certain categories of specific crimes that are recognised by Scots criminal law.

THE BASIC COMPONENTS OF A CRIME

The fundamental rule of the common law is expressed in the Latin maxim: *"actus* **10.12** *non facit reum nisi mens sit rea"*. This means that a person's act should only lead to criminal liability if that person had a guilty mind when that act took place. In order to understand the law, some Latin terminology must still be used. The wrongful act is called the *actus reus* and the wrongful state of mind is the *mens rea*. The basic equation concerning liability for a common law crime can be stated as: *actus reus* + *mens rea* = crime. (NB: later, it will be seen that this equation has to be reconsidered for some statutory crimes.)

ACTUS REUS

Any definition of *actus reus* cannot be absolute, since the criminal law involves a wide **10.13** range of specific crimes that have varied characteristics. That will be seen when those specific crimes are considered. In the meantime, it is possible to be clear about the basic principles.

In basic terms, the *actus reus* involves doing something that is wrongful. Therefore, **10.14** on its own, thinking something wrongful is not a crime. The *actus reus* has also been described as a "forbidden situation"[8] which must at least be alluded to in the facts set out in a criminal charge if the minimum requirement for a conviction is to be achieved. For a person to be responsible for a particular *actus reus*, the act must have been

---

[8] G H Gordon. *The Criminal Law of Scotland* (3rd edn) 2000, vol 1; (2001); vol 2.

something over which the person had control.[9] The act must also have been voluntary. If a person is forced to act in a certain way, their actions would not amount to an *actus reus* for which they would be responsible. However, the person who forced them to act would have a responsibility. Practically, conduct is assumed to be voluntary until proved otherwise. The *actus reus* exists in three forms.

A POSITIVE OR OVERT ACT

10.15   In this, most straightforward form, there is an act, which may be a single act or part of a series of acts. It may be a physical action or may amount only to the uttering of words. Examples of this form of *actus reus* can be found in the punch or kick that may be the basis of the crime of assault. Otherwise, it might be the setting fire to a building in the crime of fireraising.

A RELEVANT OMISSION

10.16   In this case, the *actus reus* arises from a person's failure to take action. While there is no general legal – as opposed to moral[10] – duty to act, such a duty does arise in certain specific situations. Statute does, on occasions, impose duties to act, therefore making a failure to do so actionable. Such situations arise in relation to serious matters, such as failing to report acts connected with terrorism, but they may also be observed in day-to-day matters arising in road traffic law (eg failing to report an accident, failing to insure a vehicle etc). Legal duties to act also arise under the common law. This happens in several well-defined situations.

When a special relationship exists

10.17   Where there is a clear relationship of trust and dependence between two or more people, then the person who is trusted to look after the interests of the dependent person(s) may be responsible for an *actus reus* where there is a failure to act. This has been recognised by the courts where a parent has failed to look after a child .

Where someone has chosen to assume a duty

10.18   Such a situation would arise where one person has, expressly or impliedly, volunteered to look after the welfare of another – perhaps older or infirm – person.[11]

Where the omission follows upon a prior dangerous act by the accused

10.19   Here, a person acting in a legal but dangerous manner has a duty to do what can reasonably be done to minimise that danger.[12]

---

[9] In *Hogg* v *McPherson* 1928 JC 15 the alleged criminal damage had been caused by the wind, rather than by the accused. Accordingly, there was no *actus reus*.

[10] In *George Kerr* (1871) 2 Cooper 334 a man who watched, but did not participate in, a sexual assault was adjudged not to have had any responsibility for the *actus reus*. His failure to act might have been immoral, but it was not illegal.

[11] In *R* v *Instan* (1893) 1 QB 450, the accused was convicted of the manslaughter of her 72-year-old aunt. She had been living in the aunt's house at the aunt's expense, while at the same time neglecting to provide reasonable care to the aunt, who went on to die of gangrene.

[12] In *McPhail* v *Clark* 1982 SCCR 395, a farmer was criminally liable for being "recklessly indifferent" to a fire that has been legally started, but had then gone out of control.

Where the accused has a public duty to act

The public servant has a duty to do what is reasonable in the public interest. **10.20** What amounts to reasonable action will be decided by reference to the particular circumstances.[13]

Where the accused is contractually bound to act

This category is similar to what has already been noted. However, it covers the situation **10.21** where someone contracts so as to accept a duty. This would relate to the position of a paid childminder or a swimming pool attendant.

A STATE OF AFFAIRS

In a "state of affairs", which can be distinguished from a positive act and a relevant **10.22** omission, the *actus reus* arises out of the fact that the accused has been found in a particular situation. It is illustrated by the statutory offence of driving while unfit through drink or drugs. That is to say that driving is not necessarily illegal, and neither is drinking. However, the combination of the two (ie that state of affairs) is what is being outlawed.

MENS REA

As was noted earlier, "*mens rea*" is the term used to indicate a person's wrongful **10.23** thoughts. These thoughts, when occurring along with a relevant type of action or omission, will lead to criminal liability. There are three types of *mens rea*. In order to be properly understood, they must first be defined. Care must be taken, since the terms have other – usually broader – meanings when they are used in a non-law context. It should also be noted that these forms of *mens rea*, while they refer to what was going on in the head of an accused, will either be admitted by the accused or established by interpreting the actions (or omissions) of the accused.

INTENTION

A person acts intentionally when he is aware of what he is doing and he is doing **10.24** what he wants to do. To be considered as intentional, these thoughts need to relate to something that person has a reasonable prospect of achieving, rather than being just fanciful. Importantly, intention must be distinguished from "motive". Intention requires consideration of "how" a crime has been carried out; "motive" is concerned with "why" it was carried out. While establishing motives will be important to the authorities that investigate crime and to the courts when they are considering an appropriate sentence; generally, they have no part to play in establishing criminal liability. As was noted by Lord Justice-Clerk Inglis in *Alexander Milne*:[14] "The motive may remain a mystery, while the murder is an accomplished fact."

---

[13] In *Bonnar v McLeod* 1983 SCCR 16, a senior police officer's failure to intervene in relation to an assault perpetrated by a junior officer upon a person in police custody resulted in the senior officer also being liable for assault.
[14] (1863) 4 Irv 301.

RECKLESSNESS

10.25   Recklessness also requires that a person is aware of his circumstances. Here, however, that person does not necessarily want to achieve a particular result, but is willing to take the risk that he will do so. It is the conscious taking of an unjustified risk. For instance, if it is proved that one person hit another person over the head with a stick, in order to rob him, it may not be the case that killing was the aim of the action. However, an objective analysis of the action may show it to involve the taking of a risk that this might come about.

NEGLIGENCE

10.26   In this case, a person is not aware of his circumstances, but has a duty to be aware. It should be noted that this same concept exists in the law of delict, where a person is liable for his unintentional actions that cause harm. As with the law of delict, the court will assess a person's actions, in terms of a "reasonableness" test, when deciding whether or not he has been negligent. For example, such a situation could occur where a fire causes death and the person responsible for the premises is deemed to have materially contributed to the circumstances that allowed the fire to take place or prevented persons from escaping. These facts could support a criminal prosecution and a civil action, both based upon the negligence of the responsible person. Recklessness and negligence should not be confused. Although they are used as synonymous terms in many everyday situations, they are quite different in criminal law.

APPLYING THE *ACTUS REUS* AND THE *MENS REA* TO SPECIFIC CRIMES

10.27   The basic components of crimes can be seen in the definitions of these crimes. These definitions state what requires to be proved beyond reasonable doubt, if an accused person's guilt is to be established. The crime of assault provides an example of this: "An assault is committed when one person makes an attack on the person of another with the intention of effecting the immediate bodily injury of that person or producing the fear of immediate bodily injury in his mind." From this, it is clear that the *actus reus* of an assault is an act, specifically it is an "attack". The *mens rea* that requires to be proved to exist at the time of the attack is intention. Therefore, a failure to prove that the act was intentional would deny the possibility of a conviction for the crime of assault.

STRICT LIABILITY

10.28   As has been noted, the criminal law generally demands that both the *actus reus* and the *mens rea* are identified in a given situation if criminal liability is to follow. Certain statutory crimes, however, have no requirement for *mens rea*. Such crimes are said to involve "strict liability" or "no-fault liability". In these cases, a person will be convicted of the crime if it is proved that he was responsible for the *actus reus*, regardless of his state of mind at the point when the action took place. These crimes have emerged in modern times; they often relate to areas of technical development (eg road traffic, environmental protection etc). It is argued that if the Crown were required to prove culpability in each case, it would be impossible to control many forms of anti-social behaviour adequately.

A court sitting in judgment in respect of a strict liability offence must first **10.29** scrutinise the statute that is responsible for creating the offence. This is a process that is entered into while bearing in mind that there is a general presumption in favour of *mens rea*.[15] For example, if the statute uses the words "wilfully" or "knowingly", then substantial case law indicates that knowledge of the offence and intention to commit the offence must be demonstrated.

As with any presumption, this one may be rebutted and case law has developed **10.30** rules for this. And so, where an act requires *mens rea* for some sections but not for others, it may be deemed that those other sections involve strict liability. Otherwise, in deciding whether an offence is one of strict liability – where the words of the statute do not clearly resolve the matter – the courts will consider the seriousness of the harm caused and the possibilities of the accused acting differently at the time in question. While defences are possible, their availability will be restricted. Again, the words of the statute would have to be considered. One example of this is the road traffic offence of driving without insurance.[16] A driver who has been charged with this offence will not be able to defend himself on the basis that he thought he was insured, alone. The statute is clear that the defence will only be available to employees who are driving in the course of their employment, while reasonably believing that they were insured. If this defence is accepted, the Crown's attention might then turn to the employer.

CAUSATION

It has been recognised that the *actus reus* of crimes can be distinguished from one **10.31** another. Some criminal actions concern what was done at a moment in time – for example, hitting a person; they may be termed "conduct crimes". In others, the physical part of the crime is more complicated, requiring proof of the initial conduct, along with the fact that the conduct caused a particular result – as where a person is shot and later dies. These may be termed "result crimes". A person may be liable for a result only if he can be proved to have caused that result. The link may be obvious, and so no difficulty will be encountered in proving causation. In some cases, however, an intervention of some description between conduct and result creates difficulties. The court would then have to evaluate the situation and attribute blame. In some situations, the application of the law is arguable.

The basic legal rule may be stated as: the act of the accused must have been **10.32** sufficient in itself to produce the result, provided that the result was not too remote from the original act. Other ways of saying this are that the result must be proximate to the original conduct; or that, but for the conduct, the result would not have happened. Following this principle, where the victim of an assault died soon after, but this was due to a pre-existing illness, the accused would be responsible for the assault, but not the death.

---

[15] In *Duguid v Fraser* 1942 JC 1, Lord Justice-Clerk Cooper asserted the judiciary's concerns that *mens rea* should not be too readily excluded from the definition of crime. In his view, the statute has to be closely scrutinised, in order to be sure that Parliament intends an exception to the common law approach.
[16] Road Traffic Act 1988, s 143.

TAKING YOUR VICTIM AS YOU FIND HIM

10.33   There is a rule of law that "you must always take your victim as you find him". This is also known as the "thin skull" rule. Basically, this means that an offender who is responsible for the initial conduct will also be responsible for the result, even when he had no knowledge of an inherent weakness in the victim which made the result more likely to occur. This rule operates in relation to both physical and psychological weaknesses.

10.34   The rule operated in *R v Blaue*,[17] where the victim of an assault refused a life-saving blood transfusion for religious reasons. The accused tried to argue that the victim's choice made her responsible for the result, while he was only responsible for the conduct. The court did not agree; it was not for one person who used violence on another person to be critical of a reaction to that, which was based on the victim's rational religious convictions.

BREAKING THE "CHAIN OF CAUSATION"

10.35   Where the link between act and result is interrupted significantly, this will amount to a break in the "chain of causation", with the perpetrator of the conduct not being liable for the apparent result. This is also called a *"novus actus interveniens"*. In order to achieve this status, the intervening act must be shown to have been the main reason for the supposed result coming about. An act that is in the normal course of events, so that it was expected, could not be said to amount to a *novus actus*.

10.36   However, the chain of causation will be broken by "Acts of God" – also termed *"damnum fatale"*. Though highly unlikely – and that is the point – where the victim of an assault is left unconscious, but is then killed by a lighting strike, the chain will have been broken and the offender will only be liable for the assault. Where a third party interrupts the sequence of events, then this also will amount to a break in the chain. For this to be the case, the intervention must be voluntary.[18] Where the arguable break in the chain of causation was a second criminal act – as where the original offender leaves a victim lying unconscious after an assault and the victim is then killed by a second offender who came upon him – the court would be presented with a difficult decision in attributing blame. As we will see later, there would be no problem in finding both accused liable if they are proved to have been acting in a concerted way. Otherwise, there are arguments that these quite rare situations might suggest that the person responsible for the first act would escape criminal liability for the result, though this might not seem to be morally correct.

10.37   Where the suggestion is that subsequent medical treatment was responsible for the result, this argument will only be upheld by the court where the medical treatment serves to worsen the condition of a victim and the medical practitioner acted in a manner that was unreasonable and unforeseeable. This might be accepted where a victim dies because of medical negligence, as opposed to the unfortunate consequences of reasonable, but unsuccessful, treatment. To satisfy this test, the

---

[17] [1975] 1 WLR 1411.
[18] In *R v Pagett* (1983) 76 Cr App Rep 279, the chain was not broken by a policeman's shooting of a person who was being used as a human shield. The police action, though tragic, was being taken in the line of duty.

negligent treatment must be completely independent of the original criminal act, so as to be the clear cause of the result. For this reason, medical treatment that requires to be carried out in an emergency is unlikely to break the chain.

Occasionally, it is argued that the victim has caused the result. There is not much **10.38** case law in this area. However, the principles again focus on how voluntary, reasonable and foreseeable the victim's actions were. This area is extremely arguable. Take, for instance, situations where the victim died by suicide or from an attempt to escape by jumping from a moving vehicle or from his failure to follow medical advice concerning treatment.

In conclusion, the issue of causation is one that is based on law and fact, together. **10.39** It has been suggested that courts reach a decision based on nothing more than a "gut reaction" to the question: "Who was to blame?".[19]

ART AND PART

Where more than one person participates in the commission of a crime, all of the people **10.40** involved will share in criminal responsibility. This type of liability – which may also be referred to as "complicity" – affects all those who knowingly play a part in planning, preparation, supply, assistance or perpetration in relation to a crime. Scots law does not have a separate offence of aiding and abetting. Generally, all parties involved will be equally responsible for the crime. The fact that a prosecution proceeds on the basis that the accused was the principal offender or that he was acting on an art and part basis is implied for common law and statutory crimes.[20]

ESTABLISHING CONCERT

Essentially, the rationale for art and part liability arises from two or more people **10.41** who act together in the commission of a crime being regarded in law as one entity. Specifically, they are all considered to be harmful and worthy of punishment, even if some of them had no overt involvement in the crime. Each member of the group is responsible for every action of any group member in pursuance of the group plan or purpose. Therefore, a person who was watching a crime take place, but was not involved, would not attract art and part liability. In order to be liable on an art and part basis, the accused need not have been involved in every step of the preparation for, or commission of, the crime. It is sufficient that he participated to some extent and had knowledge of some criminal enterprise. Effectively, then, the parties are agreeing to participate in this enterprise. This agreement could be expressed – in writing or verbally – but it might also be implied from the parties' actions. This is also know as establishing "concert" in relation to the various persons who were apparently involved in the commission of the crime. When someone acts voluntarily and intentionally and so assists, he associates himself with the perpetrator's *actus reus*. His *mens rea* may be inferred from his actions – unless he is able to establish a reasonable doubt.

---

[19] G H Gordon, *The Criminal Law of Scotland* (3rd edn, 2000), vol 1; (2001), vol 2.
[20] The Criminal Procedure (Scotland) Act 1995, s 293 provides authority for this in relation to statutory offences.

FORMS OF INVOLVEMENT

10.42   Art and part liability can involve an "instigator", who encourages or counsels others to commit a crime. It can also relate to an "aider", who provides some assistance prior to the criminal act occurring, so as to allow the crime to take place. This might involve the supply of firearms, for example. The liability of the instigator and the aider is derived from the eventual commission of the crime. Where two or more people are directly involved in the commission of a crime, they – as joint perpetrators – also share in liability for the crime that has been committed.

10.43   Logically, if concert cannot be proved to have existed between the accused persons, then the doctrine of art and part cannot be used by the prosecution. This happened in *Docherty v HM Advocate*,[21] in which Docherty was charged with murder while acting along with another person who had not been apprehended by the police and whose identity was not known. There was no evidence to suggest that Docherty had actually struck the fatal blow. Therefore, it was not possible to establish his guilt as perpetrator. Neither was it possible to prove concert. As a result, art and part liability was not an option and Docherty's conviction had to be quashed on appeal.

10.44   Once concert is proved, every member of the group is responsible for the foreseeable consequences of the common plan. It therefore becomes important to establish whether a particular incident was a reasonably expected consequence of the group's activity. Where an incident fails this "foreseeable" test, it will not attract art and part guilt. Instead, the perpetrator of that particular act will be solely liable. Where an action goes beyond a stated or implied common plan, the group may still be art and part liable where recklessness is exhibited by the group. The group would also be liable for all of the reasonably foreseeable consequences of their actions, taking their victims as they find them. These points are illustrated by *Boyne and another v HM Advocate*,[22] in which three men were convicted of a murder committed in the course of an assault and robbery. During the robbery, one of the parties had drawn a knife and stabbed the victim. The appeal court quashed the murder convictions against the other two. They were clearly art and part in the original assault and robbery; however, there was no evidence to show that they knew or had reason to anticipate that a knife would be used or that they carried on their attack after the knife had been used.

APPORTIONMENT OF LIABILITY

10.45   While art and part liability will result in more than one person being criminally liable, in some situations the law will distinguish between the persons in relation to the particular crime that they have committed. These situations arise where the *actus reus* is jointly achieved but there are distinctions between the *mens rea* of the accused persons. As a result of this, where two parties are initially accused of murder, the court might eventually convict one of murder while the other is convicted of culpable homicide. Indeed, it is even possible that the apparent offender is acquitted while those assisting or instigating are convicted. This occurred in *R v Cogan and Leak*,[23] where Cogan had initially been convicted of the rape of Leak's wife. Leak had made Cogan believe that his

[21] 1945 JC 89.
[22] 1980 SLT 56.
[23] [1976] 1 QB 21.

wife had consented to sexual intercourse, while he knew that she had not. On appeal, Cogan's conviction was quashed, since he lacked the *mens rea* required for the crime of rape. However, Leak's appeal was unsuccessful. His conviction stood because he had provided the *mens rea* element, which accompanied Cogan's unwitting *actus reus*, so as to form the crime. He was art and part liable in relation to a person as he had set up Cogan to commit the act.

INCHOATE LIABILITY

Literally, the word "inchoate" means "just started" or "undeveloped". In the context of criminal law, it refers to situations where a criminal enterprise has commenced, but has not been completed. It can be argued that these forms of crime are justified, as those involved in criminality are still dangerous, even if they have not yet achieved their goals. The failure to complete the crime might not have been due to their lack of effort. It can also be suggested that this form of liability may allow the investigating authorities to interfere with private lives as they investigate matters that are in their early stages of development. It is also the case that those authorities have a duty to prevent crime and provide a deterrent effect, where reasonably possible. However, interventions that are too enthusiastic can undermine the human rights of private individuals. Inchoate liability exists in three forms: incitement, conspiracy and attempts. **10.46**

INCITEMENT

This occurs where one person approaches another and invites him to participate in the perpetration of a crime. Whether or not this prompting is successful, the invitation or encouragement, alone, is enough to establish that person's liability for the completed crime of incitement. While these rules of law are part of the common law, it should also be noted that this form of liability is found in legislative crimes. **10.47**

CONSPIRACY

This inchoate crime is established where two or more enter into an agreement to do something that would be criminal if carried out by one person. It is essential that the fact of an agreement be established for liability to be founded; without express or implied agreement, there can be no conspiracy. A conspiracy is complete if there is an agreement, even if nothing is then done to implement that agreement. While there may be difficulties in proving that conspiracies exist, this form of liability may be thought of as an important means by which the authorities can try to control group-based criminal activity. **10.48**

ATTEMPTS

The Criminal Procedure (Scotland) Act 1995, s 294 provides that all crimes may be attempted and any attempt to commit a crime is itself criminal. The *mens rea* required for an attempt is the same as for the completed crime. While that seems logical in relation to crimes that involve intention, the appropriateness of being responsible for attempting to act recklessly is less clear. In any event, *mens rea* alone is not enough to **10.49** convict someone of a criminal attempt. Clearly, this requires to be accompanied by an *actus reus*, amounting to some overt act of a sufficient nature. This act indicates that a person has gone some way towards the commission of a completed crime.

10.50   The law considers the progress of the criminal endeavour from its conception to its commission. At some point along that line of progression, a person may be said to have done enough to attract guilt for the attempted offence. However, this is an area of common law and so, over the centuries, competing tests have emerged about how much requires to be done in order for a person to be guilty of an attempt. The "irrevocability" test seeks to establish whether or not the accused has gone beyond the point where he can revoke or recall the effects of his action. The "final stage" test involves the possibility of an earlier intervention, given that it relates to an assessment of whether the accused had done all that was necessary for him to do in order to complete the crime. This test takes account of the possibility that the crime was not ultimately committed, due to someone's intervention. However, the test that tends to be used in contemporary practice is the "preparation/perpetration" test. Essentially, this test asks whether the accused has moved from the stage of preparing to commit the crime to that which involves starting to actually perpetrate the crime. This begs a question of fact, not law. Of all the tests, it also allows for the earliest possible police intervention.

Attempts to do the impossible

10.51   Although it may seem odd at the outset, a discussion relating to the law of attempted crime must take account of those who attempt to do things that were never possible, for example, someone attempting to steal from an empty pocket or attempting to kill a person who is already dead. The law governing impossible attempts can be categorised on the basis of the nature of the impossibility in question. This has been considered to involve factual, legal or inherent impossibility.

10.52   The issue that is of most practical concern is factual impossibility. In this type of case, the accused would have committed a crime had he managed to do what he set out to do. That he didn't manage to achieve his goal was due to some factual circumstance. Importantly, that circumstance is something unexpected and out with the control of the accused. The modern authority in this area was provided by *Docherty* v *Brown*,[24] which affirmed that an accused would be liable for an attempt to do what was in fact impossible, so long as he had the necessary *mens rea* and had done something positive in trying to achieve the desired goal. In this way, the person who speculatively puts his hand in another person's pocket with the intention of stealing from that pocket is liable for attempted theft, even though there was nothing in the pocket.

DEFENCES

10.53   The law recognises the possibility of defences to criminal liability. These defences, if proved on the balance of probability, attack the possibility of establishing the liability of an accused. This comes about because one or both of the elements of the

---

[24] 1996 SLT 325.

common law crime are missing. An accused can be defended on the basis of denying the Crown case and putting it to the test. However, it is also possible that an accused can seek to rely on a named defence. These defences are of varying complexity. In order to understand how defences operate, it is important to categorise them, prior to considering the specific defences that may be available to an accused person.

Some defences seek to "excuse" the accused from responsibility for his actions. In **10.54** these cases, the assertion is that the accused must be acquitted because he was not able to control his actions. Other defences also accept that the incident occurred, but seek to "justify" the fact that it did. Effectively, these defences assert that the accused did not want to act as he did; however, he had no choice but to do so in the circumstances. Another category of defence can be said neither to excuse nor to justify what has happened. Instead, this category of defence indicates that some measure of liability is accepted, but seeks to "explain" what has happened.

Defences may also be distinguished from one another by focusing on the **10.55** implications of successfully using the defence. Some defences "exculpate", which is to say they remove all questions of guilt, requiring that the accused be acquitted. Other defences are said to "mitigate", meaning that they reduce the impact of, but do not remove, criminal liability. In certain situations, this might involve the accused being liable for a lesser offence. For the most part, however, the effect relates to the imposition of a reduced sentence. Otherwise, defences can be considered in relation to the effect that they have on the components of a crime.

NAMED DEFENCES

NON-AGE

In terms of s 41 of the Criminal Procedure (Scotland) Act 1995, the age of criminal **10.56** responsibility in Scotland is 8 years. Therefore, from the age of 8, a person carries full responsibility for his actions and may be found guilty of a crime. The basis for this defence is that a person who is younger than 8 is not sufficiently competent, as a matter of fact, to be considered capable of forming *mens rea*.

ERROR AND MISTAKE

There are circumstances where the criminal law recognises that a genuine and **10.57** reasonable error will excuse a harmful deed which would otherwise be criminal. The accused might have done something unintentionally; alternatively, something might have been done intentionally, but in the mistaken belief that it was justified. Here, the distinction between errors of law and errors of fact must be observed. Generally, errors as to the state of the law will not affect a person's criminal liability. As is well understood, "ignorance of the law is no defence".

However, an error relating to factual matters will amount to a defence, so long as: **10.58** the mistake affects either the *mens rea* or the *actus reus*; it is genuine and reasonable in the whole circumstances of the case; and, it is of such a character that if the circumstances were as the accused believed them to be, he would either escape liability completely or have it reduced. Where the defence of mistake is established then the accused is judged as if the circumstances were as he believed them to be. Again, this can be explained by the accused person's lack of *mens rea* in those limited circumstances. In *Owens v HM Advocate*,[25] the court was prepared to consider that the accused had acted in self-defence, since it was accepted that that form of defence could exist even where the accused had been mistaken, so long as the mistake was genuine.

10.59   Usually, the proof of the mistake will be on the basis of an objective analysis. However, given the very specific nature of the definition of the rape, the law has upheld the fact that a man accused of rape could have made an unreasonable, though genuine, mistake as to the alleged victim's consent to sexual intercourse. This, then, involves a subjective mistake, though it is dependent upon a jury believing this, as a matter of fact.[26] Where this is proved, *mens rea* is excluded.

NECESSITY

10.60   Here, the accused is claiming that he necessarily broke the law; he had a choice, and chose to break the law, in order to protect or preserve something of greater value than the harm caused. The choice was dictated by the circumstances; for example, the theft of a fire extinguisher to deal with a fire or the driving of a car while under the influence of alcohol, in order to escape the threat of an assault. The defence exists where the action taken was a reasonable method of protecting something or someone, given the time that the accused had to consider the issues. However, the closer the values attached to the act committed and the danger avoided, the less likely that the defence will be successful. Certainly, the court was not prepared to accept the defence in *R v Dudley and Stephens*,[27] where shipwrecked sailors were convicted of the murder of a cabin boy, whose body they then ate.

COERCION OR DURESS

10.61   This is similar to necessity, though here the threat is posed by people rather than events. Still, the accused has a choice, and the act is still voluntary. In *Thomson v HM Advocate*,[28] it was noted that an accused could not use the defence successfully – in relation to his involvement in an armed robbery – unless it could be proved that he had been subject to an immediate threat that could not be reasonably resisted. Further, the defence would not be available if the accused had played a central role in the commission of the crime, or if no attempt had been made to resolve matters at the earliest available opportunity.

COMPULSION OR SUPERIOR ORDERS

10.62   This defence, arising out of action taken in public services, shares some characteristics with coercion. Briefly stated, an apparently lawful order is the basis for the successful use of compulsion by a soldier or sailor on duty.

---

[25] 1946 JC 119.
[26] *Meek v HM Advocate* 1982 SCCR 613.
[27] (1884) 14 QBD 273.
[28] 1983 SCCR 368.

DIMINISHED RESPONSIBILITY

It is accepted that an accused, although not insane, can suffer from a lesser incapacity   **10.63**
which renders him less responsible for his actions. Diminished responsibility denotes a
weakness or aberration of the mind, bordering on, but not quite amounting to, insanity.
Importantly, the defence rests on a mental, rather than a personality, disorder. Medical
experts require to recognise it, but the court will conclude whether it is sufficient so
as to justify the use of the defence. It is not a complete defence to any charge; it is only
considered as a possible mitigating factor in relation to murder. If proved, it reduces
the conviction to one of culpable homicide. When this plea is entered, the judge has the
option of putting the accused in a mental hospital rather than a prison. The decision
of the appeal court in *Galbraith* v *HM Advocate (No 2)*[29] should be considered for its
statement of the contemporary law regarding diminished responsibility, which also
extends to the form of evidence that will be considered appropriate to substantiate the
defence.

INSANITY

This plea should be compared with other defences concerning aspects of mental   **10.64**
dysfunction; specifically, "automatism", "intoxication" and "diminished responsibility".
The modern law recognises that mental disorder may affect a person's ability to
understand what he does or (if it is accepted that he understands this much) his
ability to stop himself doing what he does. The mere fact that such a situation exists
will not itself justify the acceptance of the defence. The question which requires to
be answered, using psychiatric evidence, is: "To what extent has the mental disorder
affected the accused's criminal responsibility?". "Insanity" is a brutish legal term
that awkwardly attempts to sum up a variety of disorders, including, among others,
psychoses (such as schizophrenia, depression, and mania); and neurotic conditions
(such as compulsive, neurotically depressed conduct). This is an area of law where the
Scottish Law Commission – a body that researches law and make proposals regarding
future developments – has suggested significant changes to the terminology that
should be employed and the ways in which the law should operate.

The issue of insanity may potentially lead to one of several approaches being taken   **10.65**
by the law. It will affect decisions about prosecuting a case; this might not be deemed
appropriate. It could also lead to a "plea in bar of trial", which, if accepted, means that
a person is not able to be tried at that time. To do this would be unfair, since an accused
would not be able to understand the proceedings. In such a case, the accused would
be detained in a psychiatric hospital until fit to face trial. Of course, the accused might
never regain capacity, so as to allow a trial to take place.

Insanity may also be used as a special defence. (NB: with special defences, the   **10.66**
prosecution must be given notice that they are to be entered.) Here, the defence would
have the onus of proving, on the balance of probabilities, that the accused was insane
at the time the offence was committed. If the defence were accepted, the accused
person would be acquitted in relation to the charge, but then detained in a psychiatric
hospital. As with diminished responsibility, medical evidence would be required in

---

[29] 2001 SLT 953.

order to establish the mental state of the accused. Thereafter, the court would decide on the implications in a legal context. Hume defined what required to be shown as an "absolute alienation of reason". In modern times, this has been expressed as: "the total alienation of reason in relation to the act charged as the result of mental illness, mental disease, or defect or unsoundness of mind and does not comprehend the malfunctioning of the mind of transitory effect".[30]

INTOXICATION

10.67 This relates to someone's alleged loss of capacity through the ingesting of drink or drugs, or both. However, much of the crime that comes before the courts has some connection with alcohol and its abuse. Previously, intoxication was regarded as being capable of diminishing responsibility – reducing murder to culpable homicide. However, the decision in *Brennan* v *HM Advocate* emphatically altered this position. In that case, a man sought to use the defence of intoxication to excuse the fact that he had killed his father after taking a huge amount of alcohol and ingesting some drugs. He based his plea on the fact that he was incapable of knowing what he had been doing and, therefore, lacked the required *mens rea* for murder. The court rejected this, since he had voluntarily become intoxicated; he had either formed the necessary intention when doing so or, in any event, could be said to have been sufficiently reckless.

AUTOMATISM (INVOLUNTARY ACTIONS)

10.68 It may be understood that certain actions are not the products of a person's own will. In such situations, a person is not able to maintain self-control. This has already been encountered in relation to insanity, but, in this defence, the concern is with matters that are of a shorter duration. It would seem inappropriate to find such a person criminally liable for his actions or omissions. For instance, the accused could have lost consciousness or, at least, full consciousness, for some reason. This area of the law is known as "automatism". This is a state which may arise in a variety of ways; for example, where someone has a seizure or a heart attack, or is overcome by fumes. The general principle is that where someone acts involuntarily (or automatically) they are not culpable for their actions. It should be noted, though, that a person's conduct will be deemed to be voluntary unless the contrary is proved.

10.69   This defence was subject to a variety of approaches taken by judges over the course of last century. The position is now quite settled, on the basis of the decision in *Ross* v *HM Advocate*.[31] This case involved a man who attacked and seriously injured a number of people after becoming drunk at a party. He alleged that he had acted as he had because some other person, unbeknown to him, had "spiked" his drink. The appeal court determined that Ross ought to have been allowed to put his defence to the jury. It also redefined the defence, stating that it could be used where an accused was rendered temporarily incapable by some external factor. Accordingly, the defence is capable of being used in the circumstances set out in *Ross* and also, for example, where a person is overcome by fumes, through no fault of his own. However, the defence does not cover

---

[30] *Brennan* v *HM Advocate* 1977 SLT 151.
[31] 1991 SLT 564.

matters that are internal to the accused, as with an epileptic seizure. The implication is that the accused knew or ought to have known about this, allowing measures to be taken to avoid such an occurrence.

SELF-DEFENCE

Again, this is a special and complete defence. It concerns some forms of action that a **10.70** person had to take to protect himself or others. It asserts that these actions were justified. The potential use of the defence is illustrated most clearly in relation to a homicide charge. In order for the defence to be successful, the accused must show that:

- there was imminent and unlawful danger to life or an attempt to rape, in the case of a woman;
- the danger must have been such that the accused could not have affected an escape;
- the force used was not excessive. In an urgent situation the accused will not be expected to weigh up the position too carefully.

PROVOCATION

It should be noted that where someone responds to an attack or a threat, in circumstances **10.71** that do not bring their response within the criteria for self-defence, then they have the possibility of pleading provocation. Essentially, this is an acceptance that the action taken was not justified, but that it can be explained, to some extent, as an immediate – though unlawful – reaction to an extreme situation. Where this defence is accepted, it will mitigate the sentence. In the case of what would otherwise be murder, it will reduce the liability to the level of culpable homicide.

ALIBI

In this special defence, the accused is denying liability on the quite simple basis that **10.72** he was not the person responsible for the commission of the alleged crime. This is being stated emphatically, since the accused is asserting – and requires to prove on the balance of probabilities – that he was elsewhere at the material time.

INCRIMINATION

Again, this is a special defence, and again the accused is asserting that he was not **10.73** responsible for the crime. In this instance, it is being stated that another person was, instead, responsible.

SPECIFIC CRIMES

Up until now, the concern has been to state the criminal law in terms of criminal **10.74** liability and defences. In doing so, it has been necessary to refer to specific crimes, in order to illustrate the issues. Now, it is important that the most common crimes are defined and explained. Given that this is an introduction to the law, the approach taken involves only a selection of crimes being considered. It should be noted that much crime is derived from statute; though it is still the case that Scots criminal law is substantially reliant upon a wide range of common law.

CRIMES AGAINST THE PERSON

Murder

10.75 Murder is one of two forms of unlawful homicide, the other being culpable homicide. The *actus reus* of murder and culpable homicide is identical: the accused has acted positively (or failed to act when he had a duty to do so) and has thereby caused the death of another human being. Therefore, a life must have begun and a natural and legal person created if it is then to be held to have been destroyed, in terms of the definition. For this reason, the termination of a pregnancy, which might be carried out legally or possibly amount to another form of crime, is certainly not a homicide. Similarly, if the *actus reus* for unlawful homicide is to be proved, then life must have ended. Technological advances that have allowed for life support have also blurred the distinction between life and death. It has also been noted previously that murder and culpable homicide are result crimes. In this regard, it is indicated that the crimes are primarily concerned with the result of a party's conduct (as well as "causation", linking the party's conduct to that result).

10.76 Macdonald's approach to defining the crime of murder was long regarded as the standard to be followed. He stated that it is "constituted by any wilful act causing the destruction of life, whether intended to kill, or displaying such wicked recklessness as to imply a disposition depraved enough to be regardless of the consequences".[32] Traditionally, then, the crime of murder has demanded that the act be carried out subject to the perpetrator's "intention" or "wicked recklessness". In a more recent development, the law now appears to require proof of a "wicked" intention to kill. This arises out of the judgment in *Drury* v *HM Advocate*,[33] where the inference is that someone's intention would only amount to a sufficient *mens rea* for murder if it was indicative of fundamental immorality; the suggestion being that this might, for example, allow the court some latitude in a "mercy killing" situation. However, the more likely interpretation concludes that little has changed.

10.77 As far as the alternative form of *mens rea* is concerned, it is clear that for murder the recklessness must certainly be "wicked". This signifies that the recklessness must be something beyond ordinary or simple recklessness. Gordon has suggested that the wickedly reckless killer is the "moral equivalent" of the intentional killer, while the three-stage test to which Hume subscribed requires proof that:

- the accused should have meant to carry out some great and material bodily harm;
- the harm was such as might well have resulted in death; and,
- the harm showed an absolute indifference as to whether the victim lived or died.

10.78 The initially unreported decision *Miller and Denovan* v *HM Advocate*[34] is often referred to as a clear example of a situation that meets all three criteria. The two accused were

---

[32] J H A Macdonald, *A Practical Treatise on the Criminal Law of Scotland* (5th edn), p 91.
[33] 2001 SLT 1013.
[34] Unreported, 1960, noted at 1991 SLT 211.

involved in planning and committing robberies, preying upon single men in a park. One of the accused would act as a lure, encouraging the man who was being targeted to go to a quiet area of the park. The second accused would then come out from his hiding place and hit the man over the head with a stick, in order that he would be incapacitated, and that the two accused could steal whatever he had in his possession. However, on one occasion, the blow that a victim received caused his death. The two accused tried to defend themselves on the basis that they has not intended to kill. However, the court disagreed, holding that their conduct clearly amounted to wicked recklessness and was sufficient to make them liable.

Culpable homicide

Murder and culpable homicide are distinguished from one another in respect of the **10.79** *mens rea* that requires to accompany the *actus reus* so as to establish liability. The precise requirements for murder have already been noted. The position regarding culpable homicide is less straightforward; it covers those situations where there is a homicide which is not murder, but which still deserves to attract criminal liability. Briefly stated, culpable homicide arises in three situations, where:

- a homicide would have resulted in a conviction for murder, but for the operation of a mitigating defence (ie provocation or diminished responsibility);
- an accused did act intentionally or recklessly and did cause a death, but the nature and extent of the intention or recklessness fell short of that required for murder (eg an accused intended to punch the victim, but lacked the intention to kill);
- in an overtly non-criminal situation, a person is killed because of the gross negligence of the accused.

Murder and culpable homicide may also be distinguished from one another in regard **10.80** to the consequences following upon conviction. Murder carries a mandatory life sentence, while the judge has a wide discretion when it comes to imposing a sentence for culpable homicide.

Assault

This is commonly defined as the crime that occurs "when one person makes an attack **10.81** upon another with the intention of effecting the immediate bodily injury of that other person or producing the fear of immediate bodily injury in his mind". The *actus reus* involves an "attack", which has been interpreted in a very wide manner. It seems clear, however, that the use of words alone will not amount to an "attack". The injury that results from the attack can be relatively serious or trivial; indeed, a "gesture" (ie as opposed to actual contact) can amount to an assault. The attack can take place in circumstances where the victim is conscious or unconscious. Certain conduct will not be deemed to amount to an attack: for example, the reasonable force used by a person who is duty-bound to keep the peace; parents using reasonable force when disciplining children; or the actions of players in a sport which involves contact. An attack may be indirect in the sense that the perpetrator uses another person or animal to effect it. Also, the law recognises the possibility of aggravated assaults: for example, "with intent to rob"; "with a knife"; "to severe injury and permanent disfigurement" etc.

10.82   The *mens rea* which is required is intention. This has been summed up as "wicked intent"; "intention to do bodily harm"; and "intention to place a person in a state of fear or alarm as to their safety". As a result, an assault cannot be committed accidentally, recklessly or negligently. Where a person tries to assault one person, but because of their poor aim etc assaults another person, the *mens rea* of intention is preserved as the law treats the intention as having been transferred to the actual victim. That the "victim" consented to the conduct may amount to a defence in certain situations, but not in others (eg the "square go" situation will not afford either party a defence arising out of the fact that both agreed to fight; both parties will still be potentially liable for assault).

Rape

10.83   The crime of rape is very precise in its definition. It was clarified in *Lord Advocate's Reference (No 1 of 2001)*.[35] This judgment of the appeal court stated that the *actus reus* consists of a man having sexual intercourse with a female without the "active consent" of that female. The *actus reus* is gender-specific; the crime can be directly perpetrated only by a man and only a woman can be the victim. In fact, the modern law recognises that the victim may be the wife of the accused. The man must have been responsible for "genital intercourse". Therefore, there must have been penetration of the vagina by the penis. As a result, penetration of any other part of the woman's anatomy will not satisfy the definition. Neither will penetration of the vagina with any other part of the man's anatomy or with any object involve liability for rape. Ejaculation is not necessary in order to satisfy the definition, though, clearly, there will be evidential difficulties where this has not taken place. Also, the modern crime does not require the use of force.

10.84   The *mens rea* element of the crime relates to the intention of the accused to have sexual intercourse without the active consent of the female. The cases of *Meek* v *HM Advocate*[36] and *Jamieson* v *HM Advocate*[37] should be considered in relation to this; they relate to situations where the accused asserted that he genuinely believed that the female was consenting. Therefore, if a jury believed that the accused had thought the victim had consented, even though this was an apparently unreasonable interpretation of the situation by the accused, then they would acquit. However, if the jury did not believe that the accused was being truthful, a conviction would follow.

Sexual assault

10.85   Assaults of a sexual nature can be committed against males and females. Where a female is the victim, the clear suggestion is that the attack falls short of the specific demands in the definition of rape. These common law crimes are aggravations of assault. "Clandestine injury to women" is a crime that may not be prosecuted much in the future. It related to a situation where a man had sexual intercourse with a woman while she was incapacitated and, therefore, unable to give or withhold her consent. As noted above, the modern definition of rape now encompasses this situation. In any event, it can be said that the common law crime of indecent assault is recognised by the law in circumstances where "an assault is accompanied by circumstances of indecency".

---

[35] 2002 SLT 466.
[36] 1983 SLT 280
[37] 1994 JC 88.

This has been further specified as requiring an assault of a sexual character. Clearly, this definition is wide enough to encompass the several situations that were noted as falling out with the definition of rape.

CRIMES AGAINST PROPERTY INVOLVING DISHONESTY

Theft

It is theft to appropriate moveable, corporeal things belonging to another person, where **10.86** the accused knows that those things belong to another and intends to deprive him of them or use them permanently, indefinitely or (in certain circumstances) temporarily. This common law crime has been the subject of significant changes in the course of the last century. The *actus reus* used to demand "felonious taking". In connection with this, the law used to focus upon *"amotio"* (ie the taking of property from its place). However, developments in the course of the last century expanded the definition of the crime to allow it to encompass "appropriation". As opposed to the restrictive possibilities imposed by "taking", this allows for theft to encompass any situations beyond that, where a person treated items as if they were his own. This broader definition has been used in the successful prosecution of persons who appropriated items that they thought had been abandoned, such as coffins delivered to a crematorium. Anything that is the subject of public or private ownership can be stolen. Traditionally, the type of property has been restricted to corporeal moveables. However, it has also been accepted that energy can be stolen.

In terms of *mens rea*, it was traditionally the case that there must have been an **10.87** intention to deprive permanently. That interpretation has been held to include situations where a person had taken a car for the purposes of driving it around, before then abandoning it. However, even where a court does not find that the intention was one of permanent deprivation, the favoured interpretation is now that temporary deprivation will constitute the crime.

The crime of theft can be aggravated. In such cases, the convicted person's liability **10.88** is more significant, as is the likely sentence. The aggravations relate to housebreaking (where a house or other building is broken into for the purposes of carrying out the theft) and theft by opening lockfast places (where the break-in relates to a safe or some other type of container).

Reset

Hume defined this crime as "the receiving and keeping of stolen goods, knowing them **10.89** to be such, and with an intention to conceal and withhold them from the owner". A more contemporary definition would include reference to persons who are "privy to the retention" of such property. However, the cases are not entirely clear on this issue. It has been suggested that being privy to the retention of stolen goods may be suggestive of a party's "connivance". But, this may be an inappropriate conclusion in some instances. It used to be that the crime was seen as an alternative to theft; now the possibilities are wider. In terms of the Criminal Law (Consolidation) (Scotland) Act 1995, s 51: "Criminal resetting of property shall not be limited to the receiving of property taken by theft or robbery, but shall extend to the receiving of property appropriated by breach of trust and embezzlement and by falsehood, fraud and wilful imposition."

10.90 Still, it should be noted that a person may not be convicted of theft and reset in respect of the same property. In that regard, the crimes are mutually exclusive. Reset is a "relevant" crime in relation to the actual property that was stolen. Therefore, anything that may be stolen (including a child) may be subject to reset. It is thought that it may not be relevantly charged in respect of the proceeds of the sale of such items.

10.91 Scots criminal law still recognises an exception to the general rule on liability for reset: a wife cannot be convicted for the reset of goods stolen by her husband, so long as she did not take an active part in the disposal of the goods. Some have suggested that this protection might be deemed to be discriminatory.

10.92 In terms of *mens rea*, the crime is clearly one of intention. The accused must be shown to have known that the goods were stolen, and intended to deprive the rightful owner of their possession. The law does, however, recognise the possibility of "wilful blindness". *Latta* v *Herron*[38] provides a good example of this act being accepted. A solicitor was convicted of the reset of two antique duelling pistols that turned out to be stolen. He claimed that he had had no knowledge of this aspects of the items. However, he was deemed to have been sufficiently aware of the likelihood of this, since he had done the deal up a close, after midnight! In these cases, the law of evidence also operates to shift the onus of proof onto a person who is in possession of recently stolen goods in "criminative" circumstances.

Robbery

10.93 This crime is really a combination of theft and assault. To be more specific, it is a theft achieved by means of personal violence or intimidation. *Miller and Denovan* v *HM Advocate*,[39] which was noted earlier in relation to murder, can be seen as a case where an intended robbery ended up as murder. In order for a conviction to be achieved in respect of the completed crime of robbery, the actual theft must be complete. The violence used must be prior to or contemporaneous with the theft; it must also have been perpetrated for the purpose of the theft. Although the violence required may vary greatly, the incident must amount to more than "theft by surprise". Of course, as with assault, actual contact is not necessary; "intimidation" can suffice.

Fraud

10.94 This crime arises out of one person's deception, which is designed to achieve a practical goal at the expense of another person. Fraud is a result crime; therefore the *actus reus* comprises three components:

- the false pretence;
- the practical result; and,
- a causal connection between the false pretence and the practical result.

10.95 If the false pretence achieves something that would not otherwise have been achieved, then that is fraud. The false pretence must be material (ie essential) rather than just incidental to what occurred. The false pretence can be either explicit or by implication. In certain circumstances, a person's silence may even amount to misrepresentation.

---

[38] 1967 SCCR Supp 18.
[39] Unreported, 1960, noted at 1991 SLT 211.

Fraud, as a result crime, will not be completed unless it can be shown that the false pretence achieved the result. However, if the deception has not achieved the result, then the charge of attempted fraud would still be relevant. The *mens rea* of fraud relates to the accused person's "intention" to defraud. However, it might be argued that the crime should also cover situations where there was a sufficient degree of recklessness in the representation.

CRIMES AGAINST PUBLIC ORDER

Breach of the peace

This is a very broadly interpreted and commonly prosecuted crime. It is defined **10.96** as any conduct that is likely to put the lieges (ie ordinary people) in a state of fear and alarm. This covers a very wide range of possible conduct, such as shouting in public; gesturing; playing loud music in a private house, which affects others outside the house; taking off clothes in public; kerb crawling; acting as a "peeping tom"; and distributing written material. This is far from an exhaustive list; it would be practically impossible to provide this, such is the range of unlawful possibilities. Even where the only persons who witnessed the conduct were police officers (ie no member of the public was actually alarmed) the crime is still relevant, since it may still be adjudged that the conduct was likely to do so. This was expressed in *Montgomery* v *McLeod*,[40] where it was noted: "All that is required is . . . some conduct such as to excite the reasonable apprehension . . . (that the there will be a disturbance)." As was noted in *Palazzo* v *Copeland*,[41] it makes no difference if the conduct was motivated by a wish to control others, who were, themselves, thought to be acting in an alarming manner. Extending this analysis, it is a crime that has no real demand for *mens rea*.

Mobbing

This crime is named "mobbing", as opposed to "mobbing and rioting". However, it is **10.97** still commonly charged in relation to a "riotous mob". The *actus reus* has three essential elements:

- concourse (ie a gathering of persons);
- an illegal combination; and
- alarm to the lieges (ie a breach of the peace).

Therefore, mobbing requires a crowd of persons with a shared criminal purpose **10.98** which acts in a manner that breaches the peace. All the same, it might be that only one person is convicted of mobbing. That person would only be convicted if it is proved that he acted with others; they were assembled for an unlawful purpose in respect of which they had begun to act; he knew of the unlawful purpose; and, he was an active participant, not just a passive spectator.

As to the size of the gathering, Hume stated that "a great host or multitude"[42] was **10.99** required. This was based upon his view that a great number would have the power

---

[40] 1977 SLT (Notes) 77.
[41] 1976 JC 52.
[42] *Commentaries*, 416.

to intimidate and cause fear and alarm in ordinary people. Courts considering these matters in the first half of the 19th century found the charge to be relevant in relation to assemblies in excess of a thousand people. However, in the time since then, judicial attitudes have changed. As a result, the case law displays a willingness to see the crime of mobbing to be relevant to significantly smaller gatherings. This is clearly illustrated by the decision in *Hancock* v *HM Advocate*,[43] where a group of eight justified conviction. Clearly, it was considered that a small group could still be capable of significant and outrageous behaviour. This would be the case especially where the group has the appearance of greater numbers.

10.100   As has been noted, the mob must combine for a common purpose. That purpose might have been planned, but it could also be achieved spontaneously. For example, the activities that are struck at by the crime of mobbing could involve such matters as the gathering of a crowd in order to free a prisoner or the unlawful intimidation of workers in the course of industrial action. It is important to note that mobbing is a distinct charge, quite different to a breach of the peace committed by a number of persons. In this, the connections between mobbing and art and part liability should be evident. It would be usual if the mob was made up of participants with differing degrees of involvement, such as planners, activists and supporters. Principal activists are guilty of mobbing as actors. Those who are involved (but less active) planners, organisers, suppliers of equipment etc will be guilty following the normal art and part rules.

10.101   Spectators would not normally have any criminal liability, at least not if they were just observing. However, any apparent voicing of encouragement might be enough to extend liability to the spectators. The safest course for such a spectator would be to attempt to stop the mob's activities (which may well be impractical) or dissociate himself from the mob.

10.102   Those persons arrested in the course of a mob's activity (no doubt not the total mob) will be charged with mobbing while acting in respect of a common purpose. Particular crimes may also be incorporated in relation to the mob or particular individuals. As before, liability for these other named crimes will depend upon the principles of art and part, in the circumstances. This extended concept links parties to a crime through a less direct route than is normal in art and part. Membership of the mob is sufficient, so long as they acted in relation to the common purpose. A detailed analysis will depend upon a careful consideration of the common purpose. If the act in question comes within the common purpose then all involved in the mob will be liable. For example, where a killing results from the activities of one or more members of the mob, the court will ask "Was there murderous intent?". The court will also consider whether or not the mob displayed wicked recklessness. The more specific the common purpose, the more finely these matters may be weighed up.

10.103   There is no clear authority regarding the *mens rea* element of this crime. Certainly, the court must be able to infer voluntary presence in the vicinity of the riot in circumstances where there is knowledge of the common purpose and an intention to further that purpose. Some have even suggested that a person may be liable for acts committed before he joined; at least, this might be the case where he knew of these acts prior to joining.

[43] 1982 SCCR 32.

Other named crimes

In concluding this introduction to the specific crimes known to the law of Scotland, it is appropriate to make broad reference to the crimes that have not been detailed, above. As previously noted, this includes a very wide range of crimes that are statutory in origin. Also, among those that owe their existence to the common law, brief mention can be made of other crimes, some of which are rarely prosecuted.

10.104

Within that common law category concerning crimes against the person, consideration should be given to abduction (where a person is unlawfully deprived of his liberty); lewd and libidinous practices (where a young person is the victim of an aggravated assault of a sexual nature); culpable and reckless conduct (which covers a range of crimes where harm is caused, but without intention); and extortion (where apparently lawful demands are used to deprive a victim of his property). Likewise, crimes against property involving dishonesty include embezzlement (where a person dishonestly appropriates the property of another that is in his own possession).

10.105

Other categories of crime are also recognised. And so, crimes against property (ie not involving dishonesty) concern trespass (though the "freedom to roam" legislation in Scotland has asserted broad rights to access land, so long as no damage is caused); malicious mischief and its related statutory crime of vandalism (which both relate to the unlawful damage to, and destruction of, other people's property); and various aspects of fireraising. Even where a person is not physically attacked, the morality-based crime of shameless and indecent conduct covers a range of issues, including indecent exposure; the production and distribution of pornographic materials; and incest. Finally, another category, usually referred to as "honour code crimes", includes such matters as perjury (lying under oath, so as to defeat the ends of justice) and treason (which is a crime of English origin that is of little relevance in peace time, since it relates to a violation of the duty of allegiance to the State, more specifically the Queen).

10.106

ESSENTIAL FACTS

NATURE OF CRIMINAL LAW

10.107

- Criminal law is public law.
- It exists, unlike civil law, to allow the state to hold persons accountable for their allegedly wrongful and harmful actions and omissions, in so far as these are prohibited by the criminal law.
- Where guilt is established, the accused person will be convicted and punishment will usually be imposed, in the form of a sentence.

THE COMPONENTS OF A CRIME

- Common law crimes, and some statutory crimes, are made up of what is mostly described as a physical element (the *actus reus*), as well as a mental element (the *mens rea*). These elements are expressed in the definition of each crime.

- In relation to these crimes, both elements have to be proved beyond reasonable doubt, if a person is to be convicted.

- While the *actus reus* is often an act – in several discrete situations – it may also be an omission; otherwise, it can arise from a state of affairs.

- The *mens rea* of a crime will be intention, recklessness or negligence.

STRICT LIABILITY

- In some statutory crimes, Parliament has removed the need for the prosecution to prove *mens rea*. Accordingly, if a person is proved to be responsible for the *actus reus,* he will be liable.

- However, these crimes – which usually concern matters of regulation where such proof would be difficult – do still allow for limited defences.

CAUSATION

- Where a crime is principally concerned with the accused person's alleged liability for a result – as with the death of another person – it must be proved that the accused person's original conduct caused that result.

- On occasions, the accused person's responsibility for the end result will be obvious. In all cases, however, the chain of causation has to be established beyond reasonable doubt.

- Where there is a break in this chain – and the law does recognise the possibility of this in several situations – the accused will not be liable for the result. However, liability will still be possible in relation to the original conduct or some related crime.

ART AND PART LIABILITY

- Where two or more persons join together in order to commit crime, they will share in liability for these actions.

- In order to establish this form of liability, it must be shown that the persons had entered into an agreement. This could be planned, but can also be spontaneous.

- Art and part liability will extend to all of those persons who knowingly participated in the criminal enterprise, whatever their particular role.

- Although liability is shared, the sentences passed down in relation to the joint wrongdoers will not necessarily be the same. This is because the specific involvement of each party will be taken into account.

INCHOATE LIABILITY

- This form of liability relates to crimes that have not been completed, as such persons are still considered to be a sufficient danger to the public.

- This category of crime includes incitement (where one person tries to involve another person in a criminal enterprise); conspiracy (where two or more persons are involved in the planning of a crime); and, attempts to commit crime (where the person or persons move beyond the preparation stage to the perpetration phase).

DEFENCES

- The law recognises a variety of situations where the accused can seek to rely on a defence in relation to an alleged crime.

- Named defences may be considered in relation to their aims: some seek acquittal rather than mitigation; some seek to justify, while others seek to excuse or explain; and some seek to undermine the prosecution's proof of *actus reus*, while others seek to do the same in relation to the *mens rea*.

SPECIFIC CRIMES

- Many crimes arise from statute, in which case the particular statute has to be scrutinised to establish the definition of the crime.

- In relation to the common law, which still provides most of the criminal law of Scotland, crimes fall into several categories. The categories that are considered in more detail in this chapter include crimes against the person (including murder, culpable homicide, assault and rape); crimes against property involving dishonesty (including theft, reset, robbery and fraud); and, crimes against public order (including breach of the peace and mobbing).

ESSENTIAL CASES

Hogg v *McPherson* (1928): alleged criminal damage had been caused by the wind, rather than by the accused. Accordingly, there was no *actus reus*.

R v *Instan* (1893): the accused was convicted of the manslaughter of her elderly aunt, in whose house she had been living but for whom she had neglected to provide reasonable care. Held that *actus reus* could be said to have arisen from the accused's failure to take action.

Duguid v *Fraser* (1942): *mens rea* should not be too readily excluded from the definition of a crime. A statute must be closely scrutinised in order to be sure that Parliament intends an exception to the common law approach.

10.108

R v *Blaue* (1975): the victim must be taken as he is found. The court disagreed with the accused's argument that the victim's choice to refuse a life-saving blood transfusion, for religious reasons, made her responsible for the result of his assault.

R v *Pagett* (1983): the chain of causation was not broken by a policeman's shooting of a person who was being used as a human shield.

Docherty v *HM Advocate* (1945): art and part liability cannot be invoked by the prosecutors unless concert can be proved to have existed between the accused persons.

Docherty v *Brown* (1996): an accused would be liable for an attempt to do what was in fact imposssible, so long as he had the necessary *mens rea* and had done something positive in trying to achieve the desired goal.

Owens v *HM Advocate* (1946): the court accepted that the accused had acted in self-defence even where it had been shown that he had been mistaken, so long as the mistake was genuine.

R v *Dudley and Stephens* (1884): the court did not accept a defence of necessity where shipwrecked sailors were convicted of the murder of a cabin boy, whose body they then ate. The action taken had not been reasonable in comparison with the danger thereby avoided.

Thomson v *HM Advocate* (1985): an accused could not successfully plead coercion or duress unless he could prove that he had been subject to an immediate threat that could not be reasonably resisted.

Galbraith v *HM Advocate (No 2)* (2001): contained a statement of the contemporary law regarding diminished responsibility and the evidence that will be considered appropriate to substantiate the defence.

Brennan v *HM Advocate* (1977): altered the legal position on whether intoxication could be regarded as being capable of diminishing responsibility. As the accused had voluntarily become intoxicated, he had either formed the necessary intention or could be said to have been sufficiently reckless for the *mens rea* for murder to have been established.

Ross v *HM Advocate* (1991): the defence of automatism could be used when an accused was rendered temporarily incapable by some external factor, such as having had his drink "spiked".

Miller and Denovan v *HM Advocate* (1960): the court considered the concept of "wicked recklessness" as the *mens rea* for murder.

11 CONSUMER LAW

Consumer law is the specialised law which applies in the relationship between the **11.1** consumer, or private customer, and the supplier of goods and services. The main purpose of consumer law is to afford the person who is buying for private use and consumption greater rights against the supplier than those of a trade purchaser under ordinary law of contract. The main justification for this additional protection is the inequality of bargaining power between the consumer and those selling goods or services or providing credit by way of business. In many types of consumer contract the terms and conditions are dictated entirely by the seller who may use a standard form contract. This leaves no scope for the individual consumer to negotiate on specific terms of the contract. In the past 30 years there has been great expansion of consumer law in order to give consumers increased rights against businesses and a better deal when buying goods and services. Many areas of consumer law have been reserved to the Westminster Parliament but matters relating to food, agricultural and horticultural produce and fish are delegated to the Scottish Parliament. Scottish local authorities carry out much of the enforcement work for consumer protection.

SALE AND SUPPLY OF GOODS

As well as being regulated by the general law of contract, sale of goods contracts are **11.2** governed by the Sale of Goods Act 1979 as amended by the Sale and Supply of Goods Act 1994 and the Sale of Goods (Amendment) Act 1995 and the Sale and Supply of Goods to Consumers Regulations 2002. The Sale of Goods Act applies to all contracts by which the seller transfers or agrees to transfer the property in goods to the buyer for a money consideration called the price. The price may be fixed by the contract or may be left to be fixed in a manner agreed by the contract, or may be determined by the course of dealing between the parties. Where no price has been agreed the contract will still be valid and there will be a presumption that the buyer is obliged to pay a reasonable price for the goods. (Usually the current market price.)

Such a situation arose in the case of *Foley* v *Classique Coaches*.[1] Classique Coaches **11.3** agreed to purchase land adjoining Foley's petrol station, subject to the condition that they would buy all their petrol from Foley "at a price to be agreed from time to time". It was held that this was a valid sale of goods contract and it would be implied that the petrol would be supplied at a reasonable price.

---

[1] [1934] 2 KB 1.

DUTIES OF THE SELLER

11.4   The Act imposes several duties on the seller of goods by implying the following conditions into all sale of goods contracts.

Existence of the goods

11.5   The seller warrants that the goods exist (and therefore will be in breach of contract if they do not) except that where there is a contract for the sale of specific goods and, unknown to the seller, the goods have perished before the contract is concluded, the contract is void. Specific goods are goods identified and agreed on at the time the contract is made. (Eg if a customer buys the actual item displayed in a shop.)

Duty to pass a good title

11.6   There is an implied condition on the part of the seller that he has a right to sell the goods.[2] A seller was found to be in breach of this implied in the case of *Rowland* v *Divall*.[3] In May 1922 Rowland bought a car from Divall. It was a stolen car and the person who sold it to Divall had no right to sell it. It was held that Rowland was entitled to damages as Divall was in breach of the implied condition that he had the right to sell the car. The seller is obliged to ensure, for example that the goods can be sold legally into the United Kingdom.[4] There is an implied condition, that the goods are free from any charge or encumbrance not known to the buyer and that the buyer will enjoy quiet possession of the goods.[5]

Transfer of property

11.7   It can be important to ascertain the exact point at which property in the goods passes from the buyer to the seller. A number of consequences may follow the passing of property, for example:

1. Unless otherwise agreed the risk of loss or accidental damage to the goods passes to the buyer.
2. The passing of property gives the seller the right to sue for the price.
3. When property has passed the buyer can sell the goods to a third party, even though he may not yet have paid the seller.
4. If there is a difference between the passing of property and the physical taking of possession, then the person physically in possession of the goods may, despite the fact that he is not the lawful owner, pass good title on to an innocent third party acting in good faith.
5. If the seller becomes insolvent while the goods are still in his possession the only circumstances in which the buyer can claim the goods are if the property has passed (or exceptionally, if the court grants specific implement).

---

[2] Sale of Goods Act 1979, s 12(1).
[3] [1923] 2 KB 500.
[4] *Niblett Ltd* v *Confectioners' Materials Co Ltd* [1921] 3 KB 387.
[5] Sale of Goods Act 1979, s 12(2).

Criteria as to when property is to pass depend largely on whether the goods are **11.8**
unascertained or specific. Specific goods are goods which are identified and agreed on
at the time that the contract of sale is made. Obviously unascertained goods are those
which have not been identified and agreed on at the time of the contract. Unascertained
goods depend for their identification on some subsequent act of appropriation to the
contract.

Unascertained goods

Normally property cannot pass until the goods become ascertained.[6] This is shown **11.9**
in the case of *Hayman* v *McLintock*.[7] A seller had 420 sacks of flour stored in his warehouse. He agreed to sell 100 sacks to a buyer who paid but left the sacks in Hayman's
warehouse. The 100 sacks were not physically separated from the rest. The seller
went bankrupt and his trustee in bankruptcy claimed to be entitled to all 420 sacks.
His claim was upheld as the goods were still unascertained.

There are some rules which clarify when goods become ascertained **11.10**

- Where there is a contract for the sale of unascertained or future goods by
  description, and goods of that description are unconditionally appropriated
  to the contract either by the buyer with the sellers assent or by the seller the
  property in the goods thereupon passes to the buyer.[8]
- Where the seller delivers the goods to the buyer or to a carrier for the
  purpose of transmission to the buyer and does not reserve the right of disposal
  he is regarded as having unconditionally appropriated the goods to the
  contract.[9]
- Where the buyer has bought goods which are an unspecified part of a specified
  whole property will pass to the buyer when the bulk is reduced to the quantity
  to which the buyer is entitled.[10]

These rules must be read in conjunction with s 16. Therefore property would not **11.11**
pass if the goods were delivered to a carrier but were still mixed with other goods of
the same description. A precise definition of "unconditional appropriation" is very
difficult. Each case is decided according to the particular circumstances. The case of
Pignataro v *Gilroy*[11] involved the sale of 140 bags of rice. Fifteen of the bags were left
on the sellers premises ready for delivery. The buyer was asked to collect them but
a month had passed before he decided to do so. In the meantime the bags had been
stolen through no fault of the seller. It was held that there had been an unconditional
appropriation to the contract and the buyer could not claim back the price of the 15
sacks.[12]

---

[6] Sale of Goods Act 1979, s 16.
[7] 1907 SC 936.
[8] Sale of Goods Act 1979, s 18, r 5(1).
[9] Sale of Goods Act 1979, s 18, r 5(2).
[10] Sale of Goods Act 1979, s 18, r 5(3).
[11] [1919] KB 459.
[12] See also *Carlos Federspiel & Co* v *Charles Twigg & Co* [1957] 1 Lloyd's Rep 240.

Specific goods

11.12 In a contract for the sale of specific goods the property in the goods is transferred at the time intended by the parties. In order to ascertain the intention of the parties regard shall be had to the terms of the contract, the conduct of the parties and the circumstances of the case.[13] In commercial contracts sellers frequently reserve title to the goods until the price is paid in full. Such clauses are known as "Romalpa clauses" after the leading case; *Aluminium Industrie Vaasen BV* v *Romalpa Aluminium*.[14] Where no intention as to the passing of property can be found in the contract then rules 1–4 of s 18 will apply.

Rule 1

11.13 Where there is an unconditional contract for the sale of specific goods in a deliverable state, the property in the goods passes to the buyer when the contract is made. In the case of *Morison* v *Lockhart*[15] it was held that, as long as something is attached to land, it can not be in a deliverable state. "Delivery" is defined in s 61 as "the voluntary transfer of possession from one person to another". It is therefore not necessarily a physical handing over of the goods.[16]

Rule 2

11.14 Where there is a contract for the sale of specific goods and the seller is bound to do something to the goods in order to put them into a deliverable state, the property does not pass until that thing is done and the buyer notified. The leading case on this rule is *Underwood* v *Burgh Castle Brick & Cement Syndicate*.[17] A contract was made for the sale of an engine weighing over 30 tons. Its weight had caused it to sink into its cement base and it was agreed that the seller would dismantle it and detach it from the floor. It was held that the engine was not in a deliverable state and property could not yet pass.

Rule 3

11.15 Where the seller is bound to weigh, measure, test or do something to the goods in order to calculate the price, the property does not pass until that thing is done and the buyer notified.[18]

Rule 4

11.16 Where goods are sold on sale or return; the property in the goods passes to the buyer if:

1. he signifies his approval or acceptance to the seller; or
2. he adopts the transaction (eg by treating the goods as his own); or
3. he retains the goods beyond the date fixed for their return or beyond a time which is reasonable in the circumstances.

---

[13] Sale of Goods Act 1979, s 17.
[14] [1976] 2 All ER 552.
[15] 1912 SLT 189.
[16] See also *Tarling* v *Baxter* (1827) 6 B & C 360.
[17] [1922] 1 KB 343.
[18] *Nanka Bruce* v *Commonwealth Trust Ltd* [1926] AC 77.

An example of the adoption of the transaction arose in the case of *Kirkham* v *Attenborough*.[19] Kirkham had delivered jewellery to a buyer on sale or return. The buyer then pledged them with a pawnbroker. It was held that the buyer had adopted the transaction by pledging the goods. This meant that he was the owner of the goods and Kirkham could not recover them from the pawnbroker.

Transfer of risk

As you will have perceived from the last section, one of the reasons why it may be **11.17** important to establish when the property in the goods is transferred is because this often determines who bears the risk for loss or damage to the goods. The general rule is that risk passes with the property. Section 20 states: "unless otherwise agreed, the goods remain at the seller's risk until the property in them is transferred to the buyer, but when the property in them is transferred to the buyer the goods are at the buyer's risk, whether delivery has been made or not." Section 20(c) provides that where delivery has been delayed through the fault of either party the goods will be at the risk of the party at fault as regards any loss which might not have occurred but for such fault.

Transfer of title by a non-owner

Where the goods are sold by a person who is not their owner, and who does not sell **11.18** them under the authority or with the consent of the owner, the buyer acquires no better title to the goods than the seller had. This is summed up in the maxim *nemo dat quod non habet*. The consequences of this rule can be unfair to a person who has bought goods in good faith with no notice of any defect in the owner's title. There are therefore some exceptions to the general rule.[20] For example, a bona fide purchaser for value of a motor vehicle from a person in possession under a hire purchase or conditional sale obtains a good title.[21] The purchaser must be a private purchaser and not a trade or finance purchaser.[22]

Duty to deliver the goods

This does not necessarily mean "deliver" in its popular sense. The buyer may, for **11.19** example, have undertaken to collect the goods from the seller's premises, in which case " to deliver" means "to make available". The normal place of delivery is the seller's place of business. Therefore, unless the terms of the contract make some other provision for delivery, the buyer must collect the goods or arrange to have them collected on his behalf. The seller must ensure that the goods are in a deliverable state and, unless otherwise agreed, the cost of putting them in a deliverable state must be borne by the seller. A duty to deliver goods to the premises of the buyer is discharged by delivery to a respectable looking person at those premises even though it should later become evident that the person was not authorised to accept delivery. Unless otherwise agreed, delivery and payment are concurrent conditions, ie the buyer must pay for the goods

---

19 [1897] 1 QB 201.
20 Sale of Goods Act 1979, ss 24–27.
21 Hire Purchase Act 1964, s 27.
22 *Stevenson* v *Bentinck Ltd* [1976] 1 WLR 483; *Barker* v *Bell* [1971] 1 WLR 983.

the price when the goods are delivered and the seller must deliver the goods as soon as the price is paid.

Duty to supply the goods at the right time

11.20   Where there has been no time fixed for delivery, delivery must be within a reasonable time.[23] What is reasonable will depend on factors such as trade usage. If a time for delivery has been fixed, failure by the seller to deliver on time entitles the buyer to rescind the contract even if he has suffered no material loss. The importance of supplying the goods at the right time was established in the case of *Bowes* v *Shand & Co*.[24] By two contracts Shand & Co bought about 600 tons of madras rice to be shipped at Madras during the months of March and April 1874. About 4 tons were shipped in March, the remainder having been shipped in February. Shand & Co refused to accept the rice. It was held that they were entitled to do so.

Duty to supply goods in the right quantity

11.21   If the seller delivers less than the contracted quantity the buyer may reject all of the goods delivered.[25] One exception to this rule is that a buyer who is not a consumer cannot reject the goods if the difference in quality is slight and it would be unreasonable to reject the whole consignment.[26] If the buyer chooses to accept the goods he must pay for them in proportion to the agreed price. Unless he has agreed to do so the buyer need not accept delivery by instalments.[27] If the seller delivers too much the buyer may accept the contract goods and reject the rest, accept the whole delivery or reject the whole delivery. This is because the delivery of a different quantity is a new offer which the buyer may choose to accept or reject. If he accepts more than the quantity contracted for he must pay for the extra quantity at the contract rate.

Duty to supply goods of the right quality

11.22   This is the duty which gives rise to the greatest amount of litigation. There are three aspects to this duty.

Description

11.23   There is an implied condition that where goods are sold by description, the goods will correspond with that description.[28]

11.24   A sale is a sale by description if:

> (i)   the purchaser has not seen the goods, eg if they are purchased by mail order from a catalogue;
>
> (ii) the sale is of future or unascertained goods;

---

[23]   Sale of Goods Act 1979, s 29.
[24]   (1877) 2 App Cas 455.
[25]   Sale of Goods Act 1979, s 30.
[26]   Sale of Goods Act 1979, s 30(2E); *Regent OHG Aisenstadt und Barig* v *Francesco of Jermyn Street Ltd* [1981] 3 All ER 327.
[27]   *Behrend & Co* v *Produce Brokers' Co* [1920] 3 KB 530.
[28]   Sale of Goods Act 1979, s 13.

(iii) the goods are described as well as displayed, eg if they are in a package with a description or if there is a label on the goods or if the seller describes the goods.

Future goods are goods which are not yet in existence or not yet acquired by the seller at the time of the contract.   **11.25**

Unascertained goods may be;   **11.26**

1. goods to be manufactured or grown by the seller;
2. purely generic goods, eg 100 kilos of sugar; or
3. an unidentified part of a specified whole, eg 100 boxes of paper from a warehouse containing 500 boxes.

The implied condition that goods must correspond with their description applies   **11.27**
whether goods are sold in the course of a business or sold by individuals acting in a private capacity. Section 13 therefore provides a useful remedy where the remedies under s 14 are not available. The case of *Beale* v *Taylor*[29] involved a sale by a private individual. Taylor advertised his 1961 Triumph Herald motor car in *Exchange and Mart* as a "Herald Convertible, white 1961". Beale bought the car. On the rear of the car was a metal disc with "1200" on it. The vehicle proved to be unroadworthy and unsafe being made of two halves welded together. Only the back half was made in 1961 and the engine was not 1200 cc. Taylor had not owned the vehicle for long and was ignorant of these facts so there was no fraud involved. It was held that Beale was entitled to damages because the vehicle did not correspond with its description.

Satisfactory quality

Where the seller sells goods in the course of a business there is an implied condition   **11.28**
that the goods supplied under the contract are of satisfactory quality.[30] This provision has replaced the previous provision in section 14 of the Sale of Goods Act 1979, which stated that goods should be of "merchantable quality".[31] This condition does not apply to:

(i) defects shown to the buyer before the sale;
(ii) defects which the buyer should have seen when he examined the goods.

In the case of *Bartlett* v *Sidney Marcus Ltd*,[32] the buyer of a second-hand car had   **11.29**
been told that the clutch was not working properly but that a minor repair should correct it. It was held on appeal that the vehicle was not unmerchantable because the buyer knew of the defect. The implied condition that goods must be of satisfactory quality only applies when goods are sold in the course of a business. Goods are of satisfactory quality if they meet the standard that a reasonable person would regard

---

[29] [1967] 1 WLR 1193.
[30] Sale of Goods Act 1979, s 14, as amended by Sale and Supply of Goods Act 1994, s 1.
[31] The standard of satisfactory quality is a more stringent standard than that of merchantable quality and so much of the earlier case law is still relevant.
[32] [1965] 1 WLR 1013.

as satisfactory, taking account of any description of the goods, the price (if relevant) and all the other relevant circumstances.[33]

11.30   The quality of goods includes their state and condition, including:

(a) fitness for the purpose for which goods of the kind in question are commonly supplied;

(b) appearance and finish;

(c) freedom from minor defects;

(d) safety;

(e) durability.

11.31 It is hoped that the standard of satisfactory quality will prove to be easier to understand than the old law that goods should be of merchantable quality. There was often doubt about the exact meaning of "merchantable quality", although it was established in *Crowther* v *Shannon Motor Co*[34] that the condition that goods must be of the right quality could be applied to second-hand goods as well as new goods. Crowther bought a second-hand Jaguar car, 8 years old with 82,165 miles on the mileometer. Three weeks later after the buyer had driven 2,354 miles the engine seized up completely and had to be replaced. It was held that the buyer was entitled to damages.

11.32   The first Scottish case in which the standard of satisfactory quality was applied was *Thain* v *Anniesland Trade Centre*.[35] Mrs Thain had purchased a second-hand Renault car. The gearbox developed a fault after two weeks. The sellers refused to replace the gearbox and Mrs Thain rejected it several weeks later. It was held that the car was of satisfactory quality as a reasonable person would not any expect a car which had a recorded mileage of 80,000 to be durable. In a more recent case before the Inner House of the Court of Session,[36] a customer had sought to rescind a contract where a motor vehicle had a number of defects.[37] The sheriff, at first instance, had found that the vehicle was of satisfactory quality, as the faults were easy to rectify, were covered by the warranty, and would not affect the durability, longevity or value of the vehicle. The sheriff principal held that the buyer was entitled to reject the vehicle. This decision was upheld on appeal.

11.33   Goods which are unsafe will never meet the standard of satisfactory quality. Safety was an important factor in the case of *Clegg* v *Anderson*.[38] A yacht had been supplied with a keel which was much heavier than the manufacturer's specification. The heavy keel would cause the rigging to be unsafe. It was held that the yacht was not of satisfactory quality.

11.34   Where goods are sold in the course of a business and the buyer makes known any particular purpose for which the goods are bought, the goods must be reasonably fit for that particular purpose, whether or not it is a purpose for which goods of that kind are normally supplied.[39] The condition can not be relied on if the seller can prove that

[33] *Clegg* v *Anderson* [2003] 1 All ER (Comm) 721.
[34] [1975] 1 WLR 30.
[35] 1997 SLT (Sh Ct) 102.
[36] *Lamarra* v *Capital Bank* 2006 SLT 1053.
[37] This case concerned s 10 of the Supply of Goods (Implied Terms) Act 1973 by which a similar duty is imposed in the case of hire purchase transactions.
[38] [2003] 1 All ER (Comm) 721.
[39] Sale of Goods Act 1979, s 14(3).

the buyer did not rely on his skill and judgement. This condition requires only that the goods be reasonably fit for the purpose, not absolutely fit.[40]

Sales by sample

In a sale by sample the goods must be free from any defect making their quality **11.35** unsatisfactory which would not be apparent on a reasonable examination of the sample.[41] This condition applies whether or not the goods are sold in the course of a business. A sale is a sale by sample when there is an express or implied term to that effect.

In a sale by sample: **11.36**

   (i) the bulk must correspond with the sample;
   (ii) the buyer must be given a reasonable opportunity to compare the bulk with the sample.

These duties are owed by the seller of the goods any remedies exercised by the customer **11.37** will be against the seller, not the manufacturer. The seller will, however, have a right to seek compensation from the person who supplied goods to him. The extent to which the liability of the seller can be excluded or limited is governed by the Unfair Contract Terms Act 1977. The implied undertakings as to title[42] cannot be excluded or restricted by reference to any contract term. The implied undertakings as to quality[43] cannot be excluded or restricted as against a person dealing "as a Consumer".[44] In other contracts, eg contracts between businesses or contracts between private individuals they can only be excluded if it is fair and reasonable to do so.[45] The case of *Lamarra* v *Capital Bank* makes it clear that a manufacturer's warranty cannot limit the statutory rights of the buyer.[46]

DUTIES OF THE BUYER

There are two duties imposed on the buyer by the Sale of Goods Act 1979. **11.38**

Payment of the price

If it is not otherwise agreed, the buyer must pay the price as soon as the contract is **11.39** concluded as long as the seller is ready to deliver. A delay in making payment by the buyer does not justify the seller rescinding the contract. The seller need not accept payment other than by legal tender. If he accepts a cheque it is as a conditional payment and the debt revives if the cheque is dishonoured.

---

[40] *Bristol Tramways* v *Fiat Motors Ltd* [1910] 2 KB 831.
[41] Sale of Goods Act 1979, s 15.
[42] Sale of Goods Act 1979, s 12.
[43] Sale of Goods Act 1979, ss 13–15.
[44] Unfair Contract Terms Act 1977, s 20. Sale and Supply of Goods to Consumers Regulations 2002 (SI 2002/3045).
[45] Sale of Goods Act 1979, s 24.
[46] 2006 SLT 1053.

Duty to take delivery

11.40 Failure to take delivery on time does not entitle the seller to rescind the contract, but if the delay is so long as to justify the seller assuming that the buyer has abandoned the contract he may dispose of the goods elsewhere. The length of delay which will justify rescission will depend on the terms of the contract and circumstances such as the nature of the goods. Obviously, if the goods are perishable rescission may be justified after a relatively short delay. If the buyer delays taking delivery he is liable for any accidental loss of or damage to the goods which would not have occurred but for the delay.

ACCEPTANCE OF THE GOODS

11.41 The buyer is deemed to have accepted the goods when either:

1. he intimates to the seller that he has accepted them; or
2. the goods have been delivered to him and he does any act in relation to them which is inconsistent with the ownership of the seller.[47]

11.42 The buyer is not deemed to have accepted the goods until he has had a reasonable opportunity of examining them in order to ensure that they are in conformity with the contract. If, for example, a person buys a lawn mower in the January sales, he may not be regarded as having accepted the goods until he has had an opportunity to try the lawn mower to see if it works.[48] The buyer loses his right to reject the goods when he accepts them. In certain circumstances there is provision for a cooling off period during which the buyer can cancel the contract. Under the Consumer Credit Act 1974 there is a 7-day cooling-off period where a credit agreement is signed away from trade premises.[49] The Consumer Protection (Cancellation of Contracts Concluded away from Business Premises) Regulations 1987 provide a similar cooling-off period where the contract does not involves the provision of credit.[50] Where the contract is made exclusively by means of distance communication the Consumer Protection (Distance Selling) Regulations 2000[51] there is a 7-day cooling-off period which may extend to 3 months if the seller has failed to fulfil a duty to provide information to the buyer.[52]

REMEDIES OF THE SELLER

11.43 The seller has a right to action against the buyer in two circumstances.

1. Where the seller has refused to accept delivery of the goods the seller can claim damages for non-acceptance.
2. Where the buyer has failed to pay the price the seller may sue for payment of the price.

---

[47] Sale of Goods Act 1979, s 35 (as amended by the Sale and Supply of Goods Act 1994).
[48] Sale of Goods Act 1979, s 34.
[49] Consumer Credit Act 1974, ss 67–73.
[50] SI 1987/2117 (as amended by Consumer Protection (Cancellation of Contracts Concluded away from Business Premises) (Amendment) Regulations (SI 1988/985) and Consumer Protection (Cancellation of Contracts Concluded away from Business Premises) (Amendment) Regulations 1998 (SI 1998/3050)).
[51] SI 2000/2334.
[52] SI 2000/2334, regs 8–10.

An unpaid seller may also have remedies against the goods. He will be deemed to be **11.44** an unpaid seller if the whole of the price has not been paid or tendered or a cheque taken as payment has been dishonoured.[53] The seller will be classed as unpaid even if there is only a fraction of the price still to be paid. The unpaid seller who is still in possession of the goods has a right of lien, ie the right to retain possession of them until he is paid. This right exists even if property has transferred to the buyer. The lien is only for payment of the goods not for any other debt owed by the buyer to the seller. The right of lien is lost where the seller delivers the goods to a carrier for transmission to the buyer or when the buyer lawfully obtains possession of the goods or if the seller waives his right. When the buyer becomes insolvent, the unpaid seller who has parted with possession of the goods has the right to resume possession of the goods so long as they are in transit. The buyer is insolvent if he has either ceased to pay his debts in the ordinary course of business or he cannot pay his debts as they become due. The goods are in the course of transit when they have passed out of the control of the seller or his agent and are not yet in the control of the buyer or his agent. If the buyer intercepts the goods at some stage during transit the right of stoppage is lost.[54]

Once the seller has exercised a right of lien or stoppage, he may sell the goods if **11.45** they are perishable or if he gives notice to the buyer that he intends to do so and the buyer does not pay the price within a reasonable time. There may be an express term in a sale of goods contract giving the seller a right of resale in specific circumstances. As you already know, such a sale confers a good title on the second buyer.

REMEDIES OF THE BUYER

Damages for non-delivery

The amount of damages which can be claimed if the seller wrongfully neglects or **11.46** refuses to deliver the goods is the estimated loss arising naturally and directly from the breach of contract. Where the goods can be obtained elsewhere the buyer should minimise his loss by buying equivalent goods and claiming the difference in price and his expenses.

Specific implement

This remedy is only available for specific goods and where the goods cannot be replaced **11.47** in an available market.

Rejection of the goods or retention and damages

Where the seller is in breach of contract, the buyer shall be entitled either: **11.48**

1. to retain the goods and claim damages; or
2. if the breach is material, to reject any goods delivered under the contract.[55]

Any breach of any term (express or implied) as to the quality of the goods or their **11.49** fitness for a purpose, or that the goods will correspond with their description, is a

---

[53] Sale of Goods Act 1979, s 38.
[54] *Plischke & Sohne* v *Allison Bros Ltd* [1936] 2 All ER 1009; *Muir* v *Rankin* (1905) 13 SLT 60.
[55] Sale of Goods Act 1979, s 15B.

material breach. Where the buyer chooses to reject the goods he is also entitled to the return of the purchase price if it has been paid. Once the buyer has accepted the goods he loses the right to reject them but he can claim damages equal to the difference between the actual value of the goods supplied and the value which the goods would have if they had conformed with the contract. Where the defects only become apparent when the goods are used, the act of using them will not necessarily amount to acceptance of the goods. In the case of *Rogers* v *Parish (Scarborough) Ltd*,[56] it was held that a new Range Rover which had developed several defects over a period of 6 months was not of merchantable quality and the buyer was entitled to reject it.

Goods which are not supplied under a contract of sale

11.50   Where goods are supplied under a licence agreement or a hire agreement the Sale and Supply of Goods Act 1994 gives the person acquiring the goods the same rights and remedies as a buyer of goods.

Additional remedies in consumer contracts

11.51   Where there is a consumer contract in which the buyer is a consumer,[57] there is an assumption that, if the goods do not conform with the contract during a period of six months from the delivery of the goods, they did not comply at the time of the contract. This means that the buyer does not have to prove that the defect existed when the contract was formed. The right of the buyer to reject the goods, however, is more limited. The remedies of repair or replacement, reduction in price and rescission of the contract are available but the buyer does not have an automatic right to choose between these remedies.[58] Where the buyer requires the seller to repair or replace the goods he must do so within a reasonable time and without causing significant inconvenience to the buyer. The buyer cannot require the seller to repair or replace the goods where it is not possible to do so or the cost is disproportionate. If repair or replacement cannot be carried out then the buyer may seek a reduction in price or may reject the goods. Where the buyer rejects the goods the compensation may be reduced to take account of the period of use of the goods before rejection.[59]

REMEDIES AGAINST MANUFACTURERS OR SUPPLIERS

11.52   At common law persons who are injured by unsafe products, provided that they themselves bought the goods, may sue the seller of the goods in contract, using also the Sale of Goods Act 1979 principles of satisfactory quality and fitness for purpose. In addition, the injured party, whether or not they themselves bought the goods, may sue the manufacturer in delict. The leading case on the manufacturer's liability is the Scottish House of Lords case of *Donoghue* v *Stevenson*. A manufacturer supplied a bottle of ginger beer in an opaque bottle to a cafe. The product had not been opened since it left the factory. Unknown to all parties, the bottle contained the remains of a

---

[56] [1987] QB 933.
[57] Pt 5A (inserted by reg 5 of the Sale and Supply of Goods to Consumers Regulations 2002).
[58] Section 48A.
[59] This contrasts with the right to reject under s 15B, when no reduction is made.

decomposed snail. A customer ordered an ice cream drink containing the ginger beer for Mrs Donoghue. After drinking most of the ginger beer, Mrs Donoghue discovered the remains of a snail in the bottom of the bottle. She became ill, and successfully sued the manufacturer for negligence.[60] The case established for the first time that manufacturers owed a duty of care to the end-user, even where they had no knowledge of who that person would be. It was an important fact in this case that the cafe staff had had no opportunity of examining the contents of the bottle: if the retailer has a chance to examine the goods before supplying them to the customer, he too may find himself liable in delict.

Legislators have been faced with a delicate problem as there is a distinction between **11.53** goods which are unsafe in themselves and goods which are unsafe, or potentially unsafe, in use. Consequently, there are two main threads to the control of the safety of goods. These ensure that goods are safe in themselves and that sufficient information is provided with goods to prevent their being unsafe in use.

CONSUMER PROTECTION ACT 1987

Part I of the Consumer Protection Act 1987 implements the EC Directive on Product **11.54** Liability, and makes manufacturers strictly liable in delict for defective products "if the safety of the product is not such as persons generally are entitled to expect". Damages may be claimed by persons who may not have a contract with the seller, eg friends and family of the buyer. Even a person who was bystander may claim damages. Damages may be claimed directly from the manufacturer.

The claimant does not need to prove that any manufacturer or supplier has been **11.55** negligent. All that he has to prove is:

    (a) there has been injury or damage;
    (b) there was a defect in the product;
    (c) the defect caused the injury or damage.

Product

A product is defined as any goods (including components and raw materials) or gas, **11.56** water or electricity.[61] Land and buildings are not products but things used in the construction of buildings (bricks, cement, wood, glass, etc) may be products. Originally primary agricultural products were not included but following an amendment to the original Product Liability Directive, they are now included.[62]

Persons liable

Section 2 of the Act states that it is the producer who is primarily liable. A producer **11.57** may be any one of the following:

    1. the manufacturer;
    2. the abstractor of the product (eg a miner or quarryman);

---

[60] 1932 SC (HL) 31; 1932 SLT 317.
[61] Consumer Protection Act 1987, s 1.
[62] Directive (99/34/EC) amending Directive (85/374/EEC); Consumer Protection Act 1987 (Product Liability) (Modification) (Scotland) Order 2001 (SSI 2001/265).

    3. the processor of the product, where the processor has altered the essential characteristics of the product (eg a petroleum refiner);

    4. an own-brander (ie a person who puts his own name on a product – usually a supermarket chain);

    5. the person who imported the product into the EC.

11.58   The supplier of the goods may also be liable if he is unable to identify the manufacturer, own-brander or importer to the person who suffered the damage within a reasonable time of being asked to supply the information. (A supplier is defined as a person who sells goods, hires goods, supplies them under a hire purchase contract or provides them as part of an exchange, whether or not any money has been paid.)

Causation

11.59   The fact that a product fails to work is not sufficient for it to be regarded as defective. A product is defective if its safety is not what persons generally are entitled to expect. This is an objective test which takes into account the design of the product, the purpose for which it was marketed, the use of any warnings or instructions and the state of knowledge at the time when the product was supplied and any warnings and instructions which were issued. No liability would arise, therefore, if a brand of wood preservative had been marked and clearly labelled as being for outdoor use only and a customer used it indoors and was rendered unconscious by breathing the fumes. The Act states that there will be liability if the person who has suffered the damage can prove that he suffered damage caused by the defective product.

Damage

11.60   The Act defines this damage as covering death, personal injury or any loss or damage to any property. The loss or damage must be to private property, so damage to a private car may give rise to a claim but damage to a company van will not. No claim can be made under that Act if the loss or damage to property is less that £275. The producer is not liable under the Consumer Protection Act for loss of, or damage to the product itself. Any claim for compensation for damage to the product itself must be made under the Sale of Goods Act 1979. If the damage to the product is caused by a defect within the product which was supplied with the product, a claim cannot be made under the Consumer Protection Act 1987, but if the damage was caused by a component which was fitted later, a claim for the damage to the main product can be made under this act. Therefore if a computer fails because of a faulty memory chip which was part of the computer when it was supplied, the value of the computer cannot be included in a claim under the Consumer Protection Act, but if the memory chip is purchased and fitted later and causes damage to the computer a claim under this act can be made for the damage to the computer but not for the chip itself.

Defences

11.61   It is a defence to prove that the defect in the product is caused by compliance with a statutory provision.

11.62   Another defence is that the goods were never supplied. This defence only applies to goods which were intended only for the producer's own use or goods which have been stolen. It is not necessary for a claimant to show that he bought the goods. Claims cannot be made where damage has been caused in circumstances where the supply was not in the course of a business or for profit. Therefore no claims could be made if a product donated to a charity raffle caused damage.

Liability is only for defects which existed at the time of supply. A manufacturer may **11.63** claim that a product has become unsafe only after excessive use or that goods have been tampered with. A supermarket would not be liable if poison had been injected into bottles of tonic water.

Another defence is the development risks defence which can be used where the **11.64** state of scientific and technical knowledge in an industry is such that there was no way of knowing that goods were unsafe at the time when they were supplied.

The liability of the producer may be reduced if he can show that the person who **11.65** has suffered the loss, damage, or injury has himself been negligent. This is known as contributory negligence and has the effect of reducing any award of damages according the percentage of blame attributable to the victim. A person may be deemed to have been contributorily negligent if he ignores a warning on the label of a product and uses it for a purpose for which it was not supplied.

The defence of *volenti non fit injuria* applies where a person has voluntarily purchased **11.66** and used a product which is inherently dangerous such as tobacco.

LIABILITY FOR DEFECTIVE SERVICES

Many of the contracts entered into by consumers are for the provision of services; **11.67** such as furniture removal, home improvements, car maintenance, holidays, health care and professional services (eg banking, insurance, accountancy, legal services).

The provision of services has not been afforded the same attention by legislators as **11.68** the provision of goods, particularly in Scotland. In England there is a statute – the Sale and Supply of Goods Act 1982 – Pt 2 of which implies certain terms into contracts for the provision of services. This does not apply to Scotland.

Some contracts (known as contracts for work and materials) may involve both sale **11.69** of goods and provision of services. An example would be a contract to repair a motor vehicle where parts of the vehicle would be replaced by new components. It is often a matter of interpretation to decide whether the agreement should be treated as two contracts – one to provide the services and another to sell the goods or whether it should be treated as one contract for services alone.

If the materials have been supplied by the customer the repairer will not be liable **11.70** if they are defective but if he has selected goods he may be liable if they are not fit for the purpose. Even where the customer has specified the materials to be used the seller may be liable if they are not of satisfactory quality.[63]

PROTECTION OF THE CONSUMER IN CONTRACTS FOR SERVICES

In the absence of any express agreement to the contrary, the law will imply certain **11.71** terms into service contracts.

---

[63] *Young and Marten Ltd* v *McManus Childs Ltd* [1969] 1 AC 454.

That the contractor will exercise reasonable skill and care

11.72   A person is responsible for exercising reasonable skill in his trade or profession and if his work is not carried out with such skill he will be regarded as being in breach of contract. The case of *McIntyre* v *Gallacher* related to faulty plumbing work in a Glasgow tenement. A leaking pipe caused damage to property on the lower floors for which the landlord, McIntyre, was held to be liable to pay compensation to the residents. He sought damages from Gallacher and the court considered evidence that the proper and workmanlike method of sealing a pipe was to solder it. Mr Gallacher had merely hammered the ends of the pipe together. He was held to be liable for failing to carry out the job with the requisite level of skill.[64]

11.73   Where professional services are involved it may be difficult to determine whether reasonable skill has been exercised. A doctor cannot always cure his patient and a lawyer may not always win a case. The general view is that it is sufficient if he exercises the ordinary skill of an ordinary competent person carrying out that activity.

Time for performance

11.74   Consumers often complain because work has not been carried out on time. Where a time limit has been fixed the contractor will be liable for failure to complete the work on time, unless of course, the delay is caused by the customer. In the case of *T & R Duncanson* v *Scottish County Investment Co Ltd* it was held that a plasterer was not liable for a failure to complete his work in time because the client had failed to ensure that other tradesmen (carpenters, etc) had kept to their schedules.[65]

11.75   If there is no express term about time a consumer is entitled to expect that work will be completed within a reasonable time. In a case where a car had been damaged in an accident and the repair work was not carried out for eight weeks. It was held that the repairer was liable as the work had not been carried out within a reasonable time.[66]

Cost

11.76   The cost for a service will often be agreed in advance and if that is so, the agreed price must be paid even if it is not the normal price for the work. Where no price has been agreed there is a presumption that the tradesman of professional is entitled to reasonable remuneration. This principle was applied in the case of *Robert Allan and Partners* v *McKinstray*. A firm of architects had prepared preliminary drawings for a house which the client proposed to build. The client then requested more detailed information to allow a builder to draw up an estimate. The client later abandoned the project and refused to pay the architect's fees. He argued that the work done was in the nature of an estimate and since the house had not been built no fee was payable. The court held that the architect was entitled to a quantum meruit payment for the work done.[67]

---

[64] (1883) 11 R 64. See also *Brett* v *Williamson* 1980 SLT (Sh Ct) 56; *Mackintosh* v *Nelson* 1984 SLT (Sh Ct) 82.
[65] 1915 SC 1106.
[66] *Charnock* v *Liverpool Corp* [1968] 1 WLR 1498.
[67] 1975 SLT (Sh Ct) 63.

Duty to take care of goods deposited

A tradesman must exercise the standard of care which a reasonably prudent man **11.77** would take over his own property. In a case against a garage company which had left a car in an unsupervised car park with the keys in the ignition it was held that the garage company was liable to pay damages to the car owner. The car had been stolen by a drunken sailor who crashed it and caused serious damage.[68]

CONSUMER CREDIT

The laws relating to the provision of credit by way of business are mainly contained **11.78** in the Consumer Credit Act 1974 as amended by a series of statutory instruments[69] and the Consumer Credit Act 2006. The new Act will be implemented over the next 2 years but further changes may then occur as a result of a European Consumer Credit Directive

There are three principal types of credit transaction.

HIRE PURCHASE

This is an agreement by which goods are hired in return for periodic payments. Passing **11.79** of ownership is delayed pending compliance with certain conditions. (Normally this will entail making the final payment and exercising an option to purchase the goods.) Unless and until the conditions are complied with the customer does not have a good title to the goods which he can pass on to a third party.[70]

CONDITIONAL SALE

This is an agreement whereby the buyer is obliged to make a specified number of **11.80** deferred payments after which ownership of the goods will pass to him.

CREDIT SALE

This is a contract of sale in which there is a provision for deferred payment of the price. **11.81** Ownership of the goods passes according to the provisions of the contract.

The 1974 Act applies to consumer credit agreements. These are agreements for **11.82** personal credit for amounts up to £25,000 (s 8(2)). (This upper limit will be removed when the new provisions of the 2006 Act are implemented.) The 1974 Act only applies if the debtor is an individual. The term "individual" includes a partnership with less than three partners but not a company.

EXEMPT AGREEMENTS

Agreements which are exempt from the 1974 Act include: **11.83**

---

[68] *Forbes* v *Aberdeen Motors Ltd* 1965 SC 35
[69] Consumer Credit (Advertisements) Regulations 2004 (SI 2004/1484); Consumer Credit (Agreements) (Amendment) Regulations 2004 (SI 2004/1482); Consumer Credit (Early Settlement) Regulations 2004 (SI 2004/1483).
[70] *Helby* v *Matthews* [1895] AC 471.

1. loans for the purposes of house purchase given by reputable lenders;
2. agreements with insurance companies, friendly societies, charities, bodies corporate, etc, as specified in an order by the Secretary of State;
3. small agreements, ie where the amount of credit given is less than £50;
4. non-commercial agreements. (These are not exempt from all of the Act but they are exempt from Pt v which relates to formalities.)[71]

TRADING CONTROL

11.84   The 1974 Act establishes a system of licensing operated by the Office of Fair Trading. The object is to ensure that only honest persons can deal in credit. A licence is required to carry on a wide range of credit businesses. The Director General of Fair Trading has discretion as to whether to grant a licence. He will not grant one to a person who is known to have committed any offences involving dishonesty or violence or who has contravened the terms of the Act. He has power to revoke licences, to suspend them or to impose conditions.

11.85   There are strict rules on the form and content of advertisements to ensure that they give adequate information. It is a criminal offence to canvass unconnected loans (ie loans which are not linked to the supply of goods or services) off trade premises. The only defence is to prove that the visit was in response to a signed request made on a pervious occasion. It is permissible to canvass the sale of goods or supply of services on credit. It is a criminal offence to send any advertisement or information about credit or hire to persons under the age of 18, with a view to financial gain. It is a defence to prove that the sender had no reason to suspect that the person was a minor.

11.86   Enforcement is under the control of the Office of Fair Trading and the trading standards departments of local authorities. They have the following powers:

1. entry and inspection;
2. power to make test purchases.

AGREEMENT CONTROL

11.87   The 1974 Act regulates agreements in the following ways:

Regulations on the form, content and legibility of agreements

11.88   Regulations are made under the authority of the Act to ensure that consumers are provided with all of the necessary information in a legible form. The agreement must be signed by both parties. A copy of the agreement must be supplied to the customer within 7 days of its taking effect. If these provisions are not complied with, the agreement cannot be enforced by the creditor.[72] (However, the court may choose to enforce the agreement if the customer is not prejudiced. The court may vary the terms of such an agreement.)

---

[71] Consumer Credit Act 1974, s 16.
[72] *Wilson* v *Secretary of State for Trade and Industry* [2003] UKHL 40; [2004] 1 AC 816; *Eastern Distributors Ltd* v *Goldring* [1957] 2 QB 600.

Cancellation rights

Some agreements can be cancelled by the customer without his being in breach of **11.89** contract. The cancellation rights are intended as a means of protecting customers from over-persuasive salesmen, particularly in the customer's own home.

In order for the customer to have the right to cancel an agreement the following **11.90** conditions must be met.

(a) There must have been oral representations made in the presence of the customer by the creditor, the owner of the goods, or an agent, or a dealer, before the contract was made.

(b) The customer must have signed the agreement elsewhere than at the business premises of the creditor, the owner of the goods, a party to a linked transaction, or a negotiator.

The customer has a right to cancel at any time up to the fifth day following the day **11.91** on which he received his copy of the executed agreement. Cancellation is effected by written notice to the creditor, the owner of the goods, or to an agent of either.

The right to cancel gives valuable protection to the consumer and it became apparent **11.92** that the same protection against over-zealous sales persons should be given where the contract did not involve credit. Therefore regulations have been passed to give a similar protection where the contract involves payment by cash (the Consumer Protection (Cancellation of Contracts Concluded away from Business Premises) Regulations 1987). The Timeshare Act 1992 has given cancellation rights in the case of contracts involving the use of property on a timeshare basis. This right extends to contracts concluded on the premises of the owner of the property.

Creditor's liability in respect of goods and services supplied on credit

Where there are three parties to a transaction – the buyer (debtor), the seller (supplier) **11.93** and the creditor – there is often a business association between the seller and the creditor, eg between the seller of a motor vehicle and a finance company who pay him a commission to arrange finance from their company. The 1974 Act (s 75) makes the seller and the creditor jointly and severally liable for any breaches of contract, or misrepresentation by the supplier, for agreements for credit between £100 and £30,000. This provision enables the buyer to choose to exercise his rights, eg his rights under the Sale of Goods Act 1979 against either the seller or the creditor. This is very useful if the seller has gone out of business or is outside the United Kingdom. Note that these limits are different from the limits applying to the rest of the Act.

Protection of the debtor in default

According to the law of contract, the creditor has the usual remedies if the debtor is **11.94** in breach of contract, eg rescission for a material breach. The credit agreement itself may contain additional remedies such as right to repossess and sell the goods. Before he can exercise such powers, the creditor must give notice in the form of a default notice which must specify the nature of the breach, the action required to remedy it, the date by which it must be remedied and the sum required as compensation. If the breach is remedied within the time-limit it must be treated as never having occurred.

If the customer has received a default notice he can apply to court for a time order which may extend the period of repayment. Once one-third or more of the total price has been paid the creditor cannot recover possession of the goods without a court order, even if the written agreement states that he can. If he seizes the goods without a court order the agreement is regarded as terminated and all payments must be returned to the debtor.

Extortionate credit bargains

11.95   The court has power to re-open and examine credit agreements if they are considered to be extortionate. This power can only be exercised when one of the parties seeks redress in the courts. A credit bargain is extortionate if it requires the debtor to make payments which are "grossly exorbitant" or if the agreement in some other way "grossly contravenes ordinary principles of fair dealing". This provision applies to all personal credit agreements and there are no financial limits. The court has the power to vary the agreement and any related agreements so as to achieve justice between the parties. The amended provisions under the 2006 Act will allow the courts to reopen any credit agreements which are "unfair" to the borrower.[73] The meaning of the word "unfair" is unclear.

CRIMINAL LAW AS A MEANS OF CONSUMER PROTECTION

SAFETY REGULATIONS

11.96   Part II of the Consumer Protection Act 1987 allows the Secretary of State for Trade and Industry to make safety regulations for consumer goods, to ensure that such goods are safe, and that any unsafe goods do not reach consumers. A breach of safety regulations can constitute a criminal offence. Trading Standards Officers have powers to issue prohibition notices, notices to warn, suspension notices, and forfeiture orders (under which unsafe goods can be forfeited, and destroyed following an order from a court).

11.97   Part II of the Act also creates a "general safety requirement" according to which it is an offence to supply or offer to supply any consumer goods which are not reasonably safe, ie there must be no risk or a minimal risk of death or personal injury resulting from the goods. There are some defences to a charge under this part of the Act.

REGULATION OF TRADE DESCRIPTIONS

11.98   In order to protect the consumer from being induced by misleading descriptions relating to goods or services into entering contracts the Trade Descriptions Act 1968 and the Consumer Protection Act 1987 provide for the legal regulation of descriptions used by businesses to attract customers. The use of criminal sanctions under these acts

---

[73] Consumer Credit Act 1974, s 140A.

to regulate business practices is in addition to the remedies available under civil law which have been explained in the previous sections. Regulation by criminal sanctions has the advantage that it does not rely on the knowledge of the consumer as to his rights and his willingness to enforce those rights. Enforcement is by the local trading standards departments and the regulation has a deterrent effect on unscrupulous trade practices.

Applying a false trade description to goods

"Any person who, in the course of a trade or business: **11.99**

    (a) applies a false trade description to any goods; or

    (b) supplies or offers to supply any goods to which a false trade description is applied:

shall, subject to the provisions of the Act, be guilty of an offence."[74]

The term "person" includes a limited company.[75] Where an offence under this Act **11.100** which has been committed by a body corporate is proved to have been committed with the consent and connivance of, or to be attributable to any neglect on the part of, any director, manager, secretary or other similar officer of the body corporate, he as well as the body corporate shall be guilty of an offence.

"A person applies a description if he –   **11.101**

    (a) attaches it to or incorporates it with the goods themselves or anything on or in or with which the goods are supplied;

    (b) places the goods in, on or with anything which has the trade description on or incorporated with it;

    (c) uses the trade description in any manner likely to be taken as referring to the goods".[76]

An oral statement may amount to the use of a trade description. Where the goods **11.102** are described in response to a request in which a trade description was used and it is reasonable to infer that the goods were supplied as goods corresponding to that trade description, the person supplying the goods shall be deemed to have applied that trade description. Normally the person who commits the offence will be the seller, but not always. In the case of *Fletcher* v *Budgen* it was the buyer who applied the false trade description. He was a car dealer who told his customer that his car was irreparable and fit only for scrap. The dealer gave him £2 for it, carried out repairs costing £56 and advertised it for sale at £135. It was held that the dealer had applied a false trade description when buying the car.[77]

According to s 2 of the Act, a false trade description is one which is false or **11.103** misleading to a material degree as regards any of the following matters with respect to any goods or parts of goods:

    (a) quantity, size or gauge;

    (b) method of manufacture, production, processing or reconditioning;

---

[74] Trade Descriptions Act 1968, s 1.
[75] Trade Descriptions Act 1968, s 20.
[76] Trade Descriptions Act 1968, s 4.
[77] [1974] 2 All ER 1243.

(c) composition;

(d) fitness for purpose, strength, performance, behaviour or accuracy;

(e) any other physical characteristics;

(f) testing by any other person and the results thereof (eg current MOT);

(g) approval by any person or conformity with a type approved by any person;

(h) place or date of manufacture, production, processing or reconditioning;

(i) person by whom manufactured, produced, processed or reconditioned;

(j) other history, including previous ownership or use (eg the mileage of a car).

11.104 It is an offence under s 1 to supply or to offer to supply goods to which a false trade description is applied in the course of a trade or business. The application of the trade description is only an offence if it is associated with a supply of goods.[78] It is possible to disclaim a trade description in certain circumstances. The disclaimer must be as bold compelling and precise as the trade description itself, eg the disclaimer of a car's mileage must be boldly placed on the car's odometer.

Making misleading statements with regard to services

11.105 Liability for misleading statements with regard to services is established by s 14 which states that it shall be an offence for any person, in the course of a trade or business to make a statement which he knows to be false: or recklessly to make a statement which is false as to any of the following matters:

(1) the provision in the course of a trade or business of any services, accommodation or facilities;

(2) the nature of any services, accommodation or facilities provided in the course of a business;

(3) the time at which, manner in which or persons by whom any services, accommodation or facilities are so provided;

(4) the examination, approval or evaluation by any person of any services, accommodation or facilities so provided; or

(5) the location or amenities of any accommodation so provided.

11.106 This applies to statements made in advertisements brochures, and menus and to information given orally or in writing. The case of *Wings Ltd* v *Ellis* concerned a brochure which contained a false statement that a hotel in Sri Lanka had air conditioning. The mistake was discovered and steps were taken to mitigate the effect of the mistake. However a customer booked a holiday from the unchanged brochure, even though at the time he did so the tour operator was aware that the statement was false. It was held that Wings Ltd had committed an offence.[79] A well-known High Street retailer, Dixons, was convicted for offering for sale a TV set and a video recorder at an inclusive price with a "free 5 year guarantee". In fact the guarantee only applied to the TV set, although the advertisement did not say so.[80]

---

[78] *Wycombe Marsh Garages Ltd* v *Fowler* [1972] 1 WLR 1156.
[79] [1985] AC 372.
[80] *Smith* v *Dixons Ltd* 1986 SCCR 1.

Defences to a prosecution under the Trade Descriptions Act 1968

It shall be a defence for a person to prove that the commission of the offence was due **11.107** to a mistake or to reliance on information supplied to him, or to the act or default of another person, or an accident or some other cause beyond his control, and that he took all reasonable precautions and exercised all due diligence to avoid the commission of such an offence by himself or any person under his control.[81]

In proceedings for an offence of supplying or offering to supply goods to which a **11.108** false trade description is applied it shall be a defence for the person to prove that he did not know and could not with reasonable diligence have ascertained that the goods did not conform to the description or that the description had been applied to the goods.

It shall be a defence for a person to prove that he is a person whose business is **11.109** to publish or arrange for the publication of advertisements and that he received the advertisement for publication in the ordinary course of business and did not know and had no reason to suspect that its publication would amount to an offence under the Act.[82]

Enforcement of the Trade Descriptions Act 1968

Trading Standards Officers have a duty to enforce the Act within their area. They **11.110** have the power to make test purchases and to enter premises and inspect and seize goods and documents.[83]

MISLEADING INDICATIONS AS TO PRICE

It is an offence under the Consumer Protection Act 1987 to give a misleading indication **11.111** as to price in the provision in the course of a business of goods, services, accommodation or facilities.[84] A person shall be guilty of an offence if he gives an indication which is misleading as to the price at which any goods, services accommodation or facilities are available in circumstances where some or all of those consumers might reasonably be expected to rely on the misleading indication and he fails to take reasonable steps to prevent the consumers relying on the indication. It is immaterial whether he is acting on his own behalf or for another, whether he is the person from whom the goods, services etc. are available and whether the indication only misleads some of the consumers

The Consumer Protection Act defines a "consumer" as any person who might wish to **11.112** be supplied with goods for his own private consumption or to be provided with services or facilities, but not for the purposes of a business of his or to occupy accommodation, but not for the purposes of a business of his. "Price" means the aggregate of sums required to be paid by a consumer or any method of determining that aggregate. The term "misleading" includes such things as giving an indication that the price is less than it really is or that the price covers matters which it does not.[85] It is also an offence to give a misleading indication as to the method of calculating a price.

---

[81] Trade Descriptions Act 1968, s 24.
[82] Trade Descriptions Act 1968, s 25.
[83] Trade Descriptions Act 1968, ss 26–28.
[84] Consumer Protection Act 1987, s 20.
[85] Consumer Protection Act 1987, s 21.

11.113   This part of the Consumer Protection Act only applies where one party is acting in the course of business and the other is a consumer. There is a code of practice drawn up according to s 25 which has no legal force but which should assist traders to avoid contraventions of the Act and which may be used as evidence.

Defences

11.114   There is a general defence of taking reasonable precautions and exercising due diligence.[86] A disclaimer does not provide a defence but it does have the effect of negating the liability of a person giving a misleading indication. A disclaimer will not be effective in the case of a self-applied indication.

ENTERPRISE ACT 2002

11.115   Part 8 of the Enterprise Act confers powers on enforcers, such as Trading Standards Officers, to obtain court orders against traders who fail to fulfil their legal obligations to consumers.

11.116

> # ESSENTIAL FACTS
>
> ### INTRODUCTION
>
> - Consumer law is the specialised law which applies in the relationship between the consumer, or private customer, and the supplier of goods and services.
> - The main purpose of consumer law is to give a consumer greater rights against the supplier than those of a trade purchaser under ordinary law of contract.
>
> ### SALE AND SUPPLY OF GOODS
>
> - The Sale of Goods Act 1979 applies to all contracts by which the seller transfers or agrees to transfer the property in goods to the buyer for a money consideration called the price.
> - Goods are all movable property other than incorporeal rights and money.
> - The price may be fixed by the contract or may be left to be fixed in a manner agreed by the contract, or may be determined by the course of dealing between the parties.
>
> #### Duties of the seller
> 1. The seller warrants that the goods exist.

---

[86] Consumer Protection Act 1987, s 39.

2. There is an implied condition on the part of the seller that he has the right to sell the goods

3. There is an implied condition, that the goods are free from any charge or encumbrance not known to the buyer and that the buyer will enjoy quiet possession of the goods.

4. Duty to deliver the goods. The normal place of delivery is the seller's place of business. Unless otherwise agreed, delivery and payment are concurrent conditions.

5. Duty to supply the goods at the right time. Delivery must be within a reasonable time and at a reasonable hour.

6. Duty to supply goods in the right quantity.

7. Duty to supply goods of the right quality.

   (a) There is an implied condition that where goods are sold by description, the goods will correspond with that description (Sale of Goods Act 1979, s 13). This condition applies whether goods are sold in the course of a business or sold by individuals.

   (b) Where the seller sells goods in the course of a business there is an implied condition that the goods supplied under the contract are of satisfactory quality. (Sale of Goods Act 1979, s 14). This condition does not apply to, defects shown to the buyer before the sale and defects which the buyer should have seen when he examined the goods. The quality of goods includes their state and condition, including fitness for the purpose for which goods of the kind in question are commonly supplied, appearance and finish, freedom from minor defects, safety and durability.

   (c) In a sale by sample the goods must be free from any defect making their quality unsatisfactory which would not be apparent on a reasonable examination of the sample (Sale of Goods Act 1979, s 15).

Exclusion of seller's liability

The extent to which the liability of the seller can be excluded or limited is governed by the Unfair Contract Terms Act 1977. The implied undertakings as to title cannot be excluded or restricted by reference to any contract term. The implied undertakings as to quality cannot be excluded or restricted as against a person dealing "as a consumer". A manufacturer's warranty cannot limit the statutory rights of the buyer.

DUTIES OF THE BUYER

• If it is not otherwise agreed, the buyer must pay the price as soon as the contract is concluded as long as the seller is ready to deliver.

- Duty to take delivery. If the buyer delays taking delivery he is liable for any accidental loss of or damage to the goods which would not have occurred but for the delay.

ACCEPTANCE OF THE GOODS

- The buyer is deemed to have accepted the goods when he intimates that he has accepted them, or he treats the goods as his own.
- There may be a statutory cooling-off period (Consumer Credit Act 1974, ss 67–73; Consumer Protection (Cancellation of Contracts Concluded away from Business Premises) Regulations 1987; Consumer Protection (Distance Selling) Regulations 2000).

REMEDIES OF THE SELLER

- Damages for non-acceptance.
- Sue for payment of the price.
- Remedies against the goods. An unpaid seller has a right of lien. When the buyer becomes insolvent, the unpaid seller has the right to resume possession of the goods so long as they are in transit.

REMEDIES OF THE BUYER

- Damages for non-delivery; the estimated loss arising naturally and directly from the breach of contract.
- Specific implement; only for specific goods and where the goods cannot be replaced in an available market.
- Rejection of the goods or retention and damages.
- In consumer contracts the remedies of repair or replacement, reduction in price and rescission of the contract are available but the buyer does not have an automatic right to choose between these remedies (Sale of Goods Act 1979, s 48A).

REMEDIES AGAINST MANUFACTURERS OR SUPPLIERS

1. At common law the injured party, whether or not they themselves bought the goods, may sue the manufacturer in delict.
2. The Consumer Protection Act 1987 makes manufacturers strictly liable in delict for defective products. The claimant has to prove:
   (a) there has been injury or damage,
   (b) there was a defect in the product,
   (c) the defect caused the injury or damage.

- A "product" is defined as any goods (including components and raw materials) or gas, water or electricity.

- It is the producer who is primarily liable (ie the manufacturer or the abstractor of the product, or the processor of the product or an own brander, or the person who imported the product into the EC.
- A product is defective if its safety is not what persons generally are entitled to expect. This is an objective test.
- Damage includes death, personal injury or any loss or damage to any property. No claim can be made if the loss or damage to property is less that £275. The producer is not liable under the Consumer Protection Act for loss of, or damage to the product itself.

Defences

- The defect in the product is caused by compliance with a statutory provision.
- The goods were never supplied.
- The product has become unsafe only after excessive use or that goods have been tampered with.
- The state of scientific and technical knowledge is such that there was no way of knowing that goods were unsafe at the time when they were supplied.

LIABILITY FOR DEFECTIVE SERVICES

The common law principles of contract apply. In the absence of any express agreement to the contrary the law will imply certain terms into service contracts:

(a) That the contractor will exercise reasonable skill and care.
(b) If there is no express term about time a consumer is entitled to expect that work will be completed within a reasonable time.
(c) Where no price has been agreed there is a presumption that the tradesman of professional is entitled to reasonable remuneration.
(d) There is a duty to take care of goods deposited.

CONSUMER CREDIT

The Consumer Credit Act 1974, as amended by a series of statutory instruments and the Consumer Credit Act 2006, applies to consumer credit agreements. These are agreements for personal credit for amounts up to £25,000 (s 8(2)). The Act only applies if the debtor is an individual.

1. Trading control

- The Act establishes a system of licensing operated by the Office of Fair Trading.

- There are strict rules on the form and content of advertisements to ensure that they give adequate information.
- It is a criminal offence to canvass unconnected loans or to send any advertisement or information about credit or hire to persons under the age of 18.

2. Agreement control

- Regulations on the form content and legibility of agreements. The contract may be unenforceable by the lender if the rules are not followed.
- Cancellation rights. A customer has the right to cancel an agreement if there must have been oral representations and the customer signed the agreement away from business premises.
- The Act (s 75) makes the seller and the creditor jointly and severally liable for any breaches of contract for agreements for credit between £100 and £30,000.
- Before the creditor can exercise powers, such as the right to repossess, he must send a default notice. Once one-third or more of the total price has been paid, the creditor cannot recover possession of the goods without a court order.
- The court has power to re-open and examine credit agreements if they are considered to be extortionate.

OFFENCES UNDER THE TRADE DESCRIPTIONS ACT AND THE CONSUMER PROTECTION ACT

- Applying a false trade description to goods in the course of a trade or business. An oral statement may amount to the use of a trade description. A false trade description is one which is false or misleading to a material degree as regards matters such as; quantity, size or gauge, method of manufacture, production, processing or reconditioning, composition, fitness for purpose, strength, performance, behaviour or accuracy, etc.
- Making misleading statements with regard to services (1968 Act, s 14). It is offence for any person, in the course of a trade or business to make a statement which he knows to be false: or recklessly to make a statement which is false with regard to services, accommodation or facilities.
- Misleading indications as to price. It is an offence under the Consumer Protection Act 1987, s 20 to give a misleading indication as to price in the provision in the course of a business of goods, services, accommodation or facilities.

ESSENTIAL CASES

SALE OF GOODS ACT

Foley v *Classique Coaches* (1934): reasonable price.

Rowland v *Dival* (1923): breach of the implied condition that the seller had the right to sell the goods.

Niblett Ltd v *Confectioners' Materials Co Ltd* (1921): buyer's right to rescind the contract where seller did not have right to sell.

Hayman v *McLintock* (1907): property cannot pass when goods are unascertained.

Pignataro v *Gilroy* (1919): risk passes when property passes.

Aluminium Industrie Vaasen BV v *Romalpa Aluminium* (1976): title in goods can be reserved until conditions have been met.

Morison v *Lockhart* (1912): as long as something is attached to land, it can not be in a deliverable state.

Underwood v *Burgh Castle Brick & Cement Syndicate* (1922): property cannot pass until the goods are in deliverable state.

Nanka Bruce v *Commonwealth Trust Ltd* (1926): property does not pass until any weighing or measuring to ascertain the price is done.

Kirkham v *Attenborough* (1897): pawning goods amounts to adopting the transaction.

Bowes v *Shand & Co* (1877): duty to deliver at right time.

Regent OHG Aisenstadt und Barig v *Francesco of Jermyn Street Ltd* (1981): duty to deliver the right quantity.

Behrend & Co v *Produce Brokers' Co* (1920): the buyer need not accept delivery by instalments.

Beale v *Taylor* (1967): implied condition that goods will correspond with description.

Bartlett v *Sidney Marcus Ltd* (1965): no liability if customer knew of defect.

Clegg v *Anderson* (2003): satisfactory quality; unsafe goods.

Crowther v *Shannon Motor Co* (1975): difficulty in defining "merchantable quality".

Thain v *Anniesland Trade Centre* (1997): satisfactory quality.

Lamarra v *Capital Bank* (2006): satisfactory quality – right to reject.

Bristol Tramways v *Fiat Motors Ltd* (1910): reasonable fitness for normal purpose.

Plischke & Sohne v *Allison Bros Ltd* (1936): right of stoppage in transit.

Rogers v *Parish (Scarborough) Ltd* (1987): using goods may not amount to acceptance.

REMEDIES AGAINST MANUFACTURERS OR SUPPLIERS

Donoghue v *Stevenson* (1932): manufacturers owe a duty of care to the end-user.

LIABILITY FOR DEFECTIVE SERVICES

Young and Marten Ltd v *McManus Childs Ltd* (1969): even where the customer has specified the materials to be used. the seller may be liable if they are not of satisfactory quality.

McIntyre v *Gallacher* (1883): a person is responsible for exercising reasonable skill in his trade or profession.

T & R Duncanson v *Scottish County Investment Co Ltd* (1915): time of performance.

Charnock v *Liverpool Corp* (1968): work will be completed within a reasonable time.

Robert Allan and Partners v *McKinstray* (1975): assumption that reasonable payment will be due.

Forbes v *Aberdeen Motors Ltd* (1965): duty to take care of goods deposited.

TRADE DESCRIPTIONS

Fletcher v *Budgen* (1974): false trade description may be applied by a buyer.

Wings Ltd v *Ellis* (1985): false statement in a brochure.

Smith v *Dixons Ltd* (1986): misleading advertising.

12 PROPERTY LAW

Property law in Scotland is a large, complex but important area of law governing all **12.1** manner of rights and obligations in relation to land and other types of possessions. It is large because of the wide range of different types of property which can be held. It is complex because of the range of rights and obligations which can arise in these types of property. It is important because our possessions have enormous economic value and significance. Indeed, it is impossible to envisage any form of economy without property.

Not surprisingly, the principles of Scots law have ancient foundations. To a great **12.2** extent, these are derived from Roman law, with the addition of aspects of feudal law (being of particular importance in land ownership). The influence of feudal law has, however, been significantly lessened by the Abolition of Feudal Tenure (Scotland) Act 2000.

The word "property" is frequently used in two different senses: first, in the active **12.3** sense of a right over a particular object, and second, in the passive sense of the object itself over which a right or rights exist.

We shall first discuss some general concepts of the law of property and thereafter **12.4** consider the import of particular situations and types of possession.

GENERAL CONCEPTS

REAL AND PERSONAL RIGHTS

Rights in property can be further categorised as either real rights (*ius in re*) or personal **12.5** rights (*ius ad rem* or *ius in personam*). The distinction is extremely important. A real right is a right in or over a piece of property, to use it, destroy it or have the right to its fruits. A personal right, on the other hand, is a right against another person which might be created by agreement or operation of law. It has long been recognised that real rights are the more valuable – they are enforceable "against the world" as opposed to personal rights which are enforceable against a person or persons.

> " … the essential difference may be perceived between rights that affect a subject itself, which are called real, and those which are found in obligation or, as they are generally styled, personal. A real right … entitles the person vested with it to possess the subject as his own … whereas the creditor in a personal right or obligation has only a *jus ad rem* or a right of action against the debtor … but without any right in the subject".[1]

---

[1] Erskine, III, 1, 2.

12.6   The case of *Muirhead & Turnbull* v *Dickson*[2] illustrates the importance of the distinction between real rights and personal rights. The pursuers supplied a piano to the defender, who made some payments towards the total price. When the defender ceased making payments, the pursuers sued for delivery back to them of the piano, on the argument that the title (a real right) remained with them until the full price had been paid. Since the price had not been paid, they argued that they had retained ownership in the piano and were entitled to its return. However, the Court of Session decided that the transaction was properly to be construed as a credit sale, and that property (a *real* right) in the piano had passed when it was first delivered to the defender. Muirhead & Turnbull were thus left with a *personal* right to recover only the balance of the price.

12.7   You can see that as rights of property constitute a bundle of rights in Scotland, more than one right may exist simultaneously over an item of property. For example, a house may be the subject of ownership, a standard security and a lease at the same time. Real rights are the fullest and most effective form of these.

Real rights

12.8   What, then, are the real rights which exist in Scots law?

The principal real right is "ownership". According to Erskine, ownership entails the right to use and dispose of property, subject only to any restriction imposed by the law or by agreement.[3] Subordinate real rights, *iura in re aliena*, exist where a person can enforce rights over the property in the ownership of another. Examples of subordinate rights include rights in security, leases, servitudes and simple possession. These will be considered in more detail later.

Personal rights

12.9   Personal rights, as the case of *Muirhead & Turnbull* v *Dickson* shows, are rights to demand the performance of a duty or obligation by another person. They may arise from contractual agreement or from the operation of law (for example, a person who breaches a duty of care can be obliged to make a payment of damages to the injured party). In the above case, the personal right was one of making payment of the outstanding amount in the agreement.

Property and ownership

12.10   It is, of course, possible for property to be owned by more than one person. Where this is the case, the property in question will be either common property or, much less frequently, joint property.

Common property

12.11   Common property describes the situation where an item is owned by more than one person, each of whom has a *pro indiviso* share in it. Shares are generally equal, but there is no requirement that this is so. Each co-owner has a right to a share of the

---

[2] (1905) 7 F 686.
[3] Erskine, II, 1, 1.

whole property and to its use, but not to a particular part of it. Thus, two co-owners of a house have a one-half *pro indiviso* share in the house. Each co-owner is entitled to dispose of their share without reference to the other. On death, the share of the deceased will pass to the co-owner's heirs. *Pro indiviso* shares can be divided infinitely and there is therefore no limit to the number of co-owners that a piece of property may have. Each co-owner is entitled to further sub-divide their share. In addition, it is open to any co-owner to raise an action of division and sale to enforce the sale of the property and the division of the proceeds.

There are various consequences of owning property in common. For example, what **12.12** happens if there are co-owners of a house and it is necessary for the whole owners to undertake alterations and repairs to the house? In these circumstances, the general rule is that each co-owner is entitled to a say in the management of the common property. It is thus necessary to have the consent of all co-owners before repairs and maintenance can be carried out, unless the work is so minor as to be considered *de minimis*.[4] Where repairs are necessary, there is an important exception to the rule that unanimity is required.[5]

The law in relation to the ownership of common parts within a tenement building **12.13** has been altered by the Tenements (Scotland) Act 2004,[6] which removes the requirement for unanimity before work can take place.

Where there is agreement of all co-owners, any use of the common property is **12.14** possible, however, where no such agreement exists, co-owners are limited to ordinary and reasonable uses.

Joint property

This form of ownership arises where two or more persons own property but do not **12.15** have separate rights in it. The commonest example is where trustees own shares or other trust property, where partners hold partnership property, or club members hold the property of their club. They may not dispose of their rights to any other person either by a lifetime transfer or by will. In the event of their ceasing to hold the property, their right accresces to the other joint holders.

In the case of *Murray* v *Johnstone*[7] a silver cup which was won by a club could not be **12.16** given away against the wishes of a minority of the club members.

Common interest

This occurs where owners have individual rights to their own property but they must **12.17** have regard to the interests of others which occur in that property. For example, the owners of land through which a river flows ("riparian proprietors") have rights in common in the water flowing in the river. The corollary to this right is that the same riparian proprietors are under an obligation not to interfere with the natural flow of the water nor to exhaust the river of the water flowing in it.

---

[4] *Rafique* v *Amin* 1997 SLT 1385.
[5] "Necessary repairs may be carried out by any one proprietor, and costs may be recovered pro-rata": Bell's *Principles*, s 1075.
[6] The law of the tenement is considered below.
[7] (1896) 23 R 981.

Ownership and possession

12.18   It can be seen from the above that the apparently simple concept of possession is not always straightforward. With items of corporeal moveable property of a small or moderate size, physical possession is possible but for most other forms of property, and in particular with property held in common or jointly, it is frequently necessary for there to be some means of formalising ownership in documents of title.

12.19   The obvious example of this is land ownership where a recorded or registered title is a prerequisite. But other documents of title may include stock and share certificates, bank books, car and aircraft registration documents, and similar. It does not always follow that the possession of a document of title necessitates ownership. Sometimes the underlying ownership is not that of the title holder but of some other party (for example, a car registration form "V05" indicates the name of the keeper who lawfully possesses the vehicle but the keeper may not be the vehicle's true owner).

12.20   While possession is a lesser right than ownership, possession of heritable property over a period of time can result in the attainment of ownership. This type of possession is sometimes referred to as "prescriptive possession" which is further discussed below.

12.21   The possessor of moveable property is deemed to be the owner of it unless the contrary is proved.

Classifications of property

12.22   "Property", in the other sense of the word, that of objects over which rights exist, is classified as either heritable or moveable, and either corporeal or incorporeal. This results in four different classes of property, which are considered in turn.

Corporeal heritable property

12.23   Corporeal property is tangible (physical) property which means that it is capable of being physically possessed. Heritable property is land, with the buildings and other fixtures attached to the land, for example crops, trees, stones, minerals etc. Heritable property can therefore be possessed by the physical occupation of buildings and use of the surrounding land. This can be done by the owner or by his tenants or other persons with the authority of the owner. To establish ownership of corporeal heritable property, it is not enough simply to possess property, even where walls, fences and locks are used to keep others out. Ownership of such property is therefore proved by means of documents of title.

12.24   Certain limitations are imposed on ownership of corporeal heritable property. For example, mines of gold and silver are property of the Crown in terms of the Royal Mines Act 1424 and the Mines and Metals Act 1592, and the Civil Aviation Act 1982 allows aeroplanes to fly through what is, strictly speaking, property of the landowner.

Corporeal moveable property

12.25   All other tangible property is thus moveable. So, corporeal moveable property consists of goods in general. A strictly literal interpretation of "moveable property" is perhaps misleading, given that some property in this category is unlikely to be moved due to its size or weight. But, in general, corporeal moveable property comprises the sorts of things which can be physically taken and carried away and thus stolen. Title to corporeal moveable property usually depends upon proof merely of possession.

Incorporeal heritable property

In this category fall certain rights connected with land, but not being the land itself. **12.26**
Thus, leases and servitudes are incorporeal heritable property. We discuss both of these below. Also included are rights "with a future tract of time", such as pensions and annuities.

Incorporeal moveable property

This category contains rights which are not connected with land. In particular, they **12.27**
include important economic rights such as intellectual property rights, for example copyright and patents.[8]

Excluded from the above categorisation are persons,[9] items such as air, the sea **12.28**
and running water (which are deemed in law to be incapable of individual private ownership) and *res nullius* – items such as wild animals, which are ownerless until subject to *occupatio*.[10]

ACQUISITION AND LOSS OF CORPOREAL MOVEABLE PROPERTY

There are a variety of means by which original acquisition of corporeal moveable **12.29**
property may be obtained.

OCCUPATIO

Occupatio (or occupation), a Roman law term, is the doctrine whereby ownership is **12.30**
taken to property which was hitherto ownerless. The Latin maxim is *quod nullius est fit occupantis* – that which belongs to no-one becomes the property of the taker. However, there is today a scarcity of property which can truly said to be ownerless. Property which once had an owner, but which is lost or abandoned, will generally be owned by the Crown – *quod nullius est fit domini regis.*

Wild animals, birds and fish[11] are thus susceptible to acquisition by occupancy **12.31**
if they are taken and controlled. It is permissible for any person to fish for and take wild trout and other fish in rivers and streams (provided that the activity of fishing is permitted by the riparian owners). This is because such fish are *res nullius*. However, in *Valentine* v *Kennedy*[12] the accused were convicted of the theft of escaped rainbow

---

[8] Discussed further below.
[9] *Reavis* v *Clan Line Steamers* 1925 SC 725.
[10] Occupation or possession, discussed below.
[11] Excluding salmon, which are "Royal fish' and belong to the Crown.
[12] 1985 SCCR 89.

trout which they had caught in a river outside the enclosure in which the trout had been kept. Although the fish had escaped, the sheriff held that ownership in them had not been lost. They could not be regarded as *res nullius* because the fish were not of a native species and, having been possessed, were capable of being stolen.

SPECIFICATIO

12.32   The doctrine of specification deals with the situation where a new thing has been created from materials which, at least in part, belonged to another, and where the other party's property cannot be restored to him in its original form. For example, if one person's grapes are made into wine, then a new product has been made and the original grapes cannot be restored to their former owner. Questions obviously arise as to the ownership of the new thing, and as to whether compensation is due to the party who has lost his original property.

12.33   The general rule is that the new thing belongs to the maker.[13] In *International Banking Corporation* v *Ferguson Shaw & Sons*,[14] the defenders made lard from 53 barrels of oil which had been delivered to them. While the defenders were held to own the lard, they were required to pay compensation to the former owners of the oil. It should be noted that where a maker has acted in bad faith, he generally will not acquire a right of property in the manufactured product. In *Macdonald* v *Provan of Scotland Street*,[15] where a car had been made out of two other cars, one of which had been stolen, the maker claimed ownership of the resulting vehicle. In the event, the court held that specification did not occur (as it was possible to separate out the original parts of the new car) but that, even if specification had occurred, then the maker would not have acquired ownership because of his bad faith.

COMMIXTIO AND CONFUSIO

12.34   Commixture is the mixing of solids, and confusion the mixing of liquids. Where either occurs, and the resulting property cannot be separated into its constituent parts, the result is co-owned by the owners of the constituent parts, according to the proportionate share or value contributed by each part. In *Tyzack & Braefoot Steam Ship Co* v *J S Sandeman & Sons*[16] it was suggested that *commixtio* had occurred in relation to bales of jute.

ACCESSIO

12.35   Accession occurs where two items of corporeal property become attached. The lesser item, known as the accessory, is subsumed into the ownership of the greater item (commonly known as the principal). The maxim is *accessorium principale sequitur* – the accessory follows the principal.

12.36   The principal effects of accession are as follows:

---

[13] Bell's *Principles*, s 1289.
[14] 1910 SC 182.
[15] 1960 SLT 231.
[16] 1913 SC 19.

1. separate ownership rights in the accessory are extinguished;
2. the original ownership rights in the accessory do not revert to the original owner on subsequent separation;
3. property may be converted from one class to another (see "The law of fixtures", below).

On attachment, the owner of the principal becomes the owner of the whole, including **12.37** the accessory. Compensation may be due to the owner of the accessory but only where the attachment has been done by or on the instructions of the owner of the principal.

The law of fixtures

A special example of the idea of accession occurs when items of corporeal moveable **12.38** property become annexed to heritable property such as land or buildings. This is an example of the principal of conversion where property of one class (corporeal moveable) is converted into another (heritable).

For example, when moveable property such as wood and bricks is built into a **12.39** structure permanently fixed to the land, it ceases to be moveable and becomes heritable. In the case of *Brand's Trs* v *Brand's Trs*[17] mining machinery (moveable property) was brought onto land leased by a tenant. On the tenant's death, the court held that the machinery had acceded to the heritable property owned by the landlord. What had been moveable had become a fixture upon the land. The intention of the parties was held to be irrelevant.

Under the common law, a number of recognised criteria exist which indicate where **12.40** accession of moveable items to land and buildings may have taken place.

These include: **12.41**

1. degree of attachment;
2. permanence of attachment;
3. functional subordination;
4. mutual special adaptation;
5. time and expense of installation and removal;
6. the intention of the parties.

These call for some individual explication:

Degree of attachment

The greater the degree of attachment to the ground, the more likely it is that accession **12.42** will have taken place. However, it is important to note the existence of constructive fixtures such as the key of a door which, according to *Fisher* v *Dixon*,[18] is a fixture since the door into which it fits is heritable. In *Christie* v *Smith's Executrix* a summerhouse weighing about 2 tons was held to be a fixture notwithstanding that it was merely resting upon the ground under its own weight rather than attached to it.

---

[17] (1876) 3 R (HL) 16.
[18] (1843) 5 D 775.
[19] 1949 SC 572.

Permanence of attachment

12.43   Where moveable property is of a type where its installation is intended to be permanent, this indicates that it has acceded to the land. For example, in the case of *Scottish Discount Company* v *Blin*,[20] scrap industrial sheers (over 60 tonnes in weight) bolted to concrete foundations fell to be regarded as fixtures on the basis that when they were installed they were intended to be a permanent or quasi-permanent feature of the land to which they were attached.

Functional subordination

12.44   Where the accessory can be seen to serve the principal in some material way, it may be regarded as having acceded to the ground. For example, a central heating system fitted into a house will be regarded as a heritable fixture.

Mutual special adaptation

12.45   Where either the accessory or the principal has been adapted to fit the other, the accessory will be regarded as having acceded to the land. In *Howie's Trs* v *McLay*,[21] looms were placed in a shed, the dimensions of which fitted the looms. The uppermost parts of the looms were bolted to the roof of the shed. The court held that the looms were heritable by accession. Similarly, if an item is designed to fit or match existing fixtures, it will generally also be regarded as a fixture. So, where a painting is made to fit within panelling, it is likely to be regarded as a heritable fixture. However, as with all of these rules, there is some measure of ambiguity. In *Cochrane* v *Stevenson*[22] the court had to consider a painting which had been incorporated into panelling. The painting concerned would have been regarded as a fixture except that it was merely one of a set of three paintings, the other two of which were not so incorporated. The court held that because it was a member of a set, it would not be appropriate to hold that it had acceded in that instance.

Time and expense of installation and removal

12.46   The greater the time and expense which are involved in the installation of an item of moveable property, the more likely it is to be regarded as having acceded to the heritable property upon or into which it has been installed. A vehicle shredder which weighed 150 tonnes and took 3 months to install at a cost of £93,000 was held to have attached to the ground.[23]

The intention of the parties

12.47   *Brand's Trs* (above) is authority for the proposition that the intention of the parties is not relevant in determining whether accession has taken place. Thus, a contractual

---

[20] 1985 SC 216.
[21] 1902 5 F 214.
[22] (1891) 18 R 1208.
[23] *TSB Scotland plc* v *James Mills (Montrose) Ltd* 1991 GWD 39–2406.

term that certain goods will remain moveable will have no effect where the criteria for attachment have been met. In *Shetlands Islands Council* v *BP Petroleum Development*[24] it was held that "no agreement between owner and occupier can affect the matter of ownership of heritable fixtures even as between them".

12.48 There are, however, several exceptions to this general rule. Where a tenant carries on business on property owned by his landlord, he is entitled to remove trade fixtures, that is property of the tenant which was attached by him for the purposes of his trade. The tenant's right of removal exists throughout the term of the lease, not just at its conclusion.[25] This is not to say that accession has not taken place, but only that the tenant is nonetheless entitled to removal. A similar rule exists in relation to agricultural tenants whose right of removal can extend to buildings.[26] Finally, industrial crops, that is those crops which require to be sown annually, are heritable as they are attached to the land. However, where a tenant has sown such a crop, he is entitled to reap and remove that crop.

Other forms of accession

12.49 While fixtures comprise the largest category, it is possible for accession to take place between two items of moveable property, or indeed two items of heritable property. Similar rules apply as regards ownership of the new piece of property.

12.50 There will not be accession of one moveable item to another unless it is impossible to separate the principal from the accessory without damage to one or other. In *Zahnrad Fabrik Passau GmbH* v *Terex Ltd*[27] it was held that where axles and transmissions had been installed in machinery, the test as to whether they had acceded was to be judged on whether their efficiency had been reduced by removal, not by whether there was a reduction in market value.

12.51 Accession of one piece of heritable property to another is rare, but may occur where a river which forms the boundary between two properties changes its course. If this happens gradually, over a period of time, it is termed *alluvio* and one landowner will benefit from the additional land which has been lost by the neighbouring proprietor. Seasonal variations, such as caused by floodwaters, are termed *avulsio*, and have no consequences for ownership. In *Stirling* v *Bartlett*[28] the pursuer argued that a channel in the centre of a river which had been bulldozed 15 years previously should be taken as the boundary between his property and the defender's. The court held that this was not a case of *avulsio* and that the channel should accordingly be taken to be the boundary.

INCORPOREAL MOVEABLE PROPERTY

NEGOTIABLE INSTRUMENTS

12.52 Negotiable instruments are documents which entitle the owner of them to demand payment of the sum of money which is stated on the document. The definition is

---

[24] 1990 SLT 82.
[25] *David Boswell Ltd* v *William Cook Engineering Ltd* 1989 SLT (Sh Ct) 61.
[26] Agricultural Holdings (Scotland) Act 1991, s 18.
[27] 1986 SLT 81.
[28] 1992 SCLR 994.

given in s 3 of the Bills of Exchange Act 1882 which states: "A bill of exchange is an unconditional order in writing, addressed by one person to another, signed by the person giving it, requiring the person to whom it is addressed to pay on demand or at a fixed or determinable future time a sum certain in money or [to pay] to the order of a specified person or to bearer." In commercial circles, ownership of bills of exchange is easily transferred, whether by simple delivery[29] or by endorsement by the current owner followed by delivery.

12.53   The most common form of negotiable instrument is the cheque, defined by s 73 of the 1882 Act as a "bill of exchange drawn on a banker and payable on demand".

GOODWILL

12.54 The goodwill of a business is "the whole advantage, whatever it may be, of the reputation and connection of the firm".[30] It is, in brief, the likelihood that existing customers will return to make repeat purchases and that new customers will be likely to choose to purchase goods on the basis of the business's established reputation.

12.55   Clearly, a proportion of a business's turnover will relate to its goodwill. The value of goodwill is therefore quantifiable in terms of turnover generated by reputation. Where turnover due to reputation continues over a period of years, the value of goodwill can be capitalised[31] and so can be many times the value of the annual turnover. As a result, businesses wish to protect their goodwill and do so using the common law of "passing off".

12.56   To succeed in an action of passing off, the trader must first show that he owns the goodwill, that is that his reputation has been established among customers, and that the defender has sought to take advantage of that goodwill, and so deceive the public, to the extent of causing damage (loss of pursuer's turnover for which the pursuer can seek damages) or of profiting from the confusion (in which case the pursuer may seek an accounting for profits and payment of any such profits so generated). The initial step, that of the pursuer proving exclusive right to his established name or goodwill, can be problematic, and for this reason many traders wish to register their name or mark as a trademark (see below).

INTELLECTUAL PROPERTY

12.57 A third very important group of incorporeal movable rights involves intellectual property rights. Their importance is mainly due to the fact that this class of rights is economically very valuable. Because of the advent of the Internet and developments in information technology, the law at the boundaries of these rights is subject to rapid change. For example, the law concerning the liability of businesses who market P2P

---

[29] Where the bill is payable to the bearer.
[30] *Trego* v *Hunt* [1896] AC 7.
[31] For every pound invested in a business by the owners, they will expect a rate of return on their capital so employed ("ROCE"). It follows that every pound of turnover represents the income arising on an identifiable number of pounds invested. The return on capital employed in a business is usually much higher than the amount which the same amount of capital could generate when invested in a bank or in shares or other investments. By analogy, the turnover generated by the goodwill of a business can be seen to have a notional capital value which may easily be between four and twelve times the amount of turnover.

("peer-to-peer") file-sharing software for inducing copyright infringement in the files so shared by their customers is only now being clarified.[32]

Copyright

One of the earliest forms of intellectual property is that which protects creative ideas. **12.58** Strictly, it is not so much the ideas, but the fixed form in which the ideas are expressed which is protected.

The first forms of copyright, the right not to have one's work copied by another for **12.59** economic gain by that other, are to be found in the protection of printed books. The Stationers' Guild set up a register of printed books in 1556 but this only had jurisdiction in England. The Statute of Anne of 1710 was the first modern intellectual property statute and was to a great extent motivated by the desire to prevent Scottish publishers from profiting from the printing and sale of pirate copies of English books which up to that time had not been protected here. Over the years, the protections were extended from books to engravings and later to a broad range of created works. Copyright protections now extend to any form of literary, dramatic, musical and artistic work, to films, published editions, broadcasts and performances.

The principal right is to prevent an infringer from copying works for economic gain **12.60** and there are secondary rights to prevent the possession and importation of infringing works. A performer has rights to prevent the recording, copying and exploitation of performances. Moral rights also exist to protect the proper attribution of works to the original creator and to prevent derogatory treatment.

Because creators' economic rights are not the only rights in ideas, there exist **12.61** "fair use" provisions which allow a limited amount of copying for the purposes of private study and research, reporting, proper educational and public uses. These uses are defensible only when the economic interests of the copyright owner are not prejudiced.

Copyright typically lasts for a lifetime of the original creator and for 70 years **12.62** thereafter but the period of protection varies according to the type of work and rights concerned.

Designs

In the 19th century it became clear that some kind of protection was required for the **12.63** designs of industrial articles. The courts were unhappy to grant artistic copyright to this type of mass-produced commercial product and it became clear that some alternative protection was necessary.

The Registered Designs Act 1949 sets out to protect "features of shape, configuration, **12.64** pattern or ornament applied to an article by industrial process".[33] This definition is generally interpreted by means of appearance to the informed observer – what used to be called "eye appeal". The protections do not extend to aspects of the design which are imposed by a method or principle of construction, by the article's functional requirements, by a need to fit in, to or around any other article to which the article to

---

[32] *MGM Studios* v *Grokster* (2005) 545 US 913.
[33] Registered Designs Act 1949, s 1(3).

be protected relates (the "must fit" rule). These imposed aspects give no freedom to the designer to create design elements. Registered designs are not an automatic right but require to be established by an applications procedure. The protection lasts for up to 25 years.

12.65   Unregistered design right is granted by the Copyright, Designs and Patents Act 1988, s 213(1). This right protects "any aspect of the shape or configuration [internal or external] of the whole or part of an article". As a result, this form of design right is useful to protect the functionality or performance of an industrial appliance. This right is automatic and does not require any registration procedure. The right lasts for 15 years from the end of the year in which the design was first recorded or the article produced to the design. Similarly to registered designs, imposed design elements are not protected. This gives rise to the "must fit" rule which we have seen above, and to the "must match" rule which excludes from protection any aspect of the design which is imposed by the need for the article to match other similar articles to which it is to be related (say, by being part of a set of appliances of the same generic design).

12.66   In broad terms, registered design rights are most useful in protecting the aesthetic aspects of an industrial article, while unregistered design rights are most useful in protecting the functionality of industrial articles.

Patents

12.67 Patents are a monopoly granted to protect the creators of inventions, whether they be invented products or processes. The right is not automatic and must be applied for. The applicant must establish that the product or process is new (in the sense of not previously being known in the public domain), involves an inventive step (a step not being obvious to someone aware of the "state of the art" for products of a similar type), not in an excluded category, and capable of industrial application.[34]

12.68   The application procedure involves searches of the "prior art" to see whether the invention has been previously disclosed by means of use, publication, demonstration, prior patent application or otherwise anywhere in the world. If previously disclosed, then the invention cannot be patent protected. However, the type of disclosure must be an "enabling disclosure" in the sense that it is sufficient to enable a person skilled in the art to reproduce the product or process concerned. Any disclosure which falls short of being "enabling" will not disallow a patent from being granted.

12.69   The excluded areas are: a discovery, scientific theory or mathematical method, literary and other created works protected already by copyright, methods for performing a mental act, playing a game or doing business, or a computer program, or the presentation of information. For moral and public interests, certain forms of biotechnological process and product are also an excluded. Most important of these excluded forms of biotechnology involve uses of human embryos, modifying human germ line genetic identity or the modifying of the genetic identity of animals in such a way as is likely to cause the animals suffering and without any substantial medical benefit to man or animal.[35]

12.70   Patent protection lasts for 20 years (25 years for pharmaceutical products).

---

[34] An important case for establishing the meaning of some of these terms is the case of *Windsurfing International Inc* v *Tabur Marine (Great Britain) Ltd* [1985] RPC 59.
[35] *Harvard Onco-Mouse* [1992] OJ EPO 589 (Examining Division).

Trademarks

Trade names and marks are a statutory extension of recognised protections for business **12.71** goodwill. The principal form of trademark protection is the registered trademark. The Trade Marks Act 1994 defines a trademark as "any sign capable of being represented graphically which is capable of distinguishing goods or services of one undertaking from those of other undertakings".[36] As a result, trademarks have been held to include words, designs, logos, the shape of goods or their packaging, smells, sounds and even colours. There are, however, considerable difficulties in rendering smells, sounds and colours in graphic form, since such rendition must be capable of defining the characteristic specifically and being understood by the reader of the description. Attempts have been made to get around this by reference to chemical formulae and samples for smells (but samples are not capable of being rendered in graphic form), by using musical notation for sounds, and by colour samples for colours. These attempts have been rejected where they are not clearly specific or understandable to the reader.[37]

The application procedure requires searches to ensure that goods or services of **12.72** the same class have not been protected by the same or similar marks such as might cause confusion to the consumer. In addition, a trademark should not be granted where it might give an unfair advantage and as a result applications will be refused where the proposed mark indicates purpose, value, origin, time of production of goods or rendering of services, or aspects of the sign imposed by the nature of the goods or necessary to obtain a technical result, or which gave substantial value to the goods.

Registration is proof of ownership in the trademark and gives the registered owner **12.73** exclusive rights in that mark. As a result, the owner of a registered trademark is in a better position to prevent infringement and a trader who has no registered mark but wishes to protect the distinctive name of his business or goods under the common law of passing off (see above).

Confidential information

The common law recognises certain circumstances and relations where the leak of **12.74** confidential information should be prohibited. The most obvious of these concerns the protection of trade secrets. While strictly not a form of property as such, many businesses regard trade secrets and in particular recipes for their products as rights with considerable economic value tantamount to property which require protection. Again, such "property" can have a value entered on a balance sheet as a "brand".

Before information is protected, three requirements must be proved:[38]   **12.75**

(1) the information must have the quality of confidence;
(2) the information must have been imparted in circumstances implying an obligation of confidence; and
(3) the information must have been used without authority.

---

[36] Trade Marks Act 1994, s 1.
[37] In *Venootschap onder Firma Senta Aromatic Marketing's application* [1999] ETMR 429 an application was made to register the "smell of fresh cut grass" as a trademark for a tennis ball manufacturer. The board held that "the smell of fresh cut grass is a distinctive smell, which everyone immediately recognises from experience". In granting the trademark, the board observed that "the description provided ... is appropriate and complies with the graphical representation requirement".
[38] *Coco v A N Clark (Engineering) Ltd* [1969] RPC 41.

12.76   There are many different categories of a confidential relationship in which the information will be regarded as having the quality of confidence. For example, the law recognises and protects personal secrets between a husband and wife, secrets between friends, drawings by members of the Royal Family, trade secrets, State secrets, and information imparted within privileged relationships of professional confidentiality.

12.77   Information which is already in the public domain cannot be protected as secret. But if such information were imparted within a relationship of secrecy and at a time when it was not in the public domain then the person to whom it was imparted must maintain the secrecy even if the information becomes public thereafter.[39]

HERITABLE PROPERTY

12.78   As we have seen, "heritable property" broadly covers land and buildings or anything attached to land. It also covers rights connected with land and buildings such as salmon fishings, leases, servitudes and the benefit of title conditions exercisable over neighbouring property.

12.79   The sources of Scots land law derive from Roman law and also from the feudal system.

12.80   The idea behind feudalism was that all land ultimately derives from the Crown as ultimate superior. Historically, the Crown granted parcels of land to nobles in return for military and other services owed to the Crown. Such nobles would be vassals of the sovereign who would be their superior. The nobles in turn would grant parcels of land to their own vassals in exchange for services, and so on. The ultimate vassal would possess what was known as the *dominium utile* (the right of the use and enjoyment of the piece of ground) while the interest of the superior was known as *dominium directum*. Over the years, military service was abolished and by the 20th century the only service required by the vassal was the annual payment of a sum of money known as a feuduty or ground annual. In 1974 a procedure was introduced to redeem feu duties which were ultimately abolished. It will be seen that, under feudalism, any piece of ground may involve two or more interests in land at one and the same time – the interest of the vassal and the interests of superiors.

12.81   The last vestiges of feudal tenure were abolished on 28 November 2004,[40] but title conditions in the form of real burdens remain in force as forms of contractual restriction on the use of land. As a result, the proprietor of a "benefited property" may enforce a real burden against the proprietor of a "burdened property". There is no fixed list of types of real burden, but these generally relate to the preservation of the enjoyment of the benefited proprietor in their property, or the maintenance of services to the benefited property. Real burdens must confer a real benefit if they are to be valid,[41] they must not be contrary to public policy, and they must not be repugnant with the ownership of the burdened property. They must, if created since 28 November 2004, be expressly specified in deeds registered or recorded as affecting both the benefited and burdened properties.

12.82   One example of real burdens and their interplay with the common law (and now with statute) involves the apportionment of the expenses of common repairs in a

---

[39] *Terrapin Ltd* v *Builders Supply Co* [1967] RPC 375.
[40] Abolition of Feudal Tenure etc (Scotland) Act 2000.
[41] *Marsden* v *Craighelen Lawn Tennis and Squash Club* 1999 GWD 37–1820

tenement block. The common law (the "law of the tenement") traditionally stated that the owner of a maindoor flat was responsible for the upkeep of the ground and foundations under the flat (the "*solum*") and the owner of a top flat was responsible for the upkeep of the roof above the flat. This situation gave rise to considerable hardship, particularly to the top-flat proprietor who would be responsible for the whole costs of roof repairs which could be considerable. Under the common law, the top-flat proprietor could not claim relief from the proprietors of the other flats. It therefore became normal (but not invariable) practice, when tenement flats were first sold off by the builders, for the title deeds of each flat to state the share of the expenses of the upkeep of all common areas including the *solum* and the roof. This meant that when roof repairs were carried out, the top-flat proprietor could therefore recover the other flats' shares of the costs from the proprietors of those flats in the proportions stated in the title deeds. But in some titles the apportionment was not referred to in the title deeds and so the common law situation pertained. To remedy the injustice, the Tenements (Scotland) Act 2004 now regulates situations where the titles of flats in a tenement are silent on the apportionment of common repairs expenses. The Act does this by the imposition of a system of default rules specifying the parts which are deemed to be owned in common and giving a means for the sharing of maintenance responsibilities and costs.

Much of the common law, and in particular servitudes, derives from Roman law. **12.83** A servitude is a right held by the owner of a "dominant tenement" and enforceable against the owner of a "servient tenement". It is therefore similar in some respects to a real burden but it is really of an entirely different nature. A servitude right does not arise from contract but is one which is necessary to enable the owner of the dominant tenement adequately to enjoy his property. Well-known examples of servitudes include rights of access and also wayleaves for services (such as water, electricity and gas supplies, and drainage and sewage pipes and systems). Again, the class of servitudes is broad and not closed and it is thought may now include even the servitude right of parking of vehicles. A servitude may be created by express deed but may also arise by implication and use over the prescriptive period of 20 years.

Both burdens and servitudes may be extinguished or varied by express deed, **12.84** non-use or acquiescence over the relative negative prescriptive period (for which, see below), or by certain formal procedures including application to the Lands Tribunal.

The Crown retains two types of rights in land, known as *regalia majora* and *regalia* **12.85** *minora*. *Regalia majora* are inalienable public rights such as the rights of the public in the foreshore[42] (for navigation, fishing, mooring and possibly recreation), in the sea and seabed, and in navigable tidal rivers. *Regalia minora*, on the other hand, are alienable rights, for example in salmon fishings, precious metals, treasure and lost property. These can be granted to private individuals but only so far as the rights of the public are unaffected. "Precious metals" includes mines of gold, silver and lead of a specified fineness. The minerals can be granted to the landowner in exchange for a royalty. Salmon fishings are a separate heritable right from that of the landowner. When salmon fishings and land ownership are not held by the same person, the salmon fisher has certain enforceable common law rights which allow access, mooring of boats and drying of nets, but in exercising these the salmon fisher has to respect the rights

---

[42] The shore between the high- and low-water marks of ordinary spring tides.

of the landowner. Where the foreshore is granted to a person, they are entitled to make use of it and take materials such as seaweed from it, but they must at all times respect the rights of the public.

12.86   The rights of proprietors are as specified in their title deeds or title certificates. In most cases these rights are specified in "bounding" descriptions which verbally describe the boundaries, or they will be specified in deed plans. The proprietor's rights extend theoretically *a coelo usque ad centrum* which means "from the heavens above to the centre of the earth". This means that proprietors will have rights to rocks and minerals under the ground (unless these have been excluded by a grant or reservation to another) and they also have rights in the airspace above their property and so may prevent encroachment by overhanging objects (such as parts of buildings, cranes,[43] overhanging branches[44] and similar). The proprietor also has an implied right of support to prevent collapse or subsidence of his land due to operations carried out beneath the land or on neighbouring land. This is most important where the proprietor does not possess the right to mine minerals under his property. In such circumstances there may exist statutory compensation schemes.[45] A proprietor also has the right of exclusive possession of his property (excluding others) and the right to enjoy his property free of nuisances. A proprietor also may have other ancillary rights as incidents of his property rights. These common law rights include a right of access along the least inconvenient route through neighbouring proprietors' properties if the property would otherwise be land-locked.[46] Other forms of common law rights include the right of salmon fishers to access their fishings, to draw up and wash nets and to moor boats. Such common law rights are inalienable and imprescribable incidents of property in the land or salmon fishings concerned.

12.87   The ownership of land necessarily involves any buildings and other fixtures attached to the land. This derives from the principle of accession. To become a fixture, an item of movable property requires to be physically attached to the ground, functionally related to the enjoyment of the heritable property or permanently attached to the heritable property. We have seen some examples of accession of fixtures above.[47]

REGISTRATION

12.88   Interests in land required to be recorded or registered before the personal right of the owner (enforceable against his predecessors in title) becomes a real right enforceable against all persons. The effect of recording or registration is therefore to make public the interest concerned.

12.89   The Register of Sasines, a register of deeds, was set up in 1617. This system operated well for over 300 years but, since 1979,[48] has been gradually replaced by registration in the Land Register (a system of registration of titles guaranteed by the State).

12.90   The validity of any deed recorded in the Register of Sasines could be challenged and, if the deed were reduced, the proprietor of the interest granted in the deed would lose his title. As a result, the recorded deeds and searches relating to any interest in

---

[43] *Brown* v *Lee Construction Ltd* 1977 SLT (Notes) 61.
[44] *Halkerston* v *Wedderburn* (1781) Mor 10495.
[45] For example, under the Coal Mining Subsidence Act 1991.
[46] *Bowers* v *Kennedy* 2000 SC 555.
[47] See "Classifications of property" above.
[48] Land Registration (Scotland) Act 1979.

land required to be examined for a period of at least 10 years (the prescriptive period) in order to establish that the title was valid. This was a time-consuming, expensive but necessary process since the validity of the title to any interest in land flowed from the recorded deeds. One could only acquire the interest validly held by one's predecessor in title.

Registration of titles in the Land Register is intended to avoid this checking process, **12.91** since, once registered, the title specified in a land certificate is guaranteed by the State. Under registration of title, a system based on the English system, the validity of the title flows from the Land Register and not merely from the deeds.

The process of conversion from the Register of Sasines to the Land Register **12.92** involves detailed examination of the title and is therefore an expensive and lengthy process but subsequent transmissions of title should be simple and inexpensive. There are inevitably some difficulties in transferring from a Sasine title to a registered title. In some ways the Englishness of the registration system sits unevenly upon our Scottish system of land law. In particular, a verbal-based system of description does not easily transfer to one based upon annotated ordnance survey plans. Registration has therefore given rise to some unusual problems. It is not uncommon for there to be small inconsistencies between one Sasine title and those of its neighbours. These would traditionally be resolved by the extent of possession. But when one of these Sasine titles first becomes registered, its terms become definitive regardless of how the inconsistency has arisen. The possessor of the competing Sasine title loses out and can only seek compensation from the Keeper. This effect is sometimes referred to as the "invulnerability" of the proprietor in possession of a registered title. In some limited circumstances, the Keeper can rectify a land certificate. These circumstances must necessarily be limited in order that the public will have confidence that an interest which is registered is guaranteed and can be relied on.

A land certificate comprises four sections: (1) the property section, describing **12.93** the interest owned and containing an ordnance survey plan of an appropriate scale on which the interest is illustrated; (2) the proprietorship section, stating who the owner is; (3) the charges section, stating any heritable securities which exist over the property; and (4) the burdens section, showing any registered or recorded burdens (this will, of course, not show any servitudes created by implication and use alone (which together with any other unrecorded or unregistered rights, as for, say, rights of way, are known as "overriding interests")). It will be seen that the intention is that the land certificate will therefore contain all the relevant interests and restrictions and will therefore "stand alone" as a definition of the interest possessed. No reference to any other deed is generally relevant to define the interest possessed. But it is always necessary to consider the overriding interests which may exist and which can have a material effect on the value of the interest possessed and upon its enjoyment.

PRESCRIPTION

We have seen above how prescription may be the basis for the creation of implied **12.94** servitudes and it is also necessary to establish a good title in the Register of Sasines. The modern law is given in the Prescription and Limitation (Scotland) Act 1973.

Prescription means that certain classes of rights can be acquired or lost due to **12.95** use or non-use over the relative prescriptive period. Positive prescription allows for the creation of rights or the making of existing rights unchallengeable. Negative prescription serves to extinguish rights which have not been exercised.

12.96　　For example, where a person acquired a Sasine title with a general and non-specific verbal description, then, provided that the title was sufficient to cover the proprietor's possession of the land, and that the land was possessed openly, peaceably and without judicial interruption for the full 10-year positive prescriptive period, the owner's possession would fortify his right to the land. No person thereafter could successfully challenge his title to the ground so possessed. The period of positive prescription for rights in the foreshore, salmon fishing, and servitudes created by implication, is 20 years.

12.97　　Prescription has less effect in the Land Register, however; if there is an insufficiency in the description of the property, the Keeper of the Land Register may restrict the extent of the indemnity (ie restrict the guarantee of the title). Such exclusion from indemnity may be cured by the possession by the proprietor for the full prescriptive period.

12.98　　The loss of real burdens involves a negative prescriptive period of 5 years while the loss of servitudes involves a negative prescriptive period of 20 years.

LIMITS ON LAND OWNERSHIP

12.99　While "an Englishman's home may be his castle", in practice in Scotland there are a number of restrictions on the ability of a proprietor to possess his property.

12.100　　We have seen that the common law of land ownership places some restrictions upon land ownership and the exercise of rights of use and possession of the land. Just as a landowner should be able to expect to have and possess his property with exclusive possession (and so resist any attempts at encroachment or trespass) and without nuisance from neighbouring proprietors, so a proprietor must occupy his land in conformity with the common law (without encroaching or trespassing on the rights of neighbours or committing any nuisance which would detract from the neighbour's normal use and enjoyment of his property).

12.101　　Other common law rights may exist over any particular piece of property. These involve rights incidental to land ownership such as common law rights of access and the right to draw up nets and moor boats. But properties, particularly rural properties, may also be subject to the right of the public to cross the land concerned. Under common law these include rights of way which must be exercised between a definite origin and destination point. These were extended by the Land Reform (Scotland) Act 2003 which creates "access rights" in favour of the public to cross or be upon land for recreational, educational and certain other purposes.[49] In exercising these rights, the public must do so responsibly,[50] following the Scottish Outdoor Access Code,[51] and landowners must use or manage their property in a manner respecting these public rights.[52] Local authorities are charged with the responsibility of ensuring that these rights are recorded and protected.

12.102　　We have also seen that real burdens specified in the title deeds may also restrict rights of use and possession in a quasi-contractual manner. The owner of the benefited

---

[49] Land Reform (Scotland) Act 2003 ("LR(S)A 2003"), s 1.
[50] LR(S)A 2003, s 2.
[51] LR(S)A 2003, s 10.
[52] LR(S)A 2003, s 3.

property can enforce the burden against the owner of the burdened property affected. Similarly, servitudes may be enforced by the owner of the dominant tenement against the owner of the servient tenement.

While real burdens and servitudes protect the interests of immediate neighbours, there are also a number of statutory provisions which protect the interests of neighbourhoods. Of these, the most important concern planning permissions and statutory notices. Zoning for planning purposes specifies a range of permitted use classes to which properties within the zone may be put. A change of use will usually require planning permission unless it is another use permitted within the same use class. Developments to buildings usually require planning and building control permissions to which conditions may be attached. Owners of buildings in conservation areas will usually require permissions for alteration and demolition work. Planning applications must be notified to adjacent proprietors who have the opportunity to object or make other representations. However, in deciding planning applications, the local authority will consider the best interests of the wider local area and not merely of the immediately adjacent proprietors. Local authorities have the right to object to breaches of planning law for a number of years (depending on the nature of the breach concerned) and can enforce the restoration of buildings or even their demolition in extreme cases. In addition to planning regulation, local authorities have the power to issue statutory notices where buildings are dangerous, defective or not of a tolerable standard. They may even serve closing or demolition orders. The proprietor of the buildings concerned has certain rights of appeal but otherwise must carry out any specified works within the time limits prescribed for the type of notice concerned. **12.103**

LEASES

A lease is a contract whereby heritable property is hired by one party (the tenant), from another (the landlord). At common law, the tenant acquires only a personal right against the landlord, but can acquire a real right if the requirements of the Leases Act 1449 are met. A real right allows the tenant to enforce the lease against the landlord's successors in title. For this to occur, the lease must be in writing; the rent must be specified;[53] the heritable subjects must be sufficiently identified; there must be an "ish', that is a finite date at which the lease will end; and the tenant must have entered into possession of the subjects of the lease. In *Millar* v *McRobbie*[54] a landowner granted a lease to a farmer over arable land. Prior to the farmer taking up occupancy of the land, the landowner sold it. The purchaser of the land was held not to be bound by the lease, as the tenant had not taken possession, and thus had not acquired a real right. **12.104**

A real right can also be obtained where the lease is recorded or registered in the property registers (the Register of Sasines or Land Register (see below)). **12.105**

Rights and duties of landlords

Rights

In addition to the normal contractual remedies of rescission, interdict, implement, damages and eviction, the landlord has additional remedies of irritancy and **12.106**

---

[53] A right to occupy heritage without payment is a licence, not a lease.
[54] 1949 SC 1.

hypothec.[55] A landlord is entitled to irritate the lease and evict the tenant where the tenant is in arrears of rent for more than 2 years ("legal irritancy") or where specific provision for irritancy is made in the lease ("conventional irritancy"). The tenant has no right to remedy the breach which has led to conventional irritancy (for instance, payment of arrears of rent), but the landlord is probably under an obligation not to act oppressively.

Duties

12.107   The landlord must give the tenant "full possession" of the subjects. A failure to do so may entitle the tenant to reduce the lease, or at least claim a reduction in the rent. The landlord must also maintain the tenant in possession, that is, he must not derogate from his grant. In *Huber* v *Ross*[56] a tenant leased a top-floor flat to use as a photographic studio. The landlord carried out structural alterations to the remainder of the tenement which caused considerable damage to the leased flat. The tenant was held entitled not only to repairs to the premises but also damages for loss of business caused by the works. A landlord must maintain the premises in tenantable condition and keep the subjects in good repair. In *Gunn* v *NCB*[57] the tenant was found entitled to damages for loss of clothing and inconvenience and also for loss of wages stemming from asthma brought on by the dampness in the flat he leased from the defenders.

Rights and duties of tenants

Rights

12.108   The tenant, like the landlord, is entitled to rescind the lease and to seek interdict or implement to enforce the terms of the lease. The tenant may also be entitled to retain a portion of the rent where the landlord is in breach of his obligations, such as keeping the property in good repair.

12.109   Certain other types of lease, notably those relating to residential property, are governed by statute rather than common law. These types of leases are beyond the scope of this chapter.

Duties

12.110   The tenant must enter into possession of the leased premises and must plenish (furnish) the subjects. The requirement to plenish the subjects is to ensure that the landlord has sufficient security for payment of rent should he require to exercise his hypothec.[58] The tenant must only use the property for the purposes of the let: he must not "invert the possession". In *Moore* v *Munro*,[59] premises which were leased as a grocer's shop were used by the tenant as a shop on the ground floor and a

---

[55] Hypothec is considered below under "Rights in security".
[56] 1912 SC 898.
[57] 1982 SLT 526.
[58] Hypothec is discussed below under "Rights in security".
[59] (1896) 4 SLT 172.

dwellinghouse on the upper floor. The landlord was held to be barred by acquiescence from preventing the tenant using part of the property as a dwellinghouse, where the valuation roll had referred to the property as "house and shop" for 3 years. The tenant is also obliged to pay rent timeously and to look after the property. In *Fry's Metals* v *Durastic*[60] tenants who disconnected the alarm system when they left possession of leased subjects were held liable in damages to the landlord when the premises were damaged by vandals.

RIGHTS IN SECURITY

When an owner of property borrows money he is undertaking a personal obligation to repay the sums borrowed together with interest. If the debtor fails to make payment, the creditor must raise an action for payment of the outstanding amounts. However, to make sure that payment is made, a creditor often seeks security for the loan and interest by requiring that the debtor deliver up to the creditor some article of value in security for the loan. In the event of the debtor's default or bankruptcy, if the creditor has a real right in the property, then he can sell it to secure payment of the debt. If the proceeds are sufficient to settle the debt in full then any excess of proceeds is made over to the debtor or his trustee in bankruptcy. In the event of there being insufficient funds to pay the debt in full, then the creditor becomes an ordinary unsecured creditor on the estate of the debtor for the balance due. **12.111**

In many cases this delivery is no more than a power to take possession of the property in the event of default in payment. But the idea of delivery such as to create a real right in favour of the creditor, or something equivalent to delivery, is the key to understanding the idea of rights in security. The Latin maxim is *traditionibus, non nudis pactis, dominia rerum transferuntur* – real rights in property are transferred by delivery and not merely by agreement. **12.112**

There are two exceptions to the general rule concerning delivery. These are: (1) floating charges; and (2) hypothecs. In both of these cases there is security without possession. **12.113**

FLOATING CHARGES

Floating charges depend upon statute for their efficacy. Companies in Scotland (since 1961[61]) have been able to grant a floating charge over their whole assets (heritable and moveable alike). The floating charge requires to be registered with Companies House in the company's file held there. Because floating charges can range over the whole of a company's assets, including its stock, a security which required delivery would be impossible. Every time a secured item of stock were sold this would necessitate a formal release by the creditor. Instead, a floating charge does not attach to any particular assets until a prescribed event such as a winding-up occurs. On such event, the floating charge "crystallises" and attaches to the whole assets of the company. As a result, a floating charge is a very flexible form of security and is ideally suited to trading corporate businesses. **12.114**

---

[60] 1991 SLT 689.
[61] Companies (Floating Charges) (Scotland) Act 1961.

HYPOTHECS

12.115 These are types of security without delivery which arise in a number of specified commercial situations. They are commonly classified into "conventional hypothecs" and "legal hypothecs". Conventional hypothecs arise from contract. They are the creation of maritime commerce and involve rights in security granted by the master of a ship in the event of an emergency to raise funds to enable a voyage to be completed. If the security is limited to the cargo of the ship then the hypothec is a "bond of *respondentia*". If the security extends to the ship itself then the hypothec is a "bond of bottomry". There are a number of legal hypothecs, including the right of a solicitor to look to his client's costs and property recovered in a court action to secure unpaid expenses due to the solicitor,[62] the right of a landlord to look to his tenant's possessions to secure unpaid rent[63] and the right of the master and seamen to look to the ship for security for unpaid wages.[64]

RIGHTS IN SECURITY OVER MOVEABLE PROPERTY

12.116 Rights in security over moveable property where delivery is needed to create a real right may be achieved by pledges or deposits (these two are created by express contract) or liens (implied by operation of law).

12.117 With pledge, the pledger contracts to borrow money and agrees to deliver over to the pledgee the item of moveable property in security for the personal obligation. On fulfilment of the obligation, the pledgee must deliver the property back to the debtor. Delivery is therefore essential to the contract. Delivery may be:

(1) actual (when the property is physically transferred);

(2) constructive (for example, where the goods are held in a store, and the owner gives an instruction to the storekeeper to hold the goods for and if appropriate to deliver the goods to the pledgee – in which case the giving of the intimation to the storekeeper is an essential for the creation of a real right in favour of the creditor. It is essential for delivery that the storekeeper is an independent person from the pledger and not, for example, an employee of the pledger); or

(3) symbolical (for example, where a bill of lading, being a symbol for goods shipped, is delivered to the pledgee. This delivery of the bill of lading is regarded in law as effectual symbolical delivery of the goods themselves and so is capable of creating the real right in security).

12.118 Liens are rights implied by law to hold on to moveable property owned by another until that other has satisfied their debt or other obligation owed to the holder. Liens may be special or general.

12.119 A special lien involves a single contractual transaction and entitles a person holding the property to retain it until the obligation constituted in the contract is fulfilled. An example of this is where a carrier is instructed to carry goods. The carrier is entitled to

---

[62] "Solicitor's hypothec for the costs" now provided for by the Solicitors (Scotland) Act 1980, s 62.
[63] "Landlord's hypothec for rent".
[64] "Maritime hypothecs" now provided for by the Merchant Shipping Act 1995, ss 39f.

hold on to the goods and not deliver them up until his fee for the carriage is paid. This is a special lien because it is restricted to property held in relation to that particular transaction. A carrier does not have a special lien over other property held in relation to other transactions with the same debtor.

A general lien entitles the person holding the property to hold it generally in security for all obligations owed by the debtor. Usually this involves some general balance of money owed for a course of dealing involving a number of separate transactions. There are four generally recognised forms: **12.120**

1. lien of *factor*: who has a general lien over all goods, documents and money owned by the principal and coming into the factor's possession in the course of his dealings with the principal;
2. lien of *banker*: who has a general lien over bills of exchange, cheques, promissory notes and other similar negotiable instruments belonging to the customer and coming into the banker's possession in the course of his banking dealings with the principal. The lien does not extend to items deposited with the banker for safekeeping;
3. lien of *solicitor*: who has a general lien over all documents including title deeds and share certificates deposited by the client. The lien is to secure all professional fees and expenses made in the ordinary course of business on the client's behalf. A solicitor is not, however, entitled to dispose of the property and may retain it only until payment. The solicitor must produce the property if it is required in a court action. Where a client has become bankrupt, the solicitor must hand the property over to the client's trustee but will thereafter be ranked as a preferred creditor on the bankrupt's estate.
4. lien of *innkeeper*: who has a general lien over the luggage of a guest to secure the amount owed for hotel bills.

RIGHTS IN SECURITY OVER HERITABLE PROPERTY

To establish effectual security over heritable property, it is necessary for constructive delivery. The statutory form of security has, since 1970, been the standard security[65] which must be in statutory form. With it, security is granted over any interest in land which is capable of registration. The standard security can be used to secure an obligation present, future or contingent, to pay money or to perform some act. The statutory form may be in either Form A or Form B.[66] Form A includes the debtor's personal obligation, while Form B refers to the obligation being constituted in a separate deed. The function of Form B, then, is only to constitute the real right which secures a personal obligation recorded elsewhere. Form A, on the other hand, creates the personal obligation and then proceeds to secure it by creating the real right in security. **12.121**

Standard securities, unless otherwise varied, are granted under the standard conditions specified in Sch 3 to the 1970 Act which impose obligations on the debtor to maintain the value of the property which is offered in security (for example, to maintain the property in good repair, not to let out the property, not to make alterations, **12.122**

---

[65] Conveyancing and Feudal Reform (Scotland) Act 1970, s 9.
[66] Conveyancing and Feudal Reform (Scotland) Act 1970, s 9(2) and Sch 2.

to insure the property etc), and which also give certain protections to the debtor in the event of enforcement by the creditor. These protections are now to some extent reinforced by the provisions of the Mortgage Rights (Scotland) Act 2001.

12.123   In the event of default, the creditor may enforce the security in a number of ways. The initial step may be by means of the creditor serving a notice of default requiring the debtor to put right the default within 1 month. If the default is put right within the month, then the standard security continues unaffected by the default having occurred. If, however, the default is not corrected within the month, then the creditor may exercise various other remedies. Perhaps the most frequently occurring of such remedies is the calling-up: a notice which demands repayment of the whole amount of the loan within 2 months. In the event of the debtor failing to pay in full within 2 months of the service of the notice, the creditor may enforce the sale of the property. Because an enforced sale does not require court procedure or public notification in Scotland, it is indistinguishable, from a prospective purchaser's point of view, from a normal sale by a proprietor. This has the effect that an enforced sale should be achieved at true market value. This makes the Scottish system fairer than some others. In some European jurisdictions, enforced sales are conducted under the supervision of the court or after publication. Prospective purchasers know that the creditor has to sell the property and as a result such sales achieve only a fraction of the true market value. This shows that the Scottish standard security provides a uniform, flexible type of heritable security, with a fair balance being struck between the interests of creditors and debtors.

ESSENTIAL FACTS

ORIGINS OF THE LAW OF PROPERTY

12.124

- Scots property law derives from feudal law and from Roman law. This has been supplemented by statute.

REAL AND PERSONAL RIGHTS

- Rights in property can be categorised as either real rights or personal rights. A real right is a right in or over a piece of property: to use it, destroy it or have the right to its fruits. A personal right, on the other hand, is a right against another person which might be created by agreement or operation of law. *Real rights*: the principal real right is "ownership". Subordinate real rights exist where a person can enforce rights over the property in the ownership of another. Examples of subordinate rights include rights in security, leases, servitudes and simple possession. *Personal rights*: these rights are rights to demand the performance of a duty or obligation by another person. They may arise from contractual agreement or from the operation of law (for example, a person who breaches a duty of care can be obliged to make a payment of damages to the injured party).

COMMON PROPERTY

- Common property describes the situation where an item is owned by more than one person, each of whom has a *pro indiviso* share in it. Shares are generally equal. Each co-owner has a right to a share of the whole property and to its use, but not to a particular part of it. Each co-owner is entitled to a say in the management of the common property. It is thus necessary to have the consent of all co-owners before repairs and maintenance can be carried out, unless the work is so minor as to be considered *de minimis*. Where repairs are necessary, the Tenements (Scotland) Act 2004 lays out a scheme for management and apportionment of costs. Where there is agreement of all co-owners, any use of the common property is possible; however, where no such agreement exists, co-owners are limited to ordinary and reasonable uses.

JOINT PROPERTY

- This form of ownership arises where two or more persons own property but do not have separate rights in it. The commonest example is where trustees own shares or other trust property, where partners hold partnership property, or club members hold the property of their club. They may not dispose of their rights to any other person either by a lifetime transfer or by will.

COMMON INTEREST

- This occurs where owners have individual rights to their own property but they must have regard to the interests of others which occur in that property. For example, the owners of land through which a river flows ("riparian proprietors") have rights in common in the water flowing in the river. The corollary to this right is that the same riparian proprietors are under an obligation not to interfere with the natural flow of the water nor to exhaust the river of the water flowing in it.

CLASSIFICATIONS OF PROPERTY

- Property is classified as either heritable or moveable, and either corporeal or incorporeal. This results in four different classes of property, which are considered in turn.

Corporeal heritable property

- Corporeal property is tangible (physical) property which means that it is capable of being physically possessed. Heritable property is land, with the buildings and other fixtures attached to the land, for example crops, trees, stones, minerals etc. Certain limitations are imposed on ownership of corporeal heritable property. For example, mines of gold and silver are property of the Crown in terms of the Royal Mines Act 1424 and the Mines and Metals Act 1592, and the Civil Aviation Act 1982 allows aeroplanes to fly through what is, strictly speaking, property of the landowner.

Corporeal moveable property

• All other tangible property is moveable. So, corporeal moveable property consists of goods in general. Corporeal moveable property mainly comprises the sorts of things which can be physically taken and carried away and thus stolen. Title to corporeal moveable property usually depends upon proof merely of possession.

Incorporeal heritable property

• In this category fall certain rights connected with land, but not the land itself. Thus, leases and servitudes are incorporeal heritable property.

Incorporeal moveable property

• This category contains rights which are not connected with land. In particular, they include important economic rights such as intellectual property rights, for example copyright and patents. Excluded from the above categorisation are persons, items such as air, the sea and running water (which are deemed in the law to be incapable of individual private ownership) and *res nullius* – items such as wild animals, which are ownerless until subject to *occupatio*.

ACQUISITION AND LOSS OF CORPOREAL MOVEABLE PROPERTY

• There are a variety of means by which original acquisition of corporeal moveable property may be obtained. *Occupatio* is the doctrine whereby ownership is taken to property which was hitherto ownerless. Wild animals, birds and fish are thus susceptible to acquisition by occupancy if they are taken and controlled. It is permissible for any person to fish for and take wild trout and other fish in rivers and streams (provided that the activity of fishing is permitted by the riparian owners). This is because such fish are *res nullius*. *Specificatio* deals with the situation where a new thing has been created from materials which, at least in part, belonged to another, and where the other party's property cannot be restored to him in its original form. *Commixtio* is the mixing of solids and *confusio* the mixing of liquids. Where either occurs, and the resulting property cannot be separated into its constituent parts, the result is co-owned by the owners of the constituent parts, according to the proportionate share or value contributed by each part. *Accessio* occurs where two items of corporeal property become attached. The lesser item, known as the accessory, is subsumed into the ownership of the greater item (commonly known as the principal). Separate ownership rights in the accessory are extinguished. The original ownership rights in the accessory do not revert to the original owner on subsequent separation. Property may be converted from one class to another (the "law of fixtures"). On attachment, the owner of the principal becomes the owner of the whole including the accessory. Compensation may be due to the owner of the accessory. *Alluvio* occurs where one piece of heritable property accedes to another. This can occur where a river, which forms the boundary between two properties gradually changes its course, adding to the land on one side of the river by deposition and taking away the land on the other by erosion. *Avulsio* occurs where there arte seasonal variations, such as those caused by flood waters, and has no consequences for ownership.

THE LAW OF FIXTURES

- A special example of the idea of accession occurs when items of corporeal moveable property become annexed to heritable property such as land or buildings. This is an example of the principal of conversion where property of one class (corporeal moveable) is converted into another (heritable). For example, when moveable property such as wood and bricks is built into a structure permanently fixed to the land, it ceases to be moveable and becomes heritable. Under the common law, a number of recognised criteria exist which indicate where accession of moveable items to land and buildings may have taken place. These include:

  1. degree of attachment;
  2. permanence of attachment;
  3. functional subordination;
  4. mutual special adaptation;
  5. time and expense of installation and removal;
  6. the intention of the parties.

INCORPOREAL MOVEABLE PROPERTY

- This means economic rights which include negotiable instruments, business goodwill and intellectual property rights. Negotiable instruments are tradeable documents giving evidence of claims for money against a debtor. The best-known forms are cheques. Business goodwill is the expectation that existing customers will return to a business, usually expressed in terms of a capital value of that expectation. A competitor who gains economic advantage by pretending to be associated with a well-known business may be liable to that business in damages for "passing off". The most important forms of intellectual property are copyright, patents, design rights and trademarks.

HERITABLE PROPERTY

- This includes land and rights in relation to land and anything attached to it.

CROWN RIGHTS

- Some of Scots heritable property law derives from the feudal history of Scotland where the Crown was the ultimate superior from whom all other landowners derive their rights directly, or more commonly, indirectly. The Crown still holds rights known as regalia. *Regalia majora* are inalienable public rights such as the rights of the public in the foreshore, in the sea and seabed, and in navigable tidal rivers. *Regalia minora* are rights, for example, in salmon fishings, precious metals, treasure and lost property which can be granted to private individuals.

REAL BURDENS AND SERVITUDES

- A useful feature of Scots land law is the rights of benefited property owners over neighbouring burdened properties. These may be real burdens or servitudes. These rights are important to resolve issues of access, services, costs and maintenance of common areas, and so on. The ways these rights are created, transferred, varied or extinguished form an important part of Scots land law. The "law of the tenement" is an example of this.

TITLE

- Land rights are expressed in registered or recorded documents. The older system involved the recording of deeds in a central Register of Sasines. This has been replaced by a modern system of registration of title. In all cases the interests in land must be adequately described – usually by verbal descriptions and plans. A proprietor's rights theoretically extend from the centre of the earth to the heavens above. The right also includes any buildings and fixtures attached to the land. A modern land certificate has sections which specify not only the interest possessed but also the identity of the owner, any financial charges on the land, and the burdens which constrain the rights of the possessor to use the land. Defects in title can be cured by prescriptive possession. Similarly, certain ownership rights can be acquired, varied or lost by prescription – that is, by use or non-use during a specified length of time.

RESTRICTIONS ON LAND RIGHTS

- Rights to land are not absolute but may be restricted by agreement, by common law or by statute. Servitudes and burdens are an example of this. By common law and statute there may exist enforceable rights in favour of other people or in favour of the public. One example of this is the "right to roam" created by the Land Reform (Scotland) Act 2003 which gives the public access to the countryside. Other restrictions on ownership include control over uses imposed by administrative laws such as planning laws.

LEASES

- A lease is a contract whereby heritable property is hired by one party (the tenant) from another (the landlord). At common law, the tenant acquires only a personal right against the landlord, but can acquire a real right if the requirements of the Leases Act 1449 are met. This allows the tenant to enforce the lease against the landlord's successors in title. A real right can also be obtained where the lease is recorded or registered in the property registers (the Register of Sasines or the Land Register).

RIGHTS AND DUTIES OF LANDLORDS

- *Rights*: the landlord has the contractual remedies of rescission, interdict, implement, damages and eviction, and the additional remedies of irritancy and hypothec. A landlord may irritate the lease and evict the tenant where the tenant is in arrears of rent for more than 2 years ("legal irritancy") or where specific provision for irritancy is made in the lease ("conventional irritancy"). Conventional irritancy cannot be remedied by the tenant but the landlord should not act oppressively. *Duties*: the landlord must give the tenant 'full possession" of the subjects. The landlord must also maintain the tenant in possession. A landlord must maintain the premises in tenantable condition and good repair.

RIGHTS AND DUTIES OF TENANTS

- *Rights*: the tenant is entitled to rescind the lease, seek interdict or enforce the terms of the lease. The tenant may also be entitled to retain a portion of the rent where the landlord is in breach of his obligations. *Duties*: the tenant must enter into possession of the leased premises and must plenish the subjects. The tenant must use the property only for the purposes of the let he must not "invert the possession". The tenant must pay rent timeously and look after the property.

RIGHTS IN SECURITY

- To secure the payment of money and other obligations undertaken by an owner of property, it is common to secure these using the debtor's property. This enables the creditor to take possession of the property if the debtor fails to fulfil his obligations. This is usually achieved by *delivery* of the property by the debtor to the creditor. But delivery can be actual, constructive or merely symbolical, according to the type of property concerned. The best-known examples of security by delivery over moveable property are *pledge* and *lien*. Security over heritable property is achieved by the debtor registering or recording a *standard security* in favour of the creditor. An exception to the general requirement for delivery exists with floating charged and with *hypothecs*.

ESSENTIAL CASES

REAL AND PERSONAL RIGHTS

12.125

Muirhead & Turnbull v *Dickson* (1905): this illustrates the importance of the distinction between real rights and personal rights. The pursuers supplied a piano to the defender, who made some payments towards the total price. The pursuers sued for delivery back to them of the piano. The court held that the transaction was a credit sale and so a real right of property had passed to the defender when it was first delivered to him. Muirhead & Turnbull were left with only a *personal* right against the defender to recover the balance of the unpaid price.

JOINT PROPERTY

Murray v *Johnstone* (1896): a silver cup which had been won by a club was held to be joint property and so could not be given away against the wishes of a minority of the club members.

OCCUPATIO

Valentine v *Kennedy* (1985): the accused were convicted of the theft of escaped rainbow trout (a domestic species) which they had caught in a river outside the enclosure in which the trout had been kept. Although the fish had escaped, the sheriff held that ownership in them had not been lost. Rainbow trout, unlike the native brown trout, could not be regarded as *res nullius* because the fish were not of a native species and the trout in question, having once been possessed, were capable of being stolen.

SPECIFICATIO

International Banking Corporation v *Ferguson Shaw & Sons* (1910): the defenders made lard from 53 barrels of oil which had been delivered to them. While the defenders were held to own the lard, they were required to pay compensation to the former owners of the oil.

ACCESSION OF MOVEABLES TO HERITAGE

Fisher v *Dixon* (1843): this case related to the degree of attachment. A door was held to be a fixture since the doorway into which it fitted was heritable.

Christie v *Smith's Exrx* (1949): this case related to the degree of attachment. A summerhouse weighing about 2 tons was held to be a fixture even though it was merely resting upon the ground under its own weight rather than attached to it.

Scottish Discount Company v *Blin* (1985): this case related to permanence of attachment. Scrap industrial sheers (over 60 tonnes in weight) bolted to concrete foundations fell to be regarded as fixtures, on the basis that when they were installed they were intended to be a permanent or quasi-permanent feature of the land to which they were attached.

Howie's Trs v *McLay* (1902): this case related to the adaption of the items. Looms were placed in a shed, the dimensions of which fitted the looms. The uppermost parts of the looms were bolted to the roof of the shed. The court held that the looms were heritable by accession.

Shetlands Islands Council v *BP Petroleum Development* (1990): in this case the intention of the parties was held to be irrelevant: "No agreement between owner and occupier can affect the matter of ownership of heritable fixtures even as between them."

REAL BURDENS OVER LAND

Marsden v *Craighelen Lawn Tennis and Squash Club* (1999): real burdens must confer a real ("praedial") benefit if they are to be valid. This case involved a real burden which prohibited the playing of games on a Sunday. The court held that the benefit was a personal one which reflected the religious commitments of the superior and not a real one benefiting the owner of the superiority.

EXTENT OF OWNERSHIP OF LAND AND INTERESTS IN LAND

Brown v *Lee Construction Ltd* (1977): the proprietor's rights extend theoretically *a coelo usque ad centrum* which means from the heavens above to the centre of the earth. In this case the owners of a crane were prevented from overhanging the property of the pursuer.

Bowers v *Kennedy* (2000): the court held that an otherwise "landlocked" property had an implied common law right of access along the least inconvenient route through neighbouring proprietors' properties.

LEASES

Millar v *McRobbie* (1949): a landowner granted a lease to a farmer over arable land. Prior to the farmer taking up occupancy of the land, the landowner sold it. The purchaser of the land was held not to be bound by the lease, as the tenant had not taken possession, and thus had not acquired a real right.

Huber v *Ross* (1912): a tenant leased a top-floor flat to use as a photographic studio. The landlord carried out structural alterations to the remainder of the tenement which caused considerable damage to the leased flat. The tenant was held entitled not only to repairs to the premises, but also damages for loss of business caused by the works.

Gunn v *NCB* (1982): a tenant was found entitled to damages for loss of clothing and inconvenience and also for loss of wages stemming from asthma brought on by the dampness in the flat he leased from the defenders.

Moore v *Munro* (1896): premises which were leased as a grocer's shop were used by the tenant as a shop on the ground floor and a dwellinghouse on the upper floor. The landlord was barred from preventing the tenant using part of the property as a dwellinghouse, because the valuation roll had referred to the property as 'house and shop' for 3 years.

Fry's Metals v *Durastic* (1991): tenants who disconnected the alarm system when they left possession of leased subjects were held liable in damages to the landlord when the premises were damaged by vandals.

13 EMPLOYMENT LAW

CONTRACT AND STATUTE

Employment law is primarily concerned with the law which regulates the relations **13.1** between employers and employees. As will be explored in the first section, there are more employment relationships than employer–employee, and employment law is also concerned with these. At the centre of the employment relationship is the contract of employment, so that an understanding of the principles of contract law is essential. The contractual basis has also been supplemented and in some cases supplanted by statutory rights. Statutory employment rights have increased dramatically since the mid-1960s, in areas concerned with employment security, discrimination, maternity rights, industrial action and a wide range of individual rights. Part of this expansion has been caused by obligations arising out of the UK's membership of the European Union. An understanding of EU law and the relationship between it and national law is also necessary for an understanding of employment law. This chapter will examine the contractual relationship in some depth, and then outline a selection of statutory rights.

EU AND NATIONAL LAW[1]

The doctrine of "subsidiarity" places the responsibility on the Member State to **13.2** implement legislation to give effect to EU Directives. In principle, once this has been done, it is the national legislation which is the source of law in the Member State. Thus, the Working Time Regulations 1998 were introduced in order to implement the Working Time Directive 93/104. Anyone who wishes to establish what their rights are in relation to working time should look in the first instance to the 1998 Regulations.

However, the doctrine of "supremacy of EU law" gives the underlying EU Directive **13.3** a continuing relevance. National law must be interpreted so as to comply with the EU law so far as is possible, even if this may not be the most obvious reading of the words in the national law. In addition, certain parts of EC law may be of direct effect so that they can be relied on directly in the national court or tribunal. It has been established that Art 141 of the Treaty of Rome, the equal pay article, has "horizontal" direct effect, so that those employed by private as well as State employers may rely on it. In those cases where a (part of a) Directive is of direct effect it will be "vertical" only and thus only those who are employed by State employers may rely on it.

---

[1] See paras 8.7 and 8.36–8.38.

EUROPEAN CONVENTION ON HUMAN RIGHTS (ECHR)

13.4   Under the Human Rights Act 1998, courts and tribunals have had to interpret the law in such a way as to be consistent with the "convention rights" made enforceable by the Act.[2] This means that, although only employees of public authorities may raise an action against their employer under the Act,[3] indirectly the Act affects the way all employment law is interpreted, both common law and statutory. The ECHR rights are civil, not social, rights and do not apply explicitly to the workplace. However, a number of rights are relevant to employment. For example, Art 8, which provides for the right to respect for private and family life, has been found to be relevant in cases of workplace surveillance.[4] However, like many of the ECHR rights, Art 8 is qualified and interference with it may be justified in certain circumstances so long as it is proportionate and in pursuit of a relevant interest, such as the prevention of crime. In *McGowan* v *Scottish Water*[5] covert surveillance of the home of an employee who was suspected of falsifying his time sheets was found to be proportionate in the circumstances.

EMPLOYMENT TRIBUNALS

13.5   Employment tribunals (called industrial tribunals until 1998[6]) (ETs) were first established in 1964. Their primary function is to hear cases brought by individuals to enforce their employment rights under various statutes, principally the Employment Rights Act 1996 (ERA 1996) and the anti-discrimination statutes. The constitution and conduct of employment tribunals is governed by the Employment Tribunals Act 1996 (ETA 1996).

13.6   A standard tribunal hearing is heard by three people drawn from three panels: a legal panel appointed by the Lord President whose members act as chairs, and two other panels drawn up by the Secretary of State, one in consultation with organisations of employers, and the other in consultation with organisations of employees.[7] With the consent of both parties, a hearing may be heard by a chairman and one other, and in certain specific cases or where both parties agree in writing, or where the case is no longer contested, by a chairman alone.[8]

Statutory grievance procedure

13.7   An employee who wishes to raise an action against an employer must have complied with the statutory procedure established by the Employment Act 2002[9] which requires the employee to have given the employer a written statement of the complaint. The employer should arrange a meeting, in which the employee should co-operate. Failure to state a grievance will mean that the employee will lose the right to raise an action,

---

[2] Section 3.
[3] Section 6.
[4] *Halford* v *UK* (1997) 24 EHRR 532.
[5] [2005] IRLR 167.
[6] Employment Rights (Dispute Resolution) Act 1998, s 1.
[7] Employment Tribunals (Constitution and Rules of Procedure) Regulations 2004 (SI 2004/1861), reg 8.
[8] ETA 1996, s 4(3).
[9] Section 32 and Sch 2: does not apply in the case of unfair dismissal except for constructive dismissal.

and failure to co-operate fully may lead to reduction of any compensation. This applies to the types of cases referred to in the Act.

EMPLOYMENT APPEAL TRIBUNAL

It is possible to appeal against a decision of an ET to the Employment Appeal Tribunal (EAT). From there, in Scotland an appeal can go to the Inner House of the Court of Session (its English equivalent being the Court of Appeal) and from there to the House of Lords. A reference could be made to the European Court of Justice for a ruling on a point of EC law if relevant at any stage. Like the ETs, the EAT sits with three members: one, the chair, being a Court of Session judge and the other two people with special knowledge or experience of industrial relations as either employers' representatives or workers' representatives.[10] Appeal to the EAT is on a point of law only, and it is not competent to appeal against a finding of fact by a tribunal.   **13.8**

THE EMPLOYMENT RELATIONSHIP

WHO IS AN EMPLOYEE?

An employee is someone employed under a contract employment. Its legal name is a contract of service. This is a concept adopted without further definition in employment statutes.[11] Not everyone who is in employment is an employee. A person may be "employed" on a more casual basis, or may be employed through an agency or may be working for themselves. Some of these individuals, and their employers, may consider that they are "casual workers" or "agency workers" or "self-employed"; others may feel that they are in fact employees. While the terminology used by the parties to a contract is a strong indication of what their intentions were, it will not override other factors if the overall terms of the contract show otherwise.[12] It is important to identify under what sort of contract a person is employed. Some statutory rights apply only to employees. Employees are taxed under Schedule E, employers being obliged to deduct tax at source, while self-employed workers[13] are taxed under Schedule D and are responsible for their own payment of tax.[14] Employers are responsible for paying national insurance contributions for employees (in addition to paying the employee's own contributions at source), while self-employed workers are responsible for paying their own contributions.[15] An employer's common law vicarious liability is for employees only.[16] An employer owes specific common law and statutory health and safety duties to employees which are more extensive than those owed to others.   **13.9**

So far as the common law is concerned (and taxation and social security statutes), there are only two ways of categorising contracts to carry out work: either as   **13.10**

---

[10] ETA 1996, s 22.
[11] ERA 1996, s 230(1) and (2).
[12] *Dacas* v *Brook Street Bureau (UK) Ltd* [2003] IRLR 190.
[13] For tax and national insurance purposes, anyone who not an employee is a "self-employed worker".
[14] Income Tax (Earnings and Pensions) Act 2003, Pt 11.
[15] Social Security Contributions and Benefits Act 1992, ss 1 and 2.
[16] See paras 3.59–3.65.

contracts of service or as contracts for services. The parties to these contracts are respectively the employer and employee (formerly "master" and "servant"), and employer and independent contractor. This broadly is a distinction between an employee and a self-employed person. Common law and the taxation statutes do not make any finer distinction than that. Employment protection statutes, however, do make finer distinctions. While some rights only apply to those employed under a contract of employment/service, other rights apply to those who are classified as "workers". ERA 1996 contains 12 Parts which create a range of substantive rights, 11 of which apply solely to employees. Only Part 2, relating to unauthorised deductions from wages, applies to workers more broadly. Other rights, such as the right to the national minimum wage, to working time protection and equal pay, also extend to workers as more broadly defined. There is a further even broader category, those who are "in employment", who receive protection under the anti-discrimination legislation.

Workers and those in employment

13.11   The statutory definition of a "worker" includes an employee and also someone who contracts to perform work personally so long as the contract does not make the other party a professional client[17] or a client or customer of his business.[18] The element of personal service is crucial to the definition of an employee, and this is not what distinguishes a worker and an employee. Employees are dependent on their employers economically, and in a subordinate position legally. The object of creating an "intermediate" category between employees and the self-employed is to recognise that there are workers in a position of dependency who, though not perhaps in the same position of subordination as employees, are sufficiently dependent to require protection. In *Byrne Brothers (Formwork) Ltd* v *Baird*[19] the EAT found that the applicants, who were self-employed labour-only sub-contractors in the construction industry, were exactly the kind of worker for whom this intermediate status was created: workers who, although nominally free to move from employer to employer, in fact work for lengthy periods for one employer, supplying no more than their own labour. In some cases such labour-only subcontractors would be employees, even although their contract may on the face of it state otherwise, if the contract as a whole is in fact one of employment.[20]

13.12   The anti-discrimination statutes place duties on employers not to discriminate against those who are "in employment".[21] This is a similar but broader concept to that of worker. It includes the employee, and again anyone who contracts to perform personal service, but without the qualification that the other party must not be a professional client or customer.

---

[17] Trade Union and Labour Relations (Consolidation) Act 1992 (TULRCA 1992), s 296.
[18] ERA 1996, s 230(3).
[19] [2002] IRLR 96.
[20] *Ferguson* v *John Dawson & Partners (Contractors) Ltd* [1976] 3 All ER 817.
[21] Equal Pay Act 1970, s 1(6); Sex Discrimination Act 1975, s 82; Race Relations Act 1976, s 78; Disability Discrimination Act 1995, s 68; Employment Equality (Religion or Belief) Regulations 2003 (SI 2003/1660), reg 2; Employment Equality (Sexual Orientation) Regulations 2003 (SI 2003/1661), reg 2; Employment Equality (Age) Regulations 2006 (SI 2006/1031), reg 2.

The Employment Relations Act 1999[22] gives the Secretary of State power to amend **13.13** ERA 1996 and TULRCA 1992 to extend rights to workers in particular categories, but this power has not been used yet.

While there are good reasons for ensuring that employees, as dependent and **13.14** subordinate workers, have protection, it is perhaps more questionable whether the full range of rights should be restricted. The form of employment contract may not be at the discretion of the worker, who may be more or less dependent and subordinate in fact even although formally not employed under a contract of employment. Where an employment relationship is in practice one in which the worker is of employee status, the courts and tribunals are able to find that it is so in law as well, but the distinction between a contract of employment and a worker's contract can be narrow, and the difference in dependency and subordination between a worker and employee scarcely enough to justify withholding job protection rights.

HOW TO IDENTIFY A CONTRACT OF EMPLOYMENT

At common law a contract of service is distinguished from a contract for services. **13.15** While the concept of employee at common law is the same concept as is used in the employment statutes, the concepts of "worker" and "in employment" are not directly equivalent to the contract for services: both will be employed under forms of contracts for services, but this is not part of their statutory definition. The difference between a contract of service and a contract for services was expressed in *Stagecraft Ltd* v *Minister of National Insurance*[23] as follows:

> "In the contract of service the person hired agrees to place his services under the direction and control of the hirer. In the contract for services the person hired agrees to perform a specific service for the hirer, the manner of the performance being left to the discretion of the person hired."[24]

In this case a comedian, who had contracted to appear for a season in "resident variety" in theatres in Britain, was held to be employed under a contract of service. The most important factor taken account of in determining the question was the degree of control exercised over the employee by the employer. The importance of control is such that the approach to determining the question of whether a contract was one of service was at one stage based entirely on control and known as the "control" test. In *Stagecraft Ltd* this was expressed as follows: "A servant is a person subject to the command of his master as to the manner in which he shall do his work."[25] There is no longer a "control" test for determining who is an employee, but control is still an important criterion in the modern approach.

The modern approach

The most influential formulation of the modern approach is in *Ready Mixed Concrete* **13.16** *(SE) Ltd* v *Minister of Pensions and National Insurance*[26] in which the decision of the

---

[22] Section 23.
[23] 1952 SC 288.
[24] At 302.
[25] At 301, quoting Bramwell LJ in *Yewens* v *Noakes* [1880] 6 QBD 530 at 532.
[26] [1968] 2 QB 497.

Minister that a lorry driver was employed under a contract of service was overturned on appeal. Three conditions were identified as necessary for a contract of service: agreement by the employee, in consideration for a wage, to provide his own work and skill to perform service for the employer; agreement by the employee to be subject to a sufficient degree of control by the employer; and the other terms of the contract being consistent with its being a contract of service.[27] This definition is often referred to as the "multiple" or "multi-factor" test. As a definition it leaves a lot of room for interpretation, not least the third condition where there is no prescribed list of factors which are consistent and inconsistent, but a matter of common sense in each case. A different emphasis can be seen in the contemporaneous case of *Market Investigations Ltd* v *Minister of Social Security*,[28] in which the Minister's decision that a market research interviewer was employed under a contract of service was upheld. It identified a fundamental difference between an employed person and someone who was self-employed through the key question "Is the person who has engaged himself to perform these services performing them as a person in business on his own account?".[29] Although this was in the context of confirming the move away from the single "control" test, control was still an important, but not the sole, factor. Additional factors were: whether the disputed service provider provides their own equipment; whether he hires out his own helpers; what degree of financial risk he takes; what degree of financial responsibility he has; and the extent to which he can profit from sound management in performing the task.[30] This approach concentrates on issues relating to dependency, and is sometimes described as the "entrepreneurial", "small businessman" or "economic reality" test. The question to be asked was phrased in down-to-earth terms by the EAT in *Withers* v *Flackwell Heath Football Supporters' Club*[31] as: "Are you your own boss?". In that case the EAT felt that the claimant, a bar steward, would certainly have answered "No", and that he was an employee.

13.17   The generality of the "multiple" test is such that different parts of it may be given more emphasis in one case rather than another, both as a matter of law and in relation to the particular contract. In some cases control has been very prominent; in others less so. This may depend on why the existence of the contract is being asserted or challenged. The "entrepreneurial" test arose in the context of tax and national insurance; the issue of control has been particularly influential in relation to vicarious liability; while in unfair dismissal and other employment protection cases the concept of mutuality of obligation, which will be discussed below, has been prominent. This may be inevitable, and is certainly confusing. It would seem that a unitary approach to the question is what is aspired to in the courts[32] but not what happens in practice.

An "irreducible minimum"?

13.18   Although the "economic reality" approach seems closer to identifying the essence of a contract of employment, it is the "multiple" test which has been the more influential,

---

[27] At 515.
[28] [1969] 2 QB 173.
[29] At 184.
[30] At 185.
[31] [1981] IRLR 307.
[32] *Lee* v *Chung* [1990] IRLR 236; *Lane* v *Shire Roofing Co (Oxford) Ltd* [1995] IRLR 493.

particularly in the context of employment protection rights. Although it is a multi-factor test, there has been a tendency to focus particularly on two aspects: control and "mutuality of obligation". In *Montgomery* v *Johnson Underwood Ltd*[33] these two concepts were described as the "irreducible minimum" of a contract of service, while in *Carmichael* v *National Power plc*[34] Lord Irving in the House of Lords restricted it to "that irreducible minimum of mutual obligation".[35] This implies that the balancing of consistent and inconsistent factors and taking account of all the factors in the "multiple" test is conditional on the contract first meeting the requirement of mutuality (or possibly mutuality and control).

Mutuality of obligation

In this context mutuality of obligation means that the employer is obliged to offer   **13.19**
work, and the employee obliged to perform work under the terms of the contract. This can be particularly problematic in the case of casual workers and agency workers. For casual workers the problem is that a contract whose terms are that work will be offered "as and when required" and will be accepted "if suitable" does not provide the necessary mutuality. For agency workers there is a different problem: agency workers have a contract with an employment agency, which has a contract with an end-user with whom the worker is placed. The worker has a contract with the agency (who will usually be responsible for paying remuneration) but is under the control of the end-user. Thus there is no mutuality between worker and end-user.

There is a line of decisions which have found mutuality established by implication.   **13.20**
In the case of casual workers the Court of Appeal in *Nethermere (St Neots)* v *Taverna and Gardiner*[36] considered the position of part-time homeworkers sewing pockets into trousers where there was no obligation to provide or do the work. It found that, through a course of dealing over a number of years, implied mutuality of obligation had grown up. In the case of agency workers the Court of Appeal in *Dacas* v *Brook Street Bureau*[37] considered the case of a cleaner who had been working for 4 years with a local authority through the employment agency. The Tribunal had found that she had no contract with the end-user and her contract with the agency was not one of service. The EAT found that her contract with the agency was one of service since it paid her wages. The Court of Appeal, however, found that the question should not have been decided without considering whether there was an implied contract of service with the end-user as employer. Since Ms Dacas had not appealed against the finding that the local authority was not her employer, this did not become a live issue. There is no consistent approach here, and the implied contract analysis has been doubted in the Court of Session.[38] Subsequent English cases have emphasised that it will have to be necessary to imply a contract in order to give business reality to the situation.[39]

---

[33] [2001] IRLR 269.
[34] [1999] ICR 1226.
[35] At 1230.
[36] [1984] ICR 612.
[37] [2004] ICR 1437.
[38] *Toms* v *Royal Mail Group plc* [2006] CSOH 32 per Lord Glennie at para 22.
[39] *Cable & Wireless plc* v *Muscat* [2006] IRLR 354; *James* v *Greenwich LBC* [2007] IRLR 168.

Personal service

13.21 The contract is a personal one and the power to delegate is in general fatal to its being one of service. It is also part of the statutory definitions of a worker's contract, and of the concept of "in employment". McKenna J did say that "a limited or occasional power of delegation" might not be fatal[40] but it would have to be very limited, almost certainly restricted to a replacement approved by the employer. In *MacFarlane* v *Glasgow City Council*[41] a Tribunal had found that a gym instructor who, if she was unable to take a class, was entitled to send along a replacement from a register of instructors maintained by the council, and paid by the council, was not an employee because of the power to delegate. The EAT found that it had taken too absolute an approach to this and remitted it back for reconsideration, applying the correct test.

Control

13.22 Control is still an important, although not the sole, element. The definition of "control" adopted in *Ready Mixed Concrete* is: "It includes the power of deciding the thing to be done, the way in which it shall be done, the means to be employed in doing it, the time when and the place where it shall be done."[42] This can extend to the skilled worker whose employer is not capable of actually controlling the work. "It is the right of control not its exercise."[43]

SPECIAL GROUPS OF WORKERS

13.23 There are a number of employment relationships which are not governed by a contract of service. Some of them are treated for the most part in the same way as contracts of service. Civil servants, police officers and other Crown employees are not employed under contracts of service, but are given the benefit of most statutory employment rights.[44] Company directors are not employees by virtue of being directors (they are agents of the company), but may be employed under a contract of service as well as being a director. A director's employment contract is often referred to as a "service agreement".

Contract of apprenticeship

13.24 A contract of apprenticeship is not a contract of service: under such a contract the employer contracts to instruct the apprentice in a particular trade or skill and the apprentice contracts to learn. As a fixed-term contract it cannot be terminated on the giving of notice. Statutory definitions of employment in general include the contract of apprenticeship[45] along with the contract of service. While apprentices have additional protections by virtue of their status, this is not the case for those

---

[40] *Ready Mixed Concrete (SE) Ltd* v *Minister of Pensions and National Insurance* [1968] 2 QB 497 at 515.
[41] [2001] IRLR 7.
[42] At 515.
[43] Ibid.
[44] See, for example, ERA 1996, ss 191–201.
[45] ERA 1996, s 230(2) and (3).

working under training contracts which are not apprenticeships.[46] There is nothing to stop a "modern apprenticeship" from being a contract of apprenticeship so long as its terms comply with the common law concept.[47]

Ministers of religion

Secular appointments by religious bodies are in the same category as any other **13.25** employment. However the traditional approach of the courts towards ministerial appointments has been to regard them as being on a spiritual rather than a commercial basis. Since there is no intention to be legally bound, a minister of religion could not be an employee (nor even a worker). The position was recently reviewed by the House of Lords in *Percy v Church of Scotland Board of National Mission*.[48] An associate minister of the Church of Scotland raised an unfair dismissal and a sex discrimination action when she was counselled to resign as a minister following an internal inquiry. Both actions were dismissed by the ET and the appeal was pursued only in relation to the sex discrimination action, which required proof that she was "in employment", not that she was an employee. The House of Lords found that she was in employment. There was a personal obligation to execute work: the contract between her and the Mission gave her the right to be paid and it the duty to enforce her performance of the duties of an associate minister.[49] The statutory rights related to civil, not spiritual, matters. Although this decision relates to an associate minister, there is no reason why its terms should not apply to all ministers of religion. The House did not consider whether she was employed under a contract of service because it did not have to, but equally there seems no reason, once it has been agreed that the contract is not a spiritual one entirely, and is intended to be legally binding, why it would not also meet the terms of the "multiple" test.

THE CONTRACT OF EMPLOYMENT

The contract of employment is governed by the general law of contract. While the **13.26** formal common law position that a contract is a voluntary agreement entered into by two consenting (and equal) parties may not reflect the realities of economic power, it does reflect the legal status. The formation of a contract of employment is subject to the same principles as any other contract. There is no requirement for writing, so that an employment contract may be formed in writing, verbally or by actions.

The contract of employment is made up of a number of sources. It is an ongoing **13.27** contract which may therefore be varied throughout its life. The principal sources are: express terms (written or verbal); implied terms (general principles); incorporated terms; and implied terms (common law duties). Although there is no requirement for the contract to be in writing, there is a statutory requirement for there to be a written record of the terms of employment.

---

[46] *Wiltshire Police Authority v Wynn* [1981] QB 95.
[47] *Flett v Matheson* [2006] IRLR 277.
[48] 2006 SLT 11.
[49] At 28 per Baroness Hale.

DUTY TO PROVIDE WRITTEN STATEMENT OF EMPLOYMENT PARTICULARS

13.28 Employees who have 1 month's service and work at least 8 hours a week are entitled to receive, within 2 months of starting employment, a written statement of employment particulars. The statement must specify:[50]

- names of employer and employee;
- date when employment began;
- date when continuous employment began, if different;
- scale or rate of pay or method of calculating it;
- intervals when paid;
- terms and conditions of hours of work;
- terms and conditions of holidays and holiday pay;
- job title or brief description of work;
- place of work or, if various, indication of that and employer's address.

13.29 This information must all be given in one note. The following information must also be given but not necessarily in the same note:

- terms and conditions relating to sickness, including sickness pay;
- terms and conditions relating to pensions and pension schemes; [This information could be given by referring to a reasonably accessibly document.]
- the notice the employee is entitled to receive and obliged to give; [This information could be given by referring to statute or a collective agreement.]
- if the job is not permanent, the period for which it is expected to continue or the date when it is expected to end;
- any collective agreement directly affecting terms and conditions;
- if the employee is required to work outside the UK for over a month, information about work outside the UK.

If there are no particulars about any of the matters in this list, the statement must say so.

13.30 The employee must also be given a note about discipline and grievance rules and procedures, including the name of the person to whom an appeal against discipline can be made, or with whom a grievance can be lodged.[51]

13.31 If the employer has given the employee a written contract of employment covering all the required particulars, this document will count as fulfilling this obligation.[52] The employer must issue a written statement of any change in any of the particulars within 1 month of the change.[53]

---

[50] ERA 1996, ss 1 and 2.
[51] ERA 1996, s 3.
[52] ERA 1996, ss 7A and 7B.
[53] ERA 1996, s 4.

Legal status of the written statement

The written statement is not of itself contractual. It is a unilateral document drawn up **13.32** by one party only: the employer. Though this is likely to reflect the contractual terms, it may not. A contract, on the other hand, is bilateral: it is the product of the agreement of employer and employee. If there is a conflict between the contractual agreement and the written statement, it is the contract which will prevail. In *Robertson v British Gas Corporation*[54] where employees relied on a contractual letter which gave a right to a bonus, and the employer relied on a written statement which stated it was a qualified right, the contractual terms prevailed.

IMPLIED TERMS

Express terms take precedence over all other terms. An implied term may supplement **13.33** an ambiguous or partial provision, or fill a gap in a contract, but cannot contradict an express term. In *Tayside Regional Council* v *McIntosh*[55] an employee who had been dismissed from his job as a garage mechanic when he was disqualified from driving claimed that his dismissal was unfair since there had been no term in his contract requiring that he possess a clean driving licence. This had been mentioned in the advertisement for the job, the application form and at interview, but not in the contractual letter. The EAT held that, while an implied term could not have contradicted an express term, it could supplement or clarify: in this case it was, it said, an essential term because of the nature of the work the employee had to do.

Tests for implied terms

The most influential test is the "business efficacy" test. Where it is necessary to imply **13.34** a term into a contract to make it workable, such a term should be implied. This is essentially what happened in *Tayside Regional Council* v *McIntosh*. As a mechanic, it would be necessary for the employee to move or test drive the vehicle and thus a valid licence would be required. The contract, it could be argued, would be unworkable without it.

Another approach has been to imply into a contract a term which is so "obvious" **13.35** that it must be assumed that the parties would have agreed to it if they had thought about it. This is sometimes called the "officious bystander" or "oh, of course" test – if a bystander had suggested to the parties that they include a certain term in the contract, they would both have said "oh, of course", that it was obvious it should be included.[56] What this approach emphasises is that the implied term must be something which both parties agree (or would have agreed) should be obligatory.

There is a possible conflict between these two approaches. Something which may be **13.36** necessary, or reasonably necessary, to make the contract work, may not be so obvious that the parties must have agreed to it when made. It is more likely to be the employer's interests which would be allied with that of the business, so that a "business efficacy" test of some sort is more likely to help the employer's interpretation. In *Aparau* v *Iceland*

---

[54] [1983] IRLR 302.
[55] [1982] IRLR 272.
[56] *Lake* v *Essex County Council* [1979] ICR 577.

Frozen Foods[57] there had been no express mobility clause in the employee's contract of employment. When the employer was taken over, employees were asked to agree to a new written statement which stated that employees could be transferred to any store owned by the company. Mrs Aparau did not and, on transfer a year later to another branch, she resigned. Her resignation would only allow her to raise an unfair dismissal claim if it was a constructive dismissal, that is a legitimate response to a material breach of contract by her employer. While the ET had found that she had agreed to the new term by working on for 12 months without objecting, and, using the "oh, of course" test, that a mobility clause was implied in the original contract, the EAT did not agree: it held that because this was a change without immediate practical effect, working on did not imply that she had accepted the change. Nor did it agree that a mobility clause was implied in the original contract. It did not feel it was essential to make the contract work: a place of work is essential; a mobility clause makes life easier for management, but it is not always reasonably necessary.

Terms implied by custom and practice

13.37   It is possible, but not common, for a term to be implied by custom and practice. Such a custom would have to be "reasonable, certain and notorious".[58] It is important that implied contractual effect is shown. An implied agreement is not the same thing as an exercise of an employer's discretion, such as a one-off, or even two-off, enhanced redundancy pay.[59] Equally, agreement by employees on one occasion or a limited number of occasions is not the same as agreeing to contractual change, such as reduction in hours for work shortage.[60] The important thing is to establish that the custom has been followed without exception for a substantial period, that the custom has been drawn to the attention of employees, and that it is possible to infer an intention to be bound contractually.

INCORPORATED TERMS

13.38   Incorporation of terms into a contract occurs when the parties agree to make an outside source into a term of the contract. The most common source of incorporated terms is the collective agreement. A collective agreement is an agreement between an employer and a trade union or trade unions, or a group of employers and trade unions. A collective agreement is not a legally binding contract in itself between the employer and the union.[61] However, although the collective agreement itself creates no legal rights, its terms, or certain of them, may become part of an individual contract of employment through the process of incorporation, and thus enforceable by the employer or employee as between each other.

13.39   The terms of a collective agreement can be incorporated into the individual contract expressly (by being referred to in the individual contract as a source of terms), or by being implied by custom (as discussed in the previous section). Not all terms of a

[57] [1996] IRLR 119.
[58] *Devonald v Rosser & Sons Ltd* [1906] 2 KB 728; *Sagar v H Ridehalgh & Son Ltd* [1931] 1 Ch 310.
[59] *Quinn v Calder Industrial Materials Ltd* [1996] IRLR 126.
[60] *International Packaging Corporation (UK) Ltd v Balfour* [2003] IRLR 11.
[61] TULRCA 1992, s 179, but note exception.

collective agreement may be suitable for incorporation. Some agreements may relate to dispute resolution between employer and union, or general policy aims, such as how to deal with redundancies, and these may not be incorporated if they are considered too general.[62]

IMPLIED DUTIES: TERMS IMPLIED BY COMMON LAW

Both employer and employee have duties implied into the contract by the common **13.40** law. These duties were developed in the 19th century and reflect the subordination inherent in the relationship of employer and employee. There have also been more recent developments expanding the employer's duties. The duties can be seen as underpinning the essential nature of the contract whereby the employee agrees to provide work for the employer in return for a wage (the "wage/work bargain").

The implied duties of the employee

Duty to be willing to give personal service

The contract is one of *delectus personae*. As it is personal, performance cannot be **13.41** delegated to another.[63] Because the contract is personal it is not possible for either employer or employee to be compelled to adhere to the contract: an employee cannot be forced to remain in employment, and an employer cannot be forced to retain an employee.[64] This is so even where an employee has been successful in winning an unfair dismissal action.

Duty to obey lawful and reasonable orders

The employer's prerogative is to give orders to the employee which the employee **13.42** must obey. However, these orders must be within the scope of the contract, and must be lawful and reasonable. An employee need not obey an order to do something which is unlawful, nor something which is unreasonable. These two concepts came into conflict in *Buckoke* v *Greater London Council*[65] with (in that case) reasonableness taking precedence. An instruction to firefighters to cross red lights when driving to an emergency, while driving carefully in doing so, was found to be reasonable, and although, at that time, technically unlawful, one which the employee should have obeyed.

Duty of loyalty

This duty is also referred to as the duty to give faithful service, or the duty of fidelity, **13.43** and comprises a number of headings. The employee must put the employer's interests before his own in connection with the employment, and must act in the employer's interests.

---

[62] *British Leyland (UK) Ltd* v *McQuilken* [1978] IRLR 245.
[63] *Ready Mixed Concrete (SE) Ltd* v *Minister of Pensions and National Insurance* [1968] 2 QB 497.
[64] TULRCA 1992, s 236.
[65] [1971] 2 All ER 254.

13.44 **Duty of honesty.** A contract of employment is not a contract *uberrimae fidei* (of the utmost good faith), so that there is no duty to disclose material facts. The employee's duty is to be honest, but not necessarily to disclose prejudicial information if it is not asked for.[66] There may be special circumstances where it is necessary to disclose such information: it may be part of the employee's contractual duty (express or implied, perhaps as a supervisor) to report others' wrongdoing, which might also involve their own.[67]

13.45 **Duty not to make a secret profit.** An employee should not make any personal gain from his employment, without the knowledge and consent of the employer. This includes not just taking a bribe but gaining any advantage or payment from the employment.[68]

13.46 **Duty to act in the employer's interests.** This aspect of the duty of loyalty as a duty to co-operate with or not to disrupt the employer's business emerged in the case of *Secretary of State for Employment* v *ASLEF (No 2)*.[69] A "work to contract" by train drivers, whereby they obeyed the employer's rule book to the letter, was held to be in breach of contract since it was done with the intention of disrupting the employer's business.

13.47 **Duty not to use confidential information.** Employers may protect themselves by an express term in the contract from confidential information being disclosed during and after employment.[70] Even without an express term, the implied duty gives protection.

13.48 *Duty not to work for rivals.* An employee may work for whoever he wishes in his own time. However, in the case of a potential conflict between the interests of the employer and a secondary employer, there would be a breach of duty if there was danger that confidential information might be revealed.[71]

13.49 *Duty not to benefit personally.* An employee should not take advantage of his position in order to benefit his own interests for the present or the future, such as canvassing customers for a future business.[72]

13.50 *Duty not to disclose confidential information.* There is a difference in the implied duty between what an employee may not disclose while still an employee and what may not be disclosed after employment ends. The common law duty does have an impact after employment, but in a limited way. In *Faccenda Chicken* v *Fowler*[73] three categories of confidential information were distinguished: easily accessible information (which it would not be breach of contract to disclose); information which was told in confidence or which it was obvious was confidential but was part of the skill or memory of the employee (which it would be breach of contract to disclose during employment but

---

[66] *Bell* v *Lever Bros* [1932] AC 161.
[67] *Sybron Corporation* v *Rochem Ltd* [1983] IRLR 253.
[68] *Boston Deep Sea Fishing Co* v *Ansell* (1888) 39 Ch D 339.
[69] [1972] ICR 19.
[70] See para 4.64.
[71] *Hivac Ltd* v *Park Royal Scientific Instruments Ltd* [1946] 1 Ch 169.
[72] *Adamson* v *B & L Cleaning Services Ltd* [1995] IRLR 193.
[73] [1986] IRLR 69.

not afterwards); and "trade secrets", information so confidential that it should never be divulged even after employment has ended. Thus, using information in the second category, gained while an employee (such as the names of customers), would not be a breach of the implied term, but recording the information while an employee for use afterwards would be.

An employee might seek to justify or defend disclosing confidential information **13.51** by relying on a common law "public interest" defence,[74] or on the "whistleblower's" protection from dismissal or detriment introduced by the Public Interest Disclosure Act 1998.[75] It does not give a blanket protection: the disclosure must be a "qualifying disclosure" and it must be made to one of the specified categories of persons. Any court or tribunal considering this issue would also have to take account of Art 10 of the ECHR ("Freedom of Expression") which is a qualified right.

Inventions. At common law an invention which is connected with the employee's **13.52** employment is the employer's as the employee must work in the best interests of the employer. However, this position has been ameliorated by the Patents Act 1977[76] so that the employer only has ownership where the invention was made in the course of the employee's duties; or was made in the course of specifically assigned duties from which the invention might reasonably be expected to result; or was made in the course of the employee's duties, and the employee's responsibility gives him a duty to further the employer's interests.

Duty to show reasonable skill and care

If an employee does not exercise reasonable care and skill, he may be required to **13.53** indemnify the employer for loss caused by the breach.[77]

The implied duties of the employer

Duty to pay wages

If the employer pays wages, the primary duty is fulfilled: there is no duty to provide **13.54** work. As a judge said over 60 years ago: "Provided I pay my cook her wages regularly, she cannot complain if I choose to take any or all of my meals out."[78] Thus, an employer who suspends an employee on full pay will not be in breach of contract, though suspension without pay will be a breach unless there is an express contractual term permitting it.

There are limited circumstances in which an employee can demand work as well **13.55** as wages: where the failure to provide the work as well as wages could lead to a loss of reputation or publicity, usually applying in the case of actors;[79] where the wages are dependent on work, as in the case of piecework or commission; and possibly where skills need to be kept up to date by practical application.[80]

---

[74] *Initial Services Ltd v Putterill* [1968] 1 QB 396.
[75] Inserted ss 43A–H, 47B and 103A into ERA 1996.
[76] Sections 39–45.
[77] *Lister v Romford Ice and Cold Storage Co Ltd* [1957] AC 555.
[78] *Collier v Sunday Referee Publishing Co Ltd* [1940] 4 All ER 234 at 236.
[79] *Herbert Clayton & Jack Waller Ltd v Oliver* [1930] AC 209.
[80] *Langston v AEUW (No 2)* [1974] ICR 510.

Duty to indemnify

13.56   The employer has a duty to indemnify or reimburse an employee for losses or expenses incurred in the course of employment.

Duty to take reasonable care for the employee's safety

13.57   At common law an employer has a duty to take reasonable care for an employee's safety and to protect him from foreseeable risks. It is both contractual and delictual.[81]

"Mutual duty of trust and confidence"

13.58   This is a duty which has developed relatively recently. It is often viewed as the employer's counterpart to the employee's duty of loyalty. It has had the effect of placing a greater requirement for fair and reasonable treatment of the employee on the employer. It was acknowledged by the House of Lords in *Malik v Bank of Credit and Commerce International*.[82] The duty was stated to be that the employer "shall not without reasonable and proper cause, conduct itself in a manner calculated to or likely to destroy or seriously damage the relationship of confidence and trust between employer and employee".[83] In *Malik*, the employer's breach had consisted in conducting the bank's business in a fraudulent manner, which, the employees concerned alleged, had caused them to become unemployable even though they had not been involved in the corrupt practices.

13.59   The employer does not have to have intended to damage the relationship with the employee: the question is to be answered objectively, looking at whether the behaviour was likely to have that effect. The sort of behaviour caught by this duty is varied. It extends to bullying and harassment,[84] failing to take a complaint seriously[85] and insulting an employee.[86]

TERMINATION AND ENFORCEMENT OF THE CONTRACT OF EMPLOYMENT

TERMINATION BY NOTICE

13.60   Termination by the employer is dismissal; termination by the employee is resignation. At common law either may terminate a contract of employment by giving notice. What would commonly be considered to be a "permanent" employee, a term used in the Fixed Term Employees (Prevention of Less Favourable Treatment) Regulations 2002 in contrast to a fixed-term employee, has at common law a "periodic" contract. Such a contract is automatically renewed, by the principle of tacit relocation, unless one of

---

[81] See Chapters 3 and 4.
[82] [1997] ICR 606.
[83] At 621, quoting *Woods v WM Car Services Ltd* [1981] ICR 666 at 670.
[84] *Horkulak v Cantor Fitzgerald International* [2003] IRLR 756.
[85] *Bracebridge Engineering Ltd v Darby* [1990] IRLR 3.
[86] *Isle of Wight Tourist Board v Coombes* [1976] IRLR 413.

the parties gives notice to terminate it. The length of notice may be provided in the contract, but must be no less than the statutory minimum: from the employer, 1 week for every year of employment to a maximum of 12 weeks' notice; from the employee, 1 week.[87]

Wrongful dismissal

Dismissal without notice is called summary dismissal, and is justified only when **13.61** the employee is in material breach of contract. An employee who is unjustifiably dismissed may raise a common law action for wrongful dismissal. The measure of damages for wrongful dismissal will be calculated in the usual way for breach of contract, and will be sufficient to restore the employee to the position he would have been in but for the wrongful dismissal. Since the employer would have been entitled to dismiss with notice, compensation is often restricted to the amount due for notice. Unlike wrongful dismissal, the statutory remedy of unfair dismissal is available when the employer dismisses with notice and when the employer fails to renew a fixed-term contract, and damages are not restricted to the notice period.

OTHER FORMS OF TERMINATION

At common law a contract for a fixed period or a fixed task ends when the period or task **13.62** comes to an end. This is not the case so far as statutory employment protection rights are concerned: failure to renew a fixed-term contract is a dismissal so far as the law of unfair dismissal and redundancy pay is concerned.[88] Employer and employee may agree to end the contract: this is neither a resignation nor a dismissal. The contract of employment may be frustrated under the doctrine of impossibility of performance, but the courts are reluctant to apply this doctrine to periodic employment contracts.[89] Death of either party, the dissolution of a partnership or the winding up of a company will also terminate the contract, but if a business is acquired as a going concern the Transfer of Undertakings (Protection of Employment) Regulations 2006 (TUPE) will operate to transfer the contracts of existing employees to the new employer,[90] though an employee cannot be forced to transfer if he does not wish to.[91]

BREACH OF CONTRACT

Where one party materially breaches or repudiates the contract, the other is entitled **13.63** to terminate the contract without notice. It is the action of the innocent party in accepting the breach which terminates the contract, not the breach itself. Thus, where an employee materially breaches a contract of employment and the employer says that the contract is at an end because of the breach, this is a dismissal since it is the action of the employer which has ended the contract, not the breach.[92]

---

[87] ERA 1996, s 86.
[88] ERA 1996, ss 95 and 136.
[89] *Williams* v *Watson Luxury Coaches* [1990] IRLR 164.
[90] Reg 4. For transfers before 6 April 2006, TUPE Regulations 1981 will apply.
[91] Reg 4(7).
[92] *London Transport Executive* v *Clarke* [1981] ICR 355.

REMEDIES FOR BREACH OF CONTRACT

Specific implement/interdict

13.64 An action of specific implement cannot be used to compel either employee or employer to continue with a contract of employment. This common law rule is reinforced by statute.[93] There are, however, some circumstances in which it may be possible to obtain an interdict. An employer may be able to obtain an interdict to prohibit an employee working for another in breach of an express or implied contractual term, but this would only be granted if the employer is prepared to carry on with the contract, and the order is necessary to protect the employer's legitimate interests.[94] An employee might be able to obtain an interdict to postpone a contractually improper dismissal, but this would only be granted if the employee retained the confidence of the employer and would only postpone the dismissal until contractual procedures had been gone through.[95]

Withholding wages

13.65 If an employee refuses to carry out a significant part of their employment duties, this is a repudiation of contract, which would entitle the employer to terminate it. If the employer does not terminate it, he is not obliged to accept partial performance and pay for it. If the employer decides not to pay wages, he must have told the employee that partial performance will not be accepted.[96]

Unlawful deductions from wages

13.66 Where an employer fails to pay what is contractually due, there is a statutory procedure for raising an action for unlawful deductions in an ET.[97] This procedure is appropriate both where the employer has consciously made a deduction from wages, and also where the employer is simply in breach of contract in failure to pay or in the amount paid. In the former case a deduction is only lawful where it is required or authorised by statute or the contract of employment, or the worker has given prior agreement in writing to such a deduction.[98]

STATUTORY EMPLOYMENT RIGHTS

13.67 This section looks in outline at three statutory employment rights. The national minimum wage and working time legislation lay a base line for minimum pay and maximum hours. Both apply to workers as well as employees. The right not to be unfairly dismissed is an important right, giving some protection of job security. It only applies to employees. There are many other rights, principally in ERA 1996 but also in individual legislation which are beyond the scope of this chapter.

---

[93] TULRCA 1992, s 236.
[94] *GFI Group Inc* v *Eaglestone* [1994] IRLR 119.
[95] *Hughes* v *London Borough of Brent* [1988] IRLR 55.
[96] *Wiluszynski* v *London Borough of Tower Hamlets* [1989] IRLR 259.
[97] ERA 1996, Pt 2.
[98] Section 13.

NATIONAL MINIMUM WAGE

There had been minimum wage legislation since the beginning of the 20th century, but **13.68** this applied only to specific low pay sectors of the economy through Wages Councils, which were abolished in 1993. The National Minimum Wage Act 1998 (NMWA 1998) introduced a national minimum wage (NMW) applying to all sectors, supplemented by the National Minimum Wage Regulations 1999 (NMWR 1999).

Qualification

Although it is a national standard, not every working person is entitled to the NMW. **13.69** To qualify, the individual must be over compulsory school age, must be working in the UK and must be a "worker".[99] In addition to those employed under a worker's contract, the Act also applies to agency workers, homeworkers and Crown employees even if they are not otherwise workers.[100] However, there are a number of categories of workers who do not benefit. Certain classes of people have been excluded by the Regulations, including apprentices (for the first year), workers on certain government training schemes, students on work placement for less than a year and workers on schemes for homeless people or those on income support who are provided with shelter in return for work.[101] Further exclusions include voluntary workers for charities and voluntary organisations, prisoners, members of the armed forces and people living as part of a family.[102]

Rate of NMW

The rate is determined by the Secretary of State upon a recommendation by the Low **13.70** Pay Commission, and is set as an hourly rate. The rates are as follows:

- for those aged 22 and over (£5.35);[103]
- for those aged between 18 and 22 (£4.45);[104]
- for those aged 16 and 17 (but not apprentices) (£3.30).[105]

Calculation of the rate

The NMWR 1999 provide the method for calculating whether NMW has been paid. A **13.71** worker's hourly rate is calculated by dividing the total remuneration (TR) paid to the worker during the pay reference period (PRP) by the number of hours or work during that period (NHW): that is (TR in PRP)/NHW must be no less than NMW.

Total remuneration. This is determined by adding together all money payment paid **13.72** by the employer to the worker in and relating to the PRP in question. Certain payment

---

[99] NMWA 1998, ss 1 and 54.
[100] NMWA 1998, ss 34–36.
[101] NMWR 1999, reg 2.
[102] NMWA 1998, ss 37–44 and 45; NMWR 1999, reg 2.
[103] £5.52 from 1 October 2007.
[104] £4.60 from 1 October 2007.
[105] £3.40 from 1 October 2007.

is deducted from the total, including overtime or shift premium, tips or gratuities not paid through the payroll and payment of expenses due to a third party.

13.73   **Pay reference period**. The pay reference period is 1 month or, if pay is paid by reference to a period of less than a month, that period.

13.74   **Number of hours of work**. How the hours of work are determined depends on the category of work, whether it is time work, salaried hours work, output work or measured hours work. The NMWR explain how the hours are to be calculated for each category of work.

Enforcement

13.75   The NMW is enforceable as a contractual right by the individual worker. The Inland Revenue has enforcement powers which enable it to serve notice on employers who do not comply, getting progressively more serious with failure to comply, with the sanction of criminal proceedings if the failure is wilful.[106]

WORKING HOURS

13.76   The Working Time Regulations 1998 (WTR 1998) were introduced in order to comply with the EC Working Time Directive 93/104. This Directive was passed as a health and safety measure, and the WTR are viewed both as a health and safety measure and as "family friendly" measure. The EC Directive was amended in 2000 to include a number of excluded workers, including junior doctors, within its scope, and the WTR were subsequently amended to comply. Following the scope for derogation in the Directive, many of the provisions of the WTR can be varied so long as the employer obtains a "relevant agreement": in some cases a collective agreement or workforce agreement, in others individual agreement. The WTR apply to workers, not just employees. Contracting out of the obligations under the WTR, other than expressly allowed, is void.[107] For each provision of the WTR there are exclusions or variations.

Working time

13.77   Working time is defined as any period during which a worker is working at his employer's disposal and carrying out his activities or duties, and not during a rest period when not working. This includes time when he is receiving relevant training related to work.[108] On-call time, where a worker is on call and during the on-call period is required to be present at a place determined by the employer counts as working time, even if the worker is permitted to sleep.[109]

---

[106] NMWA 1998, ss 17–22; and 31–32.
[107] NMWR 1999, reg 35.
[108] NMWR 1999, reg 2.
[109] *Sindicato de Medicos de Asistencia Publica (SIMAP)* v *Conselleria de Sanidad y Consumo de la Generalidad Valenciana* [2000] IRLR 845.

Maximum weekly working time

The maximum weekly hours is 48 hours in each 7 days, including overtime.[110] This is   **13.78**
calculated as an average over a reference period. The basic reference period is 17 weeks;
special classes of worker (such as seasonal workers) have a 26-week reference period;
and a reference period of up to 52 weeks could be agreed by a collective or workforce
agreement. For young workers, that is those over compulsory school age but under 18,
the maximum working time is 8 hours a day and 40 hours a week, aggregating hours
worked for more than one employer.[111] It is the employer's responsibility to see that
each worker complies with the limit.

Individual opt-out

Unlike most other EU countries, the UK has included a provision whereby the employer   **13.79**
can obtain a worker's agreement in writing so that the 48-hour limit does not apply.
The reference period may be varied by collective or workforce agreement, but the
complete opt-out from the limit requires the individual worker's written agreement.
The EU has been attempting to restrict the use of this opt-out, but, in spite of the health
and safety arguments, the UK Government has continued to argue for the retention of
this flexibility.

Rest

Adult workers are entitled to at least 11 hours' consecutive rest in each 24-hour period;   **13.80**
young workers to 12 hours. Adult workers are entitled to an uninterrupted weekly
rest period of at least 24 hours in each 7-day period; young workers to 48 hours. An
adult worker is entitled to a minimum of 20 minutes' break where more than 6 hours
a day is worked; young workers to a minimum of 30 minutes for over 4.5 hours. For
monotonous or other work patterns that might put health and safety at risk, rest breaks
must be "adequate".[112]

Night working

A night worker is someone who normally works at least 3 hours at night, night being   **13.81**
11 pm to 6 am unless agreed otherwise by a collective or workforce agreement (but the
period must include midnight to 5 am). A night worker's normal hours of work cannot
exceed an average of 8 hours for each 24 hours, calculated either according to the 17-
week reference period, or for workers involved in special hazards or heavy mental or
physical strain their actual working hours cannot exceed 8 in any 24-hour period.[113]
Workers cannot be required to work at night without having had the opportunity to
undergo a free health assessment, and should have regular assessments. There is a
right to be transferred to day work if certified by a doctor that it is necessary.

An employer should ensure that young workers do not work during the "restricted   **13.82**
period", that is 10 pm to 6 am (or 11 pm to 7 am, according to contract).

---

[110] NMWR 1999, regs 4–5.
[111] NMWR 1999, reg 5A.
[112] NMWR 1999, regs 8; 10–12.
[113] NMWR 1999, regs 6–8.

Holidays

13.83 The WTR 1998 provide for a minimum of 4 weeks' paid annual leave. When they were first introduced there was a 13-week qualification period for entitlement but this was held to be contrary to the Directive.[114]

13.84   A question to which the Scottish and English courts gave different answers was whether "rolled up" holiday pay was permissible. This is where a worker is not paid when he takes his holiday, but the pay for hours worked includes an element for holiday pay. The Scottish answer was that this was impermissible;[115] the English that it was permissible.[116] The ECJ has given its ruling on the question in a number of cases referred from the English Court of Appeal.[117] The answer may be described as impermissible, with qualifications. Formally, it is contrary to the Directive since it may militate against workers taking holidays if they do not get paid at the time they are due to take them. However, if the situation is transparent, that is the precise proportion paid as holiday pay is made clear when it is actually paid, it may be permissible.

Enforcement

13.85 The individual worker may enforce the rest period and holiday provisions at an ET.[118] The working time and night work provisions are enforced by the Health and Safety Executive using a range of administrative and criminal sanctions.[119]

UNFAIR DISMISSAL

13.86 ERA 1996 provides a right not to be unfairly dismissed.[120] The statutory right of unfair dismissal should not be confused with the common law action of wrongful dismissal.[121]

Qualifying for the right not to be unfairly dismissed

13.87 Only employees have the right not to be unfairly dismissed. The employee must have been in employment with the dismissing employer for a continuous period of a year, working back from the date of dismissal.[122] Whether or not there is an unbroken period of qualifying service is calculated according to the statutory rules.[123] Continuity is presumed and it is up to the employer to prove that there has been a break. In cases of automatically unfair dismissal there is no qualifying period.

Dismissal

13.88 An action for unfair dismissal can only be raised if an employee has been dismissed. "Dismissal" is given an extended meaning in ERA 1996, both for unfair dismissal and for the right to redundancy pay. Dismissal can occur in three ways:

---

[114] *R* v *Secretary of State for Trade and Industry, ex p BECTU* [2001] ICR 1152.
[115] *MPB Structure Ltd* v *Munro* [2003] IRLR 350.
[116] *Marshalls Clay Products* v *Caulfield* [2004] IRLR 564.
[117] *Robinson-Steele* v *RD Retail Services Ltd* [2006] IRLR 386.
[118] WTR 1998, reg 30.
[119] WTR 1998, regs 28–29.
[120] ERA 1996, s 94.
[121] See para 13.61.
[122] ERA 1996, s 108.
[123] ERA 1996, ss 210–219.

(1) termination of the contract by the employer, with or without notice;

(2) expiry of a fixed-term contract without renewal;

(3) termination of the contract by the employee with or without notice where the employer's conduct would have entitled the employee to resign without giving notice.[124]

If there is a dispute as to whether the employee has been dismissed, the burden of proof lies with the employee to show that he was dismissed.

Termination by the employer

Tribunals have been careful to look at the reality of the situation as well as the form of words to see if the reality is that the termination was at the instance of the employer. If an employer gives an employee an ultimatum to resign or be dismissed, that will be an employer termination;[125] similarly, if an employee is pressurised to agree to resign, that will also be an employer termination. **13.89**

Non-renewal of a fixed-term contract

A fixed-term contract includes both a common law fixed-term contract (which cannot be terminated by notice before the end of the fixed term), and also a contract with a fixed termination date which can also be terminated by notice before that date, the latter being more common.[126] **13.90**

Resignation justified by employer's conduct (constructive dismissal)

The courts have adopted a common law analysis of this provision of ERA 1996.[127] At common law, and therefore under this provision, only a material breach of contract by the employer can entitle the employee to resign without notice. The breach by the employer may be of any term in the contract, express or implied. It can include a breach of the mutual duty of trust and confidence: indeed, it is in the context of the concept of constructive dismissal that this duty developed. **13.91**

The employee must resign in order to qualify as having been dismissed in this way, and should do so without delay. There may, however, be a series of actions by the employer, leading up to a "final straw" which precipitates the actual resignation. In *Lewis v Motorworld Garages Ltd*[128] an employee who was demoted continued to work, but resigned some time later after continued criticism and threats. While the ET and EAT had held that he had affirmed the contract by working on after demotion and the subsequent actions by the employer were not material, the Court of Appeal found that he could rely on the original demotion and subsequent actions cumulatively as a breach of the mutual duty of trust and confidence.[129] Note that the emloyee must have complied with the statutory grievance procedure to be entitled to raise an ET action. **13.92**

---

[124] ERA 1996, s 95.
[125] *Robertson v Securicor Transport Ltd* [1972] IRLR 70.
[126] *Dixon v BBC* [1979] IRLR 114.
[127] *Western Excavating (ECC) Ltd v Sharp* [1979] IRLR 27.
[128] [1985] IRLR 465.
[129] See para 13.7.

Reason for the dismissal

13.93   In a "standard" unfair dismissal claim the employer must show what the reason or principal reason for the dismissal was.[130] In the case of automatically unfair dismissals the burden of proof will rest with the employee.

Automatically unfair dismissals

13.94   These are dismissals for specific inadmissible reasons. They differ from standard unfair dismissals in that there is no requirement for a period of continuous employment, and once the inadmissible reason has been established the dismissal is automatically unfair without any further proof of fairness or unfairness. Among the inadmissible reasons are pregnancy and maternity;[131] trade union membership and activity;[132] official industrial action;[133] health and safety;[134] spent convictions;[135] asserting a statutory right;[136] and making a protected disclosure.[137]

Reason in standard unfair dismissals

13.95   The employer must establish that the reason falls within one of the potentially fair reasons specified in the Act.[138] These are: capability or qualifications; conduct; retirement;[139] redundancy; contravention of a statutory duty; and some other substantial reason justifying dismissal. Capability is assessed by reference to skill, aptitude, health or any other physical or mental quality.

13.96   It is the reason which the employer actually relied on when dismissing the employee which is relevant, not any reason either discovered after dismissal or elevated in importance after dismissal.[140]

Fairness

13.97   Once the reason has been proved by the employer the ET will consider whether the dismissal for that reason was fair. This will be decided according to the terms of s 98(4) of ERA 1996. Whether a dismissal is fair or unfair is to be judged in the light of the reason shown by the employer, and depends on whether in the circumstances the employer acted reasonably or unreasonably in treating it as a sufficient reason for dismissing the employee. The subsection requires account to be taken of the size and administrative resources of the employer's undertaking, and for the question to be determined by an ET in accordance with equity and the substantial merits of the case.

---

[130] ERA 1996, s 98(1).
[131] ERA 1996, s 99; Maternity and Parental Leave etc Regulations 1999 (SI 1999/3312), reg 20.
[132] TULRCA 1992, s 152.
[133] TULRCA 1992, s 238A.
[134] ERA 1996, s 100.
[135] Rehabilitation of Offenders Act 1974.
[136] ERA 1996, s 104.
[137] ERA 1996, s 103A.
[138] ERA 1996, s 98(1) and (2).
[139] From 1 October 2006.
[140] *W Devis & Sons Ltd v Atkins* [1977] IRLR 314.

Section 98(4) does not place a burden of proof on either employer or employee. **13.98**
While the burden is on the employee to prove there has been a dismissal, if disputed,
and to prove one of the automatically unfair grounds, if that is what is alleged, and
the burden is on the employer in a standard unfair dismissal to prove that it was for a
potentially fair reason, there is no burden of proof in relation to fairness in a standard
unfair dismissal.

Size and administrative resources of the employer

Small employers must behave fairly no less than large employers. Nevertheless the **13.99**
size and administrative resources could determine the kind of procedures which an
employer is able to adopt. The ACAS Code of Practice[141] suggests that it might not be
practicable for small establishment to adopt all its detailed provisions, and suggests
that some provisions[142] could be adapted for small businesses. For example, smaller
employers may not be able to adopt the same standards of independence at all stages
of a disciplinary hearing.

Equity and the substantial merits of the case

Each case must be determined on its own merits. A component of fairness is equitable, **13.100**
or consistent, treatment of employees. Nevertheless, each case depends on its own facts
and it may be that it is appropriate to treat different employees differently for the same
(mis)conduct where their personal situation or record is different.[143]

Reasonableness

The Tribunal has to decide whether a reasonable employer would have taken the **13.101**
decision to dismiss in the circumstances. It must not decide what they would have
done had they been the employer, but must decide if the employer's decision was
within the "band of reasonable responses" of a reasonable employer.[144] This presumes
that there is a spectrum of reasonable responses, with a harsh but reasonable decision
at one end and a lenient but reasonable decision at the other. The "band of reasonable
responses" test has been criticised for following rather than setting standards, and
for in effect placing the burden of proof on the employee by making the question one
of whether no reasonable employer would have decided to dismiss. The EAT decided
not to follow it in *Haddon* v *Van Den Bergh Foods Ltd*,[145] but the Court of Appeal rapidly
overruled this and reaffirmed the test in *HSBC Bank plc* v *Madden*.[146]

Reasonableness relates to whether there was sufficient reason to dismiss, and also **13.102**
whether the employer adopted a reasonable procedure in making the decision.

---

[141] ACAS (Advisory, Conciliation and Arbitration Service) Code of Practice on Disciplinary and Grievance
Procedures (Revised 2004), para 7.
[142] Paras 9 and 38–41.
[143] *Securicor Ltd* v *Smith* [1989] IRLR 356.
[144] *British Leyland* v *Swift* [1981] IRLR 91.
[145] [1999] IRLR 672.
[146] [2000] IRLR 827.

Statutory procedures

13.103 **Retirement dismissals**. An employee may be fairly dismissed because of retirement, so long as the retiral age is 65 or over, or lower so long as the employer can justify it as a proportionate means of achieving a legitimate aim and thus not age discrimination.[147] The employer must also comply with the provisions of ss 98ZA–ZF of ERA 1996, and the procedures in the Employment Equality (Age) Regulations 2006 (EEAR 2006)[148] which give a right to be considered for working past retirement age.

13.104 **Statutory discipline and dismissal procedures**. All employers, regardless of size, must comply with the statutory procedures introduced by the Employment Act 2002.[149] These apply to most dismissals, but there are exceptions, including constructive dismissals and collective redundancy dismissals.[150] These are minimum procedural standards: failure to follow or complete them, where this is the fault of the employer, will make a dismissal automatically unfair,[151] and increase the amount of compensation due to the employee. There are two minimum procedures: the standard and the modified procedures.

13.105 *Standard procedure*. This is a three-stage procedure. Before dismissing the employee, the employer must give a written statement of the circumstances which have led to his considering dismissal. There must be a meeting between the employer and employee before the decision to dismiss is taken. There must be a right to appeal against the decision.

13.106 *Modified procedure*. This is a two-stage procedure. It requires the employer to give a written statement of the alleged misconduct which led to the dismissal. There must be a right of appeal. The general rule is that the standard procedure applies. The modified procedure applies where the employer dismisses the employee without notice immediately on discovering the misconduct. The employer must have been entitled to dismiss without notice for this misconduct, and it must have been reasonable to dismiss without further enquiry.[152]

"No difference" rule

13.107 Before the introduction of the statutory discipline and dismissal procedures the House of Lords had held that it was an error of law for a Tribunal to decide, in cases where a dismissal was procedurally unfair, that the dismissal was fair because it would have made no difference if a proper procedure had been used.[153]

13.108   The position now is that failure to follow the statutory procedures will make a dismissal automatically unfair even if it would have made no difference. If an

---

[147] Employment Equality (Age) Regulations 2006 (SI 2006/1031) (EEAR 2006), reg 3.
[148] Sch 6; ERA 1996, s 98ZG.
[149] Implemented by the Employment Act 2002 (Dispute Resolution) Regulations 2004 (SI 2004/752) (EADRR 2004).
[150] EADRR 2004, reg 4.
[151] ERA 1996, s 98A.
[152] EADRR 2004, reg 3.
[153] *Polkey* v *A E Dayton Services Ltd* [1987] IRLR 503.

employer has complied with the statutory procedure, a failure in another aspect of procedure will not make a dismissal unfair, if the employer can show that he would have decided to dismiss the employee anyway even if a proper procedure had been followed.[154] The burden of proof is on the employer to show that it would have made no difference.

Conduct dismissals

The ACAS Code of Practice deals primarily with this form of dismissal. Much of **13.109** the case law is concerned with broader issues of procedure. The employer's own disciplinary procedure should be followed, and if it gives clear warning of the sort of conduct which will merit dismissal, a dismissal for that reason is more likely to be found to be reasonable.[155] However, a Tribunal can still consider whether a dismissal is reasonable even where it is in terms of the contract.[156]

The Burchell *test*

The decision of the EAT in *British Home Stores* v *Burchell*[157] has been very influential, **13.110** and although it was challenged at the same time as the "band of reasonable responses" test it was also reaffirmed by the Court of Appeal.[158] In *Burchell* an employer's decision to dismiss an employee for suspected dishonesty, when there had been insufficient evidence for a prosecution and where it was now accepted that she was innocent, was held to have been reasonable. The employer had met a threefold test: there was a genuine belief in the employee's guilt; the employer had reasonable grounds for this belief; and the employer had carried out a reasonable investigation as the basis of these grounds. This may not be fair to the innocent employee, but it focuses on the reasonableness of the employer's behaviour as s 98(4) requires.

Good practice

The importance of investigation, hearing the employee and a system of appeal has **13.111** been emphasised both in the ACAS Code of Practice and in many cases. The EAT have given helpful guidelines in some cases as to what makes good practice. General guidelines about conducting hearings are given in *Clark* v *Civil Aviation Authority*.[159] Guidelines as to the acceptable use of anonymous informants are given in *Linfood Cash and Carry Ltd* v *Thomson and Bell*.[160]

Capability dismissals

Although these are not misconduct dismissals so that a disciplinary approach is **13.112** not appropriate, the *Burchell* test of genuine belief (in lack of capability), reasonable

---

[154] ERA 1996, s 98A.
[155] *Beedell* v *West Ferry Printers Ltd* [2000] IRLR 650.
[156] *Scottish Midland Co-operative Society Ltd* v *Oliphant* [1991] IRLR 261.
[157] [1980] ICR 303.
[158] *HSBC Bank plc* v *Madden* [2001] 1 All ER 550.
[159] [1991] IRLR 412.
[160] [1989] IRLR 235.

grounds and reasonable investigation has been approved for capability dismissals.[161] A reasonable employer will consider whether assistance or training would be appropriate.

13.113   Ill health may be a reason for a capability dismissal, and such a dismissal may be fair, so long as the employer has followed a proper procedure (in addition to the statutory discipline and dismissal procedure), taking account of the nature of the illness, the length of absence, the need to get the job done, the possibility of transfer, medical advice and the views of the employee.[162] An employee who suffers from ill health may also be a disabled person and thus have the protection of the Disability Discrimination Act 1995. Unfair dismissal and disability discrimination are to be dealt with as separate issues, although a discriminatory dismissal is likely to be unfair.[163]

Redundancy dismissals

13.114   Selection of an employee for redundancy for an inadmissible reason will make the dismissal automatically unfair.[164] In other cases the question is whether or not the employer acted reasonably. The Tribunal will not in general examine the economic reasons for the redundancy. The relevant issues are whether the employee was fairly selected by objective selection criteria, fairly applied; whether the employee (and any trade union) was adequately consulted and warned; and whether the possibility of alternative work was properly investigated.[165]

13.115   Fair consultation means consultation when the proposal is still at a formative stage, giving adequate information and adequate time to respond. The statutory discipline and dismissal procedure applies to individual and small-scale redundancy dismissals but does not apply in the case of collective redundances. However, there are also statutory procedures in the case of collective redundancies requiring the employer to consult with trade union or employee representatives.[166]

Contravention of statute dismissals

13.116   If the employee's continued employment in his job would be contrary to legislation (such as if a driver was disqualified from driving), the dismissal is potentially fair. Relevant additional consideration could include the length of the likely illegality, the extent to which the employee is prevented from working and whether there is any alternative work.[167]

Dismissals for some other substantial reason

13.117   The full statutory wording is "some other substantial reason of a kind such as to justify the dismissal of an employee holding the position which that employee held".[168] Some

---

[161] *Taylor* v *Alidair Ltd* [1978] IRLR 82.
[162] *East Lindsey District Council* v *Daubney* [1977] IRLR 181.
[163] *Rothwell* v *Pelikan Hardcopy Scotland Ltd* [2006] IRLR 24.
[164] TULRCA 1992, ss 105 and 153.
[165] *Williams* v *Compair Maxam Ltd* [1982] ICR 156.
[166] TULRCA 1992, s 188.
[167] *Sutcliffe & Eaton Ltd* v *Pinney* [1977] IRLR 349.
[168] ERA 1996, s 98(1).

other substantial reason may include any reason which a reasonable employer would think necessary in the best interests of the business. A management style or personality which has led to a breakdown in relations may be such a reason.[169]

There have been a number of cases involving dismissal as a consequence of a business reorganisation. A Tribunal will consider whether the reorganisation was considered necessary for the business, whether the change relating to the employee was necessary to effect the reorganisation and whether there was adequate consultation in relation to the reorganisation and the consequences for the employee. A Tribunal will look for a balance between the effect on the employee and the needs of the employer's business.[170] However, fairness to the employee and the needs of the business may conflict and so long as the employer has behaved reasonably it will be the needs of the business which will usually prevail. **13.118**

Remedies

Re-instatement or re-engagement[171]

This remedy is not awarded very often, since the relationship between ex-employer and ex-employee has usually completely broken down on both sides by the time of the ET hearing. The relevant considerations are the wish of the employee, whether it is practicable for the employer to re-instate or re-engage, and whether it would be just to make such an order. Re-instatement means that the employee must be treated as if never dismissed; re-engagement that the employee is to be re-employed in comparable employment. If the employer does not comply, additional compensation can be awarded. **13.119**

Compensation[172]

Basic award. This is calculated according to the formula: 1½ weeks' pay for every year the employee worked and was 41 or over; 1 week's pay for every year aged 22 or over; half a week's pay for every year under 22. The maximum number of years' employment to be taken into account is 20. There is a cap on the week's pay, fixed usually annually by ministerial order: at the time of writing it is £310. There is a minimum basic award where the dismissal is for a trade union reason, or for acting as certain types of worker representative (£4,200). The basic award can be reduced by any redundancy pay awarded, a just and equitable amount if the employee had unreasonably refused reinstatement and a just and equitable amount if the employee's conduct before dismissal warrants it. **13.120**

Compensatory award. This is the amount which the Tribunal thinks is "just and equitable in all the circumstances". It is to compensate for the loss suffered as a result of the dismissal. There is a cap on this award (£60,000), except where the dismissal is for a health and safety reason or for a protected disclosure. The employee must mitigate **13.121**

---

[169] *Perkin* v *St George's Healthcare NHS Trust* [2005] IRLR 934.
[170] *St John of God (Care Services) Ltd* v *Brooks* [1992] IRLR 546.
[171] ERA 1996, ss 112–117.
[172] ERA 1996, ss 118–127.

his loss. The compensatory award can be reduced or increased if there has been a failure to co-operate by employer or employee in the statutory discipline and dismissal procedure or grievance procedure. It may also be reduced by any redundancy pay received, and by a just and equitable amount if the employee caused or contributed to his dismissal.

13.122   A Tribunal will take into account immediate loss of earnings, the financial loss caused by the dismissal, future loss of wages, loss of statutory rights, loss of pension rights and expenses.[173] The award compensates for financial loss, not distress, humiliation or damage to reputation.[174]

Interim relief

13.123 Where an employee has been dismissed for a trade union reason or one of a number of the automatically unfair reasons he may apply to a Tribunal for an order of interim relief within 7 days.[175] The effect of such an order is (if the employer is willing) re-instatement or re-engagement until the Tribunal hearing or (if the employer is not willing) payment of wages and benefits until the hearing.

DISCRIMINATION IN EMPLOYMENT

13.124 An important areas of employee protection is the protection against discrimination in employment. There are six prohibited grounds of discrimination. Many of the concepts of discrimination and equal treatment are the same across the different legislation, but there are also some important differences. It is beyond the scope of this chapter to deal with this issue in depth, but a summary of the sources of the law is included.

13.125   The prohibited grounds of discrimination are sex, race, disability, religion or belief, sexual orientation and age. Each has its own separate legislation and each is also subject to EC law. The underlying principle behind the legislation relating to sex, race, religion, sexual orientation and age is essentially the same: that of formal equality. The legislation is neutral in that it is designed to ensure equality of treatment between sexes, races etc and can be used by men, women, members of any racial group, followers of any religion or none, homosexual and heterosexual people, and young and old. With some important exceptions, it does not permit more favourable treatment of a member of a disadvantaged group since that would be to discriminate against a member of another group. This is not the case in relation to disability. The purpose of the legislation there is to provide protection for people with disabilities: the legislation does not apply to other people, and it to an extent requires positive action for people with disabilities.

13.126   The legislation is not restricted to employees. The equal pay legislation applies to workers, while all of the anti-discrimination legislation applies to those in employment.

---

[173] *Norton Tool Co Ltd v Tewson* [1973] 1 WLR 45.
[174] *Dunnachie v Kingston upon Hull City Council* [2004] IRLR 727.
[175] ERA 1996, ss 128–132; TULRCA 1992, ss 160–166.

SEX DISCRIMINATION AND EQUAL PAY

Equal pay

The Equal Pay Act 1970 (EPA 1970) was introduced before the UK joined the EU. **13.127**
It came into effect at the end of 1975. Although not introduced to comply with
EU law, it has been heavily influenced by it since, in order to comply with decisions of
the European Court of Justice under Art 141 of the Treaty of Rome (equal pay) and
the Equal Pay Directive 75/117.

The EPA 1970 only applies to gender inequality. As originally introduced, the main **13.128**
entitlement was to equal pay for like work, that is work that is the same or broadly
similar. As a result of enforcement action taken against the UK by the European
Commission,[176] an additional entitlement to equal pay for work of equal value was
introduced.[177] For an equal pay claim to succeed, a woman must identify an actual
male comparator employed by her employer, and must establish that she does like
work or work of equal value to him. It is then open to the employer to prove in defence
that the difference in pay is due to a genuine material factor, which is not tainted by
sex discrimination.

Sex discrimination

The Sex Discrimination Act 1975 (SDA 1975) places a duty on an employer not to **13.129**
discriminate against people in his employment on grounds of sex. The Act has also
been heavily influenced by decisions under EC law, in this case the Equal Treatment
Directive 76/207. The 1975 Act prohibits discrimination on grounds of an employee's
sex, applying equally to men and women. It also prohibits discrimination against
transsexuals[178] and discrimination because of pregnancy or maternity.

There are four prohibited forms of discrimination which are also found in the **13.130**
other legislation, though there are important differences in disability and age discrimination. These are direct discrimination; indirect discrimination; victimisation;
and harassment.

Direct discrimination

Direct discrimination occurs where an employer treats someone in employment less **13.131**
favourably on grounds of his or her sex than an employee of the opposite sex was or
would have been treated. Unlike under EPA 1970, it is not necessary to have an actual
comparator. Direct discrimination cannot be justified, but there are some jobs where
sex might be a "genuine occupational qualification".

Indirect discrimination

This occurs where an employer applies a provision, criterion or practice which, **13.132**
although it is neutral on the face of it, in fact places women at a disadvantage to men,
and which disadvantages the person making the complaint. An example might be

---

[176] *Commission of the EC v UK* [1982] ECR 2601.
[177] Equal Pay (Amendment) Regulations 1983 (SI 1983/1794).
[178] Introduced to SDA 1975 by the Sex Discrimination (Gender Reassignment) Regulations 1999 (SI
1999/1102).

refusing to allow an employee to work part-time hours. It could be argued that a refusal to allow part-time work would disadvantage more women than men. Unlike direct discrimination, indirect discrimination can be justified so long as the application of the provision, criterion or practice is to further a legitimate aim and is proportionate.

Victimisation

13.133 This is where the employer treats someone in employment less favourably because they have asserted their rights under the legislation, whether by raising an action, making an allegation, giving evidence in support of someone else, or doing something else which refers to the legislation. The ground of the less favourable treatment is not sex but raising the action.

Harassment

13.134 There are three types of unlawful harassment under SDA 1975. The first is common to all the grounds. It occurs where A engages in conduct which is unwanted by B and which has the purpose or effect of violating B's dignity or creating a hostile, degrading, humiliating or offensive environment for B.

13.135   There are two additional forms of harassment under SDA 1975 which relate specifically to sexual conduct, including less favourable treatment of someone who rejected (or submitted to) sexual advances.

RACE DISCRIMINATION

13.136 The UK has had race discrimination legislation for many years. An EU Directive prohibiting race discrimination was not passed until 2000.[179] The UK legislation is broader than required by this Directive since it prohibits discrimination on grounds of nationality which Directive 2000/43 does not. The Race Relations Act 1976 (RRA 1976) prohibits discrimination on grounds of race, colour, nationality, ethnic origins and national origins. "Nationality" means citizenship of a particular country. "National origins" may refer to a person's original nationality (where they have later adopted a different nationality) or might refer to a person's origins in an area which was formerly a state (such as Scotland, England or Wales). "Ethnic origins" relates to membership of a group with a long shared history and cultural traditions, and other relevant characteristics.[180] Gypsies have been held to be such a group.

13.137   The concepts of direct discrimination, indirect discrimination, victimisation and harassment in RRA 1976 are equivalent to those in SDA 1975. There are some jobs for which race might be a "genuine occupational requirement".

DISABILITY DISCRIMINATION

13.138 The Disability Discrimination Act 1995 (DDA 1995) pre-dated the EU Equal Treatment Directive 2000/78 which required Member States to legislate to prohibit disability,

---

[179] Race Directive 2000/43.
[180] *Mandla v Dowell Lee* [1983] IRLR 209.

religious, sexual orientation and age discrimination. It prohibits discrimination against people with disabilities. "Disability" is defined very closely in the Act: it arises where a person has a physical or mental impairment which has a substantial and long-term adverse effect on the person's ability to carry out normal day-to-day activities. Thus, in order to qualify as a disabled person, it must be established that there is a physical or mental impairment, that the impairment affects the person's ability to carry out day-to-day activities (defined in the Act) adversely, that the adverse effect is substantial and long term (lasts or likely to last 12 months or more).

There are five prohibited forms of discrimination under DDA 1995. These are **13.139** direct discrimination; disability-related discrimination; breach of the duty to make reasonable adjustments; victimisation; and harassment. The concepts of victimisation and harassment are equivalent to those in SDA 1975 and RRA 1976.

Direct discrimination

This occurs where a person is treated less favourably on grounds of their disability **13.140** than someone without that disability was or would have been treated. There is no parallel provision for a person without a disability. Direct discrimination cannot be justified.

Disability-related discrimination

This occurs where a person is treated less favourably than another was or would be **13.141** treated for a reason which relates to their disability. In this case the reason for the less favourable treatment would not be the disability as such, but something which relates to it, such as possible absences from work due to the impairment. This form of discrimination can be justified by the employer, so long as the reason for it is material and substantial.

Breach of the duty to make reasonable adjustments

An employer must make adjustments where a disabled worker is placed at a **13.142** disadvantage by any provision, criterion or practice applied, or by any physical feature of the employer's premises. Examples of possible adjustments are given in DDA 1995, such as making adjustments to the premises, transferring the worker to another vacant job, altering hours and modifying equipment. The duty is to do what is reasonable, which can take account of financial considerations.

RELIGIOUS DISCRIMINATION

The legislation prohibiting discrimination on this ground and the following two **13.143** was introduced to comply with Equal Treatment Directive 2000/78. The Employment Equality (Religion or Belief) Regulations 2003 (EEROBR 2003) prohibit discrimination in employment on grounds of religion, religious belief or "other similar philosophical belief". This includes no religious belief.

The concepts of direct discrimination, indirect discrimination, victimisation and **13.144** harassment are equivalent to those in SDA 1975 and RRA 1976. There are some jobs for which religion might be a "genuine occupational requirement".

SEXUAL ORIENTATION DISCRIMINATION

13.145   Sexual orientation is not covered by SDA 1975 or EC Directive 76/207 (sex discrimination Equal Treatment Directive). To comply with EC Directive 2000/78 the Employment Equality (Sexual Orientation) Regulations 2003 (EESOR 2003) were passed which prohibit discrimination on grounds of sexual orientation, whether this is an orientation towards people of the same sex, of the opposite sex, or both.

13.146   The concepts of direct discrimination, indirect discrimination, victimisation and harassment are equivalent to those in SDA 1975, RRA 1976 and EEROBR 2003. There are some jobs for which sexual orientation might be a genuine occupational requirement.

AGE DISCRIMINATION

13.147   Age discrimination is the last of the grounds covered by Directive 2000/78 to be legislated on in the UK. The Employment Equality (Age) Regulations 2006 prohibit discrimination on grounds of age. Because many distinctions were made in law on the basis of age there was longer consultation about this ground of discrimination, and there are more exceptions built into the legislation. In particular, age discrimination in NMWA 1998 is excluded, as is compulsory retirement either at 65 or over or at an objectively justifiable earlier age, but with provisions for possible extensions of employment beyond normal retiral age.

13.148   The concepts of indirect discrimination, victimisation and harassment are equivalent to those in SDA 1975, RRA 1976, EEROBR 2003 and EESOR 2003. The concept of direct discrimination differs in that it is possible to justify direct discrimination on the ground of age, using the same justification as for indirect discrimination. Thus it is made easier to discriminate on the ground of age than the other grounds.

ESSENTIAL FACTS

13.149

- Employment law is concerned with the relationship between employer and employee. It comprises a common law basis of the contract of employment and a range of statutory provisions. It is heavily influenced by EC law.

- An employee is employed under a contract of employment. The legal form of this is a contract of service. The parties are employer and employee.

- People who contract to provide work or services but who are not employees are employed under contracts for services. The parties are employer and independent contractor.

- The test adopted by the courts for deciding whether a contract is of service or for services is the "multiple" test. This is a three-part test: a contract of service requires a duty to give personal service, the existence of a sufficient degree of control and the terms of the contract being consistent with service.

- The concept of mutuality of obligation has been influential: there must be mutual obligations to give and to carry out work underpinning the contract. This may be implied as well as express.

- There are intermediate categories under legislation that attract some protection, but not such extensive protection as that of employees. These are "workers", and those who are "in employment".

- A contract of employment is made up of many sources: express terms, implied terms, incorporated terms and implied duties.

- The most common incorporated terms are those incorporated into the contract of employment from a collective agreement agreed between employer and trade union.

- The implied duties are common law terms implied into every contract. An employee has the implied duties of personal service, to obey reasonable and lawful orders, to take reasonable care and of loyalty. An employer has the implied duties to pay wages, to take reasonable care of safety, to reimburse expenses and of trust and confidence.

- Wrongful dismissal is the common law remedy where an employee is unjustifiably dismissed without notice. Unfair dismissal is a statutory remedy. It may be used by someone who has been dismissed with or without notice, by someone whose fixed-term contract has not been renewed, and by someone who has resigned because of the employer's material breach of contract.

- The National Minimum Wage Act 1998 provides for the setting and calculation of the national minimum wage.

- The Working Time Regulations 1998 provide for maximum hours of work and minimum rest, break and holiday periods.

- Discrimination in employment is prohibited where it takes place on grounds of race, sex, religion, disability, age or sexual orientation.

ESSENTIAL CASES

- *Ready Mixed Concrete (SE) Ltd* v *Minister of Pensions and National Insurance* (1968): a lorry driver buying his lorry on hire purchase from the company was found to be employed under a contract for services, not a contract of service. The case is authority for the three-fold multiple test to determine whether there is a contract of service: personal service, control and consistent terms.   **13.150**

- *Market Investigations Ltd* v *Minister of Social Security* (1969): a market researcher was found to be employed under a contract of service, not a contract for services. This case identified the underlying element of being in business on one's own account in relation to the "multiple" test.

- *Carmichael* v *National Power plc* (1999): a casual worker was found not to be employed under a contract of service. This case found that mutuality of obligation was an "irreducible minimum" of a contract of service.

- *Percy* v *Church of Scotland Board of National Mission* (2006): an associate minister was found to be "in employment" for the purposes of the Sex Discrimination Act 1975. This provided statutory rights which were civil and not spiritual matters.

- *Robertson* v *British Gas Corporation* (1983): employees were found to be entitled to a bonus provided for in the contract of employment. The statutory written statement of employment particulars is not contractual in itself and cannot override the contract.

- *Faccenda Chicken* v *Fowler* (1986): employees who set up in competition with their former employer and canvassed its customers were not in breach of the implied duty of loyalty. This case clarified the circumstances in which the implied duty not to reveal confidential information continues after employment has ended.

- *Malik* v *Bank of Credit and Commerce International* (1997): former employees of an employer which had traded fraudulently were entitled to raise an action for damages because their employment prospects had been damaged by the bank's breach of the implied mutual duty of trust and confidence. The House of Lords recognised and defined the duty.

- *Western Excavating (ECC) Ltd* v *Sharp* (1979): for the purposes of unfair dismissal law a resignation is treated as a dismissal ("constructive dismissal") only when the resignation is in response to a material breach of contract by the employer.

- *HSBC Bank plc* v *Madden* (2000): in an unfair dismissal action the employment tribunal decides the question of whether the employer has acted reasonably or unreasonably in dismissing the employee not by deciding whether in its view the employer acted reasonably, but by determining whether the employer's decision was within the "band of reasonable responses" of a reasonable employer.

- *British Home Stores* v *Burchell* (1980): in deciding to dismiss, an employer does not require proof of misconduct or incompetence to the standard which would satisfy a court. The employer must have a genuine belief in the guilt or lack of competence, must have reasonable grounds for this belief and must have established these reasonable grounds after a reasonable investigation.

14 CORPORATE LAW

This chapter will provide a brief introduction to the laws of Scotland in relation to private companies limited by shares; partnerships; and limited liability partnerships. This will be achieved by considering the current legislative framework governing each of these business vehicles, together with development of the common law.

14.1

PRIVATE COMPANIES LIMITED BY SHARES

Private companies limited by shares are by far the most common type of company. However, it is important to be aware that other types of companies also exist, including companies limited by guarantee, public limited companies and companies with unlimited liability.

14.2

LEGISLATION

Limited liability companies are primarily governed by the Companies Act 1985 (as amended) (the "1985 Act"), common law and, going forward, the Companies Act 2006 (the "2006 Act").

14.3

The 2006 Act received Royal Assent on 8 November 2006 and it represents the most extensive review of company law in the last two decades. The 1985 Act[1] is no longer the primary piece of legislation in this area and, as well as being substantially amended, it will have to work in tandem with the 2006 Act. At the time of writing, many provisions of the 2006 Act were not in force.[2] Therefore, this chapter will refer primarily to the current law (the 1985 Act) and will highlight key areas were changes will occur. The extent and implications of the 2006 Act will, in part, become fully evident only once company law is operating under a double legislative regime.

14.4

LEGAL PERSONALITY

A private company limited by shares cannot exist without the appointment of officers and the existence of shareholders. Despite this fact, a company is a separate legal entity distinct from its members. In reality this means that a company can enter into contracts, hold property in its own name, sue and be sued. This principle was first referred to in the case of *Salomon* v *A Salomon & Co Ltd*[3] and is known as the "veil of incorporation".

14.5

---

[1] The Companies Act 1985 is not applicable throughout the UK.
[2] All parts of the Companies Act 2006 will have commenced by October 2008.
[3] [1887] AC 22.

14.6   The "veil of incorporation" protects members of a company from liability; however, there are certain circumstances where the "veil" may be lifted, for example:

(1)   where a company is not a single-member company and continues to carry on its business for more than 6 months, with less than two members;[4] or

(2)   where a company has gone into insolvent liquidation and its directors thereafter become involved with another company with a similar name.[5]

Where the "veil" is lifted, the limited liability which members ordinarily enjoy is removed and they may become personally liable for their acts and/or omissions. Usually this will result in a personal contribution to a company's assets by the members concerned, who may also face criminal prosecution.

PRE-INCORPORATION

14.7   Before a company is incorporated, it has no legal status and therefore no capacity to enter into contracts. However, it is sometimes necessary, in anticipation of a company's incorporation, for transactions to be concluded and property purchased. This is often done by a promoter, who will usually become one of the first directors of a company. A promoter's relationship with a company cannot be described as one of agency, given that a company, pre-incorporation, is not a distinct legal entity. The relationship is fiduciary in nature, and as such promoters owe certain duties to a company, including a duty to disclose any benefits they personally receive in connection with the company's promotion.

PROMOTER'S LIABILITY

14.8   A promoter, while acting on a company's behalf, is personally liable in relation to all contracts entered into, unless express agreement is made to the contrary with a third party.[6] This means that where a third party relinquishes a promoter from personal liability they would be unable to sue the promoter, if the company did not subsequently comply with the terms of the contract.

UNENFORCEABLE CONTRACTS

14.9   Contracts made on a company's behalf cannot be enforced or relied upon by a company, once incorporated. Given this lack of enforceability, it is advisable that no business should be carried on prior to incorporation.

INCORPORATION OF A PRIVATE COMPANY LIMITED BY SHARES

14.10   To incorporate a company, Forms 10 and 12 must be delivered to the Registrar of Companies, together with a memorandum of association ("memorandum"), articles

---

[4] Companies Act 1985 ("CA 1985"), s 24.
[5] Insolvency Act 1986 ("IA 1986"), s 216.
[6] CA 1985, s 36C.

of association ("articles") and an incorporation fee. If the documents are accepted by the Registrar, a certificate of incorporation will be issued. It is at this point that a company is seen as a separate legal entity and can contract in its own name. The content and purpose of each incorporation document will be considered in turn:

FORM 10

(i) *Company name*: There are a number of restrictions and requirements to consider **14.11** when selecting a company name. The end of the name must include the word "Limited or "Ltd"; there cannot be a company with the same or similar name already incorporated;[7] and certain restrictions apply in relation to the use of particular words.[8]

(ii) *Registered office*: This is a company's official address. It is available to view at Companies House and will appear on all official documentation of a company, for example its annual return.[9] It is a legal requirement for a company always to have a registered office in order that communications and notices may be received directly by it. It also indicates where the company books are held,[10] which is important since the register of members is open to inspection by a company's members and/or third parties.[11]

(iii) *Directors*: Are officers of a company. It is now possible for a company to be incorporated with one director, and there is no upper statutory limit on the number of directors, provided that no restrictions exist in a company's articles. A director's personal details must be disclosed,[12] together with any previous and/or current directorships.[13]

(iv) *Company secretary*: Similarly, an officer of a company with ostensible authority to contract on a company's behalf. When a company is incorporated with only one director, the officer appointed as company secretary must be a different person. Where more than one director is appointed, any one of the directors may also hold the office of company secretary.[14]

(v) *Subscribers*: Are the first shareholders of a company. They, or an agent on their behalf, must sign and date the Form 10.

FORM 12

Form 12[15] is a statutory declaration which is ordinarily completed by a solicitor involved **14.12** in the incorporation of a company. The completion and filing of this document are

---

[7] Including limited liability partnerships.
[8] CA 1985, ss 26–34. Restrictions are also provided by the Business Names Act 1985 (this entire Act is being repealed by the Companies Act 2006 (CA 2006), and under common law ("passing off").
[9] CA 1985, s 364(1)(a).
[10] CA 1985, s 353.
[11] CA 1985, s 356, regulates the inspection of the register and index.
[12] Under CA 2006, new directors will be able to provide a "service address" rather than their home address, for the purpose of public disclosure.
[13] CA 1985, s 10(2).
[14] Under CA 2006 there is no requirement for a private company to have a company secretary, although they may do so if they wish.
[15] CA 1985, s 12.

required by virtue of the 1985 Act, and the document simply verifies a company's compliance with the statutory provisions.

MEMORANDUM OF ASSOCIATION

14.13 The memorandum can be described as the external constitutional document of a company and each subscriber must sign the memorandum, which will detail the number of shares being issued to them.[16] A memorandum provides information and guidance in relation to how a company will deal with third parties and must include certain information such as the name of the company, location of its registered office, initial share capital, liability of members, and the objects of the company.[17] Under the 2006 Act the memorandum will have a decidedly different format, and will have a more limited purpose. However, this does not negate its importance. Notably, the 2006 Act does not allow for the memorandum to be amended once a company has been incorporated.

ARTICLES OF ASSOCIATION

14.14 Articles are sometimes described as the internal constitutional document of a company. They primarily govern the relationship between members of a company, and there are no statutory requirements relating to the type of information which should be included in a company's articles. Typical articles will include details on the appointment and removal of officers of a company, and the process of convening meetings. It is not uncommon for companies simply to adopt as their articles Table A,[18] in whole or in part. Table A is found in the Companies (Tables A to F) Regulations 1985 and is essentially a template of model articles.[19] It remains possible, following incorporation, for a company's articles to be altered, provided that they do not attempt to circumvent the applicability of legislation.

MEMBERS' MEETINGS

14.15 Meetings of company members can be categorised as either general or class meetings, and are called in order to deal with the business of a company. General meetings can be further classified as either annual or extraordinary.

ANNUAL GENERAL MEETING ("AGM")

14.16 Every company is under an obligation to hold an AGM.[20] A company must convene an AGM within the first 18 months from the date of incorporation, and thereafter there cannot be more than 15 months between each subsequent AGM. If a company fails to convene the necessary AGM, the Secretary of State has the power to convene an AGM on its behalf. Often, the primary reasons for holding an AGM are to allow a company's

---

[16] Subscriber signatures should be witnessed by a third party.
[17] CA 1985, s 2.
[18] Companies (Tables A to F) Regulations 1985 (SI 1985/805).
[19] Going forward, it is intended that these default articles, for private companies, will be simplified.
[20] CA 1985, s 366.

accounts to be laid before its members, for the members to appoint auditors[21] and for the payment of dividends to be approved.

Notice

In order to convene an AGM, 21 days' notice must be given, in writing, to company **14.17** members,[22] although it is possible to convene an AGM on short notice, provided that there is unanimous consent by all members.[23] It is possible, by members passing an elective resolution, to dispense with the necessity to convene an AGM each year;[24] essentially, a company can "opt out" of this administrative burden.

Under the 2006 Act, a company will no longer be required to convene an AGM, **14.18** unless it positively chooses to do so, ie "opt in".

EXTRAORDINARY GENERAL MEETING ("EGM")

An EGM is any general meeting held by a company, which is not an AGM, and is **14.19** normally called to deal with business that cannot wait until the next AGM. An EGM is usually convened by the directors of a company when requisitioned by members who hold at least one-tenth of the paid-up share capital[25] of a company. The directors shall, within 21 days from receipt[26] of a requisition, proceed to convene an EGM and this should be held within 28 days from the date of the notice convening the meeting.[27]

Notice

Notice of an EGM must be given to all the members, in writing, 14 days before the **14.20** EGM,[28] or 21 days prior if the intention is to pass a special resolution at the EGM.[29] Similarly to an AGM, it is possible for an EGM to be called on short notice, provided that 95 per cent of the members concur.[30]

CLASS MEETINGS

This type of meeting is held by a particular class of shareholders, where decisions **14.21** affecting only that class of shares are being taken, for example varying their class rights.

Notice

The amount of notice required to be given is dependent on the type of meeting being **14.22** convened and the business to be dealt with. The notice must clearly state the location,

---

[21] CA 1985, s 384.
[22] CA 1985, s 369.
[23] CA 1985, s 369(3).
[24] CA 1985, s 366A.
[25] CA 1985, s 368(2). Shares must carry voting rights at a general meeting.
[26] CA 1985, s 368(4).
[27] CA 1985, s 368(8).
[28] CA 1985, s 369(1)(b)(ii).
[29] CA 1985, s 369(1)(b).
[30] CA 1985, s 369(4). Can be reduced to a 90% majority by the passing of an elective resolution.

time, general nature of the business[31] and type of general meeting being convened. Notice must be validly served on every member.[32]

RESOLUTIONS

14.23   A resolution records a decision made by the members (or particular class of members) of a company. There are a variety of resolutions which may be passed by members in general meetings and in certain circumstances the 1985 Act specifies the type of resolution to be passed.

Type of resolution	Voting requirements
Ordinary	Simple majority
Special	75% or more
Extraordinary	75% or more
Elective	100%

14.24   As an alternative to passing one of the above resolutions, the 1985 Act[33] provides that a written resolution may be passed in its place.

14.25   A written resolution requires the consent of 100 per cent[34] of a company's members entitled to vote on a specific matter. To be effective, each member must sign the resolution.[35]

14.26   The table below provides a number of examples of the type of resolution to be passed (and applicable notice periods) in particular circumstances:

Issue	Type of resolution	Notice (days)
Change of company name[36]	Special	21
Alteration of articles[37]	Special	21
Removal of a director[38]	Ordinary	28 (special notice)
Revoking an elective resolution[39]	Ordinary	14
Varying class rights[40]	Extraordinary	21 or 14 (depending on type of meeting)
Creditors' voluntary liquidation[41]	Extraordinary	14
Dispensing with an AGM[42]	Elective	21

---

[31] Table A, Art 38.
[32] CA 1985, s 370(2).
[33] CA 1985, s 381A(1).
[34] The procedure under CA 2006 does not require unanimity for written resolutions.
[35] CA 1985, s 381A(2). All signatures do not have to be on the same document.
[36] CA 1985, s 28.
[37] CA 1985, s 9.
[38] CA 1985, s 303.
[39] CA 1985, s 379A(3).
[40] CA 1985, s 125.
[41] IA 1986, s 84(1)(c).
[42] CA 1985, s 366A.

The articles of a company may provide additional requirements and/or restrictions **14.27** and should be consulted before any resolution is proposed.

DIRECTORS

Directors are under a duty to comply both with the provisions of a company's **14.28** constitutional documents and with current legislation. The obligations can on occasion be onerous, and may include how a director should manage the company, take major decisions or enter into substantial contracts.

Given the responsibilities placed on directors, it is perhaps unhelpful that who **14.29** constitutes a director is not clearly defined.[43] Consequently, there are a variety of recognised types of directors, other than those formally appointed,[44] and they include:

(i) de facto *director*: not formally appointed to the board but professes to act as a director of a company;

(ii) *shadow director*: an individual who has not been formally appointed as a director but who, as a matter of fact, influences the decisions of a company;

(iii) *alternate director*: appointed by an existing director to perform all the functions of the appointer in their absence; and

(iv) *nominee director*: members have a specific right to appoint, remove and/or replace one or more of these directors, eg in joint venture companies.

DIRECTORS' DUTIES

The relationship between a director and a company can be described as fiduciary in **14.30** nature. There are a number of fiduciary duties under common law[45] which a director owes to a company and they include:

(i) to act for the benefit of a company as a whole and not to fetter their discretion;

(ii) to avoid conflicts between their personal interests and the interests of a company; and

(iii) to act honestly and in good faith when making decisions affecting a company.

A director also owes a duty of care, skill and diligence to a company. This is measured **14.31** objectively, with a comparison being made with another person holding a similar directorship, and subjectively to the extent that consideration is given to what can be reasonably expected from a director with their level of experience, skill and knowledge.

Despite the wide scope of fiduciary duties established by common law, a number **14.32** of statutory duties are also imposed on directors, including a requirement to declare

---

[43] CA 1985, s 741(1).
[44] CA 1985, s 288.
[45] CA 2006 puts these common law duties into a statutory format.

any interest in contracts,[46] and to obtain membership approval before any substantial property transactions can be made between a company and one or more of its directors.[47]

CODIFICATION OF DUTIES

14.33   Directors' duties established at common law will, under the 2006 Act, be put into a statutory framework, and their underlying principles will, on the whole, remain unchanged. It is the intention that these new statutory duties will be interpreted and applied in the same way as they currently are under common law.[48]

14.34   In codifying current law, the 2006 Act introduces a new duty on a director to "act in the way he considers, in good faith, would be most likely to promote the success of the company for the benefit of its members as a whole".[49] This requires directors to give regard to the principle of "enlightened shareholder value". This new duty of promoting a company's success highlights a major shift in the way companies will have to undertake their business. It requires companies to consider, *inter alia*, six broad social factors, including the long term consequences of any decision being taken by a company[50] and the requirement to consider how the company's business may impact on the wider community and environment.[51]

PERSONAL LIABILITY

14.35   Directors become personally liable for their actions and/or omissions in circumstances where the "veil of incorporation" is lifted.[52] Personal liability of directors can occur in a variety of circumstances including where a director concludes a contract (on a company's behalf) without the requisite authority, or where a director falls foul of legislative provisions. Certain sections of the Insolvency Act 1986 (the "1986 Act"), if breached, may result in a director becoming personal liable, and include:

(i) Fraudulent trading[53]

14.36   It may be concluded that trading has been fraudulent if it appears that any business of a company has been carried out with the intent to "defraud creditors of the company or creditors of any other person, or for any fraudulent purpose"[54] during the course of winding up a company. Where a court makes this finding, it may order that any person who knowingly was a party to this fraudulent behaviour is financially liable to contribute to a company's assets to such extent as the court deems appropriate.

14.37   Only a liquidator has the power to make an application to the court in relation to a director's fraudulent trading. By way of illustration, a liquidator may pursue an

---

[46] CA 1985, s 317.
[47] CA 1985, s 320.
[48] All provisions of CA 2006 will be in force by October 2008.
[49] CA 2006, s 172, (not yet in force).
[50] CA 2006, s 172(1)(a), (not yet in force).
[51] CA 2006, s 172(1)(d), (not yet in force).
[52] For example, CA 1985, ss 221 and 222.
[53] IA 1986, s 213.
[54] IA 1986, s 213(1).

application where advance payment for goods is accepted by a company or a company gains credit, knowing that it will not be able to repay the money on the due date.

(ii) Wrongful trading[55]

In order for a director (or shadow director)[56] to incur personal liability, a company **14.38** must have gone into insolvent liquidation and at some point prior to winding up, a director "knew or ought to have concluded that there was no reasonable prospect that the company would avoid going into insolvent liquidation".[57] Provided that this test is met, the court may, on application by a liquidator, order that a director is liable to contribute to a company's assets. A director's defence, in this circumstance, is that he took every possible step to mitigate potential losses to a company's creditors.[58]

REMUNERATION

Directors do not, as a matter of course, receive remuneration for their services, although **14.39** it is not uncommon for a company's articles[59] to make provision for the method by which remuneration should be decided.

LOANS

The 1985 Act expressly prohibits companies[60] from making loans or providing **14.40** guarantees and/or security directly to directors, or for the benefit of directors.[61] If a prohibited arrangement is entered into it, will be deemed voidable. A director who authorised or arranged the loan will be personally liable to a company for any direct or indirect gain made, and shall personally indemnify a company for any losses or damages incurred.[62]

CESSATION OF DIRECTORSHIP

(i) Resignation

It is recognised that directors are free to resign at any time. However, the articles of **14.41** a company should be consulted, as they generally specify the method of resignation. If a director is an employee of a company, their contract of employment should be reviewed to ensure that resignation does not breach any terms of their contract of employment.

(ii) Retirement by rotation

The articles of a company often stipulate that a number of directors should retire at **14.42** every AGM and be eligible for re-election.[63]

---

[55] IA 1986, s 214.
[56] IA 1986, s 214(7).
[57] IA 1986, s 214(2)(b).
[58] IA 1986, s 214(3).
[59] Table A, Art 82.
[60] CA 2006 will abolish the prohibition on directors' loans (members' approval will be required).
[61] CA 1985, s 330. There are a limited number of exceptions to this rule.
[62] CA 1985, s 341.
[63] Table A, Arts 73–80.

(iii) Removal

14.43   Irrespective of the articles of a company, it is possible for members to remove a director from office by passing an ordinary resolution.[64] This process can be cumbersome, given that special notice requires to be given to a company,[65] although the articles may provide for a simplified procedure.

MEMBERSHIP

14.44   A company requires a minimum of one person to be a member at any one time. Given the contractual nature of membership, restrictions exist in relation to certain individuals becoming members of a company, for example individuals who lack legal capacity, who are of unsound mind or who have been declared bankrupt.

14.45   Provided a person is not restricted from being a shareholder and they agree to membership, there are several ways for a person to become a member of a company, including:

  (i)   subscription to a company's memorandum;[66]
  (ii) being allotted shares;
  (iii) receiving a transfer of shares from an existing member; or
  (iv) receiving a transmission of shares which occurs on the bankruptcy or death of a member and results in the transmission of their shares to a trustee or personal representative.

14.46   Membership exists only once a person's name and details have been recorded in a company's register of members.[67] Ordinarily, once registered, a company would then issue a share certificate to a member, detailing their shareholding.

LIABILITY

14.47   A member's liability[68] will be detailed in the memorandum of a company. Generally, a member is liable to pay to a company the full nominal value (and any agreed share premium) on all the shares held and registered in their name. On a minimum of 14 days' notice, directors can make calls to members of a company for payment of any outstanding sums on unpaid shares.[69]

RIGHTS

14.48   A company's articles (and memorandum) provide a membership contract between a company and its members.[70] Consequently, where resolutions are passed at general

---

[64] CA 1985, s 303.
[65] CA 1985, s 379.
[66] CA 1985, s 22.
[67] CA 1985, s 361.
[68] CA 1985, s 2(3).
[69] Table A, Art 12.
[70] CA 1985, s 14.

meetings, all members of a company are bound by the decision, whether or not they personally vote in favour of passing the said resolutions.

(i) *Foss* v *Harbottle*[71]

The principle of majority rule was expounded in the case of *Foss* v *Harbottle*, which **14.49** involved minority shareholders attempting to bring a case, on behalf of the company, alleging that the majority shareholders sold to the company a piece of land at an inflated price. The court held, *inter alia*, that the company alone was the "proper plaintiff"[72] (a company is a distinct legal entity and can bring legal proceedings in its own name).

This decision has subsequently, in part, been viewed as unacceptable. *Foss* gives no **14.50** consideration to the fact that it was the majority shareholders themselves who were responsible for the excessive price being paid by the company, yet it was their approval which was required in order to pursue an action (which in the circumstances was unlikely).

The courts now recognise a number of exceptions to the rules laid down in *Foss*, **14.51** which include the ratification of *ultra vires* acts by a company[73] (provided that the acts are not of an illegal nature), acts which do not adhere to the procedures laid down by a company's articles, fraud on the minority when perpetrated by the majority shareholder(s), and violations of members' personal rights.[74]

(ii) Legislative protection

Notwithstanding the rules provided by *Foss*, minority shareholders enjoy an element **14.52** of legislative protection in certain circumstances.[75] Minority members may make a petition to the court under s 459,[76] alleging unfair prejudice in relation to the past or present acts or omissions of a company which affect the members as whole, or some group of them.[77] If satisfied, the court may order such relief it deems appropriate,[78] for example requiring that the majority members or the company purchase the minority members' shares at a fair value.[79]

Alternatively, minority members may petition the court for a company to be wound **14.53** up, based on the "just and equitable" principle.[80] The courts will usually only consider this type of petition in circumstances where no other option is available.

CESSATION OF MEMBERSHIP

An individual's membership ceases when that is documented in a company's register **14.54** of members. This can occur in a variety of circumstances, including on the transfer or transmission of shares.

---

[71] (1843) 2 Hare 461, Ch D.
[72] English terminology.
[73] CA 1985, s 35.
[74] *Pender* v *Lushington* (1877) 6 Ch D 70.
[75] CA 2006, ss 265–269, provides statutory guidance on derivative proceedings in Scotland.
[76] CA 1985.
[77] CA 1985, s 459(1).
[78] CA 1985, s 461.
[79] CA 1985 s 461(2)(d).
[80] IA 1986, s 122(1)(g).

SHARE CAPITAL

MAINTAINING SHARE CAPITAL

14.55 The issued share capital of a company may be viewed as a fund available to creditors of a company. As a result, companies are prohibited from issuing shares at less than their nominal value[81] and any premium paid on a share must be deposited into a separate share premium account, which is non-distributable. Certain legislative provisions are designed to protect a company's capital, including regulating its reduction[82] and the purchase of its own shares.[83]

ALTERING SHARE CAPITAL

14.56 The share capital of a company may be altered,[84] if the necessary authorisation is provided in its articles. A company may:

    (i) increase its share capital by the creation of new shares;

    (ii) consolidate or sub-divide all or part of the existing share capital into shares with an increased or decreased nominal value;

    (iii) convert all or part of the paid-up shares into stock, or reconvert stock into shares; and

    (iv) cancel any authorised but unissued shares of a company (this does not result in a reduction of the share capital of a company).

14.57 When altering the share capital of a company it is necessary to pass a resolution[85] and file the necessary form with the Registrar of Companies within 1 month from the date of the resolution.[86]

ALLOTTING SHARES

14.58 In order for a company to allot shares,[87] directors must have the necessary authority;[88] this will be provided for in a company's articles or can be given at a general meeting by a company's members. Failure to have the necessary authority will result in a director facing criminal sanctions, but will not invalidate the allotment.

14.59   Statutory pre-emption rights exist in relation to the issue of new shares[89] in a company. This means that a company must first offer to the existing shareholders the new issue of shares, in proportion to their existing shareholding. This provision is designed to prevent the dilution of existing members' rights with the issue of new shares to third parties.

---

[81] CA 1985, s 100 (ie the par value).
[82] CA 1985, s 135. CA 2006 introduces a new "statutory statement procedure" for capital reductions.
[83] CA 1985, s 162.
[84] CA 1985, s 121.
[85] CA 1985, s 121(4).
[86] CA 1985, s 122.
[87] A company cannot allot more shares than its authorised share capital.
[88] CA 1985, s 80.
[89] CA 1985, s 89.

The offer of new shares to existing members must be made in writing and is open for **14.60** acceptance for 21 days.[90] If the shares are not taken up by the current members or they waive their pre-emption rights, the new shares can be offered to third parties. Once the shares have been allotted, a company's register of members should be updated and a share certificate issued in respect of the newly allotted shares.[91]

TRANSFERRING SHARES

The transfer of shares is generally undertaken voluntarily, but circumstances can arise **14.61** where there is a compulsory transfer of shares, for example on insolvency, death or termination of employment.

Unlike with the allotment of shares, statutory pre-emption rights do not exist in **14.62** relation to the transfer of shares, although it is not uncommon for a company's articles to contain pre-emption rights.[92]

On the transfer of shares a company must have delivered to it an instrument of **14.63** transfer, duly signed and stamped (ie a stock transfer form). Stamp duty is payable at half a per cent of the total consideration payable (rounded up to the nearest £5), although certain transfers are totally or partially exempt from this duty. Again, a share certificate will be issued to the transferee, and the register of members will be amended accordingly.[93]

CONSIDERATIONS BEFORE INCORPORATION

When contemplating incorporating a company limited by shares, it is important to **14.64** consider whether this type of limited company is the most appropriate business vehicle to meet your needs. While this is certainly not an exhaustive list, some advantages and disadvantages include:

ADVANTAGES

(i) A company has a separate legal personality and can enter into contracts, hold **14.65** property in its own name, sue and be sued.
(ii) Perpetual succession – there is no transfer of assets when a member joins or leaves a company.
(iii) Members have, in most circumstances, limited liability.
(iv) Can assist in raising finance.
(v) There is no maximum statutory limit to the number of members in a company (limits may be laid down in its articles).
(vi) The 1985 Act, common law and a company's constitutional documents provide a readily available source of guidance. These sources will be supplemented by the 2006 Act when it is fully in force.

---

[90] CA 1985, s 90. It is possible to disapply pre-emption rights under CA 1985, s 95.
[91] CA 1985, s 185(1)(a).
[92] Table A, Arts 23–28.
[93] The register of members will need to record the new shareholdings of both the transferor and transferee.

DISADVANTAGES

14.66   (i)   Certain expenses will be incurred in incorporating a company.

(ii) There are certain limitations on the name a company can choose.

(iii) Increased formality, which may include the holding of AGMs, passing of resolutions and completing annual returns and accounts.[94]

(iv) A company is required to file certain information with the Registrar of Companies, thus putting information in the public domain.

(v) Limited liability in certain circumstances may be illusory, for example directors may be required to provide personal guarantees.

PARTNERSHIPS

14.67   The Partnership Act 1890 (the "1890 Act") established the foundations of partnership law. Where no formal partnership agreement is entered into, disputes or misunderstandings between the partners, will be resolved based on the provisions of the 1890 Act. From both a practical and a commercial point of view, it is always advisable to reduce any agreement to writing.

14.68   The formation of a partnership is not subject to the same stringent formalities as other business vehicles and can be created verbally or be inferred by the conduct of the parties. In order for a partnership to exist, the individuals must have come together in order to carry on a business[95] with a view to making a profit.[96]

14.69   Partnerships in Scotland are seen as separate legal entities, distinct from their partners, therefore a partnership is able to enter into contracts, sue and be sued. However, partners are agents and guarantors of the partnership and are consequently jointly and severally liable for the debts and obligations of the partnership.[97]

FORMATION OF A PARTNERSHIP

14.70   The minimum number of partners required to form a partnership is two and there is now no statutory maximum number of partners.[98] Each person must have capacity to be a partner in a firm, and this would include being of sound mind and sufficient age. Furthermore, where a partnership has been formed with the intention of carrying on an illegal business, any partnership agreement will be deemed void. In circumstances where a partnership fails to comply with all the statutory restrictions, it will leave each of the partners open to unlimited personal liability in respect of all debts incurred by the firm.

14.71   Additional restrictions are provided by the Business Names Act 1985,[99] where a firm uses a trading name instead of the surnames of the partners; and common

---

[94] CA 2006 addresses some of these disadvantages and rectifies them.

[95] Partnership Act 1890 ("PA 1890"), s 45 defines "business" as including "every trade, occupation, or profession".

[96] PA 1890, s 1(1).

[97] PA 1890, s 9.

[98] CA 1985, s 716 has been repealed. The previous position was that a partnership could not have in excess of 20 partners (the exception to this rule was in relation to professional partnerships eg solicitors and accountants).

[99] CA 2006 repeals this Act in its entirety.

law ensures that the firm does not use a name which is the same or similar to an existing firm's name (this is in order to prevent third-party confusion). Where a firm ignores this duty, it may result in an interdict being sought on the basis of "passing off".

CONTRACTING WITH THIRD PARTIES

14.72 In the ordinary course of business it is unlikely that third parties will have any knowledge of the specific authority bestowed on an individual partner of a firm. Given that a partner can be described as an agent of the firm, partners can contractually bind the firm by any acts carried on in the ordinary course of the firm's business.[100] Furthermore, where a partner has authority bestowed upon him to act on behalf of the firm, and he does so in the firm's name, he is able to bind the partnership and his fellow partners in relation to third-party contracts.[101]

14.73 A partner's authority can be restricted by a firm.[102] Where a third party is unaware of the restriction, they can rely on the implied authority of a partner, when the contract concerns the ordinary business of a firm.[103] In circumstances where a partner attempts contractually to bind a firm in a transaction outwith the scope of its normal business, the partnership will not be required to comply with the terms of the contract, unless the partner concerned had been given specific authority to contract.[104] Where a third party knows or believes that a partner does not have authority, there is no valid contract, and the partner concerned is personally liable.

PARTNERS' RELATIONSHIPS AND DUTIES

14.74 The relationship between partners and a firm can be described as fiduciary in nature. Sections 28–30 of the 1890 Act provide guidance on the type of duties owed by partners; these include a duty to provide accounts of the firm's business to any partner, to account to the partnership for any personal profits derived from any transactions concerning the firm, and a duty not to compete with the partnership's business.

14.75 The rights which partners enjoy can be agreed or indeed varied by the consent of all the partners.[105] In the absence of any agreement between the partners as to their contractual rights, s 24 of the 1890 Act provides guidance that includes:

(i) entitlement to an equal share of capital and profits of a firm;
(ii) indemnification for any financial outlays or personal liabilities a partner incurs in the ordinary course of a firm's business; and
(iii) a right to be both involved in management of the partnership's business, and to inspect the partnership books.

14.76 Generally, partnership agreements will regulate the process of incoming and outgoing partners and how the firm's debts should be dealt with. Pursuant to s 17 of the 1890

---

[100] PA 1890, s 5.
[101] PA 1890, s 6.
[102] For example, in a negotiated partnership agreement.
[103] PA 1890, s 5.
[104] PA 1890, s 7.
[105] PA 1890, s 19.

Act, an incoming partner is usually not liable for pre-existing debts of a firm, and outgoing partners typically cease to have liability for any debts incurred following their departure. This can, of course, be varied by agreement.

DISSOLUTION

14.77 Partnerships may be dissolved for a variety of reasons. Circumstances[106] may include:

   (i) where a partnership was created for a fixed period of time or for a specific purpose, and the time has expired or the purpose has be achieved, the partnership naturally dissolves;[107]
   (ii) automatic dissolution on death, bankruptcy[108] or resignation of a partner, unless an agreement has been made to the contrary; or
   (iii) where it would be unlawful for a partnership to continue in its business.[109]

14.78 The 1890 Act provides a number of grounds where the court may intervene[110] and dissolve a partnership. This includes where:

   (i) a partner is found to be permanently of unsound mind;
   (ii) a partner is guilty of persistently breaching the terms of the partnership agreement; or
   (iii) the firm's business can only go forward by making a loss.

14.79 Following the dissolution of a partnership, the partners typically have continued authority to wind up the firm's business.[111] This can include completing any business the firm contractually undertook before the dissolution, since failure to do so may result in the partners being held professionally negligent. Once all the partnership's business has been concluded and debts settled, any surplus assets are shared among the partners.[112]

CONSIDERING PARTNERSHIPS

14.80 As with incorporating a company, when considering setting up a partnership, there are pros and cons. Again, there is no definitive list, and as a business vehicle its suitability will be largely dependent on a persons business needs.

ADVANTAGES

14.81
   (i) No requirement to put documents into the public domain.
   (ii) Informal and flexible business vehicle.

---

[106] Without a court order.
[107] PA 1890, s 32.
[108] PA 1890, s 33.
[109] PA 1890, s 34.
[110] PA 1890, s 35.
[111] PA 1890, s 38.
[112] PA 1890, s 39.

DISADVANTAGES

(i) Generally, partners have no personal protection against the financial liabilities **14.82**
of the partnership, therefore their personal assets may be at risk.

(ii) Dissolution is often inevitable on the death of a partner or where a dispute
arises between partners, which results in a partner's resignation.

LIMITED LIABILITY PARTNERSHIPS

The Limited Liability Partnerships Act 2000 (the "2000 Act") introduced a new **14.83**
corporate vehicle to the world of business; the limited liability partnership ("LLP").
An LLP can be described as a hybrid vehicle, between a company limited by shares
and a partnership.

SETTING UP AN LLP

As with the incorporation of a company, an LLP does not come into existence until all **14.84**
the necessary formalities of incorporation have been completed,[113] and a certificate of
incorporation has been issued by the Registrar.

In order to incorporate an LLP, an incorporation document (Form LLP2) requires to **14.85**
be completed, and sent to the Registrar with the requisite fee. Two or more individuals
are required to be the initial members of an LLP and their names and addresses must
be included on the incorporation document. A unique requirement of an LLP is the
appointment of a minimum of two "designated members". Failure to adhere to this
requirement results in all members being deemed to be "designated members".[114]

The role that "designated members" undertake cannot be found in any one piece **14.86**
of legislation. Their duties are largely administrative and are not dissimilar from the
duties carried out by officers of a company. The 2000 Act provides guidance on the
appointment and removal of designated members and the type of information that
they must file with the Registrar.

In addition, the incorporation document requires a name to be chosen for an LLP **14.87**
that ends with the words "Limited Liability Partnership" or "LLP"[115] and it must not
be the same name as any existing UK company or LLP (this can easily be checked
online at Companies House).[116] A registered office must also be selected, and one of the
subscribers or a solicitor involved in the incorporation of an LLP must acknowledge
that the LLP is being set up to "carry on a lawful business with a view to profit".[117]

A membership agreement is not a requirement in order to incorporate an LLP, **14.88**
although it is advisable for members to regulate their relationship in advance of
any issues arising. If no membership agreement is executed, the Limited Liability
Partnerships Regulations 2001[118] (the "2001 Regulations") provide guidance on how

---

[113] Limited Liability Partnerships Act 2000 ("LLPA 2000"), s 2.
[114] LLPA 2000, s 2(2)(f).
[115] LLPA 2000, Sch.
[116] Additional restrictions are stated in the LLPA 2000, Sch.
[117] LLPA 2000, s 2(1)(a).
[118] SI 2001/1090.

members' relationships with each other should be regulated. The 2001 Regulations are essentially default rules, however, they are not extensive and may not accurately reflect the intention of the members of an LLP, in relation to both its internal management and to its commercial objectives.

KEY FEATURES

14.89 An LLP is often described as a hybrid between a partnership and limited liability company, given its mix of corporate and partnership features. Some of these features are detailed below:

1. Company features

14.90 (i) An LLP has a legal personality distinct from those of its members;[119] consequently, it enjoys perpetual succession. In addition, there is no limit to its capacity,[120] therefore the doctrine of *ultra vires* does not apply.

(ii) The members of an LLP act as agents and, therefore, enjoy limited liability, as do shareholders of a company.[121]

(iii) Members can bind an LLP, in a similar way to directors of a company, and as a result LLPs can own property, enter into contracts, sue and be sued. An LLP is also liable for its own debts, up to the value of the assets of the LLP, since members are not jointly liable.

(iv) In order to offer a degree of protection to third parties, an LLP is under a statutory requirement to file documents with the Registrar, for example accounts and annual returns.

(v) Where a third party is contracting with an LLP, they can assume that a member has authority to act on its behalf. However, if they know that the member does not have such authority, or they know or believe that he is not a member of the LLP then the LLP is not contractually bound by that member's actions. The assumption of membership can continue until notice of cessation has been intimated to the third party directly or directly to the Registrar.[122]

(vi) The 1985 Act and the 1986 Act apply to LLPs[123] in a similar way to the way in which they apply to companies. Consequently, members of LLPs, like company directors, have to be fully aware of how the provisions relating to wrongful and fraudulent trading, insolvency and disqualification may be applicable.[124]

2. Partnership features

14.91 (i) An LLP does not have any directors, shareholders or share capital.

(ii) Members' autonomy is similar to that enjoyed by partners. There is little regulation governing the internal management of an LLP, therefore members

---

[119] LLPA 2000, s 1(1).
[120] LLPA 2000, s 1(3).
[121] LLPA 2000, s 6.
[122] LLPA 2000, s 6(3).
[123] The Limited Liability Partnerships Regulations 2001 apply the legislation to LLPs.
[124] This is not an exhaustive list.

can chose how decisions should be made and profits shared, and how to regulate the appointment and retirement of members.

(iii) A membership agreement is similar to a partnership agreement, in that it is optional (given that default provisions are provided by the 2001 Regulations) and there is no requirement to place the document in the public domain, by filing it with the Registrar.

(iv) Insolvency procedures for LLPs are very similar to those applicable to companies. However, the notable difference is that LLPs are subject to the "clawback' rule. This means that members have a very real personal interest in keeping abreast of the financial position of an LLP. In reality, if a member withdraws money from an LLP within 2 years prior to an insolvent winding-up and knew, or ought to have known, that, given the withdrawal, an insolvent liquidation was unavoidable,[125] the amount can be clawed back from that individual member. In this way members' personal exposure is similar to that of partners.

(v) LLPs enjoy similar tax transparency to partnerships. Generally, members will have the same income tax and corporation tax liabilities as partners and may enjoy similar benefits in relation to national insurance contributions.

CONSIDERING AN LLP

When considering incorporating an LLP, the positives and negatives associated with **14.92** this type of business vehicle should be weighed up. They include:

ADVANTAGES

(i) Substantial protection of members' personal assets.   **14.93**
(ii) Internal flexibility regarding management and structure.
(iii) Tax transparency and benefits.

DISADVANTAGES

(i) Limited financial privacy, given the filing requirements.   **14.94**
(ii) It is a relatively new entity, therefore limited case law exists, and this perhaps gives a perception of legal uncertainty, and in turn may dissuade third parties from contracting with LLPs.

---

[125] IA 1986, s 214(2)(b).

14.95

ESSENTIAL FACTS

COMPANIES LIMITED BY SHARES

Legislation

- The Companies Act 1985 (as amended), and the Companies Act 2006 will result in two substantive Acts governing company law.

Incorporation

- Pre-incorporation contracts do not bind a company or third party.
- A company, once incorporated, is seen as a separate legal entity.
- Members enjoy limited liability provided that the "veil of incorporation" is not lifted.

Members' meetings and resolutions

- Members can hold either general meetings (AGMs or EGMs) or class meetings.
- The notice period of meetings depends on the type of meeting and the nature of business intended to be dealt with.
- Resolutions are decisions taken by members of a company.

Directors

- A variety of types of directors recognised, other than those formally appointed, for example *de facto*, shadow, nominee and alternate directors.
- Directors owe fiduciary duties to a company as well as statutory duties. Directors' duties, established at common law, have been codified by the 2006 Act.
- Directors can become personally liable where the "veil of incorporation' is lifted, for example in cases of fraudulent or wrongful trading.

Members

- Membership only exists when a person's name is entered into a company's register of members.
- A member's liability is detailed in a company's memorandum.
- The key case in relation to minority protection is *Foss* v *Harbottle* (1843). Certain exceptions to the principles of this case are now accepted.

Share capital

- Maintenance of a company's share capital is important; consequently, statutory safeguards exist.

- To alter a company's share capital, a resolution must be passed and filed with the Registrar of Companies.

- Companies must have s 80 (1985 Act) authority to allot shares and statutory pre-emption rights exist (s 89 of the 1985 Act).

- Share transfers are usually voluntary, and no statutory pre-emption rights exist.

PARTNERSHIPS

- Key legislation – the Partnership Act 1890.

- A partnership can be created verbally, and a partnership agreement is optional. The minimum number of partners is two and there is no maximum limit.

- Partnerships are separate legal entities.

- The relationship between the firm and its partners is fiduciary in nature.

- Partners are agents of a firm and can bind a partnership, and are jointly and severally liable.

- Failure to comply with statutory requirements can open partners to unlimited personal liability.

LIMITED LIABILITY PARTNERSHIPS (LLPs)

- Legislation – the Limited Liability Partnerships Act 2000 (as amended) and the Limited Liability Partnerships Regulations 2001.

- An LLP can be described as a hybrid between a limited liability company and a partnership.

- An LLP is incorporated by sending an incorporation document to the Registrar, with the requisite fee.

- An LLP has a legal personality distinct from those of its members; therefore, it can hold property in its own name and enter into contracts.

- Members are agents of an LLP and therefore enjoy substantial limited liability.

- A membership agreement is optional, and default rules are provided by the 2001 Regulations.

ESSENTIAL CASES

14.96

Foss v *Harbottle* (1843): refers to the principle of majority rule. In circumstances where an alleged wrong has been done to a company, minority shareholders cannot bring an action on behalf of the company. A company is a distinct legal entity and therefore, the "proper plaintiff". It is now judicially accepted that there are certain exceptions to this principle.

Salomon v *A Salomon Co Ltd* (1887): refers to the principle known as the "veil of incorporation" which protects members of a company from liability. It is accepted that in certain circumstances the "veil" may be lifted and members may become personally liable for their acts and/or omissions.

INDEX